ez

oP

5w

Idea Books Architectural Series
Editor Andrea Branzi
Designer Anthony Mathews

English translation by C.H. Evans

Paperback edition published in 1995 by
ART DATA
12 Bell Industrial Estate
50 Cunnington Street
London

Originally published in Italy by Idea Books.
Copyright 1982, Idea Books, Milan.

ISBN 0-948835-16-8

Printed in Italy

On the cover: Villa Karma, The entrance hall with gallery.

ADOLF LOOS

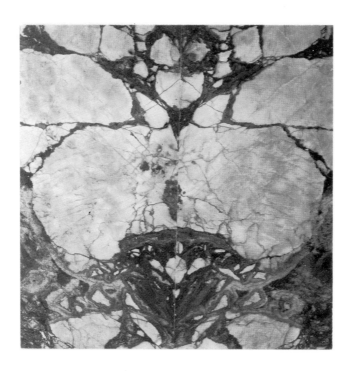

Going against a grammatical rule of the German language, the nouns
in Loos' writings have their initial letter in the lower case.
Consequently this unusual mode of writing has been adopted when
quoting passages from or the titles of Loos' original essays.

BENEDETTO GRAVAGNUOLO

ADOLF LOOS

THEORY AND WORKS

PREFACE BY ALDO ROSSI
PHOTOGRAPHY ROBERTO SCHEZEN

ART DATA

CONTENTS

The author wishes to thank Andrea Branzi, Renato De Fusco, Adriana Giusti Baculo, Nicola Pagliara, Aldo Rossi and Manfredo Tafuri for their advice and criticism. Thanks are also due to Burkhardt Rukschcio for his consultation of the documents kept in the Loos-Archiv at the Albertina, to Hermann Czech and Erhard Löcker for their kind collaboration, to Sylvia Eiblmayr for her precious assistance and to the Plan- und Schriften-Kammer of the Municipality of Vienna, the Historisches Museum der Stadt Wien and the Museum des 20. Jahrhunderts for iconographic material. Special thanks go to Massimo Patrizio De Carolis, for the long and impassioned discussions on the most problematical aspects of the culture of the finis Austriae. Maria Pia Bottone, Monika Grewenig, Giorgia Mosing and Giuliana Zeuli have collaborated on the organization of the work. Of fundamental assistance has been the hospitality of the present owners of Villa Karma, Villa Duschnitz, the Manz bookshop, the Gruener fashion-house, the Knize store and the firm J. & L. Lobmeyr, which has made it possible to visit and photograph Loos' works as they are today.

PREFACE

There is no doubt that the most interesting thing about Adolf Loos is his architecture; or rather it is the dominant aspect of his work. The way in which he carries out this work is less certain; he loves to write, to draw, to travel, to argue, to build. He claims that, like all thinkers and writers, at least ever since the Greeks, he is pursuing the truth; but as is well-known the search for truth does not necessarily follow a straight path and, above all, cannot be made into a profession.

So work and profession on the one hand and art and style on the other are the characteristic themes of Adolf Loos and his architecture. As a result a «formal» criticism of his work is split right from the start. His indifference towards the technique used is perhaps what marks him out most clearly from the architects of the Secession who, having grown up in the same culture and in the last analysis representing the same problems, do not break with its stylistic scheme, or figurative mode of expression. The «best» of them certainly break with the master of the movement, Otto Wagner, who, going against his own *Wagnerschule*, returns to the ordinary Viennese house, «the house where one is born». This is a source of wonder to Adolf Loos, and to a few others like Egon Schiele and, in a more explicit manner, Georg Trakl. Egon Schiele parts with the more orthodox schemes of the Secession, rapidly entering a more private area, not of abstraction but of obsession, where stylistic technique is almost irrelevant to its contents and problems. The repeated

breaches in the tradition» even though at the same time, «There is no development in things that have been solved for once and all... the medieval plane — see Dürer's *Melancholy* — is identical to our own».

The Doric column cannot be altered either: in architecture it is not unlike the medieval plane, a perfect fusion of form and function. And here, as in any illuministic position, lies the contradiction of Adolf Loos; if architecture begins and ends in the grave, made to measure for man's body, or rather for his corpse, what need is there in architecture for the electric light, or just what is the progress that it brings with it?

Adolf Loos draws a distinction between architecture and handicraft. «Architecture is not an art: only a small part of architecture belongs to art». And so the concrete possibility is that of the profession; «I know that I am a craftsman who must serve the men of his time. And because of this I know that art really exists».

The dilemma involved in the separation of art and craft, unknown to artists up until the 18th century (at least up until the clocks of Piermarini and the multiform activities of Schinkel) is the principal problem facing modern architects; on the more aggressive and cunning side, represented by the *Bauhaus* and the Secession, the old task of the craftsman becomes an unquestionable professional opportunity; furniture, graphics, carpeting and domestic appliances will form the body of «industrial design». The logic of this de-

THE ARCHITECTURE OF ADOLF LOOS

self-portrait, with all its narcissistic and almost obscene variations, the male or female model turned into a body/object of destructive ritual; these are seeking a form of the absolute or else of the inexpressible. In Georg Trakl, without doubt the greatest poet of this movement, the same personal problems or private obsessions tend towards silence, even if it is by means of hints and references; when the references disappear the only genuine silence is that of suicide. Compared with this silence Adolf Loos' severity still has an illuminist background; as his worldliness, his interest in things and fashions and the cynicism with which he balances his desire for the absolute, is illuminist. It is also, in the Viennese, or European culture, very easy to draw a parallel with Musil/Ulrich where «for him ethics were... the infinite complexity of the possibilities of life... He believed in a power of growth in ethics, in step with his experience and not just as is commonly understood, in step with his knowledge, and that they were therefore something stable for which man alone is not pure enough... Ethics are fantasy... the consequence of which is this: an ascending path of intelligence and its creations that rises in a more or less straight line, despite doubts, through the changes of history».

So for Adolf Loos, the human body and the tomb, which with Schiele and Trakl bring to a close and make impossible art as a form of civilization, are references to an absolute that competes with civilization in its true and illuministic meaning of the progress of things: «Therefore only modern inventions (electric light, the cement roof and so on) make

sign, which is overwhelming, is extended in its turn to architecture and the debate over function, already dear to the writers of treatises, ends up in the elimination of form or more simply of study and research. Any other experiment, like the more genuine ones of modern architecture which confront problems of style and the body of architecture itself, is obstructionist and reactionary. Today we cannot but be perplexed by an operation whose ideology was destroyed along with the collapse of the myth of welfare and social peace.

On the other, perhaps more genial and certainly more honest side, an attempt is made to recognize the division — perhaps a wreck or a catastrophe — of the elements that used to make up the profession; whether between art and craft or between art and technique, the split shows up in all its positivistic clarity, not so much in the separation of École des Beaux Arts and Polytechnic School, as in an unattainable or no longer reconcilable division between art and profession.

If Adolf Loos shows himself to be the keenest supporter of this division, others, like the Germans Heinrich Tessenow and Mies van der Rohe, are close behind him. Both these men, like the Viennese master, are familiar with the history of architecture, know that they are part of that history and judge it by the evolution of the present.

Tessenow's position is certainly the most consistent and it could be summed up in Loos' metaphor of Dürer's plane; the search for progress is only of value in so far as it is positive, and if the new is false, it is better to work with the known. Hence apparently without any polemical intent but the setting of the decisive controversy, Heinrich Tessenow follows the artisan design of the German house, to end up reuniting craft and myth or, to put it another way, profession and art. Architecture fades away in the small house and the detail, becoming almost a construction manual put together by a good master builder, but at the same time this little house salvages a timeless architecture, frozen from its beginnings in a perfection created out of small and almost invisible modifications.

For Mies van der Rohe, craft or technique is part of an absolute truth; his designs, from Berlin to America, not only do not renounce grand architecture but set out to be «grand architecture». An architecture that is born out of history, that harks back straight to Schinkel, but that seeks the essential, not a nihilistic nothing but a void that is the form of truth. Uniquely, Mies van der Rohe defines architecture by quoting St. Thomas who holds that truth is «*adequatio intellectus et rei*». Any division is therefore wiped out; architecture is an aspect of culture and of its evolution and is what gives it form. Thus the chair and the skyscraper are brought together in the same design, where a high technology makes use of the classical form, or alternatively the classical manner is made possible by the understanding of technique. By different roads, Tessenow and Mies, between Dürer's plane and the great Aquinas, seem to continue architecture, ignoring its crises and its commercial aspects alike, without separating knowing and doing.

Strangely Adolf Loos has never been set in this cultural world to which he belonged. Hence he is somehow forced into controversy with the artists of the Secession, a sharp controversy but one that was also congenial to his character, without seeing his more general position in modern architecture. As for the two architects mentioned above, who together with Loos I see as making up a trio of masters, he makes a radical denunciation of the terms that they reassemble: what makes him unique is that he does not wish to reunite them. On the contrary this declaration of their separation or conflict almost seems to be a motive of survival, just as his friend, the great poet Georg Trakl can also write that «now all this is lost»; his finest essay, and most fascinating title, *Ornament and Crime*, is an apology for ornament and therefore ends in an impossibility. Speaking of ornament in architecture, it would have occurred to no-one, before him, to think in terms of the savage's body and the tattoo, and of the tattoo as a form of degeneration on the modern body. The beauty of his ornament has disappeared; it is lost and any revival of it is only decadence. His contemporary, and pupil in architecture, Wittgenstein will say later that, «what is torn, torn must remain». This declaration of the separation of art and craft, or really that what is torn must stay torn, would not be so unusual if it had not been experienced by Adolf Loos in the first person, in the most personal sense, as a worker, since handicraft (certainly) and art (perhaps) are the well-springs of his work. In one of his answers to the readers of «Das andere» and in particular to one who asks him why, seeing his contempt for modern architects, he continues to be an architect he replies: because this job has provided me with my living. And, he specifies, because it is the job I know. Just as in America I made my living for some time by washing dishes. He adds: «One could support oneself here in some other way too». All this because his activity is not at all architectural, he claims, in an era «in which every carpet designer calls himself an architect».

Thus an important aspect of the contradiction between art and profession emerges which the idealistic position has always failed to take into account; that of the artist's means of subsistence. In this too the Viennese master reminds one of a positive trait of the great artists of the ancient world, by the way in which daily life with its problems of money, sickness and private matters is frequently given a lot of space in his letters.

I believe this to be the most critical stand taken against the moralism of the Modern Movement which always shows a redeeming attitude towards doing, an optimistic view where architecture sets itself to teach how to live.

On the contrary (and in an often irritating manner) Adolf Loos discourages every *aficionado* of architecture: everyone will live in his own house, according to his own personality, and the house will grow with him outside any style and, in the last analysis, without any imposition. But it is also likely that someone will ask for advice on this or that solution, or more simply has other things to do than decorate his own house. Now the architect, trying to do his job well, advises him. That's all. Because one job is as good as another. After this, apparently, nothing is left.

In reality it is here that Adolf Loos' architecture begins. Having cleared the field of carpenters, costume-designers, tailors and architects, in which he has accepted to earn his living in a mercenary position, there remains the other part in which «the architect is a mason who has studied Latin». In this definition, almost an epigraph, there is an emotion which reveals itself in controversy with his contemporaries and is no different from the definition of the poet that Umberto Saba was obliged to give in opposition to contemporary rhetoric. He knew that poetry did not circulate alone, and idle, through the lanes of Trieste; it had ancient forebears but its glory was academic and dusty and the poet had to walk around the city to encounter poetry in the boys playing at ball or in their sisters who sewed sadly the cheerful banners. Adolf Loos too, caught between classicism and his attack on the Secession, wanders the city and is entranced by old Viennese houses: only a great architect could have written in those times: «... And this illusion (of having deep ties with the tradition of Viennese building) was further strengthened for me by what a modern artist and enemy of mine had to say: he wants to be a modern artist and he builds a house like the old Viennese houses». This love for the old face of the city strikes one who has «... always had the illusion of having solved this problem in the manner of our old Viennese masters...».

The old Viennese masters are, like the saddler and the shoemaker, the craftsmen of their articles; the people with whom he stays and from whom he learns, and they are at the same time the great masters like Fischer von Erlach. In the expression «the old masters» there is something that is both affectionate and limiting; they are not «the ancients» and it is also probable that they are people who have not studied Latin. But it is perhaps in this passage that the old houses of the city make their first appearance in the urban landscape; these old houses destined to disappear through building speculation or through the stupidity of the administration, or to be, in what is perhaps a worse fate, preserved or embalmed, have in Loos a singularly modern taste and go back to being a condition of life. Thus this sentence has always reminded me of the old Goethe of *Poetry and Truth*, where his childhood walks through Frankfurt lead the boy to «establish a certain leaning towards the old» which, despite the academics, fades into the present, into the human condition to which the old houses, like the old engravings, bear witness: «and another taste revealed itself in the boy, to understand conditions that were simply human in their multiplicity and naturalness, without other pretence of interest or of aesthetics».

These are the elements important to an understanding of the artist or architect Adolf Loos; similarities and references that go further than this are tedious, gratuitous and discounted by any person of average learning. There can be no doubt that he belonged to Viennese culture; a culture with many interests and many personalities. The link with Karl Kraus is sure, and with his best friend Peter Altenberg too, as is evident in the analogy with the writers or artists we have spoken of before: Robert Musil, Georg Trakl, Egon Schiele. But what counts in criticism, or in critical understanding, are the differences and peculiarities. We can surely apply many of the maxims and aphorisms of his contemporaries to Adolf Loos and vice versa; but this is almost a game.

So Wittgenstein's «thought», «what is torn, torn must remain», could represent Adolf Loos' detachment from architecture but it also represents nothing. Torn or destroyed or abandoned things are not unique to Viennese culture; they form part of the ancient world towards which Loos was inclined — one has only to think of Virgil's memories of his schooldays. Just as it would be very limiting to attribute Egon Schiele's fragmented bodies to Viennese culture alone; perhaps they can be put back together in the sense of Musil's passage on ethics that was quoted above: that is, in an ascending line of intelligence which must necessarily contrast with the mountain of rubble of sentiments and ideas that are abandoned at the very moment of their conception.

Perhaps independently of all this, Adolf Loos loved the Bunker Hill monument at Charlestown, Massachusetts: a postcard of this was found among his papers, as Ludwig Münz informs us, but it was also a choice and a program for all his architecture. Perhaps this postcard will allow us to go into his architecture with more precision: the Bunker Hill monument is not very different from the Rohrbach sugar-refinery he built in Czechoslovakia in 1919. This too could be a postcard, just as we see great buildings represented in postcards. In all of the Viennese master's architecture there is the tendency to translate the monument into something customary, where what is simply old is mingled with the

antique. The «old houses» that we have spoken of get mixed up with the works of Fischer von Erlach, the Latin of the architect barely stiffens the observed world and the far from scandalous distortion of the original model offers the possibility of existence to the model itself. So Adolf Loos, who loves the classicism of Greece and Rome (shifting his position between these two poles) and admires the perfection of Fischer von Erlach, is perhaps the first architect or intellectual or mason to be excited by the American monuments.

I have always felt both admiration and respect for this almost certainly deep-felt recognition: because his admiration is neither literary nor sentimental but clearly technical. He understands that in the leap in scale, in the unheard-of proportions, in the distortion and in the repetition, there is an observation of and a respect for the classical laws. During this period he was examining Rome and not Greece, which he would come back to in the last years of is life. The classical world, seen through the Roman constructions, shows the union of technique and art, of engineering and architecture: «... Our education is based on classical culture ... Ever since humanity understood the grandeur of classical antiquity, one thought has linked all the great architects of all times. They think: I am building in the same way as the Romans would have built. We know that they are wrong; time, place, purpose and local climate forbid this. But every time architecture strays from its model at the hands of the mediocre and the decorators, the great architect reappears to bring it back to antiquity».

Roman architecture signifies here the grand construction, the possibility of a way of building that is not tied to personality; the architects apply scientific principles and let no sign of public or personal crises appear. His attitude towards classicism will be different in the big project for the «Chicago Tribune»; here the Doric column re-proposes not so much the civilization as the myth of Greece. And in fact his statement that «... no graphic drawing is capable of describing the effect of these columns», looks like a renunciation of architecture or of the capacity to practice it as a profession. The «Chicago Tribune» column is a sign of the silence to which Adolf Loos was coming and is perhaps his last great project.

What is left to say?

Only three years have passed since the model for the funerary monument to Max Dvořák: a cube of stone surmounted by steps. Almost nothing. There is little left to say about the cycle of works that draws to a close between 1930 and 1931 and Adolf Loos seems to accept his limits as a program; architecture is not an art, it is necessary to do one's job well, the problems are the same and only small variations are available for their solution. And the variations are a technological progression that the artist accepts but that has little effect on his work: the electric light, for example. But already the interpretation of this «discovery» or the application of it in architecture becomes ambiguous and has a different flavour to the usual significance attributed to it by builders contemporary to Loos. When Loos speaks of electric light it always brings to my mind something Mayakovsky said in order to explain the difference between himself and

Pasternak. It went something like this: «The difference between us is this: when we see a lamp we both experience a strong emotion; only I think of electric light and he of God» (I quote from memory). Adolf Loos, who was certainly an atheist, perhaps thought of both things at the same time; in other words he thought of a progress in things that did not depend on the individual but only on great changes in history, where technique had a strong influence over customs and on the way of life and overwhelmed the personality of the individual, who ended up as an instrument of these events and definitely not a protagonist. For this reason the parable of the master saddler who could not but make the same saddle as long as horses and riders existed and would exist with necessarily the same anatomical shapes, and the saddle would always have the same shape despite the hopes and efforts of the architect/designers of the Secession is a story that is not lacking in melancholy.

Function is not abstract and is inseparable from man; the form, whether literary or architectonic or figurative, can only comment. The description of grave architecture is no different; the more it will shape itself to the human corpse, the more it will be architecture. This function of the body of man is very different from the one that it has for his contemporaries, the «functionalists»; it seems almost to be the reduction of what is possible and its denial. This is not unlike the way in which the spread-eagled body of Chist was the simplest and most intense thing in the great baroque churches of the Jesuits and the white sheet of the sudarium their purest ornament. In the last years of his life, he expresses this function of the human body, between living and dying, in one of the finest and most sacrilegious passages not only of modern architecture but also of the modern conception of progress: «... It is well-known how all the breathless artistic lucubrations on the way to live - in any country - do not shift the dog from the warmth of the stove, that all the traffic of associations, schools, professorships, periodicals and exhibitions has furnished nothing new; thus the only revolution in modern handicraft (excluding the influence of new inventions) is fixed in one pair of eyes. And those eyes are mine. And this signifies that no-one has understood a thing. But I am not writing my own obituary; I am saying it now, myself».

The dog that will not leave the warmth of the stove is like the tattooed body of the Papuan; architecture identifies itself with the body, and aesthetics and functionality are aimed at a better way of survival.

What is left for the architect and for any civilized person? It is perhaps in answer to this that Adolf Loos places a sentence from Nietzsche at the beginning of his second volume of writings; «what is crucial happens anyway».

Let us set aside interpretation, or pick out one, perhaps progressive, aspect of it: in spite of the stupidity and conventions of this transitory world to which he alludes, made up of associations and exhibitions and professorships and periodicals, despite all this, what is crucial is destined to assert itself. This is perhaps why, as he had said when speaking of Karl Kraus, he too «fears the end of the world». Then all that is left to any civilized person is to work from

day to day, perhaps on small things, straying from the truth. As in the spiritual exercises of Saint Ignatius, where the most important thing for «fallen man» was everyday behaviour, the rules of living, the honest attitude; this was not just a defense but also a concrete possibility on which to build.

It is as this kind of artist that Adolf Loos himself lives, but above all it is the kind of artist that he prefigures; an artist who finds morality again in the infinite complexity of the possibilities of life, «... an ascending path of intelligence and its creations that rises in a more or less straight line, despite doubts, through the changes of history».

The artist will listen to the cobbler, strip away pretence, visit the wisest, walk through the city observing things and «will understand simply human conditions». It is perhaps by this unusual road rather than through his quotation of the Doric column that Adolf Loos rediscovers Socratic Greece and the changes of history that take place from day to day; like Hölderlin and Goethe, he will know how to «understand simply human conditions».

For this «simply human condition» is finally nothing but the quality and greatness of Adolf Loos the architect. It is very easy to compare him with his contemporaries, whether architects of the Secession or of the Modern Movement, in order to emphasize his stature. He too loved to do this in a polemical, aggressive and amused fashion in his youth or, with detachment, in his last years when he saw that his truth had encountered a new style; and that the white walls of functionalism were no different from the pastel colors of the Secession.

But these matters no longer concerned him: style and technique, as for all true artists, had been an opportunity. This is the meaning of his story of the mason and the carpenter: «... And while the mason joins brick to brick, stone to stone, the carpenter has taken his place by his side. The blows of the axe resound merrily. He is building the roof. What kind of roof? A beautiful roof or an ugly roof? He doesn't know. The roof».

As for Mies «less is more», so for Tessenow ornament becomes a hindrance as well: «... The deeper our pain or the keener our joy or the stronger our desire for progress, the more ornament is a hindrance; a profound involvement excludes secondary questions».

The «thing», be it pain or joy, must be expressed without hindrance; and we know that the hindrances are many and not easy to recognize. For Loos the definition draws back in the presence of the thing itself; technique is an aspect of ethics, it too grows materially and is made up of multiple experiences, it too is fantasy. It is identified with style and this gives rise to the indifference towards style of which I spoke at the beginning; the master grasps all the possibilities of the repertory of style. The most modern master of this is Schinkel; the extraordinary city that he foresaw, and built fragments of in Berlin, Munich and Karlsruhe, where styles and materials are united in the climate, in the customs, in the atmosphere and in everything that we can call culture.

So the artist takes no notice of where he wants to get to; if nothing can change he can make things wonderfully more intense. He encounters the immutability of Time in everyday time, flees from the ephemeral but also from what is corroded and his personal time constructs a place that is consoling, since he recognizes that, if not for him at least for others, art is consolatory. Architecture above all, full of contradictions, achieves this consolatory appearance; the house where the dog will not move away from the warmth of the stove is the very place where one lives in simply human conditions. Villa Karma on the lake of Geneva, the Steiner house, the Moller house, the house for Tristan Tzara, the Müller house, the Spanner house, the Khuner house. Along with these, the clothing stores and the Kärntner-Bar. The grand and never built projects as well.

Between the luxurious house at Montreux and the study for the Heuberg worker's estate the change in conditions and the course of time do not alter the rules of construction. If this was not so the very significance of his teachings would be lost; the architect, or the artist, or the technician, can only change a few things and these are non-essential. There is no doubt that they also depend on his inclinations, for example inclinations towards what we can call style. There are obvious differences in this style, or different inclinations towards «style», between the Steiner house, the Tzara house and the Khuner house. If we wish to resort to formal definitions we can see a purist accentuation in the first, a sort of terrorism of image in the second and almost a return to the alpine tradition in the last.

But it is important to repeat here what was said at the beginning: Adolf Loos uses architectonic style (and I find no definition that is more appropriate in its general applicability) in the same way as he uses different techniques. Neither identifying style with ethics nor seeing technique as a restrictive condition, he is free to make use of all the variations that different situations permit. Precisely because he has one sole idea of architecture, «I build in the same way as the Romans would have built», precisely because only a few technical innovations really change man's life, the architect uses the tools available to him only with logic and feeling.

This attitude is one of the essential aspects of Adolf Loos' modernity; ornament is crime not for reasons of abstract moralism but where it presents itself as a form of foolishness, of degeneration or of useless repetition. On the contrary form, which is no longer geometry or simple function, as in the paradigmatic case of the Doric columns, is used as an element of composition; thus the pedestal and the columns, the technique and the space in Mies' Berlin Museum are of a timeless classicism. There is no doubt that their immediate master is Schinkel, but it is also all 18th-century architecture where the design of the city, and the houses, «the old houses» as Loos liked to call them, is no different from that of the monument; the reference to Palladians all over the world is obvious.

But Adolf Loos, like all modern artists, knows that a linear continuity is not simple and is indeed not possible; the Berlin Museum and the Charlottenburg villa no longer stand on the same operative and mental plane as was the case with Schinkel. And even the almost contemporary quotation of the Gothic and of the Greek presents the same difficulties;

this is why all the extremists of the avant-garde (and I use the term extremists with admiration) seem to be in the right; artists for whom, to echo Wittgenstein, «what is torn, torn must remain».

But Adolf Loos, like Ulrich/Musil, believes in an ascending path of intelligence and of its creations that rises in a more or less straight line, despite the doubts and the changes of history. And now, after so much irony and spite directed at architecture (which we have learnt from Loos as from the masters of the past), we can say something in its defense. For the architect, because of his ambiguous mode of being, between engineer and poet, between craftsman and painter, is familiar with all the doubts that these professions bring with them.

The division between Polytechnic School and Beaux Arts had, it might be said, robbed him of his profession; 1794, when the Convention founded «Le Conservatoire des arts et métiers», is a historic and tragic year for the history of architecture, but one that was necessary to its time; at times I think of those singular characters, Baltard and Lamet, who at the foundation of the École Polytechnique were entrusted with the task of collecting models of architecture. These models are no different from collections of chemical, mineralogical and physical specimens; the avant-garde, child of illuminism, will elucidate in the most brutal manner the operation of its bourgeois ancestors. But not everything is included in these collections because they are always too restricted. It may seem a strange approach to the problem of Adolf Loos' relationship with, or if you like his enthusiasm for America. How different his America is from that of modern architectural historiography!

He is enthusiastic about the Chicago Exposition (and one regrets he did not see the great buildings, almost modern ruins, of the San Francisco Exposition) and loves the marriage and superimposition of styles and materials, of engineering and history. All this will have an influence on perhaps his most important building, the tower or great Doric column for the «Chicago Tribune». This artist, who was so personal and certainly deeply rooted in central European culture, though destined to rise above it in the course of his life, also understands, through his experience of America, that the great work of art is becoming collective once again; the meaning of its monuments, from the Pantheon to the Empire State Building, is to be found in this general understanding.

The postcard of Bunker Hill found amongst his papers is no different from the ones sent back from America by emigrants, nor is the postcard of the Pantheon different from the eternal monument of Adolf Loos' writings.

We may also think that, in the end, the gulf between art and profession, building trade and monument is bridged in the life of Adolf Loos, as in those of all great artists and simple men, in the search for simply human conditions without either pretence of interest or aesthetics. And that at the end of this search even art seems to us a hindrance or a secondary question.

Aldo Rossi

Adolf Loos - Drawing by Oskar Kokoschka (1916).

INTRODUCTION

We can only construct a building if we know how to live in it

Martin Heidegger
Bauen, Wohnen, Denken

... one is never so close to change
as when life seems unbearable even in
the smallest and most everyday things

Rainer Maria Rilke
Briefe von Muzot

To tackle the problem of underwear, of hair or dress styles, of listening to good music or enjoying a fine meal... does not form part of the traditional training of an architect. Everyday «triviality» has always been excluded from architecture's field of reference [1].

So it may come as a surprise that a «pioneer of modern architecture» — as Adolf Loos has been called — should have devoted so much persistent attention to such apparently marginal subjects [2].

Rarely has it seriously been asked if this might not be the real reason for the significant role his work has played in the history of contemporary architecture.

«Many will have been perplexed by my most recent arguments; perplexed as to the parallel that I drew between architecture and tailoring», wrote Loos in one of his fundamental theoretical essays, Architektur (1910), anticipating the predictable disdain of the critic for assertions of this kind [3]. Nor is it by chance that the radical change introduced by Loos in the very concept of the project arises from considerations which are related not to the sphere of construction but to that of habitation.

Loos understood the central role played by everyday culture in the processes of growth and transformation of civilization. In many passages from his writings he states that utilitarian objects are true emblems of a way of living. Because of their deep penetration of collective existence, the smallest things give shape to the culture of an era or a people in much clearer terms than even a work of literature or art. From this point of view, architecture is just one of the forms in which living becomes manifest. Which means that analysis of the relationship between ways of living in and ways of building a house becomes an indispensable premise of Loosian planning.

One thing stands out, though: the author of Ornament and Crime does not confine himself to observing «the world as I found it». His work aspires to be — and in its own way is — a plan for transformation of what already exists. How else can one explain his stated aim of influencing behaviour so as to modify it, his insistence on the necessity of freeing civilization from the mask, from the superfluous, which is the central theme of many of his essays, not to mention his numerous conferences on how to walk, sit, cook («always packed» as O. Kokoschka remembers) and the lessons in living held at the «wholly unique school which he ran around the café table» [4].

On the other hand, although architecture is steeped in the complex and subtle network of relationships between things, this should not cause its confusion with other dialects of living. The claim that the specific nature of architecture is technique — contained within strict limits — is another of the fundamental methodological principles of Loosian design. The contradiction between these two propositions is only apparent. The architect, in Loos' opinion, must learn to translate fundamental theoretical arguments into his own specific language. In this way the attention given to what is outside architecture is turned upside down in an unequivocal recognition of the autonomy of the architectural language, within the frame of a multitude of techniques for the expression of thought. An autonomy, therefore, which is not enclosed within an immutable system set up without reference to history, but which, on the contrary, is conceived with the aim of bringing about change from the starting point of its own specific locus. In conclusion, at the root of the difficult simplicity of his designs lies a precise standpoint with respect to the great themes of the dialectic between private and public, art and manufacture, Kultur and Zivilisation, which is the true key to interpreting his own peculiar nihilism.

«You have been a builder in the frame of an existence which, internally as well as externally, had renounced all ornaments. What you built was what you thought...», Karl Kraus will say, recognizing in the much sought-after identity between building and thinking the secret of his intellectual toil [5]. Besides the esthetical and logico-economic reasons, the denial of ornament is inspired by an undoubtedly ethical foundation, in the Kraussian sense of the term. This throws light on the uncompromising nature of such a method.

Moreover Loos has gained insight into and, in his own way, thoroughly analysed the close chain of relationships between living, building and thinking to which Martin Heidegger will later devote a famous essay, although the deductions of the «builder» differ substantially from those of the «philosopher» [6]. The real dividing line between their positions is marked by Loos' positive desire to produce, which leads him to recognize technique as the foundation of building.

Technique, understood as the essence of doing, of the ancient poiein, is adopted by Loos as something impersonal, a sort of «rules of the game» handed down from historical times and which, as such, the architect must limit himself to understanding, disclosing and applying. This is the source of his profound contempt for inventive narcissism, for the myth of the «original genius». His own description of himself as a «mason who has studied Latin» makes clear the ambitious modesty of a logic which has dispensed with fantasy.

This aspiration to realism, this desire to stick to the concreteness of a tautologically and simply technical way of building brings Loos close to Mies van der Rohe and distances him from the contemporary Viennese Secession, in much more meaningful terms than those which arise from the concept of rationality.

Clearly the rationality of Loos is only a derivative of the principle of realism. It is conceived primarily as a practical tool, a simple procedure for control of the project. There is nothing ascetic, still less dogmatic, about it. It is never raised to the level of a system. On the contrary, it is often gainsaid by transgression of the self-imposed rules. The most fascinating aspect of Loos' architecture lies in the simultaneous and contradictory presence of a thin irrational vein that is tightly bound by the rigid links of rational composition. It can make use, for example, of the unpredictability of optical illusions and visual trickery that is typical of the interiors of Loos' houses. In short, rationality, in Loos, is never brought down to the level of a fanatical functionalism.

Yet what counts for more in any interpretation of his method is the rigorous nature of the process by which architectural thought is translated into a lucid mastery over form and space. «When I see a work by Loos», Arnold Schoenberg acutely observed, «I am aware of a difference right away: here... I see a non-composite, immediate, three-dimensional conception... Here everything is thought out, imagined, composed and moulded in space without any expedient, without auxiliary plans, without interruptions and breaks; directly, as if all the structures were transparent; as if the eye of the spirit were confronted by space in all its parts and as a totality simultaneously» [7].

The rigorous formalization of his thought is what Loos has in common with other «great Viennese masters of language»: A. Schoenberg, K. Kraus, L. Wittgenstein to mention just a few. The undervaluation, on the part of the early historians of the «Modern Movement», of the links between the architecture of Loos and the cultural issues debated in Vienna «on the threshold of a new era», has given rise to a series of misunderstandings and clichés. The most wide-spread among these derives from the labored interpretation of his work in terms of the degree to which it anticipated Rationalism, or rather what was understood by rationalism in the ideological schemes of various authors. On the contrary, the topicality of Loos' thought emerges in all its problematical significance only when it is placed within the precise historical and cultural limits in which it was expressed. A significance which arises from the radical questioning of some fundamental problems of architecture, to the extent that, if anything, Loos' work shows itself to be a prescient criticism of the later «theory» of the Modern Movement.

The aim of this monograph is to use Loos to reinterpret Loos himself. In other words, it is a question of taking another look at some of the decisive areas of his work in order to understand its meaning through a parallel study of what he said — what he planned — what he built. Without wishing to jump to any conclusions about the consistency of his writings and works, it is nevertheless undeniable that a grasp of his theoretical ideas is an essential step in the understanding of his architecture.

Consequently the book is divided into two parts. The first, with the subtitle of *Loos and his time*, is the story of his intellectual progress and sets out to trace the network of interacting relationships between his work and the development of architectural, artistic and, more generally, cultural theories in that singular historical phase which stretches over the last thirty years of the 19th century and the first thirty of the 20th. Hence it is not so much a biography in the strict sense of the word as an account of the fundamental stages in his development.

The second, under the subtitle *Guide to the works*, is a systematic and chronological study of his work. In this sense it is really a chart for a «voyage», for a critical journey through his architecture. The works have been catalogued according to strictly chronological criteria, but without making any discrimination between projects which were simply designed on paper and those that were in fact carried out.

An hierarchical distinction of this nature would make no sense as far as the history of architecture is concerned. Sometimes, an architectural work that never got past the drawing board can have much more influence than one that is actually constructed, in determining a turning point, in introducing a new language, a new technique, a new theory, prefiguring constructions that will be built subsequently.

Besides, it is precisely the architectural thought, which moulds the forms and is laid down in them, that is the most important aspect to investigate. As is inevitable, Loos' architecture often appears dated to our eyes and shows the marks of time, but the theses developed in it go beyond the Modern Movement, throwing a bridge across to the present. A bridge whose theoretical framework may be reduced to a few supporting pillars. If it is in fact true that Loos' thought is by its very nature resistant to attempts to reorganize it into a system, certain recurring lines of logic exist all the same and may be singled out:

Difference: «*Adolf Loos and I, he in facts and I in words, have done nothing but show that there is a difference between the urn and the chamber-pot and that culture plays on this difference. The others however, the defenders of positive values, can be divided into two groups: those who take the urn for a chamber-pot and those who mistake a chamber-pot for an urn*» [8].

This aphorism of Karl Kraus' helps to make clear the ultimate meaning of the way in which Loos' architecture deliberately plays on differences: between monument and house, between art and useful objects, between the interior and exterior of the house itself. This play is based on the recognition of culture as Other (*das Andere*), which means to say the vindication of its separateness as an indispensable presupposition to its critical use in bringing about a renewal of civilization.

The theory of differences is particularly explicit in the clear distinction that Loos makes between the «house» and the «monument», which means between the building which must respond to broad social needs and the building which sets out to be art: «The house must please everyone», he writes in *Architektur* (1910), «unlike the work of art which does not need to please anyone. The work of art is brought into the world without there being any need for it. The house on the other hand satisfies a need... The work of art is revolutionary, the house is conservative... So the house should have nothing to do with art, and architecture should not be numbered among the arts? Exactly so. Only a very small part of architecture belongs to art: the tomb and the monument. The rest, everything which serves an end, should be excluded from the realm of art» [9].

This argument brings us to the heart of Loos' conception of inhabiting. For Loos, daily existence is dominated by necessity. Every object with a practical end must be subjected to the rigid laws of correspondence to purpose, of the *Sachlichkeit* imposed by the principle of utility. Even construction, in this sense, must limit itself to reflecting this condition. Only the monument and the tomb — literally: the architecture of memory and the architecture of death — can allude, in their contemplative quality without purpose, to the «poetic habitation» of which Hölderlin speaks. «If we come across a tumulus in a wood, six feet long and three feet wide, shaped by the spade into a pyramid, we become serious and something within us says: somebody is buried here. This is architecture» [10].

The sense of poetic estrangement produced by the monument is therefore legitimate; that profound feeling of the sublime uselessness of pure form. But a mixture of the languages is indecent. Art should not be confused with civilization. Eros should not be confused with Logos.

To put it another way, Loos believes that the pleasure principle should be kept separate from the principle of utility. This gives rise, as a corollary, to the same otherness distinguishing the inside from the outside of the house; a distinction which we will speak of shortly when discussing intimacy.

At this point it is important to pause and look at the theoretical implications that this radical and unbridgeable difference between art and the production line bears for the very concept of industrial design.

Loos likes to stress over and over again in his writings that his polemic against the artists of the applied arts should not be mistaken for a criticism directed towards art. On the contrary, it is aimed at defending art from the assaults of those who wish to prostitute her, applying her to utilitarian objects, relegating her to the subordinate function of a cosmetic. Moreover such an attempt is held to be not just pathetic, but «superfluous», since the quality of utilitarian objects depends on the degree to which they answer to their purpose. In this sense the industrial goods which are manufactured without interference from the applied arts are those which, in his opinion, attain to the highest standards of quality. And this is because in responding to market forces, the merchandise must stick to the genuine requirements of a community in their historically derived form. Hence his profound theoretical disagreement with both the *Wiener Werkstätten* (the workshops of high craftsmanship set up by Josef Hoffmann in 1903) and with the *Deutscher Werkbund* (the important association of industrial artists and architects, founded in 1907, that laid the foundations of industrial design). «The Werkbund people», he wrote in a 1908 essay, «confuse cause and effect. We do not sit like this because the carpenter has made the chair in this or that way, but, since we want to sit in this way, the carpenter has made the chair like this» [11].

We should not be put off by the questionable nature of such an ingenuous simplification of the production-consumption cycle. The real heart of Loos' argument is an indomitable criticism of any program, of any theory of synthesis. It takes the form of an irreverent sarcasm directed against anyone who tries to fuse art, craftsmanship and industry in a single «project», by proposing an improbable marriage between aspects of culture which should be kept separate. In this sense, the denial of synthesis is also a criticism, in advance, of the *Bauhaus* program.

Negation: «*The architects failed when they wanted to resurrect the ancient styles and they are failing now, after having tried without success to discover the style of our time*» [12].

Loos wrote this in an essay of 1914. As far back as 1898 he had declared: «But it is also true that this 'style', style in inverted commas, is in no way indispensable. What is this style at the end of the reckoning? It's difficult to define it» [13].

The radical nature of this thesis does not lend itself to equivocal interpretations. The negation of style is an extremely advanced concept for the period in which it was formulated. He is dismissing — as a false problem — a theme which has literally obsessed the architectural culture of his contemporaries. Loos' sarcastic attitude towards those who are frantically seeking to «invent» a consistent code of formalization for objects echoes the «panic-stricken laugh» of Nietzsche's Zarathustra. It is no coincidence that Loos will dedicate his collection of essays *Trotzdem* to Friedrich Nietzsche, opening the book with the following significant quotation: «*Das entscheidende geschieht trotzdem*» («What has to happen will happen in spite of everything»).

The language of one's time is not invented. It happens. For Loos, the quality of our time arises from the very absence of style, from the multiplicity of forms and above all, from the objects manufactured without any esthetic pretensions. Sharpening his attack on the *Werkbund*, he wrote: «But Muthesius also says that through collaboration within the *Deutscher Werkbund*, he will succeed in finding the style of our time. This is wasted effort. We already possess the style of our time. It may be found wherever the artist, that means any member of that association, hasn't yet stuck his nose in... Can it be denied that our leather goods are in the style of our time? And our cutlery and glassware?! And our bathtubs and American wash-basins?! And our tools and machines?! And everything — I repeat everything — which the artists haven't got their hands on yet!» [14].

Considerably in advance of such avant-garde movements as Futurism and Purism, Loos points to the «machine» or the so-called unplanned industrial reality, as the true sign of the new *Zeitgeist*. One cannot deny that this assumption derives from a disenchanted acceptance of the new capitalistic world as «destiny», but I would say that this should not be overestimated, either. «Taking it like a man», to echo M. Weber, is never translated in Loos into an infatuation with the «beauty» of the new engineering esthetic, as will happen later in Futurism, nor does it descend to a simple-minded mimicry of an industrial production that has usurped the role of a new Nature. This is a misunderstanding to which Purism, and Le Corbusier with it, often fell victim.

Such ideological attitudes are all a long way from Loosian disenchantment, which is particularly sceptical of mythologies of the future. Instead a realistic analysis of the present leads him to deride the nostalgia concealed behind the pseudo-progressive front of late Romantic criticism of the dreaded «soullessness» of the «mechanization of the world» [15].

Loos, in short, realized that the pessimistic attitude towards the «machine age», widespread among large sectors of European culture at the turn of the century, betrayed an irrepressible and pathetic desire to turn the clock back. As early as 1898 he wrote in this connection: «But all at once the modern style fell into disgrace. To go into the reasons for this would take us too far from the point. It suffices to say that a sense of dissatisfaction with our own era began to spread. To be modern, to feel or think in a modern way was considered superficial. The sensitive man buried himself in another era and felt himself to be happy...» [16].

So «negation» is a further and deep-rooted motive for criticism of the historicist-synthetic culture which hovers over all of Weimar research, from the *Werkbund* onwards.

The idealistic matrix of such research is unequivocally expressed by the title of a conference held by Muthesius in 1911: «On how to make German manufacture spiritual». It is precisely this spirituality which is the target of the ironic close to his essay *The superfluous*: «We need a carpenter's civilization. If the artists of the applied arts would go back to painting pictures or to building roads, we would have it» [17].

Memory: «*The present is built on the past just as the past was built on the times that went before it*» [18].

Nothing is further from the archaeological veneration of the past than the concept of tradition on which Loos states that he wants to base the teaching of his «school of architecture». Tradition is conceived, in fact, as memory which means, as a critical grasp of what has already been designed in order to leave the mind free and open to what has yet to be designed. In this sense it translates into a logical principle of economy of thought which aims to avoid the waste of starting all over again from the beginning.

In the effort to link past and present Loos discovers history as a basis on which to build the new. Once again he attacks the illusory arrogance of setting out to invent the new with «fantasy», ignoring the huge accumulation of solutions that has already been tried. But at the same time, despite the limits of an evolutionistic concept, or perhaps as a consequence of these, Loos' reflections on history give way to a fierce criticism of any nostalgic attachment to the past. Hence his simultaneous quarrel with the «two rival families» of the *Wiener Secession* and the *Heimatkunst*. If an excess of history leads to the repressive «pseudo-antique» of the *Heimatkunst*, the lively anti-historicism of the *Wiener Secession* leads as surely to the «pseudo-new».

The keystone of Loos' concept of memory is the principle of selectivity. The sideways glance he takes at the past makes necessary — in his view — the choice of precise trains of thought which link up. Without doubt the pivot on which Loos prefers to base his references is «the unsurpassable stature of classical antiquity» and in second place, the great masters of *Klassizismus*: firstly Schinkel and through Schinkel, Ledoux. But this is only the superficial result of Loos having taken a clear stand, having made a considered choice of cultural field. Yet it is obvious that he gives most of his attention to the more modest and anonymous tradition of the master-builders. It is from the *Baumeister* that Loos

wants to steal the secret of an occupation that has renounced autobiographical narcissism in order to stick to the historical process of collective memory. «And I saw how the ancients had built, and I saw how, century after century, year after year, they had been emancipated from ornamentation. Consequently, I had to take up from the point where the chain of development had been broken. One thing I knew: to stay on the track of this development I had to become still more simple» [19].

This passage throws light on one of the most significant aspects of Loos' concept of memory. The language of absence, which will be adopted shortly by some sectors of the avant-garde as a chance to break with the past, is interpreted by Loos as the point of arrival for a long tradition. So the nihilism of Loos has different roots from abstractionism. It should be interpreted as the extreme realism of giving up architectural «representation» in order to stay with the absolute materiality of the pure technological tautology. A good example of this is his impassioned comment on the logic of construction practiced by the «mason»: «He makes the roof. What kind of roof? A pretty roof or an ugly roof? He doesn't know. The roof» [20].

Tautological reduction is the indirect point of contact between architecture without ornament and Dadaist «realism», and in particular Marcel Duchamp's technique of «ready-made objects» which displays ordinary objects as symbols of themselves.

But there is another critical implication which turns Loos into an unwilling but excellent travelling companion of the most radical sectors of the avant-garde: the language of absence, in so far as it was achieved, is adopted as a point of no return. When the *rappel à l'ordre* is launched in the twenties, not only by the so-called «culture of the right», but at times — even though for profoundly different reasons — by the «culture of the left», Loos' attitude will be one of absolute and intransigent theoretical opposition to any kind of turning back. Architecture free of ornament will be proposed as the only possible «decency» for the buildings of the proletariat. His undying opposition to the *Proletarischer Stil*, that is to the eclectic and historicist style elaborated by the students of the *Wagnerschule* to be the symbolic language of «Red Vienna», is the final meaning of his brief experience of planning for the social democratic administration of Vienna [21].

Incidentally to all this, Loos' concept of memory raises the fundamental question of the impossibility of getting rid of the problems of language opened up «on the threshold of a new era» by the crisis brewing in science and philosophy, in the field of visual and especially architectural research. What is more, the problems raised at this time remain unsolved.

A further, and far from negligible, implication of the theory of memory concerns the relationship between architecture and the city. First of all it should be made clear that Loos never made any proposals for ideal-cities (unlike many masters of the Modern Movement such as Frank Lloyd Wright and Le Corbusier). This was because of the unmistakeable repugnance he felt for utopias. A repugnance that should not be taken for an indifference towards the urban question.

On the contrary, the close ties between architectural objects and the urban «locus» in which they are set is one of the fundamental principles of Loos' method of planning. The main reason underlying his adoption of this method is to be found in the fact that history shows its living presence in the city. The walls tell the story, in their shapes and materials, of the long process of historical stratification which has been laid down in them. Loos deduces a guiding standard for urban planning from this relationship with memory; a standard that is a recognition of the individual character that each city possesses. As a result, Loos' houses blend into the urban fabric by developing a dialogue with the existing structures.

But, once again, it is his grasp of the «true story» which prevents Loos from succumbing to an inferiority complex with respect to the past. In fact, Loosian town-planning sets out to continue the great cities' own «tradition of the new». Hence his profound disdain for the vulgar historicism of the defenders of the national heritage who «wish to reduce metropolises to small towns and small towns to metropolises» [22].

Intimacy: «*The building should be dumb on the outside and reveal its wealth only on the inside*» [23].

This idea goes far beyond a simple re-evaluation of the spatial component neglected by academic composition. Nor is it just a renovation of the planning method — though this is of great importance — by pointing out the priority of «building from the inside out» [24].

The real theoretical upset caused by the concept of intimacy lies in its affirmation of the absolute otherness of the interior with respect to the exterior.

The outside belongs to «civilization», the inside belongs to the «individual». The inside is where you live. The outside must confine itself to reflecting the impersonal technique of its own time. Thus the wall of the house is split into two faces: one is public, the other is private. Any ornament superimposed on the outside is «indecent», since it wants to speak where it should remain silent; it wishes to display in the silence without qualities of *Zivilisation*, in the adult dimension of the metropolis, an infantile attachment to the tattoos of the primitive village. But inside, the house is protective. It is a shell which shelters in intimacy the psyche of the person who lives there. Here even the search for lost values may find a warm reception. In his own private space each individual has the right to express and find room for his own subjective «bad taste».

It is not difficult to discern in this theorized dissociation of the silence of the façade from the habitability of the internal space, that singular interlacing of «reactionary theory and revolutionary praxis» which Walter Benjamin sees in Karl Kraus [25].

Like Kraus' writings, the architecture of Loos aims to protect the private sphere from public morality. To be sure, this defense is revolutionary: it affirms the need to preserve a space where it is permitted to think without being conditioned by the prejudices of the period. Such a defense is, in this sense, an indispensable premise for any potential plan to bring about change in the existing conditions.

This is also the reason why Loos' architecture does not adhere to the ideology of transparency which large sectors of Weimar culture made their own in the wake of the suggestive, poetic essay by Paul Scheerbart, *Glasarchitektur* [26].

Even when «glass architecture» triumphs in the twenties, Loosian houses will continue to stand opposite along the streets, with more and more solid walls, genuine protective screens separating the private from the public.

But this is not all. It could also be said that Loos' best-known methodological principle, the *Raumplan*, derives from this stand. The complex fit of spaces of different heights, contained within rigid stereometric shells, seems to have more to do with the psychologistic intention of creating an *Einfühlung* (empathy) between object and subject, between living space and the person who lives in it, than with any criterion of spatial economy. The smaller the rooms, the more intimate they are. The final goal is the «pleasure» the place gives. «Architecture then», Loos remarks, «is to give a precise form to one's state of mind. The room must seem friendly, the house liveable in» [27]. If only because of the indisputable affinity in its conception of space as genuine «lived experience», as *transhistorisches Erlebnis*, we cannot exclude the possibility that the theory of *Raumgestaltung* had an influence on the formulation of the *Raumplan*. This theory had been introduced by the art historian August Schmarsow, who had close contacts with the School of Art History in Vienna.

Repetition: «*We work as best we can without pausing for a moment to worry about form. The best form always already exists and no one should be afraid of making use of it, even if its elements derive from someone else's work. We have enough original genius. Let's repeat ourselves ad infinitum*» [28].

The radical renunciation of formalism leads to the constant reproposal of well-tried architectural elements. Hence the recurrent use of quotations and above all of self-quotations which are to be found throughout Loos' work. But the repetition tends to produce an untiring search for perfection rather than definitive solutions. His planning strategy is aimed at the rehandling and patient reworking of certain unchanging themes; themes of typology as well as of composition. Let us look at some of these:

— *the stepped terrace building scheme* which was introduced in 1912 with the Villa Scheu and re-proposed as a proven typology in the Housing unit projects for the Commune of Vienna (1923), in the Twenty Villas (1923), in the Grand Hotel Babylon... and finally in the Jordan house and Villa Fleischner of 1931. In this scheme a hint of the ancient monument (and in particular the Mausoleum of Halicarnassus «quoted» in 1921 in the design for Max Dvořák's Tomb) is blended with the logic of providing the apartments with an additional convenience, made possible by the technical conquest of the flat roof.

— *The roughly cubic monolithic block*. This is a compositional scheme which starts out from a brusque box-like stereometric lay-out, but which is balanced by a multidirectional object made up from whole volumetric blocks — as in the case of Villa Moller (1928), Müller House (1930) and Villa Winternitz (1931) — or by large empty spaces which hollow out the façades as in the house of Tristan Tzara (1926) or the sugar-refinery manager's Villa at Rohrbach (1916). Despite the elementary nature of the basic geometry, this theme of composition marks the final stage of Loos' work, culminating in the extreme simplicity of the pure cube in the Last House. For Loos, in short, the simplest solution is a point of arrival and not of departure.

— *The corner cylindrical element*, also drawn from traditional Viennese architecture, that is encountered, for example, in the project for the Grand Hotel in the Semmering (1913), in the Hotel des Champs-Elysées (1924) and in the house of Josephine Baker.

— *The column*, made use of both as an element of design and as an autonomous building pattern. It is an archetype, a *ready-made object* chosen as a symbol of the architecture of the great cities, beginning with the arcade of the Looshaus in the Michaelerplatz (1909-11), and the project for a Large Warehouse in Alexandria (1910), then the Monument to Franz Josef (1917)... until it finally takes on the consistency of an isolated individual piece of architecture, of an unheard-of building pattern, in the famous project for the «Chicago Tribune» (1922).

— *Marble*, a material prized for its veining which permits pattern without ornament, is not only used as an external covering for commercial premises (the Steiner store of 1907, the Kniže store of 1909-13 and lastly the Matzner factory of 1929-30) but is also the most widely used material for interiors — from Villa Karma (1904) to the apartments for Alfred Kraus (1905), for Emil Löwenbach (1913-14) and for Hans Brümmel (1929), to the elegant effects in the living-room of the Müller House (1930).

— *The mirror* is perhaps the most fascinating element because of its almost magical ability to multiply space, to create virtual and unexpected dimensions. Used elegantly in his very first work for the Goldman & Salatsch Store, the mirror is the favorite move on Loos' delicate chess-board and is his trademark, as is shown by the conceptual use made of it in the living-room of Leo Brummel's apartment in Pilsen (1929). It is framed by the same moulding as a picture painted in the manner of Seurat hung opposite it, its ability to gather images turning it too into a «picture».

The language of the materials: «*Every material possesses a formal language which belongs to it alone and no material can take on the forms proper to another. As these forms develop out of each individual material's potential for application and from the building procedures proper to it, they have grown up with and through the material. No material permits any intrusion on its own repertoire of forms. Anyone who still dares to make such an intrusion is branded by the world as a forger. Art has nothing to do with forgery, with the lie*» [29].

Loos understands the determinant role played by the material properties of color, grain, luminosity, thickness... of the facing surfaces in the quality of any ambience.

Reversing a long academic tradition, Loos sees form as the end-point of a chain of logic which begins with matter. To this way of thinking, form becomes support for the facing. It is the architect's task, then, to create the image of an ambience through the materials used. «There are architects who follow a different process. Their imagination creates building structures not spaces... The artist, or rather the architect, thinks first of the effect he is aiming at, then he constructs the image of the space he will create in his mind's eye. This effect is the sensation that the space produces in the spectator: which may be fear or fright... respect... pity... the feeling of warmth, as in his own house... forgetfulness, as in a tavern» [30].

Loos explicitly uses the term «spectator». If the architecture of interiors is the theater of habitation, all that is left to the architect is to direct the performance wisely. And the best spectacle results from letting the materials speak in their own tongue. Through a measured balancing of their qualities one can strengthen the emotion which an environment induces in its user. A setting is perceived, experienced and remembered more for the qualities of its materials than for the shape of its container.

This derives from a genuine love for material, such as that felt for the «sick» marble, found abandoned in a quarry, saved, and then used as a wall-covering for the living-room of the Villa Müller. For Loos, the vulgarity of the ornament results from the violence perpetrated on the material in order to make it tell a lie.

At this point one can well understand how baseless are the claims of those who see his use of marble as a sort of contradictory reintroduction of the ornament that had been denied in theory. The misunderstanding is born out of a strained comparison between the costliness of this material and the economy of the white plaster adopted by Rationalism. This does not take into account the more comprehensive view of economy developed by Loos.

Economy comes from making use of the quality intrinsic to the material, eliminating the cost of any additional ornamental work, and at the same time, from the perfect correspondence of this quality to its purpose. «Which is worth more? A kilo of stone or a kilo of gold? It seems a ridiculous question. But only to the businessman. The artist will respond: to me all materials are equally precious» [31]. Hence his great ambition is to attain to the modesty of the artisan, to speak the language of the materials by uncovering their secrets. Loos' painstaking research is wholly oriented towards the domain of techniques such as those which permitted him to obtain centimeter-thick slabs of marble and to invent the modern lining of wood panels, a technique that he picked up through an examination of the cisterns of old water-closets.

Not being up-to-date: «*Build as best you can... Don't be afraid of not being judged modern. Because centuries-old truth has much closer ties with us than the falsehood which is right next to us*» [32]. Not being up-to-date is the principle which resists the ideology of the «new» in the name of the need for the «best». The myth of modernity is replaced by the technique of a thought which reflects its own limits; a profound scepticism about the continual and linear progress of thought derives from this.

Freedom from the obligation to novelty at all costs leads to a quiet evaluation of building from a logical viewpoint. A logic founded on *Können*, that is to say on knowing how, on competence. Building, in short, is measured against possibility. An echo of Gottfried Semper's famous theory may be heard in this thesis, yet without it ever falling into the banal determinism of Semper's followers. From the dialectic between knowing and being able, between technical competence and the conditions imposed by the reality in which he works, springs, in fact, his determination to build the best. It is not possible for Loos even to conceive of an architectural object outside the historical, geographic, technical and economic possibilities of the building «site». This does not mean a paralysis of progress, but only a «reasonable limitation». Modifications in the traditional way of building are only permitted if they represent an improvement [33].

So the struggle of architecture which forgoes being up-to-date takes place on two fronts: against fanatical anti-traditionalism and against vulgar historicism. It has nothing in common either with the conservative attitude, since it admits the possibility of development, or with affected progressivism, since it avoids the breathless pursuit of cultural fashions. Direction is provided here by the constant inquiry into the reasons that have led to the establishment of any given form. No form is assumed to be definitive, but any transformation for the better is technically motivated.

The multiplicity of forms which is a hallmark of Loos' work also derives from reflection on the possibilities of the «sites». One need only consider the obvious dissonance in the elegant joining of white volumes in the Villa Müller, built in 1930, the same year as the vernacular Khuner country house.

Just when one work seems to be taking a path which leads back to the reassuring channel of the Modern Movement, another heads off towards different and unexpected goals. Besides, didn't Loos once say: «Not only the materials but also the form of the building is linked to the place, the nature of the ground and of the air»? [34]

Architecture which does not «keep up-to-date» has no center: it contradicts itself, speaks many languages, uses diverse techniques and invents conflicting images. It is a radical and precocious criticism of the myths, the value systems and the methods subsequently elaborated in the theory of the Modern Movement. Perhaps it is in this polemical scepticism, in this explosive criticism of doubts, that the greatest up-to-dateness of Loos' out-of-date architecture is to be found.

B. G.

Adolf Loos

gez. von Oskar Kokoschka, Februar 1916.

NOTES

1) *Wäsche*, Washing; *Die herrenmode*, Men's fashion; *Kurze haare*, Short hair; *Die kranken ohren Beethovens*, Beethoven's sick ears; *Arnold Schoenberg and his contemporaries*... are the explicit titles of some essays by Loos, which serve to demonstrate the wide range of subjects tackled in his numerous writings. Cfr. A. LOOS, *Sämtliche Schriften*, Vienna-Munich 1962. The reader should be warned that, contravening a grammatical rule of the German language, the nouns are written without capital letters at the beginning in Loos' writings. As a consequence this unusual custom will be adopted when quoting passages from or titles of the original essays.

2) We owe the definition of Loos as a «pioneer of modern architecture» to Nikolaus Pevsner and it is used in the title of the English translation of the monograph by L. MÜNZ and G. KÜNSTLER, *Der Architekt Adolf Loos*, Vienna-Munich 1964; Eng. trans. *Adolf Loos. Pioneer of modern architecture*, with an introduction by N. PEVSNER and a note by O. KOKOSCHKA, London 1966, New York-Washington 1966.

3) A. LOOS, *Architektur*, in *Sämtliche Sehriften*, cit.

4) Cfr. O. KOKOSCHKA, *Mein Leben - Erinnerungen an Adolf Loos*, in «Alte und moderne Kunst», no. 113, Nov-Dec 1970, pp. 4-6; R. NEUTRA, *Ricordo di Loos*, in «Casabella-continuità» no. 233, Nov. 1959, pp. 45-46.

5) K. KRAUS, *In memoriam Adolf Loos, Rede am Grab*, August 1933, Vienna.

6) Cfr. M. HEIDEGGER, *Bauen Wohnen Denken*, 1954. On the subject of Heidegger's ideas in general on the relationship between building and living see the essay by M. CACCIARI, *Eupalinos o l'architettura*, in «Nuova Corrente» nos. 76-77, 1978, pp. 422-442. A critical investigation of the relationship, just mentioned, between Loos' thought and that of Heidegger on the subject of technique is carried out in the first part of the present volume, subtitled *Loos and his time*, especially in the sections *Cultural roots* and *Sick ears and the desire for empty space*.

7) A. SCHÖNBERG, *Adolf Loos, zum 60.Geburtstag, am 10.Dezember 1930*.

8) K. KRAUS, *Nachts*, 1918, in *Bei Wort genommen*, München 1955, p. 341.

9) A. LOOS, *Architektur*, 1910, cit.

10) A. LOOS, idem.

11) A. LOOS, *Kulturentartung*, 1908.

12) A. LOOS, idem.

13) A. LOOS, *Die interieurs in der rotunde*, 1898, cit.

14) A. LOOS, *Kulturentartung*, 1908.

15) *Die Mechanisierung der Welt* (The mechanization of the world), is the subject of a fundamental essay by Walter Rathenau published in 1912 in *Zur Kritik der Seit*, S. Fischer Verlag, Berlin. For the long and articulate German debate on the conflict between mechanization and soul (*Mechanisierung und Seele*) see the anthology of essays edited by Tomàs Maldonado, *Tecnica e cultura*, Milan 1979 and MASSIMO CACCIARI, *Walter Rathenau e il suo ambiente* (with an anthology of writings and political speeches, 1919-1921), Bari 1979. The present volume also goes into this subject, in the section *The Other*.

16) A. LOOS, *Interieurs*, 1898, cit.

17) A. LOOS, *Die überflüssigen*, 1908, cit.

18) A. LOOS, *Meine bauschule*, 1913, cit.

19) A. LOOS, *Architektur*, 1910, cit.

20) A. LOOS, idem.

21) The term *Proletarischer Stil* was adopted to designate the Style of «rote Wien» by Joseph Frank, a friend of Loos and companion in arms in that «battle of language», fought and lost together, to make «simplicity» the criterion of design for the workers' housing. See in this connection the section *Architecture or Proletarischer Stil* in the present volume.

22) A. LOOS, *Heimatkunst*, 1914, cit.

23) A. LOOS, idem.

24) A. LOOS, *Meine bauschule*, 1913, cit.

25) W. BENJAMIN, *Karl Kraus* in *Schriften*, Frankfurt, 1955.

26) P. SCHEERBART, *Glasarchitektur*, Berlin 1914. This essay opens the way for the ideology of glass architecture practiced by Bruno Taut and Walter Gropius as far back as the Werkbund exhibition in Cologne, and which will become the «new style» of the Modern Movement after the war.

27) A. LOOS, *Architektur*, 1910.

28) A. LOOS, *Heimatkunst*, 1914, cit.

29) A. LOOS, *Das prinzip der bekleidung*, 1898, cit.

30) A. LOOS, idem.

31) A. LOOS, *Die baumaterialen*, 1898, cit.

32) A. LOOS, *Regeln für den, der in den bergen baut*, 1913, cit.

33) A. LOOS, idem.

34) A. LOOS, *Wiener Architekturfragen*, 1910.

Adolf Loos - Photograph by W. Weis, Vienna.

BIOGRAPHICAL PROFILE

Adolf Loos was not an architect who drew, and he built little; but he has left a strong impression on the hearts of those who knew him.

«Knowing him was not without its drawbacks for a young architect, should any right-minded elder come to know of it. I recall at least one professor at the Technical Institute who used his public lecture to rant and rave against the corruptor of youth to whom, scandalously, the municipal council of Vienna had not offered hemlock... But if Loos did not enjoy much favor among professors and government officials he was very popular with ordinary, but intelligent and active men... He showed his humanity above all in winning the hearts of women, without ever playing the Don Juan, and was constantly surrounded by the most seductive girls in Vienna. He married them too, one after another, and I don't recall anyone, not even in Hollywood, who had such happy divorces, meaning that they were concluded without any feeling of resentment towards him... To my amazement his marriages in no way hindered many girls and especially, I remember, two or three very beautiful ones, from following Loos and passing the small hours with him in the cafés and haunts of Vienna...

«Among the young people that this Viennese Socrates 'corrupted', apart from myself, were many admirers, not all of them sincere and unreserved. Some of the most gifted, such as Sigmund Freud's son, or Rudolf Schindler... Among the most devoted on the other hand, was Giuseppe De Finetti, a very young devotee of Viennese night life... Another great admirer and pupil of his was Heinrich Kulka» [1].

Here Richard Neutra makes a brief sketch of the personality of Adolf Loos — a really extraordinary personality judging by the fascination it exerted over those who knew him most intimately. And the best men of «great Vienna», cultural capital of *Mitteleuropa*, were among his friends. One thinks of writers like Karl Kraus and Peter Altenberg, of composers like Arnold Schoenberg, Anton Webern and Alban Berg, of philosophers like Ludwig Wittgenstein, of artists like Oscar Kokoschka to whom we owe one of the best portraits of Loos, and of poets like Georg Trakl who dedicated one of his most beautiful lyrics to Loos: *Sebastian im Traum*. These are the people who gave life to that group of intransigent, severe and controversial intellectuals, which Marcel Ray called the «other Austria» to underline their common passion for a radical transformation of the culture in a modern direction — in ostentatious and irrepressible opposition to the tired decadence which also existed in the Vienna of Franz Josef. This is the wholly exceptional climate in which Loos grew up and which shaped his most significant experiences.

He was born in Brno (Brünn), in Moravia, on the 10th December 1870. His father was a stone-cutter and sculptor. An attempt has been made to connect his love for materials (stone, marble, wood, the mirror...) to his childhood spent in the workshops of his father. But here we are in the realm of pure psychological supposition.

Few traces remain of his family life. There is an effective portrayal of his mother in the biography of a sort (*Adolf Loos, der Mensch*) written by Elsie Altman-Loos, one of his four wives. Some autobiographical hints of the years of his adolescence, of the family house and objects, of his sisters Hermine and Irma... can be read between the lines of his essay *Die interieurs in der rotunde* written in 1898.

He attended elementary and high school in the town of his birth, completing his high school studies at the Imperial Lycaeum run by the Benedictines at Melk in South Austria. At the age of seventeen he moved to Reichenberg in Bohemia to attend the State Technical School, where the course required an obligatory period of practical construction work, carried out during the summer vacations of 1887 at the firm of Czapka and Neusser in Brno.

It is highly likely that he did a year of voluntary military service in 1889, as a photograph of him in the uniform of an Austrian lieutenant seems to attest.

From 1890 to 1893 he studied at the Dresden Polytechnic, where an echo still survived of the teaching of Gottfried Semper (who taught at the Polytechnic from 1834 to 1848). Semper was an architect and theoretician to whose thought Loos would acknowledge not a few cultural debts. Other recognized teachers of ideas were the classicist Schinkel and above all Vitruvius, whose treatise on architecture

Lina Loos and Peter Altenberg.

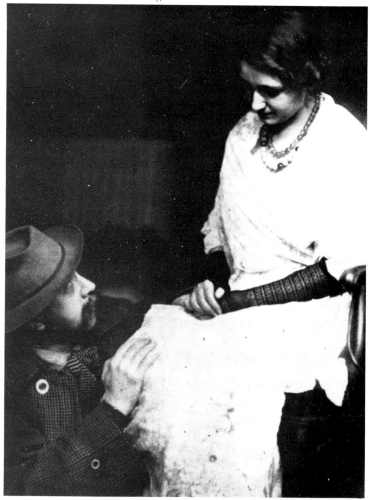

— according to O. Kokoschka — represented a veritable «Bible» for Loos.

At the age of twenty-three he left for the United States where his uncle Benjamin worked as a watchmaker in Philadelphia. He stayed there for three years and did many different kinds of work, from dish-washer to journalist. He visited New York, Philadelphia, St. Louis and Chicago — in the very year that the famous Columbian Exposition was held. America, or rather the mythical transfiguration of the New World, would have a profound influence on Loos' cultural development, but it would always remain a two-faced reality. Images of the functional universe, of the achievement of modernity, and those of the promised land for the rebirth of classicism alternate and are superimposed in his reminiscences.

In 1896 he settled in Vienna to devote himself to the profession of architect. He was twenty-six and began as an assistant in the building firm of Carl Mayreder, the husband of Rosa Mayreder. The latter was a pioneer of the Austrian movement for female emancipation (she was the author of, among other works, the text of Hugo Wolf's opera: *Der Corregidor*, 1896). It is not impossible that this acquaintance influenced his growing interest in what were then called «social questions».

The fact remains that, from 1897 onwards, Loos began to write numerous controversial essays almost all of which were published in the «Neue Freie Presse» of Vienna, assailing a wide range of problems that summed up to a certain extent all the motives behind the struggle of those years for the transformation of «everyday life», of custom, and of the «cultivation of manners». Only rarely does he speak of architecture in a strict sense.

An exception which proves the rule is the essay *Die potemkinsche stadt* (the Potemkin city), published in July 1898 in the pages of the review «Ver Sacrum», the organ of the *Wiener Secession*. This essay, because of its unmistakably sarcastic allusions, marked the beginning of a long and obstinate theoretical opposition to the then triumphant taste of *art nouveau*, developed in Vienna by the pupils of Otto Wagner, most prominent among these Joseph Hoffmann and Josef Maria Olbrich. A further, and perhaps more significant step in this direction was the construction in the following year of the Café Museum (1899), where the elimination of the superfluous had reached such an extreme that the work became known as the «Café Nihilismus», as Loos himself recalls with evident satisfaction.

In 1903 he founded the review *Das andere, Ein blatt zur einführung abendländischer kultur in Österreich* (The other, a periodical dedicated to the introduction of western culture to Austria). The paper was written entirely by Loos and only two issues were published, in 1903. The subtitle alone makes it easy to guess the controversial content of the paper, close in some ways to that singular literary production, the *feuilleton*, common in the Vienna of that time. One need only think of «Die Fackel» founded in 1899 by Karl Kraus and of the review «Kunst», edited by Peter Altenberg from 1903 onwards.

Adolf Loos - Painting by Oskar Kokoschka (1908).

Adolf Loos - Drawing by Oskar Kokoschka (1910).

The following years, up until the outbreak of the First World War, are the years in which he made a name for himself professionally and brought his theories to maturity.

In 1908 he published the essay *Ornament und verbrechen* (Ornament and Crime) which came to represent a sort of manifesto of his art as a consequence of its wide circulation, reprinting and translation. But his 1910 essay *Architektur* is better fitted to serve this end and has a more solid theoretical basis.

In the same year, work began on the construction of the House in the Michaelerplatz, set in the heart of old Vienna opposite the imperial palace of the Hofburg. The simplicity and modernity of the work stirred up such a hornet's nest of controversy, followed by a municipal order to suspend work, that Loos considered it necessary to make a public response to the attacks and insinuations at a packed meeting held at the *Sophiensaal* on the 11th December 1911. It is perhaps worth recalling that Loos was backed up in this «cultural battle» not only by his friends Karl Kraus, Georg Trakl and Peter Altenberg but also by such an authorative academic as Otto Wagner.

In 1912 he founded his *Bauschule* (school of architecture) where he held regular courses that were suspended after a short time as a result of the outbreak of war. Little evidence remains of this experience but there are, for example, some graphic works signed by Paul Engelmann (one of Loos' best pupils, who was to be the «official» architect of the house built in Vienna in 1926 by Ludwig Wittgenstein for his sister Margarethe) and an essay of 1913, with the express title *Meine bauschule*, in which Loos states the fundamental principles of his teaching.

«During the first World War, called up as an officer of the reserve, he nearly ended up in front of a court-martial for having presented himself in a uniform specially designed for him by 'Goldman & Salatsch', with an open collar instead of the usual rigid one, and leggings instead of heavy boots. The Germans lost the war because of these heavy boots: the army had sweaty feet. Loos had his own ideas». This is one of the many anecdotes with which the story of his life is studded, related by O. Kokoschka [2].

Loos lost no sleep over the break-up of the Hapsburg Empire as a result of the defeat. On the contrary — after the proclamation of the Republic of Austria on the 12th November 1918 — Loos entered into a phase of enthusiastic involvement with questions of cultural policy. In 1919 he put forward a proposal for the foundation of a «Ministry of the Arts» (in collaboration with his friends, Schoenberg, K. Kraus, M. Ermers, L. Münz and others). The *Richtlinien für ein Kunstamt* (Guidelines for a Ministry of the Arts) were published in «Der Friede» no. 62, 1919. Only Schoenberg's contribution is signed, but Loos was responsible for the essay *Der stàat und die kunst* (Art and the State) [3].

Two significant and contrasting testimonies of those years have come down to us. The first is from Ludwig Wittgenstein, who declares in a letter to Paul Engelmann that he had felt «horror and disgust» for «the stand of intellectual snob» adopted by Loos during that period [4]. We

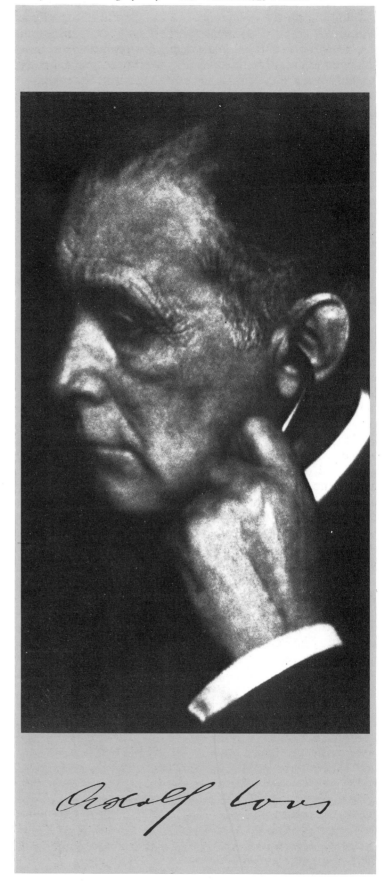

Adolf Loos - Photograph by Trude Fleischmann, Vienna.

owe the second to Alban Berg who, while describing the festivities held to celebrate A. Schoenberg's 45th birthday at Mödling on the 13th September 1919, wrote to his wife as follows: «Over the course of the afternoon greetings and telegrams arrived. It has been very pleasant. Loos especially has been in great form. I tell you, his appearance is getting finer and finer. He looks older, but his features are taking on all the signs of greatness and well-being. He talked for hours almost completely by himself, but wonderfully, on politics and culture in the easy, gracious manner of a great story-teller, almost anecdotal but with great profundity. It's a pity that you weren't there to hear him» [5].

Between 1920 and 1922 he held the post of *Chefar-chitekt des Siedlungsamtes der Gemeinde Wien* (Chief Architect of the Housing Department of the Commune of Vienna). The importance of this experience speaks for itself, if one takes into account that it occurred at the beginning of the delicate and complex attempt at a «socialist» administration of «Red Vienna» (1920-1934). It was in 1920, in fact, that the Austrian Social-democratic party (S.D.A.P.) gained a clear majority in the Viennese municipal elections. Yet Loos' employment in this specific planning sector should not be mistaken for an adherence to the ideology of Austrian Marxism. His substantial distance from this current of political thought is made clear by Loos himself at the conference *Die moderne siedlungen* held at Stuttgart on the 12th November 1926. Because of irreconcilable differences over the best ways in which to make alterations to the fabric of the city, Loos resigned as chief architect in 1922.

He then moved to France (1922-1927), dividing his time between Paris and the Riviera, but making frequent journeys to Austria, Germany and Czechoslovakia. Many events bear witness to the esteem in which he was held in French intellectual and avant-garde circles, including the republication in 1920 of a translation of his essay *Ornament und verbrechen* in the pages of «Esprit Nouveau» (the review edited by Ozenfant, Le Corbusier and Paul Dermée), his acceptance by the Parisian circle of Tristan Tzara, for whom Loos would build the House on the Avenue Junot in 1926), as well as his admission as an honorary member of the *Salon d'Automne*, where he also put on an exhibition in 1923. During this period he ran numerous conferences, among which the one held at Graz in November 1927, *Der soziale mensch und seine architektur*, is worth mentioning along with the one at Stuttgart which has already been referred to.

He returned to Vienna in 1928, though he broke his stay in Austria with trips to Paris and the Riviera in France and to Prague and Pilsen in Czechoslovakia. In the latter country especially, many of his works were built during those years. Some of his most significant works belong to this last phase, such as Villa Moller (1928) in Vienna, Villa Müller (1930) and Villa Winternitz (1931-32) in Prague and the Khuner Country-house at Payerbach in Lower Austria, works which propose a return to the monolithic nature of the architectural object in deliberate contrast to the transparency of the «glass architecture» which dominated rationalist styles in the twenties. Once again Loos continues an uncompromis-

ing expansion of certain constant postulates of his architectural thought, in contentious indifference to «fluctuations in taste».

In 1930, on the occasion of his sixtieth birthday, Loos received an important recognition of his standing as a «master» of architecture. On the initiative of the president of the Czechoslovakian Republic, Thomas G. Masaryk, the town of his birth, Brno, bestowed an annual honorific income on him in the form of a regular stipend. In the same year a weighty volume of testimonies edited by Richard Lanyi (*Adolf Loos, Zum 60. Geburtstag am 10. Dezember 1930*) and the monograph by Heinrich Kulka (*Adolf Loos, Das Werk des Architekten*) were published. The following year his collected essays were sent to the press.

In 1931 a venereal disease that he had contracted as far back as 1911 grew worse, forcing him to enter the Rosenhügel Hospital in Vienna for treatment. Troubles with his hearing, from which he had suffered since adolescence, worsened too, leaving him almost completely deaf.

In the autumn of 1932 a further worsening in his condition forced him to give up working and to enter the same hospital at first and later the Schwarzmann clinic in Kalksburg, where he died on the 23rd August 1933.

He was buried in the Kalksburg cemetery on the 25th August. In October of the following year his body was shifted to the main cemetery of Vienna, section 32 C of the graves of honor, where he lies buried beneath a simple tombstone — an elementary cube of granite — put up in 1956 by the municipal council of Vienna on the lines of a drawing by Loos himself.

B. G.

NOTES

1) R. NEUTRA, *Ricordo di Loos*, in «Casabella» n. 233, nov. 1959, pp. 45-46.

2) O. KOKOSCHKA, *Mein Leben - Erinnerungen an Adolf Loos*, in «Alte und moderne kunst» n. 113, nov. dic. 1970, p. 5.

3) *Der staat und die kunst*, in «Der Friede», 1919, n. 62, pp. 352-354.

4) Cfr. *Letters from Ludwig Wittgenstein with a Memoir*, Oxford 1970.

5) A. BERG, *Briefe an seine Frau*, München-Wien, 1965.

BIBLIOGRAPHY

CLAIRE LOOS, *Adolf Loos privat*, Vienna 1936.
ELSIE ALTMANN-LOOS, *Adolf Loos der Mensch*, Vienna-Munich 1968.
VICTOR LOOS, *Ein Gedächtnismal für den Erbauer Adolf Loos*, published by the «Haus der Technik», Vienna 1942.
LINA LOOS, *Du Silberne Dame Du, Briefe von und an Lina Loos*, Vienna-Hamburg 1966.
OSKAR KOKOSCHKA, *Mein Leben-Erinnerungen an Adolf Loos*, in «Alte und moderne Kunst», no. 113, Nov-Dec 1970, pp. 4-6.

Adolf Loos and Peter Altenberg.

LOOS AND HIS TIME

Modern architecture is a superfluity created on the basis
of the correct recognition of a lack of necessity

The others are artists of the set square
Loos is the architect of the tabula rasa

Karl Kraus
Beim Wort genommen

When one looks beyond the biographical data of a thinker-architect, in search of the fundamental presuppositions of his design strategy, the need arises to take another look at the historical background on which the «battle over language» was fought. This gives rise to the problem of defining the limits within which his individuality has played a predominant role in influencing external events. But our aim is to analyse his architectural thought; so we must consciously give up any idea of reconstructing an (unlikely) biographical identity, limiting ourselves to using the chronology of his life as a supporting structure for a discussion of his training and the development of his architectural ideas. Adolf Loos' life — so crowded with by now mythical characters — is not lacking in expressive testimonies by intellectuals or suggestive reminiscences by people who knew him well and loved him. Worth particular mention is the «poetic» volume edited by Richard Lanvi for his sixtieth birthday, which gathered together writings by Peter Altenberg, Hermann Bahr, Alban Berg, Josef Frank, Johannes Itten, Oscar Kokoschka, Karl Kraus, J.J. Peter Oud, Ezra Pound, Marcel Ray, Arnold Schoenberg, Bruno Taut, Georg Trakl, Tristan Tzara, Anton Webern, Stefan Zweig and others [1]. But even though his humanity was far from negligible in the effect that it had on the spread of his ideas, it is not this of which we wish to speak, but rather of his «architectural lesson» and its implications for theory, technique and form [2].

he goes so far as to outline the geneological tree of his predecessors.

«Ever since humanity discerned the stature of classical antiquity, one single thought has united all the great architects. They think: I am building the way the ancient Romans would have done. We know that they are wrong. Time, place, purpose, climate and setting all make this impossible.

«But every time architecture strays too far from its model at the hands of the lesser architects, the lovers of decoration, the great architect reappears to lead it back to antiquity. Fischer von Erlach in the south and Schlüter in the north were rightfully the great masters of the eighteenth century. And on the threshold of the nineteenth century there was Schinkel. We have forgotten him. If only the light of this extraordinary figure would illuminate the future generation of architects» [5].

The idea of «cyclic time», the value placed on the «Roman model», the relationship with *Klassizismus*; none of this is new. Throughout the 19th century the discipline of architecture constantly ran up against the problem of «historical awareness». What is new, rather, is the way of relating to it [6]. Historicist eclecticism had in fact reduced history to a collection of styles, and often ended up dressing the technological achievements of the 19th century in clothes borrowed from the past. This disguise concealed the naive misunderstanding involved in bestowing values which trans-

CULTURAL ROOTS

Not the biography of the man then, but the biography of his ideas. And it is a very complex thing to attempt, since it involves interpreting the evolution of his thought in all the contradictoriness of its development, tracing a path through the tangle of moments of crisis and continuity, and the relationships with the more general progress of the debate over the great themes which were the ruling passion of the decades around the turn of the century [3].

There is no doubt that Loos' architecture participated, in its own way, in the «crisis of classical reason» that came to a head in those years and 'crystallized' in the Vienna of the *finis Austriae*; even if its part in the web of problems woven in other disciplinary sectors, especially by the «great Viennese figures of language», has been to some extent exaggerated [4]. Anticipating a conclusion, it may be said that the points of convergence are more often to be found in the formulation of the problems than in a similarity of response. And yet it is in precisely this «dalliance» with disquieting inquiries, in this continual striving to find an answer to crucial questions of «language», that the singular fascination of Loos' work lies. To discover its relevance all that remains is to learn how to examine it.

If one tries to go back to the many roots of his architecture straightaway one runs across a fundamental question: his relation to history. In many passages of his writings Loos makes history and criticism of history the central pivot of his architectural meditations. In his crucial essay *Architektur*,

cend history onto the academic reconstructions of stylistic codes. This implies a weakening of the present in so far as it falls into that «excess» which F. Nietzsche defines as «antiquarian veneration» of the past [7]. All the toil and complexity of the past were impoverished by the application of too easy formulas.

The road loop known as the Ring had become the preferred backdrop for staging the eclectic 'performance' in Vienna and it is no accident that Loos will honor it with one of his most sarcastic comments in the essay *Die potemkinsche stadt* [8]. The neo-Gothic experiments of the Votivkirche by Ferstel (1853-79) and of the Rathaus by Schmidt (1872-82), the neo-Renaissance ones of the Staatsoper by Siccardsburg and van der Nüll, the neo-Hellenistic ones of the Parliament by Hansen, and many others, follow one another along the Ring in disharmonious sequence.

Otto Wagner does not go much further though he does have the merit of having introduced the *Moderne Architektur* current into Central European culture [9]. Undoubtedly Wagner makes a more complex and advanced use of the historicist vocabulary: it is based on a preliminary dismantling of the linguistic codes into their constitutive elements and then going on to an original assembly of the «pieces» collected into compositional clusters governed by new syntaxes and new hierarchical orders. If one takes into account the breadth of such a *bricolage* — which stretches from the varied melt of architectural cultures that fills the

Austro-Hungarian basin to the mimesis of features drawn from the so-called minor arts and from new technological processes — one can well understand the innovative weight of this experimental contamination of heterogeneous vocabularies.

It is true, though, that this is only the logical outcome of a nineteenth century vision where history is seen as an inventory of forms, as a sacred museum of available archetypes.

But Wagner is obsessed by an anachronistic desire to reassemble the shattered codes (a fragmentation to which he had himself contributed) into a new Synthesis, a new Style, which he incorrectly defined as *Nutzstil* [10]. The return to the past — when not free from the concept of mimesis — is again reduced to a «hurdy-gurdy tune».

The substantial conceptual «break» brought about by Loos consists in the principle of selectivity in historical reflection. The postulate from which he begins is the dilatation of the space of history, that is to say the assumption of the simultaneous coexistence of all historically produced forms. This implies a wholly different view of time that reveals — as a corollary — not only the arbitrary and conventional character of any «poetic» codification, but also the impossibility of not choosing the «rules of the game». His «sectarian» choice — of a definite line of research to take up again — is made necessary, not in spite of its arbitrary nature, but precisely because of it. To avoid running the risk of getting lost, the journey into memory can only be undertaken after the paths to be followed have been marked out. The past is dark, nothing shows itself. You can only find what you are looking for. In this sense Loos roams the disillusioned labyrinth of history without the anxiety of those who are in search of compositional systems to «repeat» or architectural vocabularies to «take back», but with the lucid persistence of someone looking for the thread.

«And I saw how the ancients had built and I saw how, century after century, year after year, they had been emancipated from ornamentation. *Consequently, I had to take up from the point at which the chain had been broken*. One thing I knew: to stay on the track of this development I had to become still more simple» [11]. Loos' traversal of *wirkliche Historie* becomes in the end a search for «historic direction». Not things then, not architectural objects intended for a new mimesis, but the broken thread of tradition: this is what anti-eclectic excavation of the past brings to light. And this submerged tradition is more exactly the handing down (*überlieferung*) of a culture of building that the *Baumeister* (one who builds) guards «with every care» against the «poison» and the «vanity» of the «false prophets» of the new who want to reduce architecture to «graphic art» [12].

Loos' disparagement of «fantasy», of the narcissistic frenzy for «invention», arises from a basic criticism of anyone who does not recognize the «historicity» of the language [13]. Hence too his conscious «humility» of wanting to

Johann Bernhard Fischer von Erlach: The Labyrinth, from «Entwurf einer historischen Architektur», Vienna 1721.

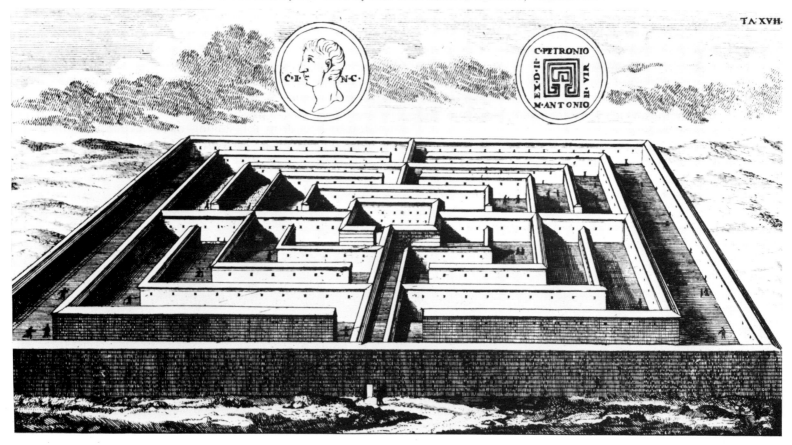

learn to build, to learn a *technè* from the holder (master) of the «secrets». «I have not fulfilled my duty as an artist by creating freely and giving free rein to my fantasy... No. Instead I tip-toed into workshops like a timid apprentice. Respectful, I watched the man in the blue apron. And I begged him: let me into your secrets! For, shyly, a large part of artisan tradition is still hidden from the eyes of the architect» [14].

Loos' architecture has an undoubted analytical bent that takes the concept of tradition as its foundation. Reflection on the past develops, in fact, out of a critical work of demolition-endless transformation which is tested only at the moment of practical design. On the test bench of 'constructed architecture' he keeps up his persistent analysis and patient manipulation of formal materials in a constant becoming. And the nodal point is precisely the recognition of this «becoming». The systematic dismantling of architecture from the past is no longer a search — as in Wagner — for «finished» elements of composition, but for the intelligibility of the deep-rooted mechanisms involved in the historical creation of «forms». If each form is the end result of a process, then it is necessary to understand its rules in order to be able to 'learn to build'; necessary — as Loos makes clear — to seek to «uncover the causes which have given rise to that form» [15]. He adds: «If progress in technique makes possible an improvement of form, it is always necessary to adopt that improvement» [16].

His criticism of the paralysing immobility of historicism and of the regressive provincialism of the *Heimatkunst* is made through a firm revaluation of «genuine history». By what is only superficially a paradox, the recognition of «historic direction» leads to a definitive surmounting of the contemplative and eclectic view of history, and therefore to its reversal from the past to the future. Loos would be able to subscribe to W. Benjamin's statement: «The past has stored up images which may be compared to those fixed on a photographic plate. Only the future can develop them: those which are so strong that the image can appear in all its details» [17].

History becomes a store of ammunition for the battles over contemporary language.

Archaeological veneration is replaced by the utilization of the past, constantly redesigned, worn out and deformed by its operative goals. It is no accident that in 1921 Loos should dedicate a superb unrealized monument to Max Dvořák — the one critic within the Vienna School of Art who takes the principle of updating history to an extreme [18]. At this point one can well understand why Loos' idea of cyclic time — in contrast to the linear conception of development — has an undeniably progressive character. Go-

Johann Bernhard Fischer von Erlach: Trajanus' square, from «Entwurf einer historischen Architektur».

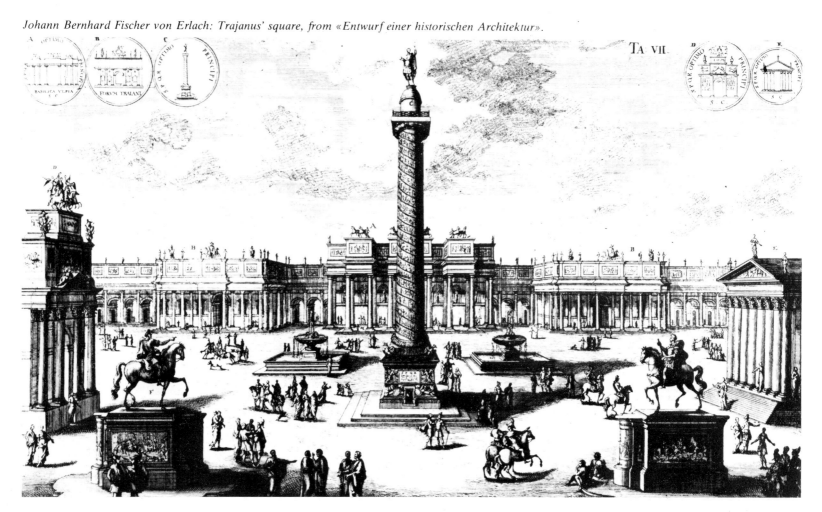

ing back to a past form never means — in this view — going back to the form itself. This return implies the very movement of becoming. History develops through «breaks», in an eternal process of de-construction and re-construction. In this sense, to repeat means to select, to get rid of all the anachronistic surface accumulations by means of an unending process of decantation. In such a radical analytical examination of the past — aimed at finding the basic principles (*Grundbegriffe*) which underly the development of western architecture — Loos gains an insight into the meaning of the recurrence of «re-births» marked by the cyclic return to the Classical.

«Our civilization is based on a recognition of the unsurpassable grandeur of classical antiquity. From the Romans we have derived the technique of our thought (*die technik unseres denkens*) and of our way of feeling. It is to the Romans that we owe our social conscience and the discipline of our soul» [19].

Later Panofsky and Saxl will write: «One of the essential characteristics of the European spirit seems to be the way in which it destroys things and then reintegrates them on new bases, breaking with tradition in order to go back to it from a completely new point of view and this is what produces the 'rebirths' in the true sense of the term... So we can say that what might be called the problem of the 'phenomena of renaissance' is one of the central problems of the history of European culture» [20].

But on what basis is the technique of thought that may be derived from Roman classical art articulated? One might answer — paraphrasing Heidegger — that the *Grundbegriff* handed down by the Romans is the principle of reflection on the already thought-of, in order to make the mind free and available for what is as yet unthought-of [21]. This is not just a principle of noetic economy (which avoids the waste of starting all over again), but above all a method of rationalizing the project based on the recomposition (and therefore change in meaning) of the formal materials inherited from history. «It is no accident», Loos adds, «that the Romans were not able to invent a new order of columns, a new ornamentation. They were already too advanced for this. They took all this from the Greeks and adapted it to their own ends... The Greeks wasted their imaginative force in the orders of columns, the Romans applied theirs in designing buildings. And someone who is able to solve great problems of planning doesn't bother with new mouldings» [22].

At this point it becomes obvious that there is no sense in supposing an elective affinity between the Roman model proposed by Loos and the re-appraisal of late Roman art fostered in those years by Riegl, Wickoff and more generally

Johann Bernhard Fischer von Erlach: The Cathedral of St. Charles Borromeo, Vienna 1715.

by the «School of art history at Vienna» [23]. At least as far as this aspect is concerned, the coincidences do not go beyond purely chronological and geographical data. Riegl's motivations for his re-evaluation of Roman architecture are profoundly different [24].

Rather it is in the realm of the Semperian theory of *Können* that the presuppositions or, if you prefer, the 'limits' of Loos' thesis are to be found. This is not just because of the reiterated and explicit declarations to this effect made by Loos himself [25], not just because of his direct familiarity with this theory dating from his attendance of courses at the

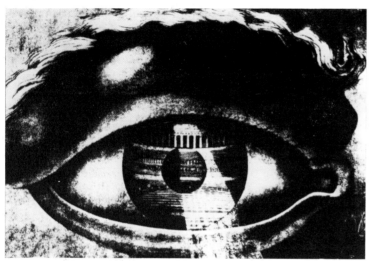

Claude-Nicolas Ledoux: «Coup d'oeil» at the theater of Besançon.

Karl Friedrich Schinkel: Interior.

Dresden Polytechnic (1890-93) and not even because of his symptomatic use of the term «technique» which Riegl himself points out as being typical of the followers of Semper, but primarily it is because there exists a substantial methodological convergence in their reflection on the limits of thought identified within a knowing how (a *Können* in fact) [26]. There is no possibility of transforming a language outside the techniques of production that are given by history: this is the point where Loos meets up again with Semper. Such a thesis, one notes, has nothing to do with a mechanical determinism of external causes in the production of forms — as has sometimes been misunderstood: it sets limits to «invention» as it recognizes a constructive principle in the chain of relationships between material, technique and purpose. Far from being inhibited, the desire for form is exalted by Loos in his constant assault on the problem of competence.

The tale of the «master-saddler» has something to tell us here. The moral of the story is unmistakable: «... The professor was able to present him with forty-nine designs for saddles... The master-saddler looked at the drawings for a long time and it all got plainer and plainer to his eyes. Finally he exclaimed: 'Professor, sir! If I understood as little as you do of riding, of horses, of leather and its working, I too could have your fantasy' [27].

The «master» is one who prefers familiarity with the tools of his own trade to the free exercise of his imagination. Any innovation in the way forms are produced must be founded on technique if it is to be a genuine one [28]. If architecture is a precise field of knowledge any change, any revolution in its disciplinary structure can only take place on the basis of a self-critical and analytical examination of its own modes of working, its own materials and its own techniques. Outside this competence there is only the ideological and fanciful smoke of mannered modernism, a smoke which is bound to be given off at any change in fashion. The reiterated and systematic attack on «fashion» — to be found over and over again in Loos' writings — is in the end an attack on the «regimes of truth» [29]. Only after having understood and totally demolished the mechanisms by which the «lie» (of pseudo-modernity) is put into circulation is it possible to go on to a re-foundation of the discipline on a new basis, on a truly modern basis.

The need for a self-critical look at the instruments, methods and historical dimension of architecture grows in step with the evolution of the long and articulate debate over the epistemological foundations of the sciences, sparked off in Vienna by the empirico-critical arguments of Mach and developed from different angles by Hertz, Boltzmann, Carnap, Popper, the *Wiener Kreis* and Wittgenstein himself [30].

One may then ask how it is possible to derive the desire for a «return to the Classical» from a realization of the eclipse of all metaphysical certainty.

In the first place it is interesting to note that Loos points to both the late-illuminism of Schinkel and Fischer von Erlach's baroque-classical as poles of reference. This fact is already of significance in that it throws into relief the simultaneous dialectical presence of both rationalism and expressionism that is never resolved in Loos' work (and is symbolically expressed by the semantic contrast between the inside and outside of his houses).

His reference to Fischer von Erlach should, probably, be interpreted as an allusion to the attempt made in the *Entwurf einer historischen Architektur* to trace a line of thematic continuity through the entire history of architecture [31]. This means, in other words, adherence to a «method» (fitting for an architect) of re-designing the past. But the great readiness of the Viennese master to experiment inevitably brings up again the question of the arbitrary nature of any «poetic choice». His attempt to reduce the field of research into form to the realm of the «abstract-geometric» is moreover a desire to go beyond the openmindedness of the baroque that is only comprehensible in terms of the cultural debate within the *finis Austriae*. But it is from Schinkel that Loos derives — strictly speaking — the strategic axis of design which leads to the «victory of straight lines» (a relative and provisory one as are all victories over form). Even before a volumetric purism, or a rigidly geometric syntax of form, comes the illuminists' «revolution» in the very concept of classicity. Through Schinkel Loos comes into contact with Ledoux, who more than anyone else was the protagonist of that «revolution» [32]. This is no small reversal of direction if one considers that — from Ledoux onwards — classicism no longer seeks an absolute harmony, a rigid hierarchy of components, but pursues — as Kaufmann puts it — the «destruction of baroque uniformity», defines composition as a «multiplicity of disconnected parts», and extols the principle of detachment of architectonic elements [33].

That it should be to this particular (illuminist and late-baroque) conception of classicity that Loos intends to refer is also confirmed by the fact that in an attempt to determine the historical antecedents to his work in the Viennese ar-

chitectural research of the last three centuries, what stands out — apart from the Liechtenstein Palace by Martinelli, the Church of the Servites by Canevale or the Pallavicini Palace by Hohenberg — is the «Flora-Gebäude» by Kornhäusel. And it is known that within the group of Viennese classicists (von Hohenberg, Montojer, von Nobile...) it was Josef Kornhäusel who developed the lessons of Schinkel and Ledoux with the greatest rigour and consistency, adopting a technique of design «... based entirely on... a composition involving the addition of simple bodies» [34].

In other words it is the *Architekturtheorie der französischen Klassik* rather than a generic *Klassizismus* that lies at the root of Loos' thought [35]. The substance of what has been inherited from the illuminist revolution was clearly expressed by Kaufmann himself, when he wrote: «No arrangement of forms, no definitive and general formula but the challenge of and the struggle for new forms and new schemes: this was the legacy of illuminism» [36].

At this point one can see how the *logos* of Loosian architecture has nothing to do with the naive rationalism of *reine Architektur* (pure architecture). It is a matter of using logic that cannot be reduced to a banal functionalism. The absence of ornament does not in fact exclude recourse to intellectually complex and refined techniques of composition such as simulation and dissonance. In this case, attempts at a trivially functionalistic interpretation of the struggles against ornament are more vociferously denied by his practice of design than by his written words. One need only look at the repeated optical fragmentation produced by the distorting play of mirrors (e.g. in the Kärntner-Bar) or at the *trompe l'oeil* of the columns without static function of the House in the Michaelerplatz (1910) or the simultaneous but contrasting presence of two or three different architectonic mannerisms in the same work to realize how far away are the logical constructions of Loos from «fanatical rationalism».

Karl Friedrich Schinkel: The façade of the Altes Museum, Berlin 1824-28.

Nor, on the other hand, is it possible to reduce Loos' «rationality» to a simple question of «taste».

Loos' motivation is at bottom theoretical, and is a dedication to the achievement of an exact formulation of language. Strictly speaking it is more correct to describe Loos' work as logical formalism and not as architectonic abstractism.

Besides, rigorous formalization of linguistic play is a much pursued theme in the Vienna of the *Tractatus logico-philosophicus* [37], a phenomenon, for example, which one comes across — although with a different stress — in the iron discipline of the writings of Karl Kraus, in the classical poetic syntax of Georg Trakl, in the limpid pictorial structure of Egon Schiele or in the compact rhythmico-serial acoustical grammar of Arnold Schoenberg. Leaving aside for the time being an appraisal of the specific differences between these poetical expressions (which are far from negligible and to which we will come back often) it is more important for the moment to get a feeling of their common denominator. An indirect key to their interpretation is offered by Wittgenstein himself in the programme which he puts forward in the preface to the Tractatus: «to set a limit to thought, or rather not to thought but to the expression of thoughts... so the limit can be drawn in the language alone, and what is outside the limit will be nothing but nonsense» [38].

Perhaps music — «heavy language» par excellence as Adorno maintains, an «intellectual form» (*Verstandesform*, says Hegel) free from any extralinguistic reference [39] — can give us a clearer insight into the direction, the limit and the course of the uncompromisingly logical construction of form developed and taken to an extreme by the radical sections of the Viennese intelligentzia. It is significant that Schoenberg, as far back as the critical years of the *finis Austriae*, should feel the need to theorize on the rules of atonal composition in his fundamental essay of 1911, *Harmonielehre* (dedicated to Gustav Mahler) [40]. The object of the essay — as L. Pestalozza makes clear — «is to subject tonal harmony to a close analysis of its formative elements. An analysis of just what there is in it and in the historical situation in which it was formed and which ordained that it should evolve in the way it did» [41].

In the text a battle is fought out between the inevitable subjectivity and the uncontainable desire for objectivity of poetic syntax. It is worth taking a careful look at the solution proposed. The element of subjectivity is confined to the basic assumption (that is to say the choice of series), the thematic development of which is dictated by inflexible criteria. The sense of this argument is caught well by Kandinsky (who attempted to make an analogous translation of it into pictorial language, which failed however) when he writes: «the greatest freedom of all, the freedom of a free art, can never be absolute. Each era attains to a certain degree of this freedom, but not even the most brilliant of geniuses can go beyond the limits of its freedom» [42]. In other words, freedom of expression is exalted by an awareness of the limits dictated by a self-imposed code, whose deep-rooted intransigence is a guarantee of historically motivated

Domenico Martinelli: Liechtenstein Palace, Vienna 1698-1711.

Ernst Koch: Drawing of the façade of the Michaelerkirche, 1792.

logical rigor and not an act of dogmatically metahistorical validity. «Tonality», writes Schoenberg in *Harmonielehre*, «is a form which offers the possibility of achieving a certain unity through uniformity», but he explains «I do not hold this to be an eternal law, a natural law of music (since) eternal laws do not exist for us, but only conditions that remain valid until they are superseded and eliminated, wholly or in part, by new conditions» [43].

Thus architecture without ornaments is mirrored not so much in the 'moral' writings of Kraus as in the atonal music of Schoenberg. Just as Schoenberg freezes *Expressionismus* by containing it within the closely packed composition of tonal intervals, Loos strips the exterior of meaning by enclosing the 'desire for habitability' in the intimate interval between the «walls» of language. Without this implosion of *Expressionismus* it would not even be possible to understand the strong intellectual and human bond between him and Oskar Kokoschka, expressionist and psychoanalytical painter [44].

What is expressible about architecture («that of which one can speak») is not — for Loos — the function, but the shape of space.

«In this way», he explains, «I have taught my pupils to think in three dimensions, to think in the cube» [45]. The architect has the «wall» at his disposal. By means of the wall he separates a space — fixing its boundaries. Inside this *Raum* one can try to live, to express one's own private existence and show one's own «bad taste». The essence of Loos' argument is to be found within this chess-game in space. Here is revealed the meaning of an architecture that is a genuine expression of «spatial thinking».

It is no accident that Schoenberg is the one who grasps it with extraordinary lucidity: «... when I see one of Loos' works I am aware of a difference right away: here as in the work of a great sculptor, I see a non-composite, immediate, three-dimensional conception... Here everything is thought-out, imagined, composed and moulded in space as if all the structures were transparent; as if the eye of the spirit were confronted by space in all its parts and as a totality simultaneously» [46].

If it is true that the specific of architectonic language is the three-dimensional shape, then it is on this scene that the representation of a thought should be appraised. Well, in the construction of space Loos' poetics shift constantly between the opposite poles of rationality and irrationality, of realism and simulation, of concreteness and abstraction. It is a play that is subtle, disillusioned, in the end cynical, a play in which the self-imposed rules always insinuate doubt, suggest transgression and entice one into making exceptions. Loos would be able to go along with Wittgenstein when he says: «I can play according to certain rules with the pawns on the chessboard. But I could also imagine a game in which I play with the rules themselves: then the rules of chess are the pawns of my game and the rules of the game are, for example, the laws of logic» [47].

The Loosian *logos* is run through with an (at times sarcastic) scepticism. He is accompanied by a whole baggage of conceptual antinomies on his intellectual adventure of which his journey to America is a stage that cannot be disregarded.

Gottfried Semper and Karl von Hasenauer: Burgtheater, Vienna 1874-88.

'As the ship on which Karl Rossmann was travelling slowed to enter New York harbor, he perceived the Statue of Liberty, which had been in sight for some time, as if suddenly bathed in a brighter light. The arm which held the sword seemed to have been raised at that very moment and the free breezes blew lightly around the figure... 'How high it is!', he said to himself — and although he had no intention of moving away, he found himself pushed little by little right up to the railing by the crowd of porters who were passing in front...».

This account of a moving arrival in the land of gigantism is the opening note of *Amerika* by Franz Kafka, and is a fitting introduction to the tone of the literary and mythical transfiguration that Loos gave to his journey to the United States, made between 1893 and 1896. He left by ship from Hamburg and landed at New York («in horrible weather and arrived in the working-class areas of lower Manhattan») [48]. He then visited Philadelphia, Chicago (where the celebrated Columbian Exposition was being held) and St. Louis, holding down a variety of temporary jobs — from draftsman to reporter to dishwasher [49].

This experience left an indelible mark on his cultural development, not only because of what he saw in reality, but also because of what he reworked and imagined in his mind. Yet it is interesting to note how his imaginary projection of the «new world» coincided for the most part with the way books, paintings and films in Europe represented the myth

raphy, had poisoned their blood...) towards realism and freedom... When he was talking about America, he sounded, to some extent, like an immigrant version of Walt Whitman» [51].

Although Loos, in his essay *Die schuhmacher* (1898) quotes expressly a poetic passage taken from *Leaves of Grass* by Walt Whitman, he would never really take the «American» point of view of the ideology of democracy [52]. In fact, that whole current of thought deriving from Jefferson would remain profoundly alien to him, a current which — although with different accents — informed the search for an autochthonous architecture by men like H.H. Richardson, L. Sullivan and F.L. Wright [53].

«Adolf Loos, my dear brother in spirit» are the words with which a famous letter from Louis Sullivan to Loos begins [54]. But it is precisely «in spirit», that is in his deepest cultural and ideological attitudes, that this profound mental distance from the «master» of the School of Chicago shows itself. The same apparent agreement with the ideas expressed by Sullivan in *Ornament in Architecture* in 1892 — stressed by Pevsner — is almost irrelevant as far as the different values they placed on the development of the forces of production and its effects on daily life are concerned [55]. Where Sullivan tries to throw a cloak of mythical «ethical values» over the skyscraper — neutral product of the free exploitation of the value of building land — transforming it into a symbol of the cultural compensation of

AMERICA

of America, seen as the place where the Modern Times could be checked out in advance. Many of the typical ambivalences of that myth — which rapidly became very widespread in Europe — recur in his writings and especially in the two issues of «Das andere» («The Other, a periodical dedicated to the introduction of western culture to Austria»): from the myth of democracy attained, to the idea of a world dominated by technology; from the pragmatic and impartial attention given to the needs of everyday life, to the 'exalted' desire for form gratified by gigantic monumental objects on an urban scale; from the overcoming of the «senile sickness» of European *Kultur*, to the optimistic «uneasiness» about the radical changes (in customs and behavior) brought about by the prefigured triumph of *Zivilisation* [50].

The demolition of the fable begins of necessity with the dismantling of its ideological supporting pillar: democracy. «For him», writes R. Neutra, «America was the land of free men, of people in touch with reality, without superstitions and false traditions... He saw that his Americans were, in general, of excellent human material, if one forgets about so-called education and culture and those things which are given an exaggerated importance in European countries, and especially in Vienna, cultural capital of Central Europe... All these people were acquiring an openmindedness and turning, unburdened by any deformity of historical origin (that in the old world, with its ancient political geog-

American architecture, Loos limits himself to observing disenchantedly the innovative potential intrinsic to advanced technological research. The ideological distance that separates Loos from such an American cultural seam — permeated by a romantic aversion to capitalism — is still more evident when compared with the extreme version offered by the organicism of Wright. The inevitable outcome of the latter's mixture of idealism and anti-urban ideology is the individualistic psychologism, whose first symbolic translation into architecture is to be found in the Prairie House [56].

Loos on the contrary regards the American urban phenomenon with amoral detachment. The high rate of growth of the forces of production — whose driving force is centered in the metropolis — seems to him a guarantee of liberation from nostalgic sentimentalism and from the cultural prejudices that have accumulated in old Europe and, at the same time, as a necessary presupposition for a gradual breaking down of the historic discrepancy between town and country.

«In our part of the world, when you travel for an hour on the railway», he writes in «Das andere» in a classic contrast between the two worlds, «and then go on foot for another hour and enter a peasant's house, you meet people who are stranger than those who live a thousand miles away across the sea. We have nothing in common with them... They dress differently, their clothes strike us in the same way as those

The illustrations of this chapter are taken from Erich Mendelsohn's well known photo-reportage Amerika, Bilderbuch eines Architekten *(1926). Although many years elapsed between Loos' and Mendelsohn's journey, the latter's photographs convey the significance of Loos' American experience (1893-96).*

New York: approaching the harbor.

seen in the Chinese restaurant of an international exhibition, and their celebration of festivities arouses the same curiosity in us as if we were watching a procession in Ceylon. This is a shameful situation. There are millions of people in Austria who are excluded from the benefits of civilization» [57].

So for Loos the positive side of American «democracy attained» lies in its extension of the process of *Kulturentwicklung* (becoming civilized) from the city to the country, that is, in the surmounting of old hierarchies and cultural barriers between different living conditions.

In this sense, the America that Loos speaks of is an America interpreted by a European, or rather, seen through the distorting lenses of German theoretical categories. His deliberate transfiguration has the function of prefiguring an advanced solution to the knotty problems of the world — worn out by the conflict between nostalgic preservation of ancient values and the growth «without qualities» of the new mode of production.

In this way America becomes «Das andere» («the Other») for Europe, an almost Freudian other, a sort of *autre* identity of the same civilization [58]. This is essential to an understanding of the provocative way in which he constantly contrasts the model of Anglo-Saxon culture with that of Germanic *Kultur* [59]. For Loos the English culture — and by extension the American one — harbors a 'dormant' German culture and, as such, is fertile ground for the growth of seeds of common origin. A passage from the 1908 essay *Kultur* is unambiguous on this subject:

«The German may not find it very pleasant to be told that he must give up his own culture in favor of the English one. But the German can find solace in this. His own culture is the one to which the English opened up their doors in the nineteenth century. It is the Germanic culture, which has been kept on ice in the island kingdom, preserved intact like a mammoth in the tundra, that, fresh and vital, now dominates all other cultures. In the twentieth century the entire globe will be dominated by a single culture (*eine kultur*)» [60].

An argument makes its appearance in this passage — side by side with the recurrent insistence on the need to tackle problems from a supranational perspective — that is worthy of special attention. The desire to be American reveals itself as a desire for a return to the original clarity of German *Kultur*.

This unique interpretation of Anglo-Saxon culture might perhaps explain the relatively independent attitude which distinguishes Loos from so many others in central Europe as far as any value judgement about the effects of the impending Americanism is concerned. Of course Loos is not alone in promoting the de-Germanization of Austrian *Kultur* [61]. Theoretical resistance remained stubborn in those years in its evaluation of America as a metaphor of the *Maschinenzeitalter* (machine age). Symptomatic of this is a passage by Rainer Maria Rilke [62]. «Now they pursue indifferent, empty things from America, semblances of things, shadows of life... A house, in the American sense, an American apple or a vine have nothing in common with the house,

Equitable Trust Building, New York.

the fruit, the bunch of grapes into which the hope and the thoughts of our ancestors had penetrated... Things, lived, experienced, familiar with us, fade away and cannot be replaced. Perhaps we are the last to have known these things» [63]. This nostalgic attachment to the delicate perfume of the past, of the enchanted objects and subtle flavors of a civilization on the wane, is only the symptom of a widespread and indomitable refusal of the dreaded *Seelenlosigkeit* (soullessness) of the industrial future [64]. On the other hand, the persistence of this ambiguity typical of the upper middle-class intelligentsia towards the *Mechanisierung der Welt* (mechanization of the world) entailed in Capitalism, is

Monadnock Building, Chicago.

demonstrated by the debate that took place around the Werkbund. Here, enthusiastic acceptance of Taylorism (imported from America as a method of rationalizing manufacturing processes) is opposed by late-Romantic attempts at a «spiritualization of work» [65].

So Loos' apology for the new world takes on particular interest when projected onto the historical background against which it was made. The American tendency to progressively reduce culture to *technique* is observed by Loos with «optimistic» cynicism. Industrially produced goods are the bearers of a new *Kultur (Industriekultur)* and of a new *Gestalt* which the modern architect must learn to recognize as such, without trying to rework it (by superimposing ancient stylings or new-false ornaments on it). There is no contradiction between industrial manufacture and art, just a difference. For this reason it is even more «superfluous» than mistaken to try and apply art to the utilitarian object. The essay *Kultur*, quoted above, concludes with words that seem to anticipate the final meaning of E. Jünger's *Der Arbeiter* about the inopportunity of any attempt to ward off the rule of technique [66]. «*Der amerikanische arbeiter hat die welt erobert. Der mann im overall*» [67].

Federal Reserve Bank, Chicago.

«The future belongs to the man in overalls»! Hence his praise for the American *Nervenleben*, hence his desire to «have modern nerves, the nerves which the Americans possess today». Modernity comes through the acquisition of a new mentality.

The implications of this assumption for the inherent features of a theory of design and of architecture are extremely important. It means that it is not so much architecture as utilitarian objects that determine the culture of an age. The merchandise of modern industrial civilization anticipates «revolutions in taste». In effect, utilitarian objects reflect the evolution of human behaviour. «We don't sit like this because the carpenter has made the chair in this or that way, but, since we want to sit in this way, the carpenter has made the chair like this» [68]. The historically determined form of an object is therefore the result of a process involving close adherence to the new needs. The architect's learning can even be an obstacle to the natural development of this «production», of this *poiein*, at the very point where he thinks he can apply his abstract cerebrations and graphic exercises, within the manufacturing cycle [69]. In his work *Hands off*, a sort of autobiography, Loos goes so far as to say: «About one thing I was certain: ... if you want utilitarian objects which conform to the spirit of your time, then poison the architects» [70]. The greatness of Anglo-Saxon civilization for Loos lies in its tendency to reduce architecture to a «superfluous» discipline. Elsewhere he adds: «At this point the perfidious English interfered and spoiled the fun for the masters of the drawing-board. The English said: it's not necessary to design but to make. Jump into life so as to discover what man needs... We are not yet at this point. But the English spirit (*englische geist*) has already infiltrated amongst our craftsmen and rebels against the pre-eminence (*vorherrschaft*) of architecture» [71]. Therefore architecture becomes a «superfluous» discipline as soon as it strays from the realm of social needs and from the concreteness of «doing» (of *poiein*) aimed at the satisfaction of these needs. By estranging himself from the manufacturing processes, the architect-artist restricts his competence to the separate field of «graphic art». The latter — in his exasperation at the independence of design from practice — becomes for Loos a synonym for «impotent will», for evasion in the realm of ineffectual self-gratification.

Insistence on the *poiein*, motivated by an empirical pragmatism, also leads him to hypothesize the superiority of handicraft in so far as it is essentially a synthesis of intellectual work and manual work. Moreover, the exaggerated value he places on the creativity of manual-mental work results — as we shall see — in an essential incomprehension of design as method («modern» and as such, «abstract») based on the displacement of elaboration from the object to the plan.

«It is time that our craftsmen», writes Loos, «trusted in their own powers and shook off their backs any unasked-for guide. Anyone who wishes to collaborate should be welcome. Anyone who, in front of the humming lathe, wearing a work apron, who, in front of the red-hot furnace, stripped

Times Square, New York.

Salmon Tower, New York.

to the waist, wants to collaborate, deserves every praise. Those dilettanti however, who think themselves able, from their comfortable artists' studios (art derives from knowing how), to predominate over those who create and prescribe what they should create, all these people are begged to stick to the limits of their field, which is graphic art» [72].

This assumed capacity of manufacturing to immerse itself in the *Erlebnis* (event) and to comply with what is needed in daily life is what provides the seed for the Loosian utopia.

What remain completely outside Loos' grasp are the alienation of the worker and the abstractness implicit in the system of circulation of money and goods, which had already been pointed out by Marx and reintroduced into the architectural debate (although in distorted terms) by William Morris [73]. It is significant here that Loos does not modify the terms of his argument when making the analytical transition from the work of the artisan to that of industry. Unlike Morris, Loos believes the split between abstract and concrete work may gradually be healed not only by craftsmanship but also by industrial manufacture. Hence his rhetoric about the man in overalls and the transfiguration of «American modernity» into myth.

His invitation to «love modern objects» is not just a sort of esthetic contemplation of their technical perfection, of their smooth surfaces or of their purity of shape (which Le Corbusier will later represent in his «purist» paintings), but it is also, and more importantly, the polemical assertion of the «reality» for which they are vehicles. «Objects» enter into everyone's daily life and modify the mental pattern of living in a more concrete manner than does literary culture. «Things» become the mirror of a civilization.

It should be stressed, however, that such an interpretative key was put into his hands, long before his American experience, by the theories of Göttfried Semper. The quotation with which he opens his essay *Glas und ton* provides evidence for this:

«'An examination of the pots made by a people will generally give us an insight into the kind of people they were and the level of culture they had reached', says Semper in the introduction to his study of ceramics. We should add, however, that this revelationary power should not be attributed solely to pots. Any utilitarian object whatsoever can tell us about the customs and the character of a people». And further on he adds: «This is what Semper asserts. Without doubt, by saying so, he has given the idealists a heart-attack» [74].

His true cultural debt to Semper consists in this «materialistic» methodological principle which Loos adopts nevertheless in all its atemporal generality, extending it from the historical analysis of Greek civilization in particular to the contemporary vivisection of *Kultur* in the age of engineering. Starting out from this premise he completely denies any regressive nostalgia for the spiritual age, making for the first time an equation (which will recur later in many writings of the avant-garde intelligentsia, and in particular in *Vers une Architecture*, 1920-21, by Le Corbusier) between the new industrial esthetic and ancient Hellas [75].

«Is there anyone left, in our time, who works in the same way as the Greeks (so wie der griechen arbeiten)? Oh yes! The English as a people, the engineers as a class. The English and the engineers are the Greeks of our time. We owe our culture (unsere kultur) to them... The Greek vases are beautiful in the same way as a machine is beautiful, as a bicycle is beautiful» [76]. Roland L. Schachel is not mistaken then, when he claims that Loos' journey to America is, in one way, a journey into the Classical; more so than a journey to Rome or Athens [77]. Mixing the suggestions of Wolfgang Goethe (who praised the «ancient» quality of modern Bohemian baskets) with the observations of the American sculptor Horatio Greenough (about the «Hellenic character» of the caravan of pioneers emigrating to the West), Loos sees the classical spirit re-evoked in the synthesis of usefulness and beauty to be found in American «things».

But in what does this evocation consist if it is not in the reproposition of the genuinely classical principle of the technè? Loos' thinking is unambiguous on this point. The engineers, the English, and we can certainly include the Americans (because of the essential and many times confirmed homogeneity of Anglo-Saxon culture), are the true shapers of modern Kultur precisely because they think technique to be the essence of construction. The objects produced by this logic are a «symbol of the incipient domination of the whole world by a single culture»: the culture, to be precise, of the rule of technè [78].

In the light of this acquisition, it becomes very clear how 'questionable' are those interpretations that tend to reduce the principle of classicity that Loos deduces from American architecture to a simple influence of the gigantism of the 'white monuments' of the World's Columbian Exposition that he visited in Chicago back in 1893. Roland Schachel himself makes this mistake in the essay mentioned above.

Loos admires in the giant scale of some urban objects in the United States the capacity to give form to Values outside time — indifferent to the daily creation of rates of exchange (commodities perish) — Values which only monuments are justified in «representing» in as much as they are a limit within which architecture tends to deny its original raison d'être for becoming Art: form free from useful function and therefore capable of hinting poetically at an inhabiting which cannot be spoken of. Perhaps the Column designed for the «Chicago Tribune» competition of 1922 is an even clearer testimony to the reinstatement of this idea picked up in the United States, than the picture postcard of the Obelisk at Bunker Hill so jealously guarded among his papers [79].

But symbolic representation is only one of the two poles between which his interpretation of American «construction» in a classical sense shuttles back and forth. The other, as has been said, is the proposition of the methodological priority of technique in the ideation of form. One might object that these two propositions are in non-dialectical opposition to each other and it is true — but from just this conceptual antithesis stems the need to theorize on the difference between «monument» and «house», between art and building. For Loos, the difference between poetically inhabiting (as Hölderlin would say: dichterisch wohnet der Mensch) and building according to the logic of the Zeitgeist is insuperable. Only memorial architecture (the monumentum) or the architecture of death (the tomb) can show the desire to speak of Values aimed towards an impossible poetic dwelling.

Building, on the contrary, must be dumb. The more it is reduced to pure technological tautology, the more logical it is, the more consistent with its lot. «And so I ask», one reads in the essay Architektur, «why do all architects, good or bad, end up washing the soap? The peasant doesn't do it. Not even the engineer... He builds the roof. What kind of roof? A beautiful roof or an ugly roof? He doesn't know. The roof» [80].

Technique forms the specific culture of building which does not tolerate «tattoos». Consequently, the engineer is the genuine upholder of the ancient building tradition precisely because he concentrates his attention on research into the tools and processes necessary for building.

In light of this, it is more plausible to assume that Loos took his inspiration from the most advanced technical and structural research on skyscrapers, rather than from the Columbian Exposition: one thinks of the shattering image of such buildings as the Jayne Granite Building designed by W.L. Johnston and put up in Philadelphia between 1849 and 1851, of the cast iron façades of the New York commercial center known as the Cast Iron District designed by D. Griffith, J. Hatch and J. Kellum or the first constructions of the so-called Chicago School: the First Leiter Building (1879) by W. Le Baron Jenney, the Tacoma Building (1887-89) from the Holabird & Roche studio and the exceptional Monadnock Block (1889-92) by D. Burnham and J.W. Root, to mention only a few of the most famous.

It would not be too bold then to claim that Loos introduces a «European» angle to the theoretical interpretation of what was going on in the American building industry, seeing it as a gradual reduction of architecture to a pure tautology of construction, an angle which Mies van der Rohe will extrapolate to its extreme consequence of, «less is more».

The silence of pure structure is the only mirror fit to reflect the absence of inhabitation [81]. Nor is it accidental that America (where the development without qualities of Capitalistic building shows itself stripped of ideological veils) is where Mies van der Rohe will carry to an extreme (putting it into effect) a design strategy that was expressed in the glass tower designed for the competition for the Bahnhof on Friedrichstrasse in Berlin as early as 1919 [82].

Can a parallel be drawn between this attitude and the extraordinary photographic reportage carried out by E. Mendelsohn that sets out to convey the unintentional charm of unplanned construction, of an urban situation in which architecture has become a «superfluous» discipline? [83].

The principle of technè, then, is the central theoretical acquisition of Loos' journey through the autre culture of the new world and will be the premise on which he will base his

Grain silos, Chicago.

effort to bring back «western culture» to Austria.

And yet there is more! Another supporting pillar of Loos' theory of architecture has its slender roots in this foreign land: the principle of the Raumplan [84].

What is the basis of this way of thinking about space, consistently and obstinately practiced by Loos right up to one of his last works (the Khuner Landhaus at Payerbach, 1930)? Any attempt to answer this question must start out from an analysis of the forms through which this idea of architecture begins to manifest itself. It is undeniable that his interior design of 1899 (see note) conspicuously displays all the morphological characteristics taken from the American pioneer's house (beams left visible on the ceiling, the conception of the living room as a fluid and unitary space onto which various smaller rooms open, the arrangement of intimate alcoves around the fire-place, the use of wood as the main material, the introduction of lively colors...) which will become some of the invariants in Loosian interior design.

Again the problem crops up — though from a different angle — of his relation to the American cultural trend which had developed on the basis of H.H. Richardson's architecture.

The similarity between the first interiors designed or carried out by Loos and those of Richardson's houses (one thinks of the Sherman house, 1874-75 — from which Wright himself drew inspiration — or of the Cheney house, 1877) is so obvious as to be inescapable [85]. In fact the similarity is not limited to morphological elements and the language of materials, but extends even to the conception of space. Moreover indirect confirmation of his intention to learn to think about space from an examination of the houses of American agriculturalists is given by the autobiographical account to be found in his essay *Abendländische Kultur*, where his description of the typology of houses with a little tower, tympanum and verandas is so precise in its details that it seems to be a «preliminary design» for the Gartenstadtsiedlung Friedensstadt project at Lainz (1920), for those of the Mustersiedlung am Heuberg (1920-22) and the Arbeitersiedlung Babí near Nachod (1931) and more generally for the constantly reproposed model of the workers' *Siedlung*.

If, however, we pause to take a look at the space, the fact which stands out from this conception of design — which Loos, one notices, even imposes on the interiors of residences situated in the center of the *Großstadt* - is the desire to build a private place in which each person can give expression to his own individual way of life.

This gives rise to an apparent paradox which is perhaps the true key to a solution of the enigma: Loos discards the neo-Romantic skin of Richardson's house and takes instead the seeds he finds inside. It is not difficult to make out, once again, the contribution made to this operation of resolution by German theoretical categories.

In this case the culture of *Einfühlung* and, in particular, August Schmarsow's theory of *Raumgestaltung* [86]. But, before making any evaluation of the degree of interaction with this specific physio-psychological view of space, it is useful to analyse further the dialectical relationship established by Loos with the «American school», as it throws a great deal of light on his fundamental ideological motivations.

The central question which marks the dividing line between different ways of thinking about architecture is still the attitude taken towards the new growth of manufacturing industry, whose driving force is to be found in the metropolis. Loos accepts «manfully» the destiny of the capitalist *Zeitgeist*, making fun of the pathetic nostalgia of those who wish to reduce «the metropolises to small towns». For good or evil, the metropolis is a point of no return. The house in the *Großstadt* — like all commodities in the abstract universe of monetary circulation — must therefore appear «naked» on the outside and display in the very technico-economic tautology of the materials of the façade the singular quality of absence. From this point of view Richardson's need — taken up and glorified by Sullivan — to dress up the skyscraper with «culture», seems to fail to the precise extent that it is «superfluous». There is significant common ground, however, when it comes to criticizing capitalistic urban development, not because it is a process of isolation but for exactly the opposite reason: because it involves taking away the dimension of «privacy» from the individual. This is the source of Loos' radical defense of the individual *Nervenleben* which he has in common with Kraus (as W. Benjamin has acutely observed) and which at the same time distances him from Sullivan if only because of the specific way he solves the problem: the solution, in fact, is to be found not outside, but inside the building.

There is a wider gap, on the other hand, separating Loos' attitude from Frank Lloyd Wright's attempts to salvage individuality outside the metropolis: in the outer suburbs of Chicago with his first experiments with the Prairie House (1890-1910), then in the desert with Octillo Camp (1927), and again in «utopia» with his invention of an alternative urban model, Broadacre (1935) or in «nature» with the famous Falling Water built in the vicinity of Bear Run, Pennsylvania (1936-39).

The myth of a happy return to an uncontaminated and regenerative Nature will remain profoundly alien to Loos' thought. On the contrary, he takes on — with all the perplexity and conflicts it brings with it — the 'modern' architect's task of creating — inside the historically determined city — a *wohnlichen Raum* (a space that is liveable in, welcoming) in which the individual can find «shelter».

To Loos' way of thinking, going back to the origin is impossible, since there exists no metaphysical essence of building-to-live-in outside the historical factors which have determined its evolution and the changes in its meaning. The architect who has truly grasped the «sense» of the *moderne Zeit* must adapt his will to build to the new anthropocentric *nature* that is the *Großstadt*. In his essay *Das prinzip der bekleidung* (1898) we read:

«The architect's task is to create a warm and welcoming space (*einen warmen, wohnlichen raum*). Carpets are warm and welcoming... But you can't build a house out of carpets.

Carpets... require the building of a floor (*ein konstruktives gerüst*) which keeps them in the right place. To invent this solid flooring is the second task of the architect. This is the correct, logical path to follow in architecture. And this is how, following this sequence, man has learnt to build (*hat die menscheit auch bauen gelernt*). In the beginning was the covering. Man sought shelter from bad weather, protection and warmth while asleep. He sought to cover himself. The roof is the most ancient architectural element. At first it was made out of skins or woven material. This meaning of the word is still recognizable in the German language. The roof (*die decke*) must have been set up in such a way that it gave shelter sufficient for the entire family! So walls were added which provided both shelter and sides. This is how architectural thought (*bauliche gedanke*) developed in humanity as much as in the individual» [87].

The walls, then, represent a leap in the development of architectonic thought. They are not dictated by mere static and functional motives, but introduce a different conception of building, by creating true barriers giving lateral protection. The social and psychological importance of these walls in so obvious as to require no further comment.

It is more important to evaluate the architectural implications of the planning program to which they give expression. In fact, a grasp of the role of «closure» given to the wall is also an essential step towards understanding the profound reasons which underlie Loos' refusal to adapt his architecture to the prevailing post-war trend towards glass buildings, to which he was opposed in theory. It cannot be by accident that in those years Loos continues to build monolithic objects and to put up solid «protective» screens for his apartments along the streets of the big cities — such as the façades of Tzara House (1926) in Paris or of Moller House in Vienna (1930) — at exactly the same time as architects like Bruno Taut and Walter Gropius, echoing the mystico-literary suggestions of Paul Scheerbart's *Glasarchitektur*, are replacing walls with large transparent surfaces [88].

But what is the result of this transparency if it is not a definitive loss of the «hidden», the secret place in which the individual can protect himself from indiscreet glances? Without intending to, the «excess of transparency» of *Glasarchitektur* ends up promoting the logic intrinsic to the technique of domination that Michel Foucault has called *panoptique* [89]. «The eye of power» watches over the well-lit figures of individuals moving around houses of glass [90]. The definitive loss of privacy can lead in the end to areas of resistance and opposition to the flow of dominant ideologies.

We cannot dismiss the possibility that this is the reason Loos' houses have the almost stone-like consistency of masses that have been hollowed out with the patient persistence of a mole. Like Chinese boxes they hold within them spaces that are as secret as they are small. The *Raumplan* has an undoubtedly psychological motive in the architecture of intimacy. The wall — the element which separates and gives shape to the *Raum* — is split in two. The outer face belongs to the world without qualities of the *Großstadt*. The inner face belongs to the life of the *individuum*. The reason is this: «The building should be dumb on the outside and reveal its wealth only on the inside» [91]. So the semantic split is deliberate. The rational bareness of the exterior should contrast with the emotional riches of the interior. Their relationship is arbitrary and founded on the principle of reticence. Le Corbusier will be the only other architect to propose — in his own way — the schizoid play of morphological contrasts between rigid stereometry outside and plastic lucidity inside, beginning with his prototype houses of the twenties [92]. But if the house must hold its tongue on the outside, on the inside it must speak, tell the *transhistoriches Erlebnis* of the person who lives there in the rhythms of its spatial sequence. In the essay *Das prinzip der bekleidung* mentioned above, Loos adds: «... the architect thinks first of the effect he wishes to achieve, then he constructs the image of the space he will create in his mind's eye. This effect is the sensation that the space produces in the spectator; which may be fear and fright, as in a prison; compassion, as in a funerary ornament; a sense of warmth, as in his own house; forgetfulness, as in a tavern. The effect is achieved by means of material and form» [93]. August Schmarsow had discussed these same themes in a text published two years earlier: *Über den Wert der Dimensionen in menschlichen Raumgebilde* (1896) [94].

The recognition that the intimate theatricality of internal space establishes an emphatic relationship between subject and object, between whoever enters and moves around in a setting and the form and materials of the setting itself, is so obvious as to leave no doubts about it being a reverberation — though indirect — of the long and articulate debate on *Einfühlung* that — beginning with the arguments of Robert Vischer, Theodor Lipps and Heinrich Wölfflin — spanned the whole field of German art and architecture at the end of the 19th century [95]. This *Gestalt* theory of physiopsychological stamp is known to have strongly influenced linguistic experimentation in those artistic movements grouped together by critics into the stylistic category of Art Nouveau, and in particular the *Jugendstil* in Germany and the *Wiener Secession* in Austria.

From all that has been said, it should appear obvious why Loos can only partially follow in the tracks of this cultural trend, containing it within the rigid boundary of the *interieur*. Any eruption of the irrational onto the external façade of a building seems «indecent» to him in so far as it is a symptom of a pathetic regression to an infantile stage of humanity, to a savagery appropriate only to the South Sea islander who is seeking his identity in the mask, extending the practice of tattooing his own face to objects of daily use. The individual, living in an adult way in the present day, must learn to confine the sphere of his own hesitant sentimentalism within four walls, in the «private» space of his own house.

In this sense Loos' *Raumplan* is closely linked in theory with only a few aspects of A. Schmarsow's *Raumgestaltung*. In the above-mentioned essay by Schmarsow we read: «Architecture is a creative relation of the human subject to his spatial surroundings, to the outside world as a spatial whole, according to the dimensions of his own true nature. In doing this, it cannot refer exclusively to man as a physical body, as is frequently believed, but necessarily proceeds according to the make-up of the human intellect, according to his spiritual constitution just as to his physical one. The result of this will be to produce the common basis, the law of the existence of space, for which man and his world are made, one for the other, and this is exactly where both the objective and the subjective value of his creation is to be found» [96].

Elsewhere Schmarsow adds that «in the rhythm of movement the driving force of the entire spatial composition...» changes the static dimension of space into a true *transhistoriches Erlebnis* [97].

It is not difficult to make out in this argument an unusual elective affinity for the theoretical presuppositions on whose basis Loos effects a significant «overturning» of the academic method of planning, giving the conception of the *interior* priority over that of the exterior. All these extraordinary coincidences are summed up in the one key point that it is precisely in the construction of space that man shows the «truer nature» of his thought, and as a consequence that the architectural space — to the extent that it is a mental construction even before it becomes a physical one — carries physio-psychological contents in its very *Gestalt*. In other terms an intrinsic semantic and psychological value is expressed in the 'form' itself of an ambience. Hence the *Raumplan* is seen as a careful balancing of emotional reactions to dimensional relationships and to the network of relations between the constitutive elements of a rhythmico-spatial chain.

'**W**ho doesn't know them, the Potemkin villages, which Catherine's shrewd favorite had built in the Ukraine? Villages of cloth and cardboard, villages whose function was to transform the desert into a flourishing landscape in the eyes of Her Imperial Majesty. But was the astute Minister ever capable of building a whole city? ... The Potemkin city, of which I wish to speak now, is our own dear city of Vienna» [98].

With these words begins the essay *Die potemkinsche stadt*, published in October 1898 in the pages of «Ver Sacrum», the review of the *Wiener Secession* [99]. And it is significant that the city should be at the center of this, his first polemic against that association of artists. The city seen as a fine mirror in which the epochal forms of collective existence are reflected in all their deceitful scenic show. Take note: the forms and not the structure.

If it is true that the city is also a cultural locus, then the definition of its image is not a dispensable element. The urban form is, in fact the «way» in which the architectural response to a wider substrate of problems manifests itself and is condensed in the physical reality of urban space. To this extent it is the vehicle of ideologies. And it is just this aspect of the urban phenomenon that is the object of Loos' criticism of the Secession! [100]

It must then be asked why Loos sees Vienna as the theatre of fraud. No satisfactory answer to this question will be found if a factor of more general historical relevance is ignored: the trauma to which the inhabitants of large cities

It is no coincidence that it was in those same years, in that same «center of the European vacuum» that was Vienna, that Sigmund Freud began the analytical studies which would lead him two years later to write the famous *Die Traumdeutung* (1899). Besides, as Freud himself was to say: « ... the poets discovered the unconscious before I did».

The incurable conflict between Eros and Thanatos, which subsides only in poetic representation-contemplation, is one of the *leitmotivs* of the culture of the *finis Austriae*. If language is the «autonomous» creation of mental worlds, then it can be used to sublimate man's uneasiness in civilization (*das Unbehagen in der Kultur*) to a certain extent. Hence the repeated recourse to the metaphor as a perverse disguise for the principle of reality.

«Whoever adds words to facts disfigures the word and the fact, and is doubly contemptible» [103]; Karl Kraus will say and this is one reason for his break with the writers of the Café Griensteidl (Hofmannsthal, Schnitzler, Bahr...).

Quite apart from any «moral» criticism, the ambiguous allure of the 'mask' remains the recurrent theme around which a large number of Hugo von Hoffmannsthal's works turn: from *Lucidor* to *Arabella*, to *Andreas oder die Vereinigten*. The latter novel is set in Venice, the city *par excellence* of the lie, the «city of adventure» as Simmel will call it, where the Schopenhauerian «duplicity of life» is realized in the ostentatious falsity of the «façades» [104]. Venice, mirror of Vienna! Hofmannsthal's last work will be *Der Turm*, a drama of the illusion of the existence, of the dream. The

VIENNA, CITY OF CLOTH AND CARDBOARD

are subjected by the rapid transformation of European capitals into metropolises towards the end of the 19th century. This is the existential trauma caused by the uprooting of the values of the paleo-industrial city, which is expressed by the poets in all its lacerating lyrical gloom.

Just as Trakl in *Abendland* sings a hymn to the imminent agony of the «great cities/raised out of stone»[101], Rilke in the tenth *Duinesian Elegy* describes the anguish of the *Großstadt*'s impotence: «True, alas, how foreign are the streets of the city/torment/where in the false silence made of noise/loud, showing off, that pouring of the mold of/emptiness/that gilded roar that is the monument exploding» [102].

But what does the research of the *Wiener Secession* amount to if not an attempt to design a «gilded» mask behind which to hide the «inhuman» face of the new Age? *Tragödie* is the explicit title of an allegory of the «New Destiny» (in which a woman with androgynous features holds a grotesque mask in her hands) painted by Gustav Klimt in 1897, the very year of the Secession's foundation.

Tragödie, indeed: Klimt seems to be conscious of the tragic dimension to which an art condemns itself when it sets out to relieve distress, drowning it in the refined voluptuousness of symbolic forms that transcend reality by transmuting it into a projection of dreams. This apparently evasive «savage delight» — which H. Broch has incorrectly defined as «gay apocalypse» — is rooted in the painful eruption of irrational currents.

artists of «young Vienna» seem to be consciously climbing the interminable steps of this ivory tower of language. The symbol which dominates the entrance gate to the House of the Secession is a mask, the expressive outcome of a collaboration between Klimt and Olbrich [105].

Like Andreas, Klimt wants at all costs to traverse the broken ground of existence, expressing it, displaying it in all the absurdity of its conflicts. In this connection the explanatory note that he wrote himself for one of his monumental works is illuminating: the «Frieze of Beethoven» was conceived as a figurative comment on the XIVth Exhibition of the Secession held between April and June in 1902. In the great hall of the *Haus der Secession*, dominated by the imposing sculptural group of Beethoven — the work of Max Klinger (who stated his intention of emulating the mythical chryselephantine statue of Jove carved by Phidias) — the evocative images painted by Klimt are ranged along the walls decorated by Josef Hoffmann. «First long wall», he explains, «facing the entrance: the desire for happiness... Shorter wall: the hostile forces. The giant Thyphoeus... the three Gorgons. Sickness, madness and death. Pleasure, luxury, excess. Gnawing anguish. Above the affections and desires of men fly away. Second long wall: the desire for happiness is assuaged in poetry. The arts lead us to the ideal realm where we can find absolute peace, absolute happiness, absolute love. Choir of the angels in Paradise. 'Joy, marvelous divine spark'. This kiss for all the world» [106].

Art, then, as Schopenhauer's contemplative «redemption»: untrammeled creation as a relief from the «agitations» of young Vienna. This vision of the world fuels the excessive manipulation of form and the overloaded polychromy of precious materials which is characteristic of the *Wiener Secession*.

Der Zeit ihre Kunst. Der Kunst ihre Freiheit. To Time its Art. To Art its Freedom. These words are written on the main façade of the *Haus der Secession* (built in Vienna by Josef Maria Olbrich in 1898) [107]. Art can permit the extreme liberty of an internal journey in search of a labyrinthine infancy where autobiographical memory encounters remote collective myths. Theseus against the Minotaur: the young will to live struggles against the darkness of the old evil. Klimt outlines this theme with extraordinary clarity as a «manifesto» for the first exhibition on the Secession. Only later, after his mystical «journey through the Byzantine mosaics» of Ravenna (1903), does his pictorial matter become dense, drenched with unreal gold, studded with gems, while from the viscous background surface barely sketched human faces are suspended among maniacal ornaments. The journey goes on towards unforeseeable goals.

All this is «legitimate» in the absolute subjectivity of art. But what happens when «art is confused with culture» (*Man verwechselt hier Kunst und Kultur*) [108]? When the difference between poetic transfiguration and naked reality is not grasped? To smear the blank walls of the city with childish scrawls, to project ancestral myths onto the screens of the house façades: to Loos this is «indecent» mystification, pathetically regressive ideology. At the exhibition on the «inner tragedy» in urban public places, Loos counters the implosion of pathos, on the «gilded lane» ...

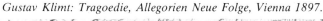
Gustav Klimt: Tragoedie, Allegorien Neue Folge, Vienna 1897.

with quiet reserve. «Yet those who know that art exists to lead men ever forwards, ever higher, to make them like unto God, find that the confusion of material goals with art is profanation of the Highest» [109].

In short, his fundamental objection to the *Wiener Secession* is that it has not understood that the modern *Zeitgeist* makes necessary the separation of languages, the independence of specializations. To attempt hybrid marriages creates ambiguous parodies. Any language offers possibilities for lying. «If something cannot be used to tell a lie, then it cannot be used to say anything at all» [110]. So even the language of architecture can become a vehicle for false ideologies.

«Anyone who makes himself out to be different from what he is in reality», he writes in *The Potemkin city*, «comes to be thought of as a scoundrel and incurs general contempt, even if by acting in this way he has caused harm to no-one. But what happens when someone seeks to obtain the same result by using fake building stones and other camouflage of this kind... Only a small number of people are aware that his is an immoral action, a deception» [111].

It doesn't help to lower one's gaze when faced with the metropolis. On the contrary, it is necessary to learn to observe the present from the perspective of life, and to work with the tools of architecture inside the *Großstadt*, articulating the abstract language that is best suited to it: this is the controversial plan of action for the city announced by Loos as far back as 1898. His words are followed by actions. In 1899, on the corner of Operngasse and Friedrichgasse, close by the *Haus der Secession*, Loos builds the *Café Nihilismus*, a true paradigm of the «architecture of absence». The assumption that the metropolis is the necessary historical result of the growth of civilization (in so far as it can only change in a progressive direction) is the presupposition from which one may deduce his indirect, but substantial distance from the urban theory formulated by Camillo Sitte in *Der Städtebau nach seinen künstlerischen Grundsätzen* (1899) [112]. As is well known, the director of the Vienna *Staatsgewerberschule* favored the hypothesis of a widespread diffusion of art in the processes of building the city as an antidote to the «schematism of the modern system» [113]. The inevitable outcome is the reproposition of anachronistic models for the shaping of the environment on which Le Corbusier will later heap scorn by describing them as the «cult of the donkey path» [114].

Once again there is an attempt to apply art in an operative sector that is structurally alien to it. In a Vienna «where even the streets are paved with culture» (K. Kraus), where Otto Wagner dedicates a never-built and bizarre monument to *Kultur* (1909), the rigorous claim for the *autonomy* of art — that is to say for its recognition as an «other» place for the expression of thoughts out of kilter with the needs of everyday praxis — takes on the meaning of a fundamental theory of discrimination [115].

Haven't the eclectic architects, by calling for a return to the «artistic» conformation, reduced the Ring to a farcical representation of nostalgia, to a pathetic parody of the past? «When I walk along the Ring», Loos remarks, «I always get the feeling that a modern Potemkin has wanted to create the impression in the visitor to Vienna that he has arrived in a city inhabited exclusively by nobles» [116].

Apparently dictated by simple military reasons, the construction of the Ring (1858-72) — along the State-owned belt of the Glacis — marks a fundamental stage in the transformation of the Hapsburg capital, not only because it offers an optimal solution for the network of road connections between *Innere Stadt* and *Vorstadt*, but because it establishes at the same time a different urban hierarchy between public facilities and residential buildings with the opening of new property markets. And yet — as Loos realizes — the architectural fulfilment of the programme cannot be mechanically ascribed to the logic of land revenue and property speculation, as it is founded on a singular *waste* that is both typological and ornamental [117]. On the contrary, the strident contradiction between the technical and functional «modernity» of the urban plan and the backwardness of form of the artisan building industry is obvious. This backwardness can only be understood as the role played by ornament in compensating the unrequited nostalgic attachment to an idealized «noble» past. The eclectic façades — redundant with pseudo-culture — hide the *Seelenlosigkeit* (soullessness) of the metropolis behind screens, offering the urban crowd consolatory altars for the evocative rite of a spectral history.

So much for the Ring! But why go on tacking on masks? Why disguise the New Destiny when it brings with it new construction methods, new techniques, new materials, in short a new *Gestalt*? Wouldn't it be more «genuine» (*am wahrsten*) to display the new language just as it is, without tattoos'? In vain Loos repeatedly confronts the *Wiener*

Josef Maria Olbrich: Haus der Secession, Vienna 1898.

Josef Maria Olbrich: Haus der Secession, a detail.

Secession with these polemical questions; in vain because a profound gap separates the two different *Weltanschauungen*. *Nuda Veritas* is an enigmatic allegory painted — in homage to Schiller — by Gustav Klimt in 1899: it depicts a woman, a serpent and a mirror, an allusion to the reality that is unknowable except through the ambiguous appearance of its reflected image. The question is answered by another question: *quid est veritas*?

This problem of Schopenhauerian ancestry is entirely alien to the limpid *logos* of Loos. Sharpening the fine blade of his humor, Loos systematically uncovers, in his essays, the wounds pre-dating the Secession, arrogating to himself the intellectual superiority of one who sticks to the Krausian concreteness of «facts», of one who illuminates bitter truths without diluting them in the sweetness of metaphors.

The *Großstadt* is an intrusive presence in everyday existence that no poetic alchemy can conceal. Beyond the principle of true and false, the architect must necessarily measure the instruments of his discipline against this new urban dimension, finding a new foundation for his own intellectual labour.

Besides, Otto Wagner himself made it plain when he said: «The task of the modern architect is the metropolis» [118]. In his own way, Wagner is the most competent Viennese architect working in the fields of theory and planning, and he goes on trying to rationalize the processes of urban change, from the reorganization of transport systems to the selection of new areas for residential expansion.

His participation in the Competition for a Town Plan for Vienna (1892), his consequent drawing up of the General Plan (1893), the construction of about eighty kilometers of railway line and of about forty stations of the Underground (1894-98), his extraordinary Plan for Vienna-unlimited-metropolis... remove any doubts about the advanced technical and urbanistic level on which his planning research was based.

But on the strictly architectural plane one observes the failure of an esthetic attitude, aimed at counteracting alienation by turning it into a decadent hedonism for what August Endell defines as the «beauty of the metropolis». By means of an artistic and cultural reworking, the new technological processes are brought back within the reassuring realm of empathy. It is this tendency to beautify which the *Wagnerschule* selects from the versatile experience of the master and develops to absurd lengths. The modern architect's mandate is substantially infringed. The technical and functional foundation that can still be detected at the bottom of Wagner's planning is systematically spurned in favour of a surrender to the fantastic.

Olbrich, even more than Hoffmann, starts on a line of research which will inevitably lead him outside the *Großstadt*. But not incidentally Josef Hoffmann's experiments with the Liberty style were carried out on the edges of the city, where in the highly residential district of Hohe Warte he built villas for artists like Karl Moll and Kolo Moser (1901-04) in a vaguely fabulous style, in which reminiscences of Austrian rural architecture are mixed up with

G. Klimt: Design for the cover of «Ver Sacrum», 1898.

Kolo Moser: Drawings, 1898.

elegant influence from the contemporary work of the Scotsman Charles R. Mackintosh. These villas reveal — as do the later Health Resort at Kaasgraben or the luxurious Villa Ast (1910-11) — a veneration for a craftsmanship that is so refined as to be unrepeatable — as the swan song at the sunset of an age can only be. It is the last-ditch resistance of the aristocrat to the inevitable advent of industrial supremacy, in deliberate opposition to the foundation of the *Wiener Werkstätte* (1903). A partial involvement of Hoffmann — and of other important exponents of the *Wagnerschule* such as Karl Ehn and Leopold Bauer — in Viennese town-planning affairs will have to await the defeat of the empire.

Josef Maria Olbrich advances along the mythical route

mapped out by the *Sezession* with more durate consistency, abandoning the metropolis for the splendid isolation of a «village of cloth and cardboard»: the *Künstlerkolonie* established at Darmstadt by grand-duke Ludwig von Essen in 1899. Here the esthetic of the synthesis sought between art and existence finds partial expression in fragments of utopia attained [119].

If irony — as Goethe has said — is thought finding its freedom in detachment, then it is this kind of «sarcastic indifference» that maintains Loos' disenchantment. Its Goethian classicity is nothing but a jumping-off point for a precautionary renunciation of illusions. The houses «without ornament» mirror the nihilism of the metropolis which — for Loos — is not tragic in itself but only appears so to those who are constantly trying to do away with it, covering it up with the veils of ornamental deceit.

Consequently the categorical imperative of his research into technique and design becomes the need to lay bare the essence of the new times. This essence is the definitive loss of the center. No style exists — nor can there any longer — no *langue* for the new era, but rather many languages that contradict each other. The preferred setting for this plurality is the *Großstadt*. The simultaneous presence of many separate practices, which nevertheless interact, clearly emerges here. Architecture too, in so far as it is «scientific knowledge», enters into this play of forces. Its capacity to influence the processes of urban change derives exclusively from the wise use of appropriate techniques and instruments, and therefore from an awareness of the limits of its own field. It is possible to formulate theorems that enter into a dialectical relationship with the city only to the extent that they are based on a rigorous logical organization of materials and forms. The decision to insert into urban settings strategic architectural works of a controversial nature, aphorisms of a transformation that can only be carried out by «parts», is dictated in the end by a realization of the impossibility of exerting any planning control over the urban phenomenon in its totality.

It is no accident that Loos never designed abstract models of ideal cities. Neither a desire to find a new center in an anachronistic *Stadtkrone* (which obsesses the revolutionary expressionism of Taut in the early post-war years), nor an optimistic faith in a methodical rationality able to resolve urban contradictions through the creation of perfect city-machines (which is the goal of Le Corbusier's impatient research from the twenties onward) will ever atract Loos' interest. A deep-rooted scepticism leads him just as far away in his ideas from the desire for a return to an idealized past as from prophecy of an improbable future.

Impervious to nostalgia and utopia alike, Loos' urban planning tends, deliberately, to apply logic to the design of single objects rather than to projects for the whole city. But this choice does not mean a lack of interest in the relationship between architecture and city, which on the contrary is invariably to be found underlying all his work, from the emblematic project for the Commemorative Church for the Emperor's Jubilee (1899) to that of the Werkbundsiedlung

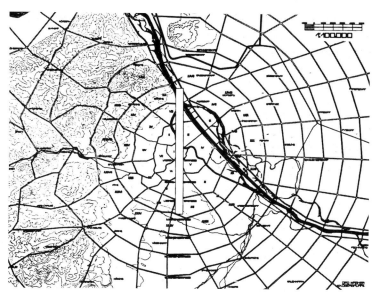

Otto Wagner: Plan of «Vienna, the Unlimited Metropolis» (1910-11).

Otto Wagner: A monument to Kultur, Vienna 1909.

in Vienna (1932). Loos' architecture is always deeply rooted in the soil of historico-cultural relationships that have accumulated in the *topos* where it is sited. On the «hunting-ground» — so to speak — he reconstructs the route taken by the local building culture from traces in the dirt and almost imperceptible details. Even difficult conceptual constructions such as the house built on the Avenue Junot in Paris for the Dadaist poet Tristan Tzara (1926) are incomprehensible outside an analysis of the close topological relations evident in the material and conceptual split between the stone base — linked to the well-tried typological structure of the place — and the abstract white square of the façade above.

But — unlike Otto Wagner — Loos does not believe in the hypothesis of a *Rationalisierung* of the virtually unlimited growth of the metropolis. For this reason he does not draw «plans». Without waiting for a unitary co-ordination of the multiform reality of the city, his «maieutic» architecture springs up in the existing urban fabric, at times contrasting with it, more often following the lines of a submerged trend which it resumes. This derives from a singular theoretic aphorism: the modern language of absence is interpreted as the inevitable end-point of a long historical process of evolution. «And this illusion has been even more strongly confirmed for me by what an artist enemy of mine has to say: he wants to be a modern architect and builds a house like the old Viennese houses» [120].

In tradition Loos found, in short, the seed of the evolutionary trend leading to abstraction. In this sense his architecture seeks to marry past and present by taking on one of the central and most characteristic problems of European culture: the relationship with memory.

Their distant origin in history prevents the great European cities from becoming absolute metropolises, that is to say sites for the pure generalization of rates of exchange. The permanence of quality becomes in the event an obstacle to the victory of merely quantitative logic. The modern architect must of necessity take this store of history into account. A good example of this is the Looshaus (1910-11), built in the Michaelerplatz in the ancient heart of the *Innere Stadt*, yet which — as Loos likes to stress — «is a building that can only exist in a metropolis» [121]. Here the inflected abstract language of the floor on which the living-quarters are situated (consistent with the new dimension of the metropolis) is significantly presented as a stage in the evolution of the memory rooted in the site. Yet he cannot avoid the inevitable compromise of form turning on a substantial dissociation of language. The nihilism of the blank surface of the living-quarters, pierced by simple and regular geometrically-shaped holes, is contrasted with the graphic richness of the marble base crowded with historical references and figurative allusion. The absence of ornament, then, should not be confused with the absence of history. Besides, as Kraus has explained: «The aphorism never coincides with the truth; either it's a half-truth or it's a truth and a half» [122].

It is also possible to draw on history for provocative *objets trouvés* which make fun of the continual progress of thought. Just as the gigantic Doric Column of the «Chicago

Tribune» (1922) contrasts the metahistoric permanence of the monument with the flux of perishable rates of exchange in the metropolis, his design for the Modena Gründe (1922) dusts off medieval patterns so as to offer feelings of unaccostumed pleasure to the urban masses.

One may object that this unbroken link with the past makes room for an unresolved theoretic antinomy that prevents Loos from carrying his nihilistic poetics to its final, uncompromising consequences as, for example, Mies van der Rohe will do on the «new continent» of America. Which is undoubtedly true. It is proved by the deep-rooted «sense of history» revealed in proposals such as the one for the reorganization of the Karlsplatz (1908) — where seven intentionally neutral walls simply act as wings to emphasise the view of the Karlskirche — or again the extreme, senile intellectual refinement of the «glass bead game» played in his head and retrospectively entered as a project for the competition for the never-built Kärntnertorplatz of 1859 [123]. So Loos contradicts himself. His technique for making alterations to the city constantly shifts back and forth between the two opposite poles of memory and negation. But, to be fair, this contradiction is in the nature of things. It is the effect of a delicate phase of historical transition between two different systems of urban values. Loos does nothing but let it show. What he has in common, despite everything, with the *Wiener Secession* is the involvement with this crisis in the traditional model of the city. The difference lies in his own peculiar way of coming up with answers. If these events are not referred back to the historical situation in which they occurred, it is difficult to understand why — despite the ambivalence or rather precisely on the strength of it — Loos' urban planning reveals a complexity of theme that is not reducible to formulas. A complexity that derives from his adoption of a critical method able to cope with the individual character of the urban settings, without indulging either in *a priori* solutions, or in nostalgic mimesis.

A group picture showing the Wiener Secession (Vienna 1902): Anton Stark, Gustav Klimt, Kolo Moser, Adolf Böhm, Maximilian Lenz, Ernst

r, Wilhelm List, Emil Orlik, Maximilian Kurzweil, Leopold Stolba, Carl Moll, Rudolf Bacher, and two house-painters.

Looking back, 1903 seems to have been particularly important to an understanding of the dialectic between the two different theoretical trends, coexistent in Viennese architectural culture during the years prior to the *finis Austriae*. This was the year, in fact, when Loos had the two issues of the review «Das andere» (The Other, a periodical for the introduction of western culture to Austria) printed, and Josef Hoffman (with the collaboration of Kolo Moser and with generous financial backing from Fritz Wändorfer, a patron of art and literature) set up the *Wiener Werkstätte* [124]. There is no overtly polemical link between these two events, and yet it is possible to make some deductions about their irreconcilable ideological «otherness».

In some ways «Das andere» fits better into the peculiar literary category of the *feuilletons*, which were very common in the Vienna of that period, than into the genre of architectural reviews in the strict sense of the word. The subjects tackled are about as far as they could be from the discipline as it is traditionally understood. The titles of the articles themselves tell us as much: «What is sold to us», «What is printed», «What we read», «What we see and what we listen to», in short, «How we live» [125]. They deal with every subject under the sun; from the scenery painted by Alfred Roller for Gustav Mahler's version of *Tristan* to problems relating to infantile sexuality raised by Frank Wedekind's *The awakening of spring*; from the typographi-

This open «war on custom» derives from the attitude taken towards the role of intellectual work [129]. Loos sees the intellectual — as does Kraus — not as a «defender of positive values», but as a critic-destroyer, a bringer of disorder, who looks askance at the society in which he lives. «Noble» destruction serves to set in motion processes of change in the status quo. Hence otherness becomes a constant questioning of acquired value systems which leads to the radical subversion of the discipline of architecture.

Although Loos will not begin to criticize the *Wiener Werkstätte*, the *Werkbund* and, more generally, any attempt to apply art to handicrafts and industrial manufacturing until later, such criticism is only comprehensible on the basis of the more general theoretical choices and precise judgements about life disclosed in the pages of «Das andere». In particular, it should be stressed that, as far as the subject under discussion is concerned, the rhetorical emphasis placed on *abendländische Kultur* is dictated by a determination to contrast what had been widely discredited, with technique, understood in the wider sense of the mode of production (*poiein*) that is at the root of a way of living and thinking and that, as such, is not reducible to organization of the industrial cycle alone. (The latter is more the effect than the cause of this wider phenomenon).

It is in fact this same disrepute that inspires the foundation of the Wiener Werkstätte. The application of art to

THE OTHER

cal characters employed for the subtitle of the review to anti-Semitism; from street decorations to vegetarian restaurants.

Echoing «Die Fackel», the review founded in April 1899 by Karl Kraus, «Das andere» develops a systematic criticism of everyday existence. What the two periodicals have in common is the «destructive» program advanced right from the first issue of «Die Fackel»: «Not a noisy what we are doing, but an honest what we want to get rid of» [126]. The mechanism to be dismantled is that of the culture of Kakania with all its encrustation of prejudices, of false habits and of nostalgic resistance which prevents Austro-Hungarian culture from establishing itself on those idealised levels of modernity that Loos attributed to Anglo-Saxon culture (assumed to be the true repository of «*abendländischer Kultur*»). The legitimacy of this «desire to demolish» will be defended by Loos at a conference in 1926: «The majority of human works are made up of two parts: destruction and construction. And the greater the destructive part is, indeed when human work is solely destructive, only then does it really become a natural, noble, human work» [127].

The destruction of the «culture of the empire» is necessary even if «it damages the reputation of Austria». Loos will reply to a reader resentful of the insult implied by the subtitle of «Das andere»: «If a man has bad breath, he should be told. He may find a remedy. It is certainly better to tell him than to shun him» [128].

handicraft is nothing but an utopian attempt to stave off the dreaded «rule of technique». This crux of the theory throws light on the real meaning of Loosian polemics. However paradoxical it may seem, what Loos and Hoffmann have in common is *the exaggerated value they place on craftsmanship*. But the motivations for this evaluation are profoundly different, and consequently, so are its implications. Taking up where William Morris' ideology leaves off and with an eye to the English experience of *Arts and Crafts* (especially the organisational structure set up by Ashbee) as well as to the German one of the *Deutscher Werkstätte* (founded by Karl Schmidt in 1898), Hoffmann sees the *Wiener Werkstätte* as an extreme «nostalgic resistance to the system of industrial manufacture».

A passage written in 1923 leaves no room for misunderstanding: «It is true that over the past decade, work has been largely ruined by the introduction of machines. But here a noble contempt prevails for the industrial product, made on a production line; the ideal of the true occupation as the creation and execution of work by a single person still exists. We believe that our work must be beautiful because the joy of living is reborn...» [130].

So Morris' «joy in labor» — elevated by its ideological substrate of struggle against the alienation of abstract work — is translated into a mythology of the beauty of working with the hands. As Th. W. Adorno remarks, the German word *Handwerk* (like its English equivalents handicraft or handiwork, made up of the terms for hand and work) in itself «refers to modes of production proper to a rudimentary economy that have been lost in the triumph of technology and degraded by their picturesque disinterment by representatives of the Modern Style» [131]. But in Hoffmann this potentially regressive outlet is consciously pursued with surprising ardor. A recurrent theme in his writings is his enthusiasm for the «sensation of hands at work, precious instruments that are not void of feeling like a machine» [132].

The problem of social division and working techniques — already present in this proto-capitalistic kind of production — is not even faced, or rather it is hastily resolved in a demagogic «double signature» (that of the artist-inventor and that of the craftsman-executor) put on the objects produced. In this way the theoretical difficulties already implicit in Morris' theory are aggravated further. On one side, in fact, the craftsman's hands remain a pure and simple (although human) instrument for carrying out the ideas of the artist, and on the other the production of unique and unrepeatable objects incurs such high costs that the products are invariably destined for a well-to-do class (thus betraying the stated social intent of this opposition to the machine). No mask can cover up the nakedly aristocratic face of a conception of culture linked to the pleasures of the «last days» of the empire. Thus the demise of the *Wiener Werkstätte* in 1933 could be foretold from its anachronistic premises, despite the high levels of formal elegance reached at times by objects made from precious materials and designed with a wealth of detail by the intellectuals of the *Fledermaus* cabaret (staged by Hoffmann himself between 1907 and 1909), where the *Kunstschau* exhibition was held and avant-garde performances put on like «dancing» Beardsley and «singing» Wedekind. At this point it should be asked how Loos, though starting out from an in some ways even more 'conservative' defense of handicraft, arrives instead at conclusions of singular modernity. The answer to this question should probably be sought in the peculiar falsification of the analysis. The specific nature of craftsmanship revealed by Loos is that it is impersonal. This — in his opinion — is the aspect to be saved in contrast to the «ladies' fashion fantasy» of the *Wiener Werkstätte* artists [133]. If the craftsman were

freed from the creative dictatorship of the artists of the applied arts, he would make objects that conform to the modern spirit. The secret of this — for Loos — lies in the fact that craftsmen base their work on technical thought, in the same way as the ancient Greeks and the contemporary engineers. From this point of view the genuine modernity of this *poiein* — of this ancient mode of production — results from a renunciation of the fetish for autobiographical reification in the unique object, in favor of work which tends to give form to the essence of the way of using the object itself, adapting it to the historical changes brought about by the evolution of civilization itself. The impersonal character of the artisan's trade is well suited to the collective nature of the evolution of *Kultur*. His basic criticism of the *Wiener Werkstätte* makes its target «the excess of the playful instinct» that leads to the paper castles of «mannered novelty», a long way from the solid logic of a technically based transformation of things. The following passage by Loos throws some light on this subject: «At this point I would like to say a few words about the technique of carpentry... In place of the fantastic forms of past centuries, in place of the ornamental art which flourished in the past, should be substituted pure and simple construction. Straight lines, right-angled corners: this is how the craftsman works who has nothing in front of him but his materials, his tools and his predetermined objective» [134]. This analysis ascribes to craftsmanship a geometrical simplicity already linguistically predisposed to reproducibility on the mechanized production line. From what has been said up to now there wouldn't seem to be much sense in checking on its reliability. It is more important to grasp the underlying meaning of such a concept, which finds the *technè* to be the supporting pillar common to both the artisan (in Loos' sense of the word) mode of production and the industrial one. For this reason Loos finds no theoretical contradiction between the defense of *Handwerk* and a positive attitude towards the machine. Putting a distance between himself and the followers of Morris (though not so much from Morris himself) — «in a city where artists have always treated our industrial products with contempt» [135] — he stresses over and over again in his writing the necessity of recognizing the genuine language of the new times in indus-

A. Loos: The cover of «Das andere», no. 2, Oct. 1903.

trially manufactured objects. Take note though: not in all industrial objects; just in those produced without interference from the artists of the applied arts. This distinction is of crucial importance in understanding his criticism of the *Deutscher Werkbund* (the important association of industrialists, artists, technicians and politicians set up in 1907).

On the occasion of one of the first exhibitions organized by this association, the one held at Munich in 1908 (at which the *Typenmöbel* proposals for mass-produced furniture by Bruno Paul and the gardens designed by Richard Riemerschmid drew the attention of the critics), Loos wrote his caustic essay *Die überflüssigen* («The superfluous»).

«There they are back together again at a meeting in Munich. Once again they have demonstrated their importance to our craftsmen and our industrialists. In the early days — ten years ago — they justified their existence by explaining that their mission was to bring art into handicrafts. Something the craftsman would never have been able to do. Just so, he was too modern to do it. Modern man looks on art as divine and would have thought it a crime against art to have prostituted her for the manufacture of utilitarian objects...

«Then they contend that their aim is to help culture back onto its feet. This doesn't seem to make sense either. A cohesive culture (*gemeinsame kultur*) — and no other kind of culture exists — gives rise to cohesive forms. And the forms of van de Velde's furniture differ considerably from those of Josef Hoffmann. So which kind of culture should the German turn to? That of Hoffmann or that of van de Velde? Of Riemerschmid or of Olbrich?

«I don't believe culture has anything to do with it. For it is already rumored that the fertile activity of the 'artists of the applied arts' is a problem of national economy which concerns the State and the Manufactures... What I'm asking is this: do we need the 'artists of the applied arts'? The answer is no.

«All the industries that have succeeded, up till now, in keeping this 'superfluous' phenomenon out of their workshops, have reached their highest level. Only the products of these industries represent the style of our time. They express the style of our time so well that we don't even notice we have a style. They have grown up together with our way of thinking and feeling. Our coach-makers, our glass-industries, our optical instruments, our umbrellas and walking-sticks, our suitcases and saddles, our cigarette cases and silverware, our jewels and clothes are modern. And they are modern because no unwelcome instructor has turned up yet to lord it over their workshops.

«There is no doubt that the products of our culture have nothing to do with art» [136].

These caustic criticisms will be further developed and reinforced in the essay *Kulturentartung* of the same year, where the attack is centered on the thought of Muthesius (1861-1927), a protagonist of the renewal of German ar-

Ludwig Wittgenstein (1889-1951).

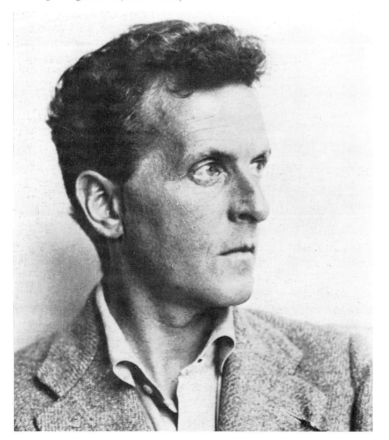

Georg Trakl (1887-1914).

chitecture at the beginning of the century, author of three fundamental essays on English residential typology (*Das englische Haus* 1904-08) and moving spirit of the *Werkbund*. There can be no doubt that Loos very effectively exposes the late-romantic ambiguities that riddle the contradictory program behind the foundation of the *Werkbund*. A program in which chauvinistic motives aimed at promoting the German economy and advanced technical attempts at reorganization of the production-consumption cycle are mixed up unconstrainedly with idealistic yearnings for the «spiritualization» of work and with anachronistic pretensions of preserving the artistic individuality of commodities. The basic mistake — and it is significant that it is repeated in the report made by Muthesius to the 1911 Congress whose theme was «The spiritualization of German production» — lies in having forgotten — as Loos points out — Goethe's warning about the damage caused by confusing art and the utilitarian object («Art, which paved the earth for the ancients and brought back the vault of heaven into the Christians' churches, is dissipated today in vases and jewellery. These times are a great deal worse than is thought» [137]) and — as Th. W. Adorno adds — the verses of Hölderlin («Which never more, from this time on/will serve the sacred»). But it is a much more complex and divided problem than would appear from Loos' ironic simplification which only has a bearing on one of the many «moving spirits» that coexisted in that association.

Cover page of «Die Fackel» no. 1, Vienna 1899.

Karl Kraus (1874-1936).

Arnold Schönberg (1874-1951) - Photograph by Man Ray.

Josef Hoffmann: Purkersdorf sanatorium, 1903.

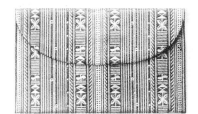 

Josef Hoffmann: Handbags, 1911.

It is no accident that the *Deutscher Werkbund* was called the «union of closest enemies». Along with Muthesius — theorist of the *Typisierung* — and the supporters of *Reine Zweckkunst* (pure functional art) such as Peter Behrens, Mies van der Rohe and Walter Gropius, one finds architects who envisage a return to elementary forms like Heinrich Tessenow and others who give expression to pre-expressionistic tendencies such as Poelzig, Berg, Marz, Stoffregen and Olbrist.

In some ways Loos' criticism, in as much as it is a criticism of the ideology of synthesis, shows a great deal of similarity to the arguments put forward by F. Naumann in 1914 on the necessity of recognizing that quality depends on the extent to which merchandise is adapted to its utilitarian function. This results in a positive and progressive elimination of the hangovers of ideological repression that are still

to be found in the special conception of the *Typisierung* which Muthesius sets against the principle, in its turn idealistic, of the indispensability of «free» artistic invention supported by van de Velde at the celebrated Cologne Conference [138].

It should be pointed out, by the way, that Muthesius had come much closer to Loos' thesis of the indispensable separation between art und utility in his essay *Das Formproblem im Ingenieurbau* (1913). Yet the realism of Loos' arguments betrays an uncritical acceptance of «civilization» as a natural phenomenon.

«But the *Werkbund* people», one reads in *Kulturentartung*, «confuse cause and effect. We don't sit like this because the carpenter has made the chair in this or in that way, but because we want to sit in this way, that is how the carpenter has made the chair. As a consequence — to the

Oskar Kokoschka (1886-1980) - Photograph by Brassaï, 1931.

Josef Hoffmann: Cutlery, 1904.

relief of all those who love our civilization — the activity of the *Werkbund* has absolutely no effect» [139].

Through the filter of consumption, the social community distills the production of goods until objects are reduced to their chemically pure essence, making them answer prefectly to «real» needs. The concept of *gemeinsame Kultur*, that is to say the unitary conception of culture, is clear proof of this. In short, what escapes such an analysis is a grasp of the multiform and changeable character of contemporary mass culture. It is, in fact, not a phenomenon anonymously given as it is, but it is simultaneously producer and product of the social transformations deriving from the dialectics between differing interests.

What is — so to speak — «heroic» about the utopia of the *Werkbund* is its attempt to interfere in this dialectic by trying to qualify it on the basis of an ethical and esthetic

Egon Schiele (1890-1918).

«plan». Muthesius says: «Considering how things stand at present, it is more necessary than ever to recognize that industry is today on the side of progress. Because it is a fixed political and economic law that there is a close reciprocity between consumer and manufacturer even in questions of taste, in that the number of shops selling goods of bad taste is always in proportion to the number of buyers with bad taste... So education from bad to good taste should always be directed towards two sources. Only gradually can these mountains which loom over us be removed from both sides» [140].

The failure of this program is also the result of a reactionary conception of the intellectual as an educator, that is to say as someone who prefigures all possible forms of representation, rather than as a technical producer of change within his own field of knowledge.

This does not take away the fact that such «heroism» is the source of some of the crucial questions linked to the birth of modern industrial design that are brought to light by Loos.

Firstly there is the problem of *Qualitätsarbeit*, clearly expressed by Fritz Schumacher in his discussion of the foundation of the *Werkbund*, where he describes its purpose as an attempt to «overcome the alienation between the worker of the material and the inventor, seeking to heal the split that emerges» [141].

It goes without saying that this alienation cannot — in «qualitative» terms — be eliminated since it is intrinsic — as Karl Marx had already pointed out — to the capitalistic mode of production. It is nevertheless an unavoidable problem — bound up with the more general question of social division and working technique — which any project for bringing about change in modern industrial society that has social aims must take into account.

Having stayed on the threshold of these problems, not having crossed it with all its inherent ambiguities and unresolved contradictions is, in the end, a strength but also a limit that historically dates Loos' thought [142].

Ornament und verbrechen (Ornament and Crime) is a text that is of crucial importance to an understanding of Loos' thought. Written in 1908, it was republished in Berlin in 1902 by the review «Der Sturm», which had links with avant-garde expressionistic groups, and then in Paris in 1913 in the pages of «L'Esprit Nouveau», the «Revue de l'Activité Contemporaine», at that time edited by the Dadaist poet Paul Dermée as well as by Ozenfant and Le Corbusier [143]. So it ended up becoming a true manifesto of Loosian poetics. The arguments expressed therein probably owe some of their wide and rapid diffusion to the way in which his writing plays on logical paradoxes and sacrilegious sarcasm; so effective a style that Loos' notoriety was for a long time more closely tied to the persuasive force of his ideas than to any direct familiarity with his works. But this also gave rise to misunderstandings, due to the very immediacy of the title-slogan which favored the reduction of his thought to banally simplified formulas.

To free Loos from too easy a label it is necessary to analyse in detail the motivations for his open war against ornament. In synthesis it may be asserted that these motivations can be traced back to an ethical/esthetic/economic argument. The interplay between these three lines of logic is obvious, but complex and in part confused, and it is worth separating them in order to untangle the knots.

One of the central themes of his criticism of ornamentation — too often left out of the explanations of the «Modern

«Ornamentation is wasted effort and therefore a waste of health. It has always been so. But today it means a waste of material as well, and the two things together mean a waste of capital» [145].

Although in simplified terms, Loos fully catches the «dynamic history» of ornament in this passage [146]. What had been historically justified and functionally motivated at the level of artisan manufacture can become anachronistic and superfluous accumulation in the logic of the new industrial cycles. Persistent reliance on decoration is therefore a sign of a reactionary attitude which tends to make a fetish out of objects and to ignore working conditions.

Indirectly this tells us a little more about the reasons for his repeated attacks on the later outcome of the ideology of William Morris that is so tiredly resuscitated by the *Wiener Werkstätte*. Loos seems to accept with equanimity the irreversible consequences of the historical break caused by the capitalistic mode of production and in part he makes its logic his own.

The quality of an object cannot be judged in abstract terms, but should be evaluated on the basis of the time, costs and techniques required in its manufacture. An amount of work that exceeds the possibilities for adequate disposal of the goods on the market will inevitably be paid for either in terms of low working wages or in those of a waste of capital. This means that the elimination of ornament serves to simplify the mass-production of utilitarian objects and

THE REMOVAL OF ORNAMENT

Movement» — concerns economic questions [144]. It is an attempt to demonstrate logically the absurdity of decoration by tackling comprehensively the problem of purpose, of costs and of techniques of production in modern industrial civilization.

«Since ornament», Loos writes, «is no longer a natural output of our culture, and therefore represents a phenomenon of backwardness or a manifestation of degeneration, the result is that the worker who produces it is no longer paid a fair price for his work.

«The working conditions of wood-carvers and turners and the wages of embroiderers and lace-makers are well-known. The decorator has to work twenty hours to earn the same amount as a modern workman does in eight. Ornament, as a rule, increases the cost of the object and yet the fact is that an ornate object that requires, as can be shown, three times as much work, is offered at half the price of a plain object made from equally expensive materials. The absence of ornament means less work and so an increase in earnings. The Chinese carver works sixteen hours, the American worker eight. If I pay the same price for a plain box as for an ornate one, the difference comes down to the length of time required to produce the object. And if there was no more ornamentation in this world — something which may not happen for millenia — man would have to work four hours and not eight, since half of man's work today is lost in ornamentation.

hence is a sort of social economy. But it is interesting to note that there are elements of naïvety in this unusual line of argument. In his defense to the bitter end of the «utilitarian value» of goods, against their reduction to mere «market value», Loos involuntarily and unconsciously places himself outside the logic of capitalist production, which in other ways he accepts as inevitable and natural. What stands out, in the end, is his essential failure to understand the mechanisms of planned and rapid obsolescence of merchandise, dictated by the need to increase and accelerate the consumption of products. What seems to escape Loos is that — in the words of Th. W. Adorno — «in society any benefit is distorted, bewitched. That society makes things appear as if they existed for people, this is the falsehood; they are produced for profit and only incidentally do they satisfy needs; needs which are themselves generated and shaped by the interests of profit» [147].

Thus to adopt the principle of utility as a basis for sanctioning the requirement for «non-perishability» of the utilitarian object (to be made from the «best materials» and with the «greatest care») means in reality to go against the logic of production which he has elsewhere made his own. Moreover the very concept of utility is in its turn historically relative and consequently would have required just as critical an appraisal.

Above and beyond its explicitly economic motivation, Loos' criticism of ornament takes on all the characteristics of an ethical choice. Ornament is crime not only because it involves a dual waste of material and work (and therefore of capital), but above all because it betrays a regressive nostalgia sublimated in the desire to mask. By introducing intuitively elementary considerations about the psychogenesis of ornamentation. Loos interprets it as a symbolic trasfiguration of erotic undertows [148].

«The impulse to decorate the face and anything else within reach», we read in *Ornament und verbrechen*, «is the origin of figurative art. It is the first stutterings of painting. All art is erotic. The first ornament to have been invented, the cross, was of erotic origin. It was the first work of art, the first manifestation of art which the first artist scrawled on a wall, to express his own exuberance. A horizontal stroke: the woman lying down. A vertical stroke: the male who penetrates her. The man who created this sign experienced the same impulse as Beethoven, was in the same heaven as the one in which Beethoven created the Ninth. But the man of our time who for some private impulse smears the walls with erotic symbols is a delinquent or degenerate. It is natural that this impulse should seize the man with such degenerate tendencies when he goes to the toilet. The level of civilization of a people can be judged by the state of the walls in their latrines. This is a natural manifestation in the child: to scrawl erotic symbols on the wall in his first artistic expression. But what is natural in the Papuan or in the child is a sign of degeneracy in modern man. I have discovered and given to the world the following notion: the evolution of civilization is synonymous with the elimination of ornament from the utilitarian object» [149].

The disapproving attitude with which Loos disparages decorative «degeneration» makes one think of the «judging» role that Walter Benjamin recognizes to be the fundamental element of even the grammar of Karl Kraus [150]. There is something in Loos' essay which reminds one of the tone of Kraus' *Sittlichkeit und Kriminalität* (Morality and Criminality), which had already appeared in the pages of the review «Die Fackel» and been reprinted in 1908, as well in the first collection of essays published by Rosner [151]. In one sense Loos seems to share with Kraus the principle of deep division between public morality and private morality, but he draws conclusions from it that are in some ways even more authoritarian than those of Kraus himself.

What is permissible in intimate surroundings, can become «indecent» in public ones! It is significant that while Kraus concentrates on the first assertion, Loos insists instead on the second. Ornamentation is «indecent» just where it ends by dirtying the «white walls» of the city streets with «erotic symbols».

The natural place for the expression, or better, sublimation of overabundant fantasy should be — in his opinion — the private sphere of art. In this sense the desire to project one's own erotic fantasies onto the entire range of utilitarian objects is interpreted as infantile regression or a symptom of barbarism.

For Loos, as for Freud, civilization is synonymous with the repression of erotic instincts. Yet once again this as-

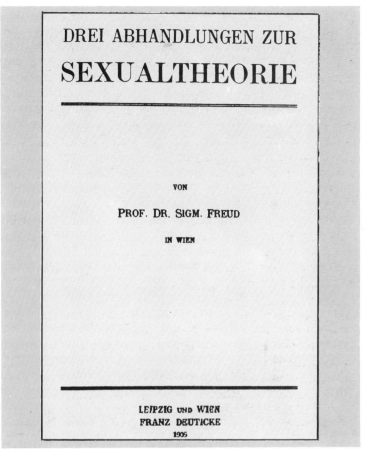

Title-page of «Three Essays on the Sexual Theory».

Sigmund Freud - Drawing by Emil Orlik.

sumption takes on moralizing overtones in Loos. Associating the psycho-biological infantile phase — which in Freudian terms could be called pre-Oedipal — with the anthropological primitive one of the Papuan, he derives an ethico-rational criticism of the perverse and polymorphous sensuality of the man who «covers with tattoos his own skin, his boat, his paddle, in short anything he can lay his hands on» [152]. To be clear about this, Loos goes on to say that the Papuan «is not a delinquent. But the modern man who tattoos himself is a delinquent or a degenerate» [153].

It is worth asking at this point why Loos feels that the tattoo — 'natural' in infancy — becomes scandalous in modern civilization. Well, no answer will be found to this question without relating his criticism of ornamentation to the model of rational civilization with which it is ideally contrasted.

«By civilization I understand», Loos explains elsewhere, «that balance inside and outside man that is only guaranteed by thought and rational action» [154].

Statements of this kind — recurrent in his essays — offer to some extent an explicit clue to the interpretation of his arguments. So it is the principle of rationality — assumed to be the sole guarantee of civilization — that demands the elimination of ornamentation from the utilitarian object, that in other words banishes the pleasure principle outside the ambit of utility. And it is the so-to-speak manly and adult adoption of social logic that limits the excess of fantasy to the only two realms in which it is held to be legitimate: the infantile-primitive dimension or the poetic dimension of art stripped of practical goals.

In the light of this, one should really speak of the removal of ornament rather than its elimination.

Although it is probably only a casual coincidence, it is nevertheless significant that there happens to be an indirect and relative affinity on this particular issue between the arguments of Loos and those put forward by Sigmund Freud.

A conference was held on the 6th December 1907 at the premises of the publisher H. Heller in Vienna: *Der Dichter und das Phantasieren* (The Poet and Fantasy). On that occasion Freud put forward the hypothesis that «both poetic activity and day-dreaming form a continuation of and sub-

stitute for the primitive children's game». He then went on to make some remarks about the pathological nature of the unresolved «desire for fantasies» in the adult individual that are worth quoting here at length: «The adult is ashamed of his fantasies and hides them from others, nurturing them within himself as absolutely private and intimate things: in general he would rather confess his own faults than communicate his own fantasies... It should be said here that the happy man does not fantasize; only the unsatisfied man does so. Unsatisfied desires are the driving force of fantasy... the young man must learn to repress the excess of conceit that is the inheritance of infantile caressing. Excess of effusion and intensity of fantasy form the conditions conducive to a fall into neurosis or psychosis...

«Such fantasies, when we hear them, arouse a certain repugnance or at most leave us cold. But when the poet performs his dramas for us or tells us what we are inclined to interpret as his personal waking dreams, we experience the keenest of pleasures that seems to flow from many sources, How the poet succeeds in doing this is his very special secret; the true *ars poetica* consists in finding a technique to overcome our repugnance, which is certainly linked to the barriers that are set up between each individual ego and all the others» [155].

Repulsion for that fantasy which exceeds the confines of art or of childish games is common to both these Viennese men. It should be noted, however, that whereas in Freud this consideration remains at an analytical level and is consequently toned down by the recognition of the widespread and ineradicable character of erotic symbolism in the implements of daily existence, in Loos it takes on the tone of a categorical imperative. If it is true that his architectural choices are in one sense derived from choices relating to the «cultivation of behavior», then one cannot accept the authoritarianism intrinsic to such a bias towards the removal of ornament from utilitarian objects.

To set as a limit to the area of excess, the maze of infantile-primitive games, and to contain the symbol within the confines of pure art is consequently an utopian concept. It is the utopia of absolute rationality, of the radical denial of all nostalgia and of the adaption of production to the bourgeois ethic of utility [156].

Adolf Loos: Chair, 1900 ca.

Adolf Loos: Detail of a table, 1900 ca.

The removal of the superfluous that appears a «definitive» conquest of modern civilization to Loos, in reality only represents a passing phase in the development of taste. So it is not a question of an elimination but of a negation of ornament dictated by the adoption of a poetics based on the principle of rationality. The esthetic motivation for his criticism of ornament, although less explicit, is the easiest one to identify precisely because of its limits.

Karl Kraus has already remarked: «That somebody is a murderer proves nothing against his style; but his style can prove that he is a murderer» [157].

The negation of ornament is above all a question of style: only superficially is it linked to the problem of functional coherence between the form of the objects and their intended poetic purpose. In its true essence the anti-ornamental attitude tends to become a search for syntax and, as such, a specific problem of language; a problem which is of not incidental concern to large areas of artistic work in those years «on the threshold of a new era».

It has already been mentioned that even an abstract art like music was at that time the subject of research aimed at a rigorous formalization of tonal syntax. For Schoenberg — as for the other Viennese composers of the *Neue Musik* — any element of sound that goes beyond the closed serial development of the theme is ornament. In the same way any metaphor that escapes the *logos* is ornament for Kraus and for other protagonists of Viennese literature. Almost en-

Adolf Loos: A detail of the Looshaus, Vienna 1909-11.

Adolf Loos: Table, 1900 ca.

tirely in harmony with the way in which Loos relates the production of form to erotic symbolism, Kraus states in *Sprüche und Widersprüche* (1909): «In the art of language one calls metaphor that which is used to convey a meaning other than its own. Therefore metaphors are the perversions of language and perversions are the metaphors of love» [158].

In tackling the question of ornament, then, Loos is dealing with a subject central to the culture of his time. This is proved by the widespread interest stirred up by his essay. To be sure, his nihilistic criticism — although deeply rooted in the same soil as that of the «great Viennese masters of language» — transcends the limits of the culture of the *finis Austriae* and links up, though only tangentially, with a theme discussed in those same years by the most advanced researchers into visual languages, that is the negation of representation.

Marcel Duchamp: Bicycle wheel, 1913.

Is not proposing the elimination of the ornamental option from architecture equivalent to abolishing — at least in intent — the symbolic and representational content that is superimposed on pure and simple construction? What is architecture without ornament if it is not an object that demonstrates in its tangible immediacy the semantic self-sufficiency of the material, and that postulates the superfluity of any attempt at description superimposed on it. The only task that Loos concedes to the architect is the logical organisation of form and material, leaving the role of communication to the primary language of these last.

This is the point on which there is unwitting conceptual agreement with some more or less contemporary experiments of the avant-garde.

A. Loos: Sketches of a Lancia motor-car (ca. 1924).

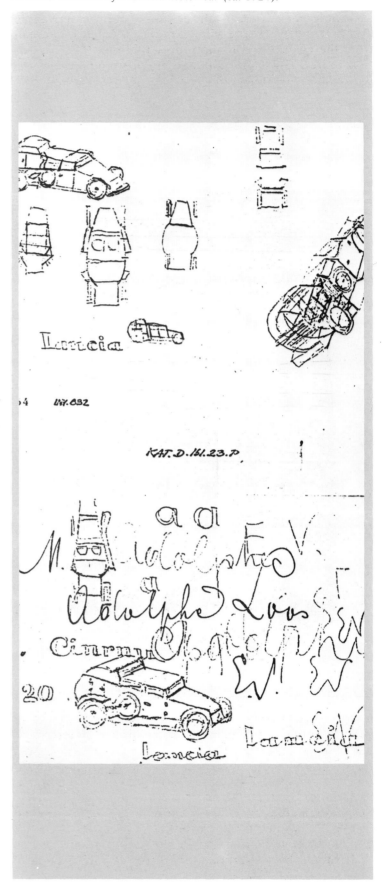

As is well-known, Kazimir Malevich, painted his famous «Black square on a white background» in 1913, achieving — as he himself declares — «the ecstasy of non-objective freedom», that is to say the culmination of the liberation of art from the «world of will and representation»[159]. The same year Marcel Duchamp exhibited in Paris the *Bicycle wheel*, the ready-made object that marks a decisive turning-point

some significant points in common with Duchamp's negation, even though the declared «destructive» intent of Duchamp's gesture is in apparent opposition to the declared «constructive» intent of Loos' project. Apparent because, on one hand Duchamp's negation turns into its opposite when by its deconsecration of the outmoded values of art it leads to a more progressive «statute» consistent with the

Adolf Loos: Cupboard, Vienna 1900.

A. Loos: Chest of drawers (Turnowsky apartment), Vienna 1900.

in the history of visual thought. To exhibit an object instead of representing it means in fact to abolish the intercession that language makes between things and the naming of those things, introducing a whole cargo of logical paradoxes and of semantic ambiguities connected with the use of an object as a symbol of itself.

Consequently, these two parallel experiments indicate the two limiting points for the abolition of «representation»: extreme abstraction or extreme realism.

It should be no surprise to find that Loos' ideas have

dominion of absence in the new machine age, and on the other Loos' rigid definition of the limits of his design as a pure and simple control over «construction» implies the opening up of the same semantic dimension introduced by the tautological ambiguity of ready-made objects.

Architecture without ornament can be better ascribed to the category that we may define as «negative realism» than to that of abstraction; a realism that is founded on the concreteness of things instead of on symbolic representation.

'D espite their carefully prepared strategies the Austrians lost the war because of the stiff boots that were part of the army uniform: the army has sweaty feet» [160].

This paradoxical reflection on the war — recounted by his friend Oscar Kokoschka — reveals, behind its veil of irony, the shape of a structured *forma mentis*. Not even the outbreak of the great conflict could make Loos forget the long and stubborn cultural battle he had fought, ever since his return from America, for the de-Germanization of German culture. Typically, che military defeat is interpreted by Loos as a cultural defeat. The defeat, that is, of a decadent world anchored to historically outdated forms that had been superseded by the modern, rational, western culture. This is why the dissolution of the Austrian Empire did not arouse in Loos the feeling of nostalgic attachment to the «*belle époque*» of *Austria felix*, too often metamorphosed into myth by the fictional evocations of Viennese men of letters. One thinks of the unrestrained melancholy for the past that stands out ostentatiously from the novels of Joseph Roth, or that is more subtly concealed, diluted in the affectionate parody of the *Kakania*, in *Der Mann ohne Eigenschaften* by Robert Musil [161].

Loos also reveals the impolitic character of his attitude towards culture.

This attitude is close in some ways to that train of thought developed by «bourgeois» German intellectuals,

and 1922 as Chief Architect of the Housing Department of the Municipality of Vienna. The fact that Loos was the first technician to hold such a high level post in the planning authority of «Red Vienna» (it was in fact in 1920 that the SDAP gained a decisive majority in the municipal elections) should not make us draw any false conclusions about his agreement with the strategies for intervention in the city, worked out, after a long and articulate debate, by «Austromarxism» [166].

It was to be Loos himself, at the conference *Die moderne siedlungen*, held in Stuttgart on the 12th November 1926, where he made a sort of retrospective self-analysis of that experience and polemically underlined his ideological differences with this political groundwork [167]. Apart from his explicit statements, a substantial difference of intentions seems to be already evident in the very premises of his method of planning, though it is only from 1923 onwards that direct municipal intervention in the building sector settles into the choice of precise patterns of operation and so it is only then that the inacceptability of Loos' ideas becomes clear in practical terms. This inacceptability has its source more in questions of architecture than in ones of ideology.

But in order to understand the meaning of Loos' projects it is essential to set them against the background of historical problems in which they were formed. As is well known, for a variety of concomitant factors the «housing question» becomes the central subject for theoretical discussion and for

ARCHITECTURE OR PROLETARISCHER STIL

which Thomas Mann interprets so extraordinarily at the time in *Betrachtungen eines Umpolitischen* [162].

This lack of prudence is borne out by the ingenuous' and contradictory way he deals with the new problems raised by the Proclamation of the Republic of Austria on the 12th November 1918 [163].

In 1919 Loos — along with his friends Arnold Schoenberg, Karl Kraus, Max Erners, Ludwig Münz and others — put forward a proposal for the establishment of a «Ministry of the Arts», where in expectation of direct intervention from the State in this specific cultural sector the presupposition of the repeated polemics of the pre-war years is impugned in support of the absolute autonomy of art. It is given the value of intellectual work that is distinct and separate from the contingent aims of social utility [164]. This episode aroused «horror and contempt» in Ludwig Wittgenstein, as he had to say in a letter to Paul Engelmann in which he derides «the air of intellectual snob» assumed — in his opinion — by Loos at that time [165].

One may not go along with the harshness of Wittgenstein's judgement, but it remains a fact that not long afterwards, this sudden and enthusiastic commitment was largely refuted by the stand he took over questions of urban policy.

A contempt for politics — as deliberate and open as possible — is in fact the key to understanding not only the originality of his concepts, but also the theoretical limits of the singular experience that he underwent between 1920

the techniques of urban intervention under the social-democratic administration of Vienna (1920-33) [168]. Without doubt, the increasing shortage of housing that was the result of the distorted mechanism of urban growth in the 19th century plays a decisive role in dictating this priority of intervention [169]. The abnormal urbanization of the imperial city (that saw a quadrupling of its population in half a century: from 440,000 inhabitants in 1840 to 1,643,000 in 1900) must be seen in the context of a situation where the housing available to the working-classes was made up entirely of the speculative building projects of the *Mietkasernen* (that is to say compact blocks of very small houses for rent, often lacking in the most basic of conveniences). The consequences of such a massive exploitation of the building industry were to emerge in all their dramatic clarity from a census on housing conditions carried out in 1917, which revealed that around 73% of the entire residential fabric of the city was made up of minimal low-standard housing at high rental cost. (Rent in fact swallowed about 25% of the average working wage) [170].

From all that has just been said, it is obvious that the «miserable standard of housing» — already the subject of philanthropic concern and searching enquiry on the part of scholars like Emil Sax and Eugen von Philippovic at the end of the 19th century — represented in reality the most serious social evil inherited from the defunct Hapsburg Empire and, as such, was bound to become the most urgent objective of

Austromarxist plans for a transition to «socialism» [171]. So much so that in the essay *Der Weg zum Sozialismus* that he wrote in 1919, Otto Bauer indicates «the right to housing» to be an indispensable tactical move in the complex political game played on the chess-board of the «program for socialization» of the economy [172]. The means of implementing such a plan are identified here with a process of gradual appropriation of land and housing (through a system of taxation that would effect an indirect expropriation and equal redistribution of inherited property) and with self-administration of the property by tenant associations.

In line with these suggestions, the Council of State issued a «Decree for the requisition of housing» on the 13th December 1919 that would permit the Municipal Council of Vienna to acquire the substantial number of 44,838 lodgings between 1919 and 1925. This measure was followed by two other important legislative initiatives which marked the fundamental stages in the process of solving Vienna's housing problem: at the national level, the approval of the «Bill for rent control» on the 7th December 1922 and on the local level, the launching of the «Five-year plan» for housing construction on the 21st December 1923 that envisaged the building of 5,000 apartments a year [173].

The exit of the SDAP from the governing coalition (in 1920, following the failure of attempts to nationalize the main industries) and the large amount of administrative autonomy allowed to Vienna and its *Landrat*, created the conditions for the choice of the former imperial capital as a proving ground, and at the same time, a source of propaganda for Austromarxist ideas. From this point of view the construction of housing takes on an indisputably symbolic connotation. It has already been noted that the political limit of this heroic building up of the city which was a symbol for «social-democracy achieved» lies in the lack of any correspondence between this regional administration of the urban problem and a more comprehensive administration of the national economy and, secondly, in a relative underestimation of the problem of financing the expropriations, that was the cause in the end of an abrupt interruption of the experiment.

Without going into complex evaluations of political economy (which would take us a long way from the line of

Proclamation of the Republic in Vienna, 12th November 1918.

argument pursued up to now in this monograph) it is perhaps worth pausing to take a look at the more specifically architectural aspects of the «housing question». Evidence that problems of form are anything but irrelevant to Austromarxist housing policy is provided not only by the rhetorical emphasis with which the apologists for *Rote Wien* insisted on promoting the *neue Baustil*, but also by the close attention paid by the administration under Karl Seitz to architecture, in the sense of a technique for intervention in the city [174]. It is no accident that the «Five-year plan» of 1923 was accompanied by an efficient re-organization of the municipal structures responsible for building (with the setting up of a special «section of municipal architecture») and was preceded by a fierce debate over the typological models to be employed. The choice lay between the model of the *Siedlungen* — quarters of low density single-family housing with gardens — and the model of the *Höfe* — huge residential blocks with large courts in which the basic communal services are concentrated: from kitchens to wash-houses to nurseries. The choice of the model of the *Höfe* was certainly determined by the role of «monumental propaganda» entrusted to the «red fortresses».

This fact would emerge from the International Congress of Housing and Town-planning (*Internationaler Wohnungs - und Städtebau-Kongress*) held in Vienna from the 12th to the 19th September 1926 where the functional and typological drawbacks of the «superblocks» were to be stressed on many sides (in particular the lack of space, light and air in the apartments — ill-concealed by the «apparent luxury» of the façades) [175]. Following this congress the model of the *Höfe* underwent considerable modifications (largely involving an expansion of the «courts») but the lack of concern for typological aspects of the apartments would remain; an indifference that is still more indicative when it is contrasted with the highly advanced studies on the *Existenzminimum* that were being conducted in Europe at that time [176].

The architectural solutions to the housing problem proposed by Loos differ radically from the ideological basis of the model of the *Höfe*. It is no coincidence that the latter choice was confirmed at the same moment as Loos resigned as Chief Architect of the Housing Department. His proposals are largely based on extensive suburban building plans, making use of the model of the *Gartensiedlungen* (of Anglo-Saxon origin) — although Loos himself would continue to draw up plans for compact superblocks of communal housing like the stepped Housing Unit of 1923 (that remained on the drawing-board) and the Otto-Haas-Hof (built between 1924 and 1925 in the area bounded by Pasettistrasse and Leystrasse) [177].

The fact remains, however, that until 1922 Loos' housing projects are those of the *Gartensiedlungen*. These are as follows: that of Hirschstetten (never built and only recently come to light), that of Lainz (divided up into eight houses in a group, built only in part between 1921 and 1922) and the one of Heuberg (also only partially realized, over the same period, near Röntgenstrasse) [178].

On the whole, we are dealing with constructions modulated around lay-outs of extremely simple composition that

Karl Ehn: Karl-Marx-Hof, Vienna 1929. Two views of the inner court.

make use of elementary technological processes (including for example, wooden beams of standard length resting on the common external walls of two adjacent houses). The scheme of composition belongs to the typology of «group housing» (two-story buildings with the sleeping area on the first floor). A high degree of flexibility in the internal arrangement is obtained by the use of rudimentary systems of movable partitions (such as curtains, cupboards or wood panels). It is not difficult to discern a hint of his memory of American suburban houses in the architectural image of the exterior. The towers that rhythmically punctuate the street façade of the Siedlung am Heuberg are so similar to his description (made in «Das andere» in 1903) of the houses he visited in the neighborhood of Philadelphia, as to make it appear something of a preliminary design for the former [179].

Another important element is the vegetable garden, thought of as an essential extension of the dwelling, to which Loos assigns a role of «primary importance», sanctioning

the obligation to cultivate the land in order to promote the growth of a self-sufficient economy [180]. This is also the logic behind the absence of sanitary services (with the aim of encouraging the production of manure) [181].

Despite these limits it would be a mistake to consider the proposal of the Siedlungen model as «regressive ideology».

It is very true that as early as 1869, Emil Sax (in *Die Wohnungszuständ der arbeitenden Klasse und ihre Reform*) had proposed — from an unmistakably «bourgeois» progressivist point of view — the principle of the *Siedlungen* as «the highest and most important point in the reform of the house» [182]. In 1919, Leopold Bauer would promote the principle of the Siedlungen in opposition to Austromarxist plans for socialization (in *Gesund wohnen und freudig arbeiten. Probleme unserer Zeit*) with arguments that balance the conservative defense of private ownership of land and the formal inspiration of Camillo Sitte's canons of urban estheticism [183]. The naïvety of the underlying aims of Loos' projects is not hard to see, with his confused, but determined ethical bias towards social goals, and the desire for a «realistic» appraisal of the habits of life of the worker-peasant.

It should be noted, however, that the adoption of «poor technologies» is totally foreign to any shades of romantic populism, being dictated exclusively by the need to contain construction costs as much as possible. Moreover the total lack of elements drawn from the repertoire of folklore of the *Heimatkunst* in these projects is not fortuitous. On the contrary, the modern flat roof is adopted as a deliberate step towards the deruralization of its architectural image. Proof that Loos dedicated a great deal of attention to the problems of economy in building is given by, among other things, his arguments about the social utility of keeping the costs of construction low, on the basis of which he justifies — somewhat over-enthusiastically — the registration of a patent for a «system for building houses with only one wall» in December 1921 [184].

In fact, the effects of the historical conditions in which this planning drive took place should not be underestimated, conditions that were marked by runaway inflation and a serious shortage of food supplies, especially in the big cities. Aware of the nature of this economic crisis the Municipality of Vienna published in 1919 a pamphlet on the *Grundsätze für einen Wettberwerb zur Erlangung von Vorentwürfen für eine Gartensiedlung in Wien* (Principles of a competition to draw up preliminary schemes for a garden-district in Vienna) [185]. In this context, there is nothing rash about Loos' idea of creating on the periphery of the city a transition area between city and countryside capable of a certain degree of autonomy in agricultural production. This is even more true when one considers that the single-family house with a vegetable garden attached was proposed as one of the possible solutions to the «housing question» left unresolved by the bourgeois city of the 19th century — perhaps the most urgent but in any case not the only one. There is no lack of spontaneous incidents in the struggle for housing to confirm this urgency, including the occupation of the former imperial park in Lainz by a group of workers determined to raise — by cutting down the trees and selling the wood — the funds necessary to build the *Siedlung* planned by Loos.

Previously there have been historians who testified to how widespread and deeply-rooted was the aspiration to the semi-rural single-family house among the Viennese working-class itself. Proof of this is afforded by the foundation in 1883 of the *Verein für Arbeiterhäuser* (Workers' housing society) which drew up a full building program for *Siedlungen*, carried out only in part with the Favoriten Cottage (18 single-family houses) solely because of the scarcity of funds that could be raised out of very low workers' wages. [186]. On the other hand, the principle of the Siedlungen would be adopted as an appropriate technology for building within the city, in the more or less contemporary experiments in «democratic» urban management carried out in Germany under the Weimar Republic. One need only think of the *Trabantenprinzip* used by Ernst May as an urban model for the «new Frankfurt», or of the *Siedlungen* built by Bruno Taut in Magdenburg, by Otto Haesler in Gelle and by Martin Wagner in Berlin [187].

It is evident from this that the concept of the *Siedlungen* is not at all foreign to social-democratic ideology, and that it cannot in itself be accused of being «reactionary» by taking it as an indication of lower middle-class aspiration to an exaggerated individualism in conflict with the collective ideal embodied in the *Höfe*. On the contrary, in so far as it is an attempt at reclamation of the urban periphery, it represents rather an alternative idea to the model of the bourgeois city, perhaps even more radical than the *Höfe* which largely follow the pattern of the *Mietkaserne*, disguising it with the *éclat* of the *Proletarischer Stil* (as Josef Frank would sarcastically name this style in his essay *Architektur als Symbol* [188].

From what has been said up to now it seems evident that the basic reasons for the incompatibility between Loos' intentions and the ideological administration of «Red Vienna» should be looked for not so much in those aspects

Otto Bauer (1882-1938).   *Karl Seitz (1869-1950).*

relating to political questions but rather in those specific to questions of architecture.

Consistently with his arguments for the denial of any omni-representative Style and any symbolic tattooing of the architecture, Loos proposed to the social-democratic administration of Vienna objects that are marked by a controversial but logical simplicity. The design of the superblocks provides even more unequivocal and significant evidence for this than does that of the *Siedlungen*. So, in another light, the central theoretical question of the «removal of ornament», practiced in the years prior to the *finis Austriae* for a «clientele refined enough to accept that supreme architectural quality that is the renunciation of ornament», now faces a difficult test in the plans produced for the new 'socialist' clientele [189]. Before his move to Paris he did, in fact receive a commission to draw up plans for the Otto-Haas-Hof (1924-25, in collaboration with Karl Dinhuber, Franz Schuster and Grete Schütte Lihotzky): a superblock

of ·50 apartments put up at a stone's throw from the Winarskyhof (the work of Peter Behrens, Josef Hoffmann, Josef Frank, Oskar Strnad and Oskar Wlach).

Loos took advantage of the occasion to demonstrate his theorem of the rational construction of architecture in deliberate constrast to the rhetorical search for a «proletarian style». The wing of the building that he designed is as different — in its strict geometrical purity — from the exaggerated plastic play of the two horizontal lines that shape the corner of the Otto-Haas-Hof (designed by Karl Dinhuber) as it is from the expressionistic symbolism of the entrance to the nearby Winarskyhof (the work of Peter Behrens). A densely packed but extensive narrative rhythm gives order to the square window-openings that dominate the composition of the bare façade looking onto the Durchlaufstrasse. The roof is deliberately recessed and therefore invisible. Only within the court do the massive volume of the Kindergarten, furrowed by the high windows cut into the thick wall, and the repetitive element of the towers, break up the austere rigidity of the composition.

The use of rationality as a method is also clearly visible in the never-built Housing unit designed in 1923. Having de-

termined the optimal form for the cells of habitation, Loos confines himself to a clear and simple assembly of these modules into a «stepped» scheme of composition that follows the lines of the scheme tried out for the Villa Scheu, though on a much larger scale. The sole plastic effect is obtained through the slight bending of the block so as to follow the curve of the street. Whilst the building, in its undeniable «grandiosity», preserves an unadorned and anti-populistic «simplicity». No giving in to nostalgia, no concession to historical codes: this is the essential characteristic of the «working-class» architecture designed by Loos. But this is precisely his means of dissent. In his unflagging dedication to «architecture without ornament», Loos deliberately shies away from the «ideological» need of Austromarxism to discover a *Proletarischer Stil*, reflecting the dominance achieved — or if you like, sought — by the working-class.

It is up to Peter Behrens (skilled constructor of symbolic structures and already successful, first, in his attempt to represent the myth of the beautifying of existence sought by grand-duke Ludwig von Hessen in the *Kunstlerkolonie* of Darmstadt, and then in «giving shape» to the new image of the *Industriekultur* at the behest of the electrical monopoly of the Rathenaus) to show the way to «socialist realism» in Austria in the calculated semantic expressivity of the Winarskyhof [190]. The students of the *Wagnerschule* (H. Gessner, R. Oerley, R. Perco, O. Schöntal, E. Hoppe, K. Ehn, J. Hoffmann and others) follow this road to its end, drawing their morphological material from historicist styles, especially from that of the petit bourgeois *Biedermeier*, and passing it through the fine sieve of the artful lesson of the Secessionists. The symbolic quality of their games with allusive forms is the point at which they deliberately take flight. An example affording proof of this is the triangular element which interrupts the horizontal skyline of the Karl-Marx-Hof, an element whose ostentatious absence of functional motivation shows it to be an expressive substitute for the «lost roof» — almost a dreamlike transfiguration of the house. This «triangle» is also an explicit quotation from a solution already adopted by J. Hoffmann in the Klosehof (1924) — just as the design of the doors set between two great arches that pass underneath alludes to the style introduced by Behrens in the Winarskyhof (1924). There is in short a sort of consonance in this effort to find a design which blends individual inventiveness with the collective imagination. And, by dint of the rediscovered connection between subjectivity and symbolic representation, the «red fortresses» take on the appearance of concrete forms of sociality achieved. In other terms, the patient reworking of highly expressive elements of style (arches, towers, clocks, tympana, cornices, junctions of volumes and large colored surfaces) results in one of the most effective inventions of a national popular style, or alternatively one of the most alluring accentuations of a nostalgia for an unresolved past.

Typical of this style — perhaps even more so than the Karl-Marx-Hof — is the Karl-Seitz-Hof (1926-27, by Hubert Gessner). Josef Frank will not unreasonably poke fun at its populist rhetoric by calling it a *Volkwohnungspalast*, which may be freely translated as a Working-class Palace [191]. In his sarcastic attitude towards this pathetic and ugly exemplar of the residential model of «decadent aristocracy» an echo may be heard of Loos' arguments attacking ornamentation. And yet that «crime», that populist rhetoric represents in fact the release of a suppressed desire on the part of large numbers of the masses to take possession of the ornaments of power, to taste the luxury of the *ancien régime* that has been the object of so much hatred and so much myth-making. The glorification of the deposed is perhaps the source of the misery, but also of the grandeur of the architectural adventure in *Rote Wien*.

This is also where the profound theoretical distance from contemporary events in architecture under the Weimar Republic can be detected. As is well known, social building became the preferred field of application in Germany for the most advanced technological processes of standardization in the construction industry, for the improvement of typological models on the basis of the very diligent studies carried out on the *Existenzminimum*, and for innovations in form derived from the linguistic workshops of the avant-garde movements in figurative art.

A fundamental question is raised at this point: whether the «rational» forms that can be produced by the most advanced techniques of language or the expressive mannerisms drawn from historicist codes are the most suitable to represent the «new» culture of the proletariat? *Architecture or Proletarischer Stil*?

The artistic and architectural debate which spans the entire gamut of events taking place in those societies moving towards socialism during the twenties will shift back and forth between these two poles. This occurs in post-revolutionary Russia, Germany under the Weimar Republic and Austria under the Austromarxists. There can be no doubt that Loos' solution to the dilemma leans towards the first of the two alternatives. And in this sense it is an impolitic solution, since it does not take into account the greater degree of practicality that derives from the mass consensus available through the use of already familiar codes of communication, but it is also a far-sighted solution because it presents to the new «historic subject» a language appropriate to modern times precisely in so far as it is based on technique.

P. Behrens, J. Hoffmann, J. Frank, and others: Winarskyhof, Vienna 1926.

'The middle-classes were scandalized by his compositions. 'However', they said, 'what a pity, this man has sick ears. His mind conceives frightening dissonances. Yet he claims them to be sublime harmonies — and bearing in mind the easily demonstrable fact that our ears are healthy — it means that his ears are sick. A real shame!'... A hundred years have passed since that time and the middleclasses listen with emotion to the works of this sick, crazy musician... Now everybody has Beethoven's sick ears» [192]. When Adolf Loos read in 1918 — on the occasion of the second of ten rehearsals for Schoenberg's *Kammersymphonie op. 9* — this tale of Beethoven, in the hall of the *Konzerthaus*, the audience burst into hearty applause. But perhaps few of them grasped its deep meaning. These words «full of irony and passion» (as Alban Berg describes them) can be taken as a metaphor for the last years of his intellectual labor [193].

The secret of a technique of thought is hidden in these words, as is a suggestive autobiographical identification.

Like Beethoven, Loos conceives «frightening dissonances». Like Beethoven, Loos is «deaf». He does not listen to the uproar of the new trends that emerge and establish themselves in the twenties. His mind works in a state of relative isolation, concentrated on a process of re-elaboration of his own ideas.

Even those architectural works that appear similar in form to that kind of linguistic *koiné* known as the Modern

rules is a fact that cannot be eliminated in an achitecture which plays on differences. It is not difficult to see how in works like the House of Tristan Tzara in Paris (1926) he makes contextual — in the same «text» — use of three different syntaxes of composition. From this impartial manipulation of a multiplicity of planning techniques derives his profound theoretical distance from the late-illuminist dream of finding salvation from chaos in synthesis and of exorcising the fear of contradictions in a system.

Hence, in other terms, his distance from Walter Gropius, who adopted rationality over the same period as a «method» (consistently applicable from the smallest scale of the industrial product to the largest scale of the city) and from Le Corbusier, who sees rationality as a «system» (on the basis of which he designs his «models» of ideal cities aimed at an idealised clientele). In 1928 A. Schoenberg wrote «I can't complain, not everything has gone badly for me. Not only have I always had as friends men like Adolf Loos, but I have always had as enemies men like Walter Gropius». Remarks like this take on, apart from any incidental personal bias, the nature of a polemical stand against the Weimar culture which tries to reconcile unavoidable polyphonies of meaning in the synthesis of forms [194]. Such statements may be interpreted as a precise «choice» of cultural field, that is in a clear-cut discrimination between enemies and friends on the basis of fundamental theoretical presuppositions. Schoenberg seems to recognize in Loos the elective affinity of

SICK EARS AND THE DESIRE FOR EMPTY SPACE

Movement differ greatly, when looked at closely, in their theoretical basis. Most of the time we are dealing with compositions that adhere so closely to theses formulated during the pre-war years as to appear post-dated. As theorems, they develop, on the basis of a logical chain of deductions, certain consistent postulates of his thought.

If for no other reason than this obstinate repetition, Loos' work cannot be made to fit into naïvely linear interpretations of the history of the Modern Movement (schemes that tend to trace improbable continuities of evolution: from Morris to Gropius, from Ledoux to Le Corbusier, and so on). An unreasonable attempt has been made to interpret his «architecture without ornament» as an anticipation of Rationalism.

An esthetic attitude that — as such — once it had fulfilled its historic task no longer had any reason to exist and was fated, as a consequence, to melt away in the triumph of abstract styles in the twenties. On the contrary, by a paradox that is only apparent, the up-to-dateness of his architectural thought stands out because of the way it obstinately reproposes rigorous self-imposed limits, an up-to-dateness deriving from the doubts, rather than certainties, that invade the very meaning of the discipline. The analytical reflection of thought that enquires into itself results, in short, in the awareness of the limits of rationality. Rationality is seen as an instrument of design, useful for the organization of the material, but never as a dogma. Transgression of linguistic

taking dissonances to extremes, even at the cost of alienating the consensus, even at the cost of not being up-to-date.

At a time when the eagerness for certainty pushed some «masters» of the Modern Movement to prefigure the *langue* of the new world, Loos laid down the rules that prevented him from forcing his architectural compositions into the syntactic norms of a unified code. «Build as best you can... Don't be afraid of not being judged modern» [195]. The limit to architectural thought is set in the realm of practice, in the very essence of building. The concrete possibility offered by context is what dictates the rules of the game. Outside the possibilities of the context one cannot even think of the architectural object. Any abstract and a *priori* methodology is doomed to ineffectuality, unless one wants to leave the construction process deliberately out of consideration. Consequently: «In heavily forested mountains one will build in wood, on a rocky mountain one will use stone» [196]. Which amounts to claiming that no one *langue* exists, but only a multiplicity of languages, techniques and materials.

Loos would be able (in his own fashion) to go along with proposition 2.0121 of Wittgenstein's *Tractatus logico-philosophicus*: «Just as we can in no way conceive of spatial objects outside space or temporal objects outside time, we cannot conceive of any object outside the possibilities of its connection to others. Although I can conceive of the object in the context of the state of things, I cannot conceive of it outside the possibility of this context» [197].

What puts the search for a unitary *langue* out of the running is the very heterogeneity of works like the «Chicago Tribune» Column (1922, deliberately «out-of-date» in the improbable manner that it blows up an archaeological archetype to gigantic proportions), the House of Tristan Tzara (1926, given a surprisingly modern appearance by the advanced application of avant-garde techniques), the Villa Moller (1928, «surreal» in its classical frontal symmetry) and the Khuner country house (1930, «vernacular» in its up-dated use of familiar elements of peasant culture).

Introducing over and over again the Kraussian play of contradictions into his architecture, Loos carries out in reality a laicization of the discipline, stripping it of that ethical *bias* which the critic Edoardo Persico had recognized as the true matrix of German Rationalism [198]. But Loos' «deafness» is not limited to the present. It is also the intellectual choice of refusing to listen to the «irresistible promise of pleasure» of the «gay return» to a mythical past represented as still alive («rather than being used as material for progress») [199]. Loos reacts to the «Siren song» by stopping up his ears. «If the Sirens know everything that happens, they ask for the future in exchange, and the gay return is the fraud by which the past captures the nostalgic» [200]. In throwing light on the seductive trap which is hidden behind symbolic and contemplative representation of the past, the exegesis by M. Horkheimer and Th. W. Adorno of the mythical Homeric story makes clear the mechanism by which the «mystique» that surrounds the language is reproposed when it enters on the nostalgic paths of a «historicism without history».

And this is precisely the point. Disappointment in the failure of urban planning in «Red Vienna» had led solely to this negative certitude. The crisis that occurred «on the threshold of a new era» could not have been avoided, or erased simply by the ideological desire to put things back together. Not even the «Proletarian style» could have exorcized it by transcending it. It was no longer possible to naïvely turn back.

But in order not to turn back it is necessary to know exactly where you are. Loos was obliged to make an evaluation of the problems opened up by that historical break which, starting out from the processes of crisis and search for a new foundation in the disciplines of science and philosophy, had spread into art and architecture itself.

The translation in 1920 of his essay *Ornament und verbrechen* in the pages of «L'Esprit Nouveau», his exhibition at the *Salon d'Automne* in Paris in 1923, his adoption as an honorary member of that temple of the French intelligentsia

A. Loos: Interior of Moller House, Vienna 1928.

(even more significant for a citizen of a nation with which France was at war) and his regular attendance in the Paris circle of Tristan Tzara are biographical data which bring up again the question of his relationship to the avant-garde. Moreover Loos had already built up relationships with German radical groups in the pre-war years, through the intercession of A. Schoenberg.

And yet it has already been pointed out that it is not possible to find common ground between Loos and all of the avant-garde movements, and especially not with the constructive ones that feed off the late-illuminist myth of the «continuous progress of thought». It only exists, in an indirect and involuntary sense, with the negative movements, characterised by doubt and by a radical renunciation of synthesis. Indirect because it is an intersection that occurs along essentially different cultural routes. The starting point — but also the point of arrival — of the course that Loos takes is the radical questioning of some fundamental «problems of language» raised in the cultural climate of the *finis Austriae*. In its final phase, in short, Loos' line of thought seems to rejoin the «parabola of fragmentation» that had traversed and shaken «great Vienna». The problems then debated have become once more a source of concern [201].

«But who is man, that he can make plans!» one reads in *Ein Brief* (1901-02) by Hugo von Hofmannsthal [202]. The tragic awareness of the impossibility of expressing reality through language is indicated, in the introduction, by the author himself, as the ultimate meaning of the text. «This is the letter that Lord Philip Chandos... wrote to Francis Bacon... to justify himself to his friend for his total renunciation of literary activity» [203]. The reason for this renunciation is given in the following telling words: «I have felt with a certitude that is not entirely free from sorrow, that in the coming years, and in those following, and in all the years of my life, I shall not write any more books, either in English or in Latin... because the language in which I would have set myself not only to write but perhaps also to think, is not Latin or English or Italian or Spanish, but a language of which I don't know a single word, a language in which dumb things speak...» [204].

The desire for silence, or alternatively the gradual elimination of the mediation between language and things to go back to a sort of «first naming» (to echo M. Foucault) in which those «dumb things» speak: this is the goal of the unlikely journey on which Loos embarks along with some «great Viennese figures of language» like Hofmannsthal, Kraus and others [205]. Georg Trakl is one of the others and it is no coincidence that he dedicates to Loos one of his most beautiful poems: *Sebastian im Traum* (1914) which includes the lines «in silence / dies the lonely harping of the unquiet soul» [206].

But Loos — the «mason who has learned Latin» — seems rather to observe the simultaneous multiplicity of the voices of the material with detachment. If architecture is in its essence a «building technique», the problem of language is posed in different and definite terms in this field. What else can a tendency towards the elimination of language in architecture mean if not to impose a strict self-limitation on subjective imagination? To do away, in short, with all that weight of deliberate creative arrogance which believes it has the right to distort «the facts» in order to chase after private «fantasies», to neglect the intrinsic qualities of materials and forms proven over a long period of use?

As far back as 1898 Loos pointed, in his essay *Das prinzip der bekleidung*, to the «language of materials» as the only genuine grammar of architecture. The architect must learn the «script of things». He must let the material speak, limiting himself to structuring the «form» which supports it. So «technique» is the sole legitimate principle of construction.

On this point Loos finds himself in agreement with Mies van der Rohe who arrives by other roads at an analogous reduction of architecture to pure technical tautology, to pure assembly of materials.

Emblematic of this is the German pavilion at the Universal Exhibition of Barcelona in 1929, where it is not difficult to detect a «quotation» from the Viennese master in the language of materials (slabs of onyx, reflective surfaces of water, marbles and chromed metals). But even before the architecture he built, his essay with the significative title *Building* — written in 1923 at a time when he belonged to the «G» group — polemically enunciates the minimalist program: «we want building to really mean building and nothing else» [207].

In taking the language of things to its «limit», the architecture of negation — that of Loos as much as that of Mies — leaves a fundamental question hanging in the air: why build?

«We can only build a house if we are capable of living in it» warns Martin Heidegger [208]. On the other hand what does living somewhere mean in the universe of *Zivilisation*, in the metropolis without qualities, in the center of the vacuum of values? This question does not — cannot — have a satisfactory answer. No abstract essence of inhabiting exists. It is unknowable outside the possibilities of its appearance. If architecture is the technique of building, then it should limit itself to producing, to bringing into appearance the way of living itself. This is the underlying thesis of Loos' projects.

In its final phase this thesis undergoes a further radicalization. In an essay written in 1914 Loos had already said:

Paul Engelmann and Ludwig Wittgenstein: Interiors of the house for Margaret Wittgenstein Stoneborough, Vienna 1926.

«The building should remain dumb on the outside...». The reticence of the façade should reflect, in its silence, the *Nihilismus* of the metropolis. In line with this assertion, Loos' last houses accentuate the bareness and the closedness of their exteriors. As fortresses «of private dwelling» they oppose the public space of the street with solid walls, barely pierced by only the most functionally unavoidable openings. Here — as has already been said — the contrast with the contemporary «glass architecture» (practiced in Germany — following a path indicated by Paul Scheerbart — by W. Gropius, B. Taut and Mies van der Rohe himself) is radical and implacable [209].

But, towards the end of the twenties, even Loos' interiors become «dumb». They are pervaded by an unrestrainable desire for empty space. One need only think of the internal space of Villa Moller or of the alterations made to Hans Brummel's apartment in Pilsen where the rarefaction of space is taken to its limit.

The meaning of this aspiration for empty space has been grasped by Peter Eisenman who, in an imaginary letter *From Adolph Loos to Berthold Brecht*, has the Austrian architect write the following significative words: «While the architectural system may be complete, the environment of the 'house' is almost a void. And quite unintentionally — like the audience of the film — the owner has been alienated from his environment. In this sense, when the owner first enters 'his house' he is an intruder; he must begin to regain possession — to occupy a foreign container. In the process of taking possession the owner begins to destroy, albeit in a positive sense, the initial unity and completeness of the architectural structure. By acting in response to a given structure, the owner is now almost working against this pattern. By working to come to terms with this structure, design is not decoration but rather becomes a process of inquiry into one's own latent capacity to understand any man-made space» [210].

It is necessary to understand the ambiguity of the relationship between building and inhabiting: the two terms of the relationship tend to an opposite separateness. Architecture — in so far as it is a hierarchical relationship between spaces and their shells — tends to an absolute autonomy that does not take intrusion from the public that uses it into consideration.

It is left up to the person who invades the space to demolish «the structural order of things», to impose — against this *logos* — his own life-style. But the task of the architect is exclusively to build — to build in order to build — leaving the way of living in the building out of consideration. How can one forget the similar attitude adopted by Arnold Schoenberg, in a letter of the 23rd March 1918, in answer to an objection by Zemlinsky about the «consideration owed to the listener»? «I ignore this consideration», he writes, «just as the listener ignores any consideration for me. I know only that the listener is present, although for acoustic

Mirror-paneled door.

The doors are much higher than the average size.

81

reasons I cannot give him up entirely (in an empty hall, in fact, there is no resonance)» [211].

In later years, in short, even the utopia of private dwelling — that had characterised Loos' interiors — yields ground to the pre-eminence of empty space. The interiors, like the exteriors, speak the language of absence. Only the «lively» component of the chromatic play of materials preserves a trace of what has been called the «feminine grandeur of Loos».

It is not impossible that he was influenced in this reversal of trend by the «architectural lesson» given him indirectly by Wittgenstein when he built the house for his sister Margarethe Stonborough in 1926. (It is no accident besides that the plans were drawn up in collaboration with Paul Engelmann, a pupil of Loos) [212]. Wittgenstein turns the interior as

Ludwig Mies van der Rohe: German pavilion, Barcelona 1929.

well into an inflexible logical mechanism that plays on binary choices which the visitor can take in along guided routes. The symmetry that governs the composition is dictated by rigorous logico-mathematical criteria. The doors themselves — transparent, opaque, or reflective like the unusual mirror-door of his sister's bedroom — are used as «switches» that regulate the system of distribution. The only ornament is the noise that reverberates from the floor and from the metallic fixtures.

One notices, however, that Loos never goes so far in his negativity as Wittgenstein, even when his interiors start to empty. What stops him is a Kraussian faith in the «concreteness» of the facts, or if you like, an intuitive grasp of the language of things. «... Anyone who has something to say goes ahead and holds his tongue» Kraus had said [213].

«Silence» turns language upside down. Where words keep silent, things speak. Architecture communicates by means of the wall and of space. A meaning is laid down in these that transcends even the original intentions of the plan.

Here lies the «ineffable» limit to building. Hence, again, the aspiration to the «impersonality of the technique» necessary to produce building itself. Like Hans Karl — Hugo von Hofmannsthal's «difficult man» — Loos is conscious of «speaking in a vacuum» (*Ins leere gesprochen*), but he is also moved by the desire to speak, to build «in spite of all» (*trotzdem*) in the profound silence of his sick ears. Nothing remains, then, but to try to listen to this silence.

NOTES

1) For other accounts of Loos, cf. *Du silberne Dame Du* (Briefe von und an Lina Loos), Vienna-Hamburg, 1966; CLAIRE LOOS, *Adolf Loos privat*, Vienna 1936; ELSIE ALTMANN-LOOS, *Adolf Loos, der Mensch*, Vienna-Munich 1968; VICTOR LOQS, *Ein Gedächtnismal für den Erbauer Adolf Loos*, published by the «Haus der Technik», Vienna 1942; VV.AA., *Adolf Loos, Zum 60. Geburtstag am 10. Dezember 1930*, Vienna 1930; OSKAR KOKOSCHKA, *In memory of Adolf Loos*, preface to *Adolf Loos, Pioneer of Modern Architecture*, London 1966, New York-Washington 1966; OSKAR KOKOSCHKA, *Mein Leben-Erinnerungen an Adolf Loos* in «Alte und moderne Kunst», n. 113, Nov.-Dec. 1970; ALBAN BERG, *Briefe an seine Frau*, Vienna-Munich 1965; PAUL ENGELMANN, *Ludwig Wittgenstein, Briefe und Begegnungen. Herausgegeben von B.F. McGuiness*, Vienna-Munich 1970; VV.AA. *Hommage à Adolf Loos* (writings by G. Besson, Le Corbusier, Gropius and others), Paris 1931; KARL KRAUS, *Rede am Grab*, 25th August 1933, Vienna 1933; EDOARDO PERSICO, *In memoria di Loos,* in «Casabella», Milano, oct. 1933.

2) RICHARD NEUTRA, *Ricordo di Adolf Loos,* in «Casabella», n. 233, Milan 1959.

3) It is obvious that this inquiry — in a sense a genealogical one — cannot go beyond the representation of a hypothetical picture. Any pretence at describing the linear genesis of ideas, or at tracing close causal links between heterogeneous historic and cultural events, would be destined to failure from the start. These links, precisely because of their transverse nature, can only be theoretical presuppositions and not absolutely objective in a philological sense. In other words it is not always possible to provide evidence of Loos' direct familiarity with certain texts, or his explicit adherence to an ideology, in order to prove elective affinities or thematic convergence — at times unconscious or unadmitted — which often arise out of a sort of historicity of thought that is transmitted through channels of communication which are often capillary in nature. As Foucault says: «Genealogy is not opposed to history as the haughty and profound vision of the philosopher is opposed to the mole-like vision of the scholar; it is opposed on the contrary to the metahistoric spreading of ideal meanings and indefinite teleologies.» M. FOUCAULT, *Nietzsche. La généalogie, l'histoire*, in «Hommage a Jean Hyppolite», Paris 1971, pp. 145-146.

4) Due merit should, in any case, be given to certain contributions and essays for having introduced and fully explored this indispensable inquiry into the relations between Loos' architecture and the Viennese cultural setting. An early implicit attempt in this direction was made in ALDO ROSSI's essay *Adolf Loos, 1870-1933* in «Casabella-continuità», n. 233, Milan 1959 (today also in A. ROSSI, *Scritti scelti sull'architettura e la città*, Milan, 1975, pp. 78-107). Other efforts in this direction should be pointed out in the volume by A. JANIK and S. TOULMIN, *Wittgenstein's Vienna*, 1973, and the monographic issue of «Critique», nos. 399-340, Paris 1975, dedicated to *Vienne, début d'un siècle*. But the «philosopher» who has tackled this theme with the greatest attention to its problems is MASSIMO CACCIARI in his essays: *Oikos da Loos a Wittgenstein*, Rome, 1975; *La Vienna di Wittgenstein* in «Nuova Corrente», nos. 72-73, Milan, 1978; *Interno e esperienza (Note su Loos, Roth e Wittgenstein)*, in «Nuova Corrente», nos. 79-80, Milan, 1979 and *Dallo Steinhof*, Milan 1980.

5) A. LOOS, *Architektur* (1910) in *Sämtliche Schriften*, Vienna 1962, pp. 302-318.

6) On the contrary it may be claimed that the problem of history is a central theme in the wider and more complex philosophical debate of the 19th century. On this subject, Friedrich Nietzsche had already warned in his «second untopical reflection» (1874): «Of course we need history, but our need for it is different from that of the refined idler in the garden of knowledge, even if he looks down his nose at our hard and awkward circumstances and necessities. We need it, that is, for life and for action... Only in so far as history serves life, are we willing to serve history». F. NIETZSCHE, *Unzeitgemmässe Betrachtungen, Zweites Stück: Vom Nutzen und Nachteil der Historie für das Leben*, Leipzig 1874, p. 3.

7) The terms «excess of history», «antiquarian veneration» and «weakening of the present» are recurrent in the essay by F. Nietzsche mentioned above.

8) «When I walk along the Ring I always get the impression that a modern Potemkin has wanted to create in the visitor to Vienna the impression that he has arrived in a city inhabited solely by nobles». A. LOOS, *Die potemkinsche stadt* (1898) in *Sä... Sch...* p. 153-156.

9) *Moderne Architektur* is the significative title of a fundamental essay by OTTO WAGNER published in Vienna in 1895, two editions of which were subsequently reprinted in 1899 and 1902. A fourth edition in 1914 was retitled *Die Baukunst unserer Zeit*. The arguments in the book had already been touched on in the opening lecture of his university course in 1894 (the year in which Wagner was appointed professor at the Vienna Academy of Arts). This set in motion an important trend of architectonic renewal known as the *Wagnerschule*, which numbered among its pupils Joseph Maria Olbrich, Joseph Hoffmann, Leopold Bauer and Josef Plečnik - to mention just a few of the most well-known.

10) *Nutzstil* may be literally translated as Useful-style. About this Wagner writes: «Need, purpose, construction technique and ideals are consequently the original germs of artistic life. Reunited in a single conception they represent a sort of necessity for the birth and existence of any work of art: this is the meaning of the phrase *artis sola domina necessitas*» (Cfr. OTTO WAGNER: *Die Baukunst unserer Zeit,* Vienna 1914, p. 58. Yet his practice of design — permeated by decorative formalism — systematically contradicts the functionalist slogans recurrent in Wagner's writings. Moreover their common «Semperian» training often leads to remarkable coincidences between the «theoretical» statements of Loos and Wagner. But the facts are not consistent with the words, and the buildings they constructed provide the best litmus paper to evaluate the «differences» in their concepts. For Wagner's architectural work see, apart from the above-mentioned text by A.G. BACULO; the comprehensive and illustrated monograph by H. GERETSEGGER, M. PEINTNER, *Otto Wagner,* Salzburg 1964.

11) A. LOOS, *Architektur,* (1910). in *Sä... Sch...* pp. 302-318.

12) Idem, pp. 245-246.

13) « ... language is not invented - if it does not reveal a history, a tradition, *at the very moment that it transforms it or revolutionizes it,* it expresses nothing and it communicates nothing». MASSIMO CACCIARI, *La Vienna di Wittgenstein,* in «Nuova Corrente», nos. 72-73, Milano 1977, p. 60. On this subject see also the paragraph *Mahlerische Kunst,* in the essay by the same author: *Krisis, saggio sulla crisi del pensiero negativo da Nietzsche a Wittgenstein,* Milano 1976, pp. 113-124.

14) A. LOOS, *Architektur,* (1910) in *Sä... Sch...,* PP. 302*318.

15) A. LOOS, *Regeln für den, der in den bergen baut* (1913) in *Sä... Sch...,* pp. 329-330.

16) Ibidem.

17) WALTER BENJAMIN, *Gesammelte Schriften,* Band I (1-3), Frankfurt 1974, P. 1238.

18) Anyone wishing to investigate the arguments of Max Dvořák (1875-1923) is referred to his principal works: *Storia dell'arte come storia dello spirito,* 1924 and *Storia dell'Arte italiana nell'epoca del rinascimento* (published posthumously, in 1927). On the theoretical aspects concerning «operative criticism» cf. MANFREDO TAFURI, *Teorie e storia dell'architettura,* Bari 1970, pp. 165 et seq.

19) A. LOOS, *Architektur, in Sä... Sch...,* pp. 302-318. As is well-known, Loos «violates» in his essays the German linguistic convention of writing nouns with an initial capital letter. Quotations from the original texts will respect, from this point on, Loos' technique of writing.

20) ERWIN PANOFSKY and FRITZ SAXL, *Classical Mythology in Mediaeval Art* in «Metropolitan Museum Studies», 1933, n. 2, pp. 228-280.

21) «Whatever we seek in any moment to think about, and in whatever way we want to think, we always think it in the limits of tradition. It is alive, if it frees our reflection on things, by projecting it in a thought that has nothing to do with mathematical calculation. Only when, thoughtful, we dedicate ourselves to the *already-thought-of,* will we then be open to that which is *as-yet-unthought-of*». MARTIN HEIDEGGER, *Identität und Differenz,* Neske, Pfullingen, 1957.

22) ADOLF LOOS, *Architektur.*

23) This argument has been upheld by MARIA GRAZIA MESSINA, *L'opera teorica di Adolf Loos,* in «Annali della Scuola Normale Superiore di Pisa», series III, vol. III, issue I, 1973, p. 271 - and, with different motivations, by MASSIMO CACCIARI, *Oikos, da Loos a Wittgenstein,* Rome 1975, pp. 49-51.

24) Reworking the dialectical scheme of Hegelian Esthetics, Alois Riegl interprets the conquest of *total spatiality* achieved by the Romans as a synthesis of two previous «phases» or «stages of vision»: the tactile (two-dimensional) vision of the Ancients and the tactile-optical (three-dimensional) vision of the Greeks. The «full three-dimensionality» of the Romans would represent — in other terms — a gnosological acquisition that derives from just this recognition of «space» as «intuitive form of the intellect». What stands out clearly in this «teleological» interpretation is the succession without evaluation of the different schemes of vision understood as epochal *Kunstwollen,* but the question of the re-thinking of the already-thought in the logical and methodological terms set up by Loos is not touched on. Cf. ALOIS RIEGL, *Spätrömische Kunstindustrie,* Vienna 1901. As is well known the concept of *Kunstwollen* (artistic will) was preceded by the idea — of Hegelian derivation — of *Kunstgeist* (artistic spirit) in Riegl's previous essay *Stilfragen* published in 1893. For a critical guide to the work of Riegl (1858-1905) see LICIA COLLOBI RAGGHIANTI, introduction to *Arte tardoromana.* For the more specific influence of this theory on the architectural debate see RENATO DE FUSCO, *L'idea di architettura,* Milano 1968, pp. 37-50. In this view the Roman constructions would carry to its conclusion a «mental process» whose development is already implicit in the initial dialectics between the «creation of space» (understood as «negation of matter and, therefore, a nothing») and the «creation of the limits of space» (that is of the material shell that gives it shape). Cf. ALOIS RIEGL, op. cit.

25) Cfr. A. LOOS, *Glas und ton* (1898), in Sä... Sch... pp. 55-61. Gottfried Semper (1803-1897) — author of an essay that is fundamental to the understanding of the dawning of contemporary architecture: *Der Stil in den technischen und tektonischen Künsten* — left an indelible mark on the Dresden Academy of Architecture, where he held a chair from 1834 onwards. Engaged in the same city in the construction of the Court Theater, he joined the revolutionary movement in 1848, designing barricades for the insurgents. Deported from Germany, he later taught at the Polytechnic in Zurich and in Vienna, where he built (in collaboration with C.F. Hasenhauer) the neo-Renaissance Hofburgtheater (1974-88). His theoretical and architectural work exerted a lively influence on the 19th-century artistic debate in the German-speaking cultural area.

26) «*Kunst kommt von Können*», Art comes from knowing how, Loos writes in his essay *Glass und ton*, in A. LOOS, Sä... Sch..., Vienna-Munich 1962, p. 59. The German word *können* can be translated by *knowing* but also by *being able*. In synthesis it is a know-how founded on skill.

27) A. LOOS, *Der sattlermeister* (1903), in *Sä... Sch...,* pp. 219-220.

28) The conception of architecture as *Beruf,* which brings Loos close to Tessenow, is at bottom motivated by a lucid criticism of the false awareness of modernity. Cf GIORGIO GRASSI, (edited by): *Heinrich Tessenow. Osservazioni elementari sul costruire,* Milan 1974.

29) «The 'truth' is circularly linked to the systems of power that produce and support it, and to the consequences of power that it induces and that reproduce it: 'Regimes' of truth». MICHEL FOUCAULT, *Microfisica del potere,* Torino 1977, p. 27, foreword to the Italian edition.

30) A searching analysis of epistemological questions goes beyond the scope of the present essay. As a consequence I refer the reader to the above-mentioned text by Massimo Cacciari and to A. JANIK and S. TOULMIN, *Wittgenstein's Vienna,* 1973, and to the ample bibliography of the subject contained therein. Yet it is already significant that L. Wittgenstein recognizes A. Loos' power of thought in a passage that is worth quoting here: «I do not believe that I have ever invented a train of ideas; on the contrary it has always been given to me by someone else. I have only seized on it at once with enthusiasm for my work of clarification. In this way I have been influenced by Boltzmann, Hertz, Schopenhauer, Frege, Russel, Kraus, Loos, Weininger, Spengler, Sraffa... All that I invented are new *similes*». L. WITTGENSTEIN, Frankfurt 1977.

31) JOHANN BERNHARD FISCHER VON ERLACH, *Entwurf einer historischen Architektur,* Vienna 1721, (the original is in the Albertina of Vienna). This was the first large-scale history of architecture in pictures (recently republished in paperback as part of the series «Die bibliophilen Taschenbücher» (1978). On the work of Fischer von Erlach (1856-1723) — chief protagonist of Viennese baroque and architect of, among other works, the *Karlskirche* (1715-21, completed in 1737 by his son Josef K. Emanuel) — see: HANS SEDLMAYR, *Johann Bernhard Fischer von Erlach,* Vienna-Munich 1956, which is perhaps the most complete and well-documented monograph on the author.

32) KARL FRIEDRICH SCHINKEL (1781-1841) had an undoubted influence on the development of some protagonists of modern architecture, including Mies van der Rohe himself. His «lesson» harks back explicitly to the themes of the architecture of Illuminism, and of Ledoux in particular. Cf. N. PEVSNER, *Schinkel,* «R.I.B.A. Journal», LIX, January 1952.

33) EMIL KAUFMANN, *Von Ledoux bis Le Corbusier,* Leipzig-Vienna 1933.

34) Cf. *Josef Kornhausel (1782-1860), Revolution und Biedermeier,* in «Bauwelt», n. 44, Berlin, nov. 1965, pp. 1231-1237.

35) Cf. EMIL KAUFMANN, *Die Architekturtheorie der französischen Klassik und des Klassizismus,* in «Repetorium für Kunstwissenschaft», 1924. Another way to put this would be: at the root of Loos' thought is the Classical rather than Classicism.

36) EMIL KAUFMANN, *Architecture in the Age of Reason,* Harvard 1955.

37) Although the draft of the *Tractatus logico-philosophicus* was completed in Vienna in August 1918 (and published under the title *Logisch-philosophische Abhandlung* in 1921) the themes of the research are already present in the Viennese debate of the years preceding the *finis Austriae.* Cf. A. JANIK, S. TOULMIN, op. cit.

38) LUDWIG WITTGENSTEIN, *Tractatus logico-philosophicus,* (German and English with an introduction by Bertrand Russell), London 1922, p. 189 («International Library of Psychology, Philosophy and Scientific Method»).

39) Cf. ADORNO, *Philosophie der neuen Musik,* Tübingen 1949; GEORG WILHELM FRIEDRICH HEGEL, *Ästhetik,* Berlin 1955 (first edition: Berlin 1836-1838).

40) ARNOLD SCHOENBERG, *Harmonielehre,* Vienna 1911.

41) LUIGI PESTALOZZA, introductory essay to ARNOLD SCHOENBERG, *Stile e idea,* Milan 1975, pp. 234-235.

42) Idem.

43) ARNOLD SCHOENBERG, *Harmonielehre,* op. cit.

44) Cf. OSKAR KOKOSCHKA, *Mein Leben-Erinnerungen an Adolf Loos,* in «Alte und moderne Kunst», n. 113, Nov.-Dec. 1966.

45) A. LOOS, *Meine bauschule* (1913), in *Sä... Sch...,* pp. 322-325.

46) A. SCHOENBERG, in *Adolf Loos, zum 60. Geburtstag,* cit.

47) Quoted in F. WAISMANN, *Wittgenstein und der Wiener Kreis,* Oxford 1977.

48) In this connection read Loos' autobiographical account dealing with his experience on board ship during the voyage from Hamburg to New York, in an article from the column *Wie Wir Leben (Etikettefragen)* in the review «Das andere» (1903); reprinted in A. LOOS, *Sä... Sch...,* op. cit., pp. 215-251. The description of his arrival in New York (quoted in parentheses) is from R. NEUTRA, *Ricordo di Loos,* in «Casabella», op. cit., p. 48.

49) The effect of Loos' stay in Chicago and St. Louis was first stressed by RICHARD NEUTRA, *Amerika,* in «Neues Bauen in der Welt», Vienna 1930.

50) On this subject Tafuri has written: «America, seen and praised by Loos in the far-off 1890, is a country with two faces: the one which shows is capacity to absorb and recreate on a gigantic scale the Europen ideology of Order, of Form outside time — the United States of the Columbian Exposition — and the one which complies impartially with the laws of everyday existence». MANFREDO TAFURI, *La montagna disincantata*, in VV.AA., *La città americana*, Bari 1973, p. 431.

51) RICHARD NEUTRA, *Ricordo di Loos*, op. cit., p. 46.

52) A. LOOS, *Die schuhmacher*.

53) For a critical analysis of American architectural ideologies see VV.AA. *La città americana*, op. cit.

54) On the relationship of mutual esteem between Loos and Sullivan cf. ESTHER Mc COY, *Letters from Louis Sullivan to R.M. Schindler*, in «Journal of the Society of Architectural Historians», 1961, vol. XX, n. 4.

55) Cf. NIKOLAUS PEVSNER, *Pioneers of the Modern Movement from William Morris to Walter Gropius*, London 1936.

56) The Prairie Houses represent Frank Lloyd Wright's first experiment largely carried out in the suburbs of Chicago. These works (1893-1909), which express the basic principles of Wright's architectural composition, were published in Berlin in 1910, evoking a strongly sympathetic response among young European architects.

57) A. LOOS, *Abendländische kultur*, «Das andere» (1903), in *Sä... Sch..., p. 215-219.*

58) J. LACAN, *Le Seminaire de Jacques Lacan, Livre I, Les écrits techniques de Freud*, Paris 1975, report of the 3rd February 1954.

59) As has already been mentioned, the idealized contrast between Europe and America is a recurrent theme in the German cultural setting. It is moreover significant that it was brought up again by Max Weber himself in his famous essay *Wissenschaft als Beruf*.

60) A. LOOS, *Kultur* (1908), in *Sä... Sch..., p. 263-266.*

61) One need only think — if we stick to the disciplinary field of architecture — of the exhibitions of English handicrafts organised by councillor von Scala at the Österreichisches Museum or of the arguments brought forward by Joseph August Lux.

62) Rilke was, in other ways, just as «detached», as far as the literary tradition and technique of German writing is concerned, as were the majority of central European intellectuals of Slavonic origin, such as Franz Kafka and Robert Musil. Loos — born in Brno — shares with the Czechoslovak writers this attitude of detached critical analysis of the German culture and language. «Rilke, Trakl, Weiheber», wrote Mittner, «have Slav blood in their veins. Prague in particular, nerve center of Austria in the period prior to its collapse, which was in its turn nerve center of a Europe close to the end of its age-old dominion over the whole world; Prague then, with its suggestive and disturbing Slavonic-Germanic-Jewish atmosphere ripened the 'ante litteram' existentialism of Rilke and Kafka; nearby Brünn (Brno) shaped the youth of Musil. From the diaries, the letters and also from the juvenile works of these three authors emerges a singular and very important coincidence: having always heard a language spoken around them that was not German, but Bohemian or even Yiddish, they lost faith in the validity or even the reality of the German tongue». LADISLAO MITTNER, *La letteratura tedesca del Novecento*, Turin 1960, pp. 177-178.

63) RAINER MARIA RILKE, *Brief an Wiltold van Hulewicz* in *Briefe an einen jungen Dichter* 1929, Eng. trans. *Letters to a Young Poet*, 1954.

64) F. Nietzsche had already mercilessly criticized the alienation of American life. *Gay Science* has this to say on the subject: «There is a wholly Indian savagery, typical of Redskin blood, in the way in which Americans thirst after gold; and their furious work without a moment's rest — the vice peculiar to the new world — already begins to infect the old Europe with savagery and to spread over it a prodigious lack of spirituality... And just as all forms are visibly ruined in the worker's haste, so too does the meaning of form itself, the ear and the eye for harmony of movement, go to ruin. The proof of this is to be found in the course clarity demanded everywhere». FRIEDRICH NIETZSCHE, *Die fröhliche Wissenschaft*, Leipzig 1887. Ernst Bloch will later write: «The machine has succeeded in making everything as dreary and subhuman in its details as are our residential districts as a whole». ERNST BLOCH, *Die technische Kälte* in *Geist der Utopie* (1918-1923), Frankfurt 1973, P. 21.
The criticism — of aspects relating to architecture — made by the Frankfurt school of the principle of *Sachlichkeit* and of *reine Architektur* will follow the lines laid down here.
Such a striking contradiction is already implicitly contained — as Robert Musil points out — in the opposing character of the theoretical categories *Kultur* and *Zivilisation*. The term *Kultur* is usually translated by the English word *culture* though at times *civilization* is used. The German word *Zivilisation* often has a negative connotation in as much as it alludes to the vulgar materialism imposed by industrial development. For a discussion of this conceptual dichotomy cf. ROBERT MUSIL, *Das hilflose Europa oder Reise vom Hundertsten ins Tausendste* (1922), in *Gesammelte Werke - Essays und Reden*, Hamburg 1979. This dichotomy was totally rejected by Sigmund Freud. Cf. SIGMUND FREUD, *Das Unbehagen in der Kultur*, Vienna, 1929.

65) See SAMUEL HABER, *Efficiency and uplift: scientific management in the progressive era, 1890-1920*, Chicago 1964; J.M. NADWORNY, *Scientific management and the union 1900-1932* (Cambridge, Mass. 1955) especially pp. 1-42; F.W. TAYLOR, *Scientific management. Testimony before the special house committee* (New York, 1911); C.B. THOMPSON (editor) *Scientific management. A collection of the more significant articles describing the Taylor system of management* (Cambridge, Mass. 1914). On Taylor himself: F.M. COPLEY, *Frederick Winslow Taylor* (New York, 1923). For the controversy over the application of Taylorism: H.G.J. AITKEN, *Taylorism at Watertown arsenal* Cambridge, Mass. 1960).

66) Cf. ERNST JÜNGER, *Der Arbeiter*, Stuttgart 1932.

67) «The American worker has conquered the world. The man in overalls» A. LOOS, *Kultur* (1908), in *Sä... Sch..., pp. 263-266.*

68) A. LOOS, *Kulturentartung (1908), in Sä... Sch..., pp. 271-275.*

69) The fundamental limit of Loos' analysis lies precisely in his open «indifference» to the processes of manufacture of goods (whether they are industrial or handcrafted), preferring to base his judgement on the value of the finished product itself. He wrote in fact: «The origin of merchandise is irrelevant to me. The essential thing is that the dealer should be able to furnish certain goods, packaged in a certain way. Whether he possesses his own workshop or he spreads the work over several different outside workshops is of no importance to the value of the goods themselves. My criticism is aimed at these alone». A. LOOS, *Wäsche* (1898), in *Sä... Sch..., pp. 113-120.*

70) A. LOOS, *Hands off!*, (1917), in *Sä... Sch..., pp. 342-347.*

71) A. LOOS, *Glas und ton* (1898), in *Sä... Sch..., pp. 55-61.*

72) Ibidem.

73) «Interpellating on Marx's theory of value, Morris makes use of the *forms* of capitalism, drawn, in his opinion, from classical English economy, and he changes them into concepts, on which to base political action. But, in turning all of Marx's scientific concepts into moral ones (plus value = theft), not only does he bring socialism back to its petit bourgeois origins, but he reduces the political struggle to impotence». All his zeal seems to foreshadow such an outcome. MARIO MANIERI ELIA, *William Morris e l'ideologia dell'architettura moderna*, Bari 1976.

74) A. LOOS, *Glas und ton (1898), in Sä... Sch..., pp. 55-61.*

75) Cf. R. BANHAM, *Theory and Design in the First Machine Age*, London 1960-62.

76) A. LOOS, *Glas und ton* (1898) in *Sä... Sch..., pp. 55-61.*

77) «Mag sein, dass er dort mehr an antikischem Formgut kennenlernte, als er in Rom oder Griechenland hätte finden können. Sicher aber ist, dass das Leben im Amerika der Jahrundertwende ein wichtiger Schlüssel für Loos' Verständnis klassischen Geistes wurde. ROLAND L. SCHACHEL, *Adolf Loos, Amerika und die Antike*, in «Alte und moderne Kunst», 1970 n. 113, p. 7.

78) Cf. A. LOOS, *Glas und ton* (1898), in *Sä... Sch..., pp. 55-61.*

79) Ludwig Münz in particular has stressed the importance of the postcard of the Obelisk at «Bunker Hill» in Charlestown Mass, found among Loos' papers, taking it to be the key to interpreting his project for the *Kaiserjubiläums-Gedächtniskirche* (1899). Cf. LUDWIG MÜNZ, *Über die Grundlagen des Baustils von Adolf Loos*, in «Aufbau» n. 10, Vienna 1958, pp. 393-95.

80) A. LOOS, *Architektur* (1910) in *Sä... Sch..., p. 302.*

81) It has been acutely pointed out that: «The Seagram once again makes use of the curtain wall, the glazed façade continues... The absoluteness of the object is total here: to the maximum of structurality of form corresponds the greatest absence of images. This language of absence is projected onto a further void which mirrors the first and makes it resound... The renunciation, the classical *Entsagung* is definitive here. To express it, *Mies takes a step back and remains silent*». MANFREDO TAFURI and FRANCESCO DAL CO, *Architettura Contemporanea*, Milan 1976, p. 346.

82) Making use of less radical concepts, but still following the path marked out by Loos when he drew attention to the irreversible decline of mystique, a few Austrian architects who had emigrated to America will appear on the scene, including J. Urban. R. Schindler and R. Neutra: Representative of these is the essay *Wie baut Amerika?* (1927) by R. Neutra, which marks a decisive step towards an unbiased analysis of the technological potential of the new construction systems by defining a rigorous compositional syntax that is directly connected to the production capacity of the local building industry. Cf. RICHARD NEUTRA, *Wie baut Amerika*, Stuttgart 1927.

83) Cf. ERICH MENDELSOHN, *Amerika, Bilderbuch eines Architekten*, Berlin 1926. The esteem which Mendelsohn and Loos held for each other is well known, despite the difference between their poetics of design. Cf. R. BANHAM, op. cit.

84) The interpretation given by Heinrich Kulka — and supported by Ludwig Münz — to this founding principle of Loos' methodology of design, although drawing the «obvious» conclusions, takes a limited view of it as it reduces the *Raumplan* to a pragmatic criterion of spatial economy, that is to say a way of making spaces of different heights fit together (within the unitary box-like volume) that is dictated entirely by functional motivations. Cf. HEINRICH KULKA, *Adolf Loos*, Vienna 1931; LUDWIG MÜNZ, *Der Architekt Adolf Loos*, Vienna-Munich 1964. What's more L. Münz and G. Künstler, in the monograph that has already been cited, unite in identifying the date at which the *Raumplan* was first adopted as 1922, in the Rufer House interior.
In reality the *Raumplan* is not only based on more complex theoretical motivations than those of trivial functionalism, but it also has a far longer period of gestation (though it is only in the twenties that it begins to find opportunites for a complete and explicit architectural expression). Strictly speaking it is already discernible in the colored drawing of a living-room, with fireplace and gallery, he made in 1899 and in the *American interiors* he realized in Vienna in the early years of the 20th century: one thinks of the alterations to Leopold Langer's apartment (1901), of the living-room of his own apartment (1903) or of the dining-room of the house of Alfred Kraus (1905).

85) For the reception given Richardson's lessons in Europe see the essay by LEONARD K. EATON, *American Architecture Comes of Age. European reaction to H.H. Richardson and Louis Sullivan*, MIT Press, Cambridge (Mass.) 1972; especially the chapter: *Adolf Loos and the Viennese Image of America,* pp. 109-142.

86) For the influence of the theory of *Einfühlung* in the architectural field see: RENATO DE FUSCO, *L'idea dell'architettura*, op. cit., pp. 25-36.

87) A. LOOS, *Das prinzip der bekleidung* (1898) in *Sä... Sch...*, pp. 105-112.

88) The essay *Glasarchitektur* by the poet Paul Scheerbart (1863-1915) was published in Berlin in 1914 and provoked an immediate response in architecture, inspiring works like the *Glass pavilion* by Bruno Taut and the *Maschinenhalle* by Walter Gropius and Adolf Mayer at the Exhibition of the Deutsche Werkbund in Cologne held in the same year. But it is above all in the years immediately following the war that Scheerbart's arguments profoundly penetrate the architectural esthetics of the expressionistic groups. On the subject of *Glaskultur*, see also the recent essay by MASSIMO CACCIARI, *Note su Loos, Roth e Wittgenstein*, in «Nuova Corrente», nos. 79-80, Milan 1979, pp. 372-375.

89) Cf. MICHEL FOUCAULT, *Surveiller et punir. Naissance de la prison.* Paris 1975.

90) Cf. MICHEL FOUCAULT, *L'oeil du pouvoir*, preface to the reprint of JEREMY BENTHAM, *Le Panoptique*, Paris 1977.

91) A. LOOS, *Heimatkunst* (1914), in *Sä... Sch...*, pp. 331-341.

92) Typical of this is the Obus plan for Algiers (1930), where the split between the «field of technique» and the «field of emotion» is clearly and unmistakably expressed. The «rational» organization of urban structure is left up to the technician-planner, while «fantasy» is relegated to the private sphere. *Within* his own allotment of space, each user can give free play to his individual creativity, fitting — if you like — exaggeratedly kitsch forms into the rigid structural grid. The substitution of individual cells does not in fact change the given urban conformation.

93) A. LOOS, *Das prinzip der bekleidung* (1898), in *Sä... Sch...*, pp. 105-112.

94) Cf. AUGUST SCHMARSOW. *Über den Wert der Dimensionen in menschlichen Raumgebilde,* Leipzig 1896.
As well as known, A. Schmarsow (1853-1936) developed his esthetic theories in close connection with the Vienna School and in particular with Riegl and Dvořák. Considering Loos' links with Dvořák, it is not impossible that he was indirectly familiar with the theory of *Raumgestaltung*. For a critical analysis of Schmarsow's work see H. SORGEL, *Einführung in die Arkitektur-Ästhetik*, Munich 1918; R. SALVINI, *La critica d'arte moderna,* Florence 1949; G. NICCO FASOLA, *Ragionamenti sull'architettura*, Città di Castello 1949; G. MORPUR-GO-TAGLIABUE, *L'esthétique contemporaine,* Milan 1960, as well as the above-mentioned works by RENATO DE FUSCO.

95) Cf. RENATO DE FUSCO, op. cit.

96) Cf. AUGUST SCHMARSOW, *Über den Wert der Dimensionen im menschlichen Raumgebilde,* op. cit., p. 45.

97) Cf. AUGUST SCHMARSOW, *Kompositionsgesetze romanischer Glasgemälde*, Leipzig 1916.

98) A. LOOS, *Die potemkinsche stadt* (1898), in *Sä... Sch...*, pp. 153-156.

99) The review «Ver Sacrum» first appeared in 1898 and became the main show-case for the Secession up until 1906. Gustav Klimt was the pre-eminent figure on the editorial board. The program of the review was rhetorically expressed by Max Burckhardt in the first issue: «Now we turn to you, without distinction of class and social status. In art there is no difference between rich and poor». As well as Burckhardt, who acted as «assistant literary consultant», outstanding figures from Viennese literary life such as Hermann Bahr contributed to the review.

100) The *Vereinigung bildender Künstler Österreichs* (Union of Austrian figurative artists) better known as the *Wiener Secession* (Viennese Secession) was set up on the 27th March 1897, and made much of by the theater critic Ludwig Hevesi. The association started off with forty founding members. The elderly painter Rudolph von Alt was the honorary President but its true leader was Gustav Klimt. The first general assembly was held on the 21st June of the same year. As well as painters such as Kolo Moser, Carl Moll and Klimt himself, the architects Joseph Maria Olbrich and Josef Hoffmann, and later even Otto Wagner, belonged to the association.

101) You great cities / raised out of stone / on the plain! / You dying peoples / pale wave / that breaks against the beach of night, falling stars!. G. TRAKL, *Abendland, in Gesange des Abgeschiedenen.*

102) «Freilich, wehe, wie fremd sind die Gassen der / Leid-Stadt; / wo in der falschen, aus Übertönung gemachten / Stille, stark, aus dem Gussform des Leeren der Ausguss / prahlt: der vergoldete Lärm, das platzende Denkmal». R.M. RIKE., *Duineser Elegien.*

103) K. Kraus quoted in W. BENJAMIN, *Illuminationen*, Frankfurt 1977, pp. 353-384.

104) Cf. G. SIMMEL, *Venedig* (1907) in *Zur Philosophie der Kunst*, Potsdam 1922.

105) The collaboration between Klimt and Olbrich in the «House of the Secession» project is demonstrated by, among other things, the watercolors recently exhibited at the *Wiener Stilkunst um 1900* show put on at the *Historisches Museum der Stadt Wien* in Vienna (cf. Catalogue nos. 202-209). It is significant to note that the final outcome of the construction represents a compromise in form between the two design proposals. In fact it is in some ways closer to the compositional layout designed by Klimt than to the one proposed by Olbrich.

106) By quoting the well-known phrase taken from the essay dedicated by Richard Wagner to Ludwig van Beethoven — «My kingdom is not of this earth» — as the motto of the frieze, Klimt provides further evidence of his inclination towards poetic estrangement rather than everyday banality. G. KLIMT, *Catalog of the XIV Exhibition of the Secession*, Vienna, 1902.

107) The building covers an area of 12,000 m², a gift of the Municipality of Vienna, a short distance from the Academy of Arts.

108) A. LOOS, *Architektur* (1910), in *Sä... Sch...*, op. cit., p. 316.

109) Ibidem, p. 254.

110) U. ECO, *Trattato di semiotica generale*, Milan 1975.

111) A. LOOS, *Die potemkinsche stadt* (1898).

112) C. SITTE, *Der Städtebau nach seinen künstlerischen Grundsätzen*, Vienna 1889.

113) Ibidem.

114) LE CORBUSIER, *L'urbanisme,* Paris 1925, p. 9.

115) K. KRAUS, *Beim Wort genommen,* Munich 1955.

116) A. LOOS, *Die potemkinsche stadt* (1898).

117) On this subject Loos observes: «The speculator would prefer the façades of the houses to be plain from top to bottom. It costs far less. And doing this he would act in a more genuine, more correct and more artistic way. But people don't want to live in houses like that. And to increase the chances of renting the house the owner is forced to attach to this façade, yes, really to this façade, new features to cover it again...!» On the typological aspect he adds: «Everything which Renaissance Italy expressed in its noble palaces has been plundered with the aim of enchanting his majesty the populace with a new Vienna inhabited only by people who are able to own an entire mansion from foundation to cornice. The stables on the ground floor, the servants' quarters on the mezzanine — the lowest, subordinate part — the reception rooms on the first floor — architecturally the highest and richest part — and the living-rooms and bedrooms on the upper floors. The owners of Viennese houses derived great satisfaction from possessing a mansion of this kind and even the tenant was content to live in a mansion. The ordinary man, who just rented a room and a toilet on the top floor, was satisfied by the feudal splendor and the lordly grandeur of his house when he looked at it from the outside. Doesn't even the owner of a fake diamond look at it lovingly through a sparkling lens? Oh, the swindled swindlers!» A. LOOS, *Die potemkinsche stadt.*

118) This is the fundamental thesis of the essay *Moderne Architektur* taken up subsequently and further developed in *Die Grossstadt* of 1911, Cf. OTTO WAGNER, *Moderne Architektur*, Vienna 1895.

119) There is a subtle but detectable thread running through the different experiences of his intellectual adventure. «A direct continuity exists between the drawings collected by Olbrich in the volume *Ideen* (1900)», wrote Tafuri, «and the Darmstadt Colony. The unlikely village of Darmstadt has the air of a 'magic mountain'. Eros rules there. The symbolic statues at the sides of the great gateway to the palace of the grand-duke speak clearly: the unstemmable tide of existence forces crystallization, impels you to enter — like the gaping mouth of the building — into the labyrinth of the spirit where there is no margin of alienation, compels you to abandon yourself to the absolute truth inherent to the vitalism that gives up nothing and absorbs everything... The 'magic mountain' can only represent itself as tragedy. And this is not all: to come down from that mountain and return to the city will have fatal consequences. To preserve the enchantment of Klingsor's garden it is necessary to tear away the mask from the myth, to make the 'suspended tonality' fall into the abyss on whose brink it performs its acrobatics. This is what happens to Olbrich when, having left the Darmstadt Colony, he returns, disarmed, to the metropolis... After the Dionysian orgy that had compromised any form of pursuit of the unstemmable existential tides, after the abandonment of the protective 'mask', there is nothing left but the cult of the Apollonian». Cf. M. TAFURI, *Ordine e disordine*, in «Casabella» n. 421, Milan 1977, pp. 37-37.

120) A. LOOS, *Eine zuschrift über das haus auf dem Michaelerplatz* (1910), *Sä... Sch...*, p. 293 ff.

121) A. LOOS, *Heimatkunst* 1914), *Sä... Sch...*, pp. 331-341.

122) K. KRAUS, op. cit.

123) The project is documented in the Loos-archiv by a drawing with the title *Plan einer Erweiterung der inneren Stadt Wien auf Grund des Bestandes vom Jahre 1859* - signed by Paul Engelmann but carried out under the direct supervision of Loos around 1912-13.

124) On the foundation of the *Wiener Werkstätten* the following anecdote recounted by Rochowalski is of interest: «In one of the hours of idle chatter passed at the Café Heinrichshof in front of the Opera, where the most lively young artists used to gather with Hoffmann and sometimes even Wagner, a guest turned up one day by the name of Fritz Wärndorfer. He was just back from a trip to England, where he had spent time with Mackintosh and his group and was able to recount a great deal about him and Morris' movement. His enthusiastic account and description of the activity of those liberal groups of artists caused much excitement among the young Viennese present who, as was their nature, immediately set about making plans and building castles in the air that could never have been carried out, and were, at first, chaotic. To Wärndorfer's question as to what they really wanted, Kolo Moser responded

briefly: 'If we had five hundred crowns, we would know where to start'. Then something incredible happened: Wärndorfer took his wallet out of his pocket and put down on the table the far from insignificant sum. None of the young men present had ever seen so much money. Enthusiasm mounted, and they hastened to give shape to their own ideas: the day after they had already found and rented premises, but of the money there was nothing left. Wärndorfer provided them with another five hundred crowns; the sole duty of Josef Hoffmann and Kolo Moser was that of creating an ideal, a profound justification for the work. This is how the *Wiener Werkstätte* was born and from that time on the monogram of the double 'W' was one of the most sought-after signatures by collectors and museums». Quoted in GIULIA VER-ONESI, *Josef Hoffmann*, Milan 1956, pp. 18-19.

125) Cf. A. LOOS, «Das andere» (1903), in *Sä... Sch...* pp. 215-251.

126) KARL KRAUS, «Die Fackel», n. 1, April 1899, p. 1.

127) A. LOOS, *Die moderne siedlung*, in *Sä... Sch...* pp. 402-408.

128) A. LOOS, «Das andere» (1903), n. 2. in *Sä... Sch...* pp. 215-251.

129) A. LOOS, *Wäsche* (1898), in *Sä... Sch...* pp. 113-120.

130) GIULIA VERONESI, *Josef Hoffmann*, op. cit., p. 20.

131) Th. W. ADORNO, *Funktionalismus heute*, in «Neue Rundschau», Berlin n. 4/1966, pp. 585-600.

132) G. VERONESI, idem, p. 10.

133) A. LOOS, *Josef Viellich* (1929), in *Sä... Sch...* pp. 436-442.

134) A. LOOS, *Hands off* (1917), in *Sä... Sch...* pp 342-347.

135) A. LOOS, «Das andere» (1903) in *Sä... Sch...* pp. 215-251.

136) A. LOOS, *Die überflüssigen* (1908), in *Sä... Sch...* pp. 267-270.

137) Cf. A. LOOS, *Kulturentartung* (1908). in *Sä... Sch...* pp. 271-276 and Th. W. ADORNO, op. cit.

138) «This is where the *Werkbund* is bound to fail... in programming *imbalances* between the sectors... This is the source of the crisis in the *Werkbund*. This, and certainly not the clash between the *Typisierung* of Muthesius and the 'free, spontaneous creativity' of van de Velde, is the real issue debated at the 1914 Congress. The clash between Rule and Form, as Scheffler summarizes it, is in reality the collision between an *idea* of economic necessity and a utopia of Form as an all-inclusive 'new Style'.
«The truth is that no-one grasps the concrete question that Naumann raises about capitalistic development. When Muthesius speaks of *Typisierung* he means the 'classical' sublimation of the industrial product — its form becomes Rule — the perfect synthesis of function and form. The synthetic utopia of van de Velde, and of Scheffler, is definitely not the target of his polemics. On the contrary, Muthesius accuses it, in fact, of making the synthesis incomplete again, keeping the figure of the creative spirit 'autonomous'. This struggle takes place within the same trend.
«But Naumann's intent is completely different. For a long time now, the fable has no longer expressed the relationship between form and function. It is resolved *in the facts*. Form is destined, in the Nietzschian sense of the word, to be integrated with the processes of capitalistic growth. 'Here there is nothing to get better or worse'». MASSIMO CACCIARI, *Metropolis*, Rome 1973, pp. 42-43.

139) A. LOOS, *Kulturentartung* (1908).

140) H. MUTHESIUS, Lecture given at the Werkbund Conference, Cologne 1914.

141) Quoted in *Werkbund* (edited by L. BURCKHARDT), Venice 1977, p. 8.

142) A further problem is the *Maschinenstil* which, although beset by a number of misunderstandings resulting from its historicist and synthetic cultural foundations, brings up nevertheless the qustion of adapting methods of formal design to serial manufacturing processes. The consequences of the *Typisierung* will be subjected to unexpected, but significant control by the *Deutsche Industrie-Normen* for the standardization of industrial products, imposed for economic and military reasons during the war. It is significant that in the post-war years the *Din-format* will come to represent a constant parameter of reference for the modular research carried out by the *Bauhaus*. Cf. R. BANHAM, *Theory and Design in the First Machine Age*, London, 1960.
The utopia of the *Deutscher Werkbund* will run up against yet another and perhaps even more important question: the *Rationalisierung* — beginning with the assembly line — of the whole manufacturing system. This derives — for some of the protagonists of this experiment — from an optimistic reception of «American» innovations in manufacturing processes including the more strictly technical ones of Taylor and the more loosely ideological ones of Ford. Cf. CHARLES S. MAIER, *Tra Taylorismo e Tecnocrazia: le ideologie europee e la visione della produttività industriale negli anni '20*, in «Quaderni del progetto», n. 1, Padua 1974, pp. 80-120.
Friedrich Naumann's contribution to the 1914 Congress hints at this and also indicates that it is necessary to adapt the role of intellectual work to the implications arising from changes in the *mode* of production: « ... the artist must know for whom and for what purpose he is creating. We need artists who have such a good grasp of America that they work in a German way on behalf of America! This is the greater task and in the last analysis it means: *Werkbund* and world economy. We Germans have taken and received an infinite number of things from other peoples... What others have given us we must now give to them». Cf. FRIEDRICH NAUMANN, *Werkbund und Weltwirtschaft* report to the 1914 *Werkbund* Conference, in J. POSENER, *Anfänge des Funktionalismus*, Berlin-Frankfurt-Vienna, 1964.

This means, then, an impartial open-mindedness to foreign ideas and their reworking and restitution. There is no doubt that one of the most important «constructive» trends in Weimarian architecture that aims to extend the rational plan of the assembly line to the building site, and even to the city, is indebted to American ideology. It is no coincidence that a leading figure like Walter Gropius should quote at length from the thought of Henry Ford in an essay entitled «The development of modern industrial architecture» that he wrote in 1913. He ended by saying: «We need artists who take the requirements of the industrial system into account and teachers who are familiar with it». Cf. WALTER GROPIUS, *Die Entwicklung moderner Industrie-Baukunst*, in the «Jahrbuch des deutschen Werkbunds», Jena 1913.
It is interesting to note that the uselessness of the synthesis between art, handicrafts and industry, so lucidly argued by Loos ever since the turn of the century, will become a recurrent motif in the attacks on Weimar culture made by the most radical sections of the intellectual avant-garde. Somewhat surprising in this context is the following polemic against the Bauhaus written by Georg Grosz:
«But they are also still trying to save that beautiful word art, and instead they compromise it. The furniture of the Weimar Bauhaus is probably excellently constructed. Yet one would rather sit on chairs made by some totally anonymous carpenter, as they are comfortable, than on those designed by the builders of the Bauhaus, whose technique is so romantically self-congratulatory. Taken to its logical conclusion, constructivism leads to the abolition of the artist, just as is taking place with modern forms... What to do then? Everything that has been said up to now points to one conclusion: do away with art!».
It would not be rash to claim that this passage echoes (consciously or unconsciously) the more sarcastic appeal with which Loos concludes an essay he wrote in 1908: «We need a *civilization of carpenters*. If the artists of the applied arts would go back to painting or to sweeping the streets, we would have one». Cf. A. LOOS, *Die überflüssigen* (1908), in *Sä... Sch...* pp. 267-270.

143) The review «Der Sturm», directed together with the gallery of the same name by Herwarth Walden, published five more essays by Loos as well as *Ornament und verbrechen* in 1912. Cf. SCHREYER, WALDEN, «Der Sturm», Baden-Baden 1954.

144) It is only recently that as informed a critic as Massimo Cacciari has brought to light the central importance of the economic aspect. «This formulation», one reads in *Oikos: da Loos a Wittgenstein*, Rome 1975, «can and should be criticized from an economic point of view. This is Loos' fundamental theme in *Ornament and Crime*. This *economic* reasoning, in terms of Occam's razor, serves as a general criterion: it is handled as in the pages «to come» of Wittgenstein's *Tractatus*. Quality cannot be separated from the present totality of the mode of production and distribution of goods». MASSIMO CACCIARI, *Metropolis*, op. cit., p. 15.

145) A. LOOS, *Ornament und verbrechen*, (1908) in *Sä... Sch...* pp. 276-287.

146) On this subject Th. W. Adorno notes: «Search for the necessary and resistence to the superfluous are constituent elements of the work of art... With the formula of aimless purpose as an element in judging taste, Kant has given a philosophical basis to this standard in his *Criticism of Judgement*. Only it conceals the dynamic of history: what shows itself still to be necessary in a certain sphere of materials in the traditional language, becomes superfluous, in effect ornamental in a negative sense, as soon as that language — what is called style — ceases to be legitimate». THEODOR W. ADORNO, *Funktionalismus heute* in «Neue Rundschau», Berlin, n. 4. 1966, pp. 585-600.

147) Idem.

148) Banham has rather hastily derided the ingenuous nature of these arguments by calling them «café-Freudianism, café-anthropology, café-criminology». Cf. R. BÀNHAM, *Ornament and Crime. The Decisive Contribution of Adolf Loos*, in «The Architectural Review», London, Feb. 1957, p. 186.

149) A. LOOS, *Ornament und verbrechen*, (1908) *Sä... Sch...* pp. 276-287.

150) Cf. WALTER BENJAMIN, *Karl Kraus* (1931) in *Illuminationen*, Frankfurt 1977, pp. 353-384.

151) KARL KRAUS, *Sittlichkeit und Kriminalität* (1902).

152) A. LOOS, *Ornament und verbrechen*, in *Sä... Sch...* pp. 276-287.

153) Ibidem.

154) A. LOOS, *Architektur* (1910), in *Sä... Sch...* pp. 302-319.

155) SIGMUND FREUD, *Der Dichter und das Phantasieren*, Vienna 1907.

156) In fact as Adorno remarks: «The opportunity for expression may only schematically be relegated to art and separated from the utilitarian object; even when it is not present it exacts a tribute in the effort required to avoid it... There is no form that does not have a symbolic aspect side by side with its aptitude for use; this has already been demonstrated by psychoanalysis for the archaic images of the unconscious, among which the house holds a pre-eminent position. According to Freud there is a symbolic intention at work right from the start in a technological form such as that of the dirigible... Utilitarian objects... have a much more immediate affinity with the pleasure principle than have works which are responsible only to their own laws... According to the bourgeois ethic of work, pleasure is wasted energy. Loos agrees». THEODOR W. ADORNO, *Funktionalismus heute*, cit.

157) KARL KRAUS, *Maximilian Harden* (1907), in *Die chinesische Mauer*, Munich 1964, p. 56.

158) KARL KRAUS, *Sprüche und Widersprüche* (1909), in «Beim Wort genommen», Munich 1955, p. 26.

159) MALEVICH K., *Suprematismus - Die gegenstandslose Welt* (German version),

Cologne 1962.

160) Cf. OSKAR KOKOSCHKA, *Mein Leben - Erinnerungen an Adolf Loos*, in «Alte und moderne Kunst», n. 113.

161) Hermann Broch will use the term *Gemeinschaft* to designate the end of the spiritual «community» felt by central European intellectuals to be an element in the strength of the multinational unity of the empire. Cfr. H. BROCH, *Hofmannsthal und seine Zeit. Eine Studie*, in *Gesammelte Werke, Dichten und Erkennen, Essays*, Vol. I, Zurich 1955. On the nostalgic effects of the decline of that cultural *Koiné* echoed in Viennese literature, see: C. MAGRIS, *Il mito asburgico nella letteratura austriaca moderna,* Turin 1963.

162) Cf. T. MANN, *Betrachtungen eines Unpolitischen*, Frankfurt, 1956. For a critical analysis of the theme of *imprudence* cf. A. ASOR ROSA, *Thomas Mann o dell'ambiguità borghese,* Bari 1971.

163) For a historical analysis of political events in the Republic of Austria see: C.A. GULICK, *Austria from Hapsburg to Hitler*, Berkeley-Los Angeles, 1948; cf. also L. BRÜGEL, *Geschichte der Österreichischen Sozialdemokratie*, Vienna, 1922-1925.

164) Cf. A. LOOS, *Die stadt und die kunst*, preface to *Richtlinien für ein kunstamt*, in «Der Fried», 1919, p. 62, now in A. LOOS, *Sä... Sch...*, I, Vienna 1962, pp. 352-354

165) Cf. *Letters from Ludwig Wittgenstein with a Memoir*, Oxford 1970, (letter 21, of the 2nd Sept. 1919).

166) «The name 'Austromarxists' referred to a group of young Austrian comrades involved in scientific work: Max Adler, Karl Renner, Rudolf Hilferding, Gustav Eckstein, Otto Bauer and Friedrick Adler were the most well-known of these. They were united not by any particular political trend but by the peculiar nature of their scientific work. They had all grown up in an era in which men like Stammler, Windelband and Rickert combatted Marxism with philosophical arguments; so these comrades felt the need to measure themselves against modern philosphical currents. If Marx and Engels had started out from Hegel, and later Marxists from materialism, the younger 'Austromarxists' started in part from Kant, in part from Mach». O. BAUER, *Austromarxismus*, in «Arbeiter-Zeitung», 3rd November 1967, p. 1. For a definition of the fundamental presuppositions of such an important school of political thought see also O. BAUER, *Max Adler, Ein Beitrag zur Geschichte des «Austromarxismus»*, in «Der Kampf» (Prague), yr. IV, 1937, as well as the above-mentioned volume by Giacomo Marramao (accompanied by an ample bibliography on the subject).

167) As an example of his contentious stand it is worth quoting the following passage: «Anyone who, like me, is an evolutionist and wishes to avoid revolutions, must bear in mind what follows: the possession of a garden by the individual cannot but have a provocative effect and those who do not stay in step with the times are responsible for all the revolutions and all future wars». «In my capacity as chief-architect of the technical office for the *Siedlungen* of the city of Vienna, I laid down the condition that only those who have shown themselves to be capable of cultivating a garden for many years, have the right to possess their own houses. Because, although everyone is ready to do it, only a few really succeed. But someone who spontaneously sets himself, after his eight hours of daily work, to work at producing his own food, should also have the possibility of building his own house. He should not obtain it by public means, as spongers are not permitted in human society. In my opinion, if we want to solve the financial problem, the horticulturist should be able to obtain both the land for building and the land for cultivation with public subsidy, but the house he should buy himself. By maintaining this principle I naturally clashed with the social-democratic party, which has no intention of encouraging private property, but this is irrelevant to me as I am not a party man». A. LOOS, *Die moderne siedlung*, in *Sä... Sch...* pp. 402-228.

168) Fundamental to a critical analysis of the vicissitudes of town-planning in «Red Vienna» are the essays by Manfredo Tafuri, *Austromarxismo e città. «Das Rote Wien»*, in «Contropiano», n. 2, May-Aug. 1971, Rome, pp. 259-311 and *«Das Rote Wien». Politica e forma della residenza nella Vienna socialista 1919-1933*, introductory essay to the volume *Vienna Rossa* (edited by Tafuri himself), Milano 1980. The essay is accompanied by an ample bibliography on the subject to which the interested reader should refer. For a basic reading we shall limit ourselves to calling attention to the following: *Die Wohnungspolitik der Gemeinde Wien*, Vienna 1926, second ed. revised and expanded in 1929; C. AYMONINO, *Gli alloggi della municipalità di Vienna, 1922-1932,* Bari 1965, republished in *L'abitazione razionale*, Padua 1971, pp. 13-14; H. BOBEK, E. LICHTENBERGER, *Wien. Bauliche Gestalt und Entwicklung seit der Mitte des 19. Jahrhundersts*, Graz-Cologne 1966.

169) On 19th-century changes in the urban fabric of Vienna see G. FABBRI, *Vienna* in VV.AA., *Le città capitali del XIX secolo: Parigi e Vienna,* Rome 1975, cf. also H. BOBEK and E. LICHTENBERGER, *Wien, Bauliche Gestalt und Entwicklung seit der Mitte des 19. Jahrhunderts*, op cit.

170) Cf. C. AYMONINO, *L'abitazione razionale*, op. cit., pp. 16-17.

171) Cf. M. TAFURI, *Das Rote Wien*, in *«Vienna Rossa»*, op. cit.

172) Cf. O. BAUER, *Der Weg zum Sozialismus*, Vienna 1919.

173) The figure was raised in 1927 to a total number of 30,000 apartments, to be integrated with a further 30,000 envisaged for the five-year period from 1928 to 1933.

174) HANS RIEMER in particular made use of the expression *«ein neuer Baustil»* to designate the architecture of the mythologised *«rote Wien»* in the essay: H. RIEMER, *Album von Röten Wien*, Vienna 1947.

175) A special issue of the review «Der Aufbau», n. 6, July 1926, was devoted to this important Congress, at which 1,100 participants came together from all over the world.

176) A conclusive example of this typological indifference is the building and symbol of the Karl-Marx-Hof itself. «The 1382 apartments are of varying size, from the 21 m² of the single-room apartment to the approximately 57-60 m² of the apartment with three bedrooms, of which one is only 9 m². The inconveniences of these apartments include the lack of any disengagement between the rooms, the lack of transverse ventilation, the positioning of the rooms in simple straight-line series, the excessively small apartments and poor exposure to sunlight». Cf. *Vienna Rossa*, op cit., p. 26.

177) This is a fact that should put informed critics on their guard against making any too hasty separation of architects into opposing camps (such as: A. Loos, J. Frank and F. Schuster, stubborn supporters of the *Siedlungen* - and, on the other side, P. Behrens, J. Hoffmann and K. Ehn, proponents of the *Höfe*). Cfr. M. TAFURI, «Das Rote Wien» in *Vienna Rossa*, op. cit., p. 26.

To be sure, such undeniable differences in theory and planning are dialectical in nature and moreover are centered on themes very different from a mere choice between models. So much so that even Joseph Frank and Franz Schuster will make an anything but negligible contribution to the design of the «superblocks» - as too Karl Ehn is responsible for the plans of the «Hermeswiese» Siedlung (1923, distinguished by his gaudy use of pseudo-rustic and *Biedermeier* stylistic features).

178) Cf. H. KREBITZ, *Adolf Loos - unbekannte Bauten*, in «Bau», Vienna, nos. 1-2, 1966, pp 25 et seq. An important biographical account on the subject of the Lainzer Siedlungen is to be found in: E. ALTMANN LOOS, *Adolf Loos, der Mensch*, Vienna-Munich, pp. 102-108.

179) «Along the road were many villas, charming single-storey houses with a small tower, tympanum and verandas. They were the houses of the farmers». A. LOOS, «Das andere» I. Jahr (1903), now in *Sä... Sch...*, I, op. cit., p. 215.

180) «Not every worker has the right to possess a house and garden, but only those who feel driven to cultivate a vegetable garden... The garden is the most important thing, the house is secondary». A. LOOS, *Die moderne siedlung*, in *Sä... Sch...*, I, op. cit., pp. 105, 107, 108.

181) «Let us first of all ask ourselves what rooms there should be in a house of this type. In the first place the latrine which permits the collection of manure. The *Siedlung* cannot be provided with water-closets as all the refuse of the house, including human faeces, are necessary for fertilization of the soil... In America eighty per cent of people go to the toilet in this manner. And in regions that are very cold as well; but there men still have a way of life that is closely linked to the natural order». Idem.

182) «The principle of the *Siedlung* epitomizes and embraces in the most complete way all the detailed aspects of the problem and turns it into an organic and well-ordered whole. The construction of large residential districts on extensive sites according to rational and functional criteria allows all the necessary care and attention to be paid to works of canalization, construction of water-mains, of tree-lined avenues, of gardens, etc.: the low costs of the building land permit a reduction in building density; the grouping of cottages in large residential units and the construction of similar works on a large scale substantially reduces total building costs; acquiring possession of the apartments is a natural consequence of this system of construction. To sum all this up in a few words: the construction system we have briefly described answers perfectly to all requirements of a hygienic, sanitary, functional and economic nature and offers a whole series of valuable conveniences». E. SAX, *Die Wohnungszustände der arbeitenden Klasse und ihre Riform*, Vienna 1869, p. 103.

To the compartmentalized solution of the housing problem, based on an essential acceptance of the mechanism of urban revenue as a fact «of nature», Engels opposes his well-known claim that this particular problem of town-planning can only be solved by the most comprehensive revolutionary transformation of the economic system.

Cf. F. ENGELS, *Zur Wohnungsfrage* (1872-1873) Berlin 1887.

183) Cf. L. BAUER, *Gesund wohnen und freudig arbeiten. Probleme unsere Zeit*. Vienna 1919.

«The title of the publication - To live in a healthy way and to work with joy is already symptomatic: its merit lies in taking sides, without prevarication or moralization, with capitalism, understood as the bearer of civilization and 'capable of exploiting the productivity of human labour to the maximum'». This comment is made by M. TAFURI in *Austromarxismo e città. «Das Rote Wien»* in «Contropiano», op. cit, p. 285. In this essay Tafuri makes a direct connection between Leopold Bauer's arguments in 1919 and the proposals put forward by Loos over the same period, but in my opinion, his analogies are confined to such general questions as to become vague, while the differences between the pupil of the *Wagnerschule* and the theoretician of «Ornament and Crime» are deeper in specific questions of architecture.

184) In making clear the intentions that underlay his invention of the *Konstruktionsschema aus der Patentschrift* in 1921, Loos writes: «The invention serves for the production of low cost housing... The high costs of building materials and of labor, together with the need to build because of the shortage of housing, make it urgent to keep construction costs to a minimum... If the cost of land, of building materials and of labor remain constant, the only way to build cheap housing is through a saving on materials and on labor. Cf. L. MÜNZ, G. KÜNSTLER, *Der Architekt Adolf Loos*, op. cit., pp. 149-152.

185) Cf. L. MÜNZ, C. KÜNSTLER, *Der Architekt Adolf Loos*, op. cit., p. 145.

186) Cf. H. BOBEK and L. LICHTENBERGER, op. cit. p. 55.

187) The basic similarity in the proposals for finding «an alternative to the decay of industrial periphery of the cities» to be found in the *Trabantenprinzip* adopted by Ernst May for the «new Frankfurt» and in the hypothesis of the *Siedlungen* advanced in Vienna by Loos, has been backed up by Giorgio Grassi. Cf. *Das neue Frankfurt 1926-1931* (edited by G. GRASSI), Bari 1979, especially paragraphs 4 and 5 of the introduction, pp. 12-18.

188) Cf. J. FRANK, *Architektur als Symbol, Elemente deutschen neuen Bauens*; Vienna 1931, pp. 115-116.

189) The quotation is from Manfredo Tafuri, *Vienna Rossa*, op. cit., p. 26.

190) From 1922 onwards Peter Behrens taught at the Vienna Academy. His teaching activity is documented in *Peter Behrens und seine Wiener Akademische Meisterschule* (edited by K.M. GRIMME, with an introductory essay by Peter Behrens himself) Vienna-Berlin-Leipzig, 1930. For aspects more strictly pertaining to the plans he drew up as architect for the Municipality of Vienna see: P. BEHRENS, *Die Gemeinde Wien als Bauherr*, «Bauwelt» 41, 1928. Useful for gaining a wider picture of Behrens' work are: VITTORIO GREGOTTI, *Peter Behrens*, in «Casabella» 240, 1960, pp. 5-8; J. POSENER, *L'oeuvre de Peter Behrens*, in «L'architecture d'aujourd'hui» V, n. 2, 1934, pp. 8-29; H.J. KADATZ, *Peter Behrens*, Leipzig, 1977; T. BUDDENSIEG and H. ROGGE, *Peter Behrens und die Aeg*, Berlin 1979.

191) J. FRANK, *Der Volkswohnungspalast*, «Der Aufbau» n. 7, August 1926, pp. 107-111.

192) A. LOOS, *Die kranken ohren Beethovens* (1933), in *Sä... Sch...*, pp. 326-327.

193) The testimony of Alban Berg, who was present at the rehearsal, is highly significative. In a letter to his wife he writes: «But now comes the beautiful part: before the second complete rehearsal Loos got up on the podium and read a very brief essay: «The sick ears of Beethoven» (even Schoenberg stood back a little in the orchestra and listened). To put it briefly: Beethoven's music had seemed unhealthy to his contemporaries who attributed it to his sick ears; now many people are enthusiastic about it. There can only be one explanation: listening to this music for a hundred long years has made the ears of the bourgeoisie sick as well. These words full of irony and passion received tumultuous applause...». A. BERG, *Briefe an seine Frau*, op. cit.

193) A. SCHOENBERG, *Testi poetici e drammatici* (edited by L. Rognoni), Milan 1967, p. 211.

194) *Aphorismen, Anekdoten, Sprüche; Texte zu Kanous*, Vienna 1928.

195) A. LOOS, *Regeln für den, der in den bergen baut*, (1913), in *Sä... Sch...*, pp. 329-330.

196) A. LOOS, quoted in H. KULKA, *Adolf Loos, neues Bauen in der Welt*, Vienna 1931, p. 18.

197) L. WITTGENSTEIN, *Tractatus logico-philosophicus*, 2.0121.

198) «The 'practical' content of the new architecture», writes Persico, «is only an ideal force, and above all a moral outburst, and not yet a realistic preoccupation with needs. Our architects (...) will always ignore the secret of Haesler, or of Ernst May, the town-planner of the new Frankfurt, that is in essence a religious secret... The new German architecture, as content, is expressed solely by this religious impulse».
E. PERSICO, *Punto ed a capo per l'architettura*, in «Casabella», nov. 1935, now in *Oltre l'architettura, Scritti scelti e lettere* (edited by R. MARIANI), p. 220. Persico's argument is reckless and in part unreasonable but, despite this, it does grasp the undeniable *morality* that underlies the idea of the «integral project» in Frankfurt as in Celle. It is against this ethic of synthesis that Adolf Loos' *architecture of difference* struggles.

199) M. HORKHEIMER, Th. W. ADORNO, *Dialektik der Aufklärung*, Amsterdam 1947, p. 41.

200) Ibidem.

201) Cf. A. JANIK, S. TOULMIN, *Wittgenstein's Vienna*, For a more up-to-date account of the Vienna of the *finis Austriae* see the volume by MASSIMO CACCIARI, *Dallo Steinhof, Prospettive viennesi del primo Novecento*, Milano 1980.

202) «Was ist der Mensch, dass er Pläne macht!» HUGO VON HOFMANNSTHAL, *Ein Brief*, Vienna 1901-1902.

203) Idem.

204) Idem.

205) Cf. M. FOUCAULT, *Les mots et les choses*, Paris, 1966.

206) «*In der Stille/Erstirbt der bangen Seele einsames Saitenspiel*» in *Sebastian im Traum: Unterwegs*, in *Die Dichtungen*, Salzburg 1930. Note that the lines quoted are not from the poem expressly dedicated to Loos, but from one of the poems in the collection *Sebastian im Traum*. Emblematic of this is the German pavilion at the Universal Exhibition of Barcelona in 1929, where it is not difficult to detect a «quotation» from the Viennese master in the language of materials (slabs of onyx, reflective surfaces of water, marbles and chromed metals). But even before the architecture he built, his essay with the significative title *Building* — written in 1923 at a time when he belonged to the «G» group — polemically enunciates the minimalist programme: «we want building to really mean building and nothing else».

207) MIES VAN DER ROHE, *Bauen*, in «G», september 1923.

208) Cf. M. HEIDEGGER, *Bauen, Wohnen, Denken*, English trans. in «Lotus», n. 9, February 1975.

209) Cf. the chapter *America* in this book.

210) P. EISENMAN, *To Adolph Loos & Bertold Brecht*, in «Progressive Architecture» 1974, n. 5, p. 92.

211) A. SCHOENBERG, *Ausgewählte Briefe 1958*, (ed. by Erwin Stein), eng. trans. *Letters*, 1964.

212) On the cultural rapport between Paul Engelmann and Adolf Loos, cf. V. SLAPETA, *Paul Engelmann und Jacques Groag die Olmützer Schüler von Adolf Loos*, in «Bauwelt», n. 40, 1978, pp. 1494-1499.

213) K. KRAUS, quoted in WALTER BENJAMIN, in *Illuminationen*, Frankfurt 1977, pp. 353-358.

GUIDE TO THE WORKS

Loos swept right beneath our feet,
and it was a Homeric cleaning — precise,
philosophical and logical. In this, Loos
has had a decisive influence on the
destiny of architecture.

Le Corbusier
«Frankfurter Zeitung», 1930

EBENSTEIN FASHION HOUSE

Kohlmarkt 5, Vienna 1

1897

Although for a long time «unknown», the alterations made for the fitting out of the rooms of Ernst Ebenstein's large tailoring concern were the first work carried out by Loos in Vienna, on his return from his long stay in America (1893-1896). The attribution of the work to Loos is confirmed by a passage from *Mein Leben* by Oskar Kokoschka, where one reads that Loos was acquainted with the best Viennese tailors, whose shops he had fitted out, and among them, the court tailor, Ebenstein. [1]

The alterations involved the reconstruction of the entire floor intended for the workshop and sales. The work, however, has undergone considerable modification in subsequent alterations, including a major one in 1927. It is not impossible that the exclusion of this work from the early monographs by H. Kulka and L. Münz is in fact due to the lack of either photographic or graphic documentary material. [2]

The only recognizable elements of the original version that still remain are the entrance doorway (made out of mahogany and glass) and a few details — including the stucco frieze that runs above the wooden (oak) paneling of the walls. The pattern of leaves in this frieze (into which is inserted the tailor's symbol of an open pair of scissors) shows quite a few similarities to the one used in 1898 for the bathroom of the Goldman & Salatsch Store. Apart from this detail, which is typical of central European tradition, the decoration of the rooms has an unmistakably Anglo-Saxon cast. The design of the wall fittings and of the furniture is reduced to essential lines, so that the impression of quality is conveyed solely by the intrinsic chromatic value of the materials (oak and polished brass) and the perfection of the execution.

NOTES

1) One reads: «(...) aber er kannte die besten Schneider in Wien, für die er die Geschäfte einrichtete. Zum Beispiel den Hofschneider, Herrn Ebenstein». O. KOKOSCHKA, *Mein Leben*, Munich 1971, p. 65. Another and precise indication in support of this attribution has been supplied by the engineer G. Rizzi and collected and evaluated by B. Rukschcio — present curator of the Loos-Archiv at the Albertina in Vienna — in his «Dissertation» that is included below in the bibliography.

2) Cf. H. KULKA, *Adolf Loos, Das Werk des Architekten*, Vienna 1931; L. MÜNZ, G. KÜNSTLER, *Der Architekt Adolf Loos*, Vienna-Munich 1964 [English trans. *Adolf Loos, Pioneer of modern architecture*, London 1966, New York-Washington 1966].

BIBLIOGRAPHY

O. KOKOSCHKA, *Mein Leben*, Vienna 1971, p. 85.
B. RUKSCHCIO, *Studien zu Entwürfen, Projekten und ausgeführten Bauten von Adolf Loos*, *(1870-1933)*. Dissertation an der Universität Wien, 1973, pp. 6-9.

Detail of the door.

Entrance.

Store interior.

PROJECT FOR A 4000 - SEAT THEATER

Vienna

Drawn up by Adolf Loos at the age of twenty-eight, this design already expresses a clear idea of architecture that contains quite a few elements novel to the typology of the theater. The composition hinges essentially on a division into three parts:

a) *The area of the stalls*, which (breaking with a hoary tradition of 17th-century derivation, the so-called Italian model) is conceived as a unitary, encompassing space. By expanding upwards and being reflected back off the ceiling, the curvilinear matrix of the plan makes room for an elliptical space in the unheard-of shape of an egg.

b) *The orchestra*, proposed in the perfectly circular shape of the ancient Greek chorus (reminding one of the theater of Epidaurus from 350 B.C.), is the true pivot of spatial articulation and at the same time the most expressive cultural element.

c) *The stage area*, which is conceived as an autonomous setting contained within a box-like volume clearly detached from the elliptical one of the hall.

The most interesting feature of this sketch lies in the method of design that it follows, a method which will become a *leitmotiv* of Loos' research: the invention of the new by means of a return to the ancient.

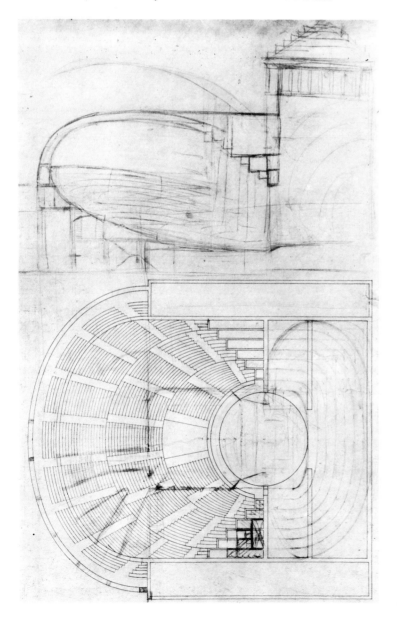

The surprising modernity of this architecture — that stands out in all its clarity when compared with the plans for theaters drawn up in the twenties by H. Poelzig and W. Gropius — derives, in fact, from a thoughtful reproposal of the classical Greco-Roman model.

To get to the bottom of the project's meaning it is necessary to take account of the historical situation in which it was formed.

During the years of Loos' training, the German-speaking cultural world was pervaded by a renewal of interest in an exploration of the origins of the theater, dominated by the Nietzschean and Wagnerian current of thought. F. Nietzsche in *The Birth of Tragedy from the Spirit of Music* (1871-1872) had stressed the central role played by the chorus — in the origins of Greek drama — as the most genuine expression of the Dionysian *Zeitgeist* and, at the same time, as a fundamental element of mediation between the audience and the symbolic, Apollonian performance in the action that unfolds on the stage. R. Wagner in his turn — reappraising the role of the chorus in a romantic key — had also drawn up precise proposals for a redefinition of the typological pattern in *The Theater for the Drama Festivals of Bayreuth* (1875, text accompanied by drawings) — in which a reunification of audience and stage is postulated and a leveling of all the spectators in front of the spectacle of Art.

Acceptance of these theories in Vienna is demonstrated by — among other things — Hugo von Hofmannsthal's search for a means of realizing the *Gesamtkunstwerk* (total work of art). We are dealing here with a true evocation of the ancient Greek theater by means of an intimate fusion of poetry, drama and music. Starting with his rewriting of *Elektra*, carried out in close collaboration with Richard Strauss, H. von Hofmannsthal proposed many adaptions of classical works that were often staged by Max Reinhardt. It is significant that Reinhardt had used the ring of the Schauman circus as a stage for the performance of *Oedipus Rex* in 1910. This indirectly demonstrates a response to a cultural demand for the circular chorus borrowed from the Greeks and placed at the center of A. Loos' theater-on-paper. In fact, despite the advanced level of innovative cultural proposals, the typology of theaters built at the end of the 19th century still followed in the footsteps, as has been pointed out, of the so-called Italian model, a model which envisaged the space for the audience divided into different sections (on the basis of a precise social hierarchy — the boxes, galleries and stalls — and the orchestra atrophied into a pit concealed from view). These limits are also encountered in the architectural works of Gottfried Semper — the architect and theoretician recognized as a «master» by Loos — who more than anyone else collaborated with Richard Wagner, designing, among other works, a theater in Munich (1865-1867) on behalf of Ludwig II, that was explicitly intended for staging the operas of the great musician. Both in the Dresden theater (1837-1841) and in the Burgtheater (1874-1888, built in Vienna in collaboration with Karl von Hasenauer), Semper still shows all the weight of 19th-century baggage that he carries with him. It will be Loos himself who gives a modern form to the new idea of the theater that had ripened in the German cultural climate in the same year that the Burgtheater was completed. The road followed to arrive at such a result is a long way away from the one chosen some years later by Peter Behrens for the staging of *Das Zeichen* by G. Fuchs and W. de Haan, on the occasion of the inaugural ceremony for the Exhibition of the *Darmstadt Künstlerkolonie* (1901). Where, in fact, Behrens takes as a backdrop for the stage performance the flight of steps designed by J. Olbrich for the Ludwigs-Haus (aiming in this way to bring together art-architecture-life), Loos on the contrary reproposes the «theater» as a fixed place for staging performances.

The course preferred by Loos is a journey into the past that recapitulates the evolutionary stages of this typology. And it is by following in the footsteps of Palladio's Olympic Theater (Vicenza, 1580) that Loos rediscovers an up-to-date method of planning. If one compares Palladio's vertical sections with the drawing of the 4000-Seat Theater, the similarities of form, as far as the stepped profile of the stalls is concerned, are obvious. In both cases the reference model is the Greco-Roman theater. But the similarity of form does not go beyond this aspect. Without conceding anything to archaeological veneration of the past, Loos bends the vertical line along a curve in order to answer better to acoustic requirements, changes the plan into the shape of an ellipse, adds on the chorus and detaches the volume of the stage. All that remains in common in the end is a similarity of method. [1] Loos' design seems to prefigure many of the typological solutions of the thirties, from Hans Poelzig's Grand Theater in Berlin to the Jahrhunderthalle of Max Berg, to the *Totaltheater* of Walter Gropius. There is no doubt, for example, that the theater-machine designed by Gropius in 1927 for Erwin Piscator is much more articulate and complex and achieves a technical or spatial synthesis of different scenic forms that is as yet unsurpassed. But the very fact that in the end, whether consciously or not, the Gropius-Piscator proposal returns to the pattern of an elliptical eggshaped space, a circular stage and an encircling amphitheater-pit demonstrates, if not the farsightedness of Loos' project, at least the intelligence of the method adopted.

NOTES

1) On this subject, it is perhaps useful to refer to a statement by his close friend, the great expressionist painter Oscar Kokoschka: «The work of Palladio has been his Bible and his Law. Loos understood the ancient order not as a model to be copied, as did the classicists and academics, but as a representation of the human proportions in relationship to the world that surrounds them, as an image of man's relationship with life». Quoted in VV.AA., *Adolf Loos*, Catalog edited by the Faculty of Architecture, Rome 1965, p. II.

BIBLIOGRAPHY

B. MARKALOUS, *Adolf Loos*, in «Prednasek o Architekture» 7, Prague, 1925, p. 17.
Adolf Loos 1870-1933, Catalog of the Würthle Gallery, Vienna, 1961, figs. 1-2.
L. MÜNZ, G. KÜNSTLER, *Der Architekt Adolf Loos*, op. cit., p. 16-20, figs. 1-3.

DESIGN FOR A TOMB

1898

The design of tombs is a recurrent theme in Loos' work. One thinks of the project for Peter Altenberg's gravestone (in 1919), of the one for a mausoleum for Max Dvořák (in 1921) or for his own tombstone (in 1931). It is worth stressing that there is nothing romantic or crepuscular for Loos in such a theme. It is a typically architectonic theme which leads to the search for an absolute purity of form in order to achieve a signified, discreet and lyrical monumentality. It is interesting to note how the composition of the tomb undergoes a process of constant distillation in time until it arrives at the elementary and primordial shape of the pure cube in his own tombstone of 1931. This first design for a tomb still shows a wealth of added details and a delight in the play of mass and volume which dates it more surely than any philological verification. [1]

NOTES

1) The date of 1898 attributed to this drawing by L. Münz and G. Künstler seems to be reliable since Loos drew on the same sheet of paper the signboard for the Goldman & Salatsch Store, of the same year. Because of the reliability of this source, it has been adopted here as a probable dating. Nevertheless no logically «certain» information exists that would enable us either to reject or to unconditionally support this hypothesis. A serious objection has, all the same, been raised by B. Rukschcio (op. cit., p. 8) drawing attention ot the fact that a sketch connected with the Kärntner-Bar is recognizable on the other side of the sheet bearing the drawing of a tomb. So it is not impossible that the drawing in question should be post-dated to a later period, around 1907.

BIBLIOGRAPHY

L. MÜNZ, G. KÜNSTLER, *Der Architekt Adolf Loos*, op. cit., sheet n. 3, p. 183.

GOLDMAN & SALATSCH MEN'S CLOTHING STORE
Graben 20, Vienna 1 (no longer in existence)

1898

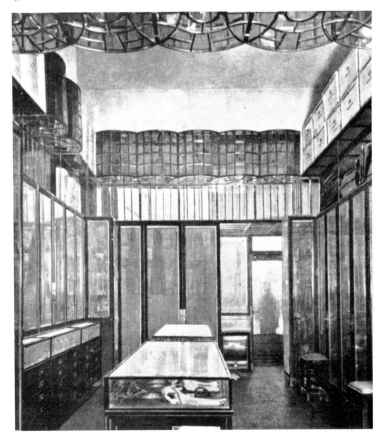

Despite the small scale, the alterations made to this store are of great importance. Many of the themes that Loos was developing in his theoretical writings during those years fall into place here. For the first time, his ideas about modernity, about beauty and about the uselessness of searching for a new style are translated into architectural facts. In fact, a total absence of the «superfluous» is achieved in the severity of the geometric scansion and the elegant use of materials.

On the ground floor, intended for use as a salesroom, Loos entrusts the design of the walls to the close, regular and repetitive pattern of the modular cupboard-showcases. Their splendid polished frames (of dark Guyanese wood) mark out the rhythmic pattern of the large, reflective, glazed walls. In their turn, the glass counters, the shiny brass of the handles, the molding which cuts in two the height of the room, the refractive ceiling of white plaster, in a word, all the elements together contribute, in their amalgam of transparency and reflections, to the luminous elegance of this interior.

One element which plays a key role in the language of materials used by Loos must not be overlooked. This is the mirror, placed on the rear and one side wall. It fulfills the dual function of allowing the customer to look at himself and, more important, of appearing to multiply space. On the upper floor, the mirror once again determines the predominant image of the room, used for trying on clothes. Here, in dividing up the large room, Loos adopts a flexible system of separation made up of specular panels (set in a square grill of white wood) interspersed with panels of dark cloth (to which hooks for hanging up clothes are attached). The height of the panels optically reduces the excessive size of the room. A movable curtain completes the flexible system of division.

Thus the design of the Goldman & Salatsch Store is based on criteria of the greatest simplicity, economy and rationality.

But the full extent of the controversial and innovative character of this work cannot be grasped unless one takes into account the cultural climate in which it was produced. It forms part of the fundamental phase of renewal in Viennese architectural culture set in motion by the publication of Otto Wagner's essay *Moderne Architektur* (1895) and by the foundation of the *Wiener Secession* in 1897. The innovative content can be schematically reduced to three interwoven motifs.

First of all, there is an indirect, but explicit, polemic against the *art nouveau* taste that the Viennese Secession had made its own and that was triumphant throughout Europe at that time. Even before his written essays, the radical simplification to which each element of architecture is subjected demonstrates, in solid fact, his profound theoretical distance from the «gay» manipulation of form of the *Wiener Secession*. In the second place, there is an idea of classicity, reproposed in a modern key as rationality. This is confirmed in an essay of 19 June '1898, entitled *Das Sitzmöbel* (The chair) in which Loos, echoing a well-known axiom of Leon Battista Alberti, defines «beauty» as the «most complete harmony» that is attained by «an object which nothing may be added to or taken away from without compromising its perfection». [1] A third motif has been caught well by the editor of the review «Das Interieur» (1901) when, in describing the rooms, he spoke of «English elegance». [2]

And, in fact, it is easy to discern a clear cultural reference to the quality of English craftsmanship — rather than a mimicry of precise prototypes. During those years, Loos had been favorably struck by the efforts to deprovincialize Viennese handicrafts made by Councillor von Scala in the exhibitions held at the Österreichisches Museum. «By reproducing English furniture, he (von Scala) has shown», Loos writes in the essay *Interieurs*, «that the public would be prepared to buy furniture invented by furniture makers, conceived by furniture makers and executed by furniture makers. This furniture had no ostentatious moldings or pillars

and made its effect solely through its comfort, its solidity, its material and the precision of its execution. They were Viennese cigarette cases translated into furniture». [3]

NOTES

1) Although Loos does not explicitly mention Leon Battista Alberti, his reference to the famous definition given by the Renaissance writer of treatises in the Sixth Book of *De Re Aedificatoria* is evident. Cf. A. LOOS, *Das Sitzmöbel*, in *Sämtliche Schriften*, op. cit.

2) *Ein Wiener Herrenmodesalon*, «Das Interieur», vol. II, Vienna 1901, pp. 145-151.

3) A. LOOS, *Interieurs*, in *Sämtliche Schriften*. Von Scala, as director of the Österreichisches Museum, played an important role of cultural promotion by laying the foundations for the renewal in Viennese handicrafts. Despite the hostility of the environment (one thinks of the Archduke Rainer, who withdrew his patronage of the Museum's activity), von Scala succeeded in getting a new statute approved for the institution. The exhibitions that he organized, often accompanied by fierce controversy, are considered by many historians to have been the premise for the foundation of the *Wiener Werkstätten* (1903). Loos refers here to the exhibition of December 1897 (at which furnishings by Otto Wagner were also displayed).

BIBLIOGRAPHY

Ein Wiener Herrenmodesalon, «Das Interieur», vol. II, Vienna 1901, pp. 145-151.
A. LOOS, *Wohnungswanderungen*, (privately printed) Vienna 1907.
H. KULKA, *Adolf Loos. Das Werk des Architekten*, Vienna 1931, fig. 1-2, with captions.
L. MÜNZ, G. KÜNSTLER, *Der Architekt Adolf Loos*, Vienna-Munich 1964, pp. 21-24, fig. 4-6.

CAFÉ MUSEUM
Elisabethstrasse 6, Vienna 1 (radically altered today)

Café Nihilismus: there could be no more appropriate definition for the work than this one first given by Ludwig Hevesi and which became the commonly used name among his architect contemporaries, as Loos recalls with ill-concealed satisfaction. [1] This work is, in fact, a mature architectural expression of Loosian negation, of the theorized renunciation of style. Moreover, by a kind of ironic coincidence, the Café Museum was situated only a short distance from the Haus der Secession (1897-1898), the «manifesto» of Austrian *Art Nouveau* completed shortly before by Joseph Maria Olbrich. And it was inevitable that Loos should make the fullest use of the strategic importance of the site to translate his polemics against the *Secessionsstil* into architecture, an attack that had already been clearly formulated, in theoretical terms, in the essay *Die potemkinsche stadt*, published the year before in the pages of «Ver Sacrum». [2]

The demonstrative and polemical intent is also stressed by Loos himself who, in an essay written in 1908, has this to say on the subject: «Ten years ago, at the time of the Café Museum, Josef Hoffmann, who

1899

represents the *Deutscher Werkbund* in Vienna, did the decorations for the store of the Apollo candle factory on the am Hof square. The work was lauded as an expression of our times. No one would say that today. From a distance of ten years we recognize that it was a mistake. And in the same way it will be clearly seen in ten years from now that whatever may be produced today along the same lines has nothing in common with the style of our time. Certainly, Hoffmann, after the Café Museum, has given up fretwork and, as far as buildings are concerned, has moved closer to what I do myself. But he still believes today that he can embellish his furniture with strange chiselings and with applied and inlaid ornaments. Yet modern man finds the untattooed face more beautiful than the tattooed one, even if the tattoos are the work of Michelangelo himself. And he feels the same way about his bedside table.

«To succeed in finding the style of our time you have to be a modern person. But the people who want to change those things that are already in the style of our time or who want to replace them with different forms —

as is happening with cutlery for example — show themselves to be incapable of recognizing the style of our time. They run after it and seek it in vain. If there is one thing that modern man recognizes with clarity, it is that the confusion of art with the utilitarian object is the greatest humiliation to which she may be subjected». [3] In this passage Loos is trying to indicate that the renunciation of any kind of ornamental redundancy is the salient fact that characterizes work in a modern sense. And the exterior of the Café Museum shows this *Nihilismus* in all its clarity. Here the supre-remacy of absence comes into its own.

A smooth and solid surface of white plaster envelops in a homogeneous manner the façade, which is rhythmically punctuated by windows reduced to pure rectangular slits in the solid wall. This white, abstract, «untattooed» wall holds a direct dialogue with the *Grossstadt*. In this it is shown to be an «object without qualities». As M. Cacciari has written: «The Café *Nihilismus*, the *Nihilismus* House... are of necessity situated in the *Nihilismus* City: it is the Metropolis where all the social circles of the *Gemeinschaft* have been broken». [4]

But the Café Museum (unlike the houses) extends *Nihilismus* to the interior as well. The difference between outside and inside — which will later be a characteristic of Loos' houses (the Steiner House in particular, but also the Haus am Michaelerplatz) — is very attenuated in this public setting. In some ways the interior of a café belongs to the public realm as well and is an integral part of the urban continuum. Probably this is also why Loos — as Hevesi remarks — avoids anything that might be called art in this early work. He wants to create something that is purely an object for use. [5]

In short, by bringing every object back to its purely utilitarian value, Loos is developing the theory of the predominance of technique, but he is at the same time affirming the aesthetic principle of the equation of beauty and utility. Reduction to the barest technically possible essentials is, in fact, the law which governs the design of the furnishings, from the lighting system to the choice of furniture. The only elements used to pattern the vault of the ceiling are the strips of brass which serve a dual functional and visual role in conducting the electrical system. The bent tubes that support the wires from which simple lamps are suspended in space are also made out of brass. Thus the technical innovation of electricity is given its first modern aesthetic interpretation in this setting.

Significant too is the use of the Thonet chairs, adopted as a symbol of the modern era. [6] It is not difficult to hear in this choice an echo of his arguments about the uselessness of the invention of newer and newer models, typically expressed in his sarcastic criticism of the chair designed by Otto Wagner for the room he had decorated, two years earlier, for the Christmas Show of the Österreichisches Museum, in 1897. [7] For Loos the best shape for any object is the one that has been proven by use.

His opposition to the mythology of the new finds confirmation in the way that he makes use of an already proven distributive layout in the Café Nihilismus, one that was in fact developed from a layout typical of Viennese cafés. Right from the start the premises had the characteristic L-shape. In line with tradition, Loos places the game room and the billiard room in the long arm — separating them by a modern partition covered with mirrors — while he intends the short arm to be used as the reading and conversation room. The cylindrical cash-desk, set at the meeting point of the two arms, in line with the entrance, becomes the pivot of the composition; it is made of mahogany as is the strip that skirts the base of the walls, knitting them together in a single gesture. Behind the cash-desk a play of mirrors: nine tall and narrow reflective surfaces, facing alternately towards the inside and outside. The reflected image is thus repeated to infinity, alluding perhaps to the unreliability of perception, to the deceptiveness of vision. [8]

NOTES

1) «When I was permitted for the first time to do something — which was quite difficult, because as I have said, the work as I conceive it cannot be represented graphically — I was sharply criticized. It happened twelve years ago: the Café Museum in Vienna. Architects called it the 'Café Nihilismus.' Yet the Café Museum still stands today, while all the other modern furnishings designed by a thousand other architects have been thrown in the attic a long time

Interior of Café Museum in its original state.

ago. Or they must be ashamed of the ones that haven't. That the Café Museum had more influence on our manufacture of furniture than all the previous works put together, may be confirmed by a glance at the 1899 issue of «Dekorative Kunst» of Munich, where this interior was reproduced — I think this must have happened through an oversight of the editorial board. But those two photographic reproductions were not what exercised an influence at the time — they went completely unnoticed. Only the strength of the example has exercised an influence. That strength with which the old masters acted.» A. LOOS, *Architektur* (1910), *Sämtliche Schriften*, Vienna 1962.

As has been mentioned, the name Café Nihilismus was coined in an article by L. Hevesi, where one reads: «Adolf Loos shows himself to be a sincere 'non secessionist' with his Café Museum; not an enemy of the Viennese Secession but something different, because after all they are both modern..., Loos has been to America and he has often described it with precision and elegance in a series of architectural essays.... Loos is safe now, because he has done well. It may be to some extent nihilistic, or even very nihilistic, but is is attractive, logical and practical.» L. HEVESI, *Kunst auf der Strasse*, in «Fremden-Blatt», 30 May 1899, Vienna.

2) A. LOOS, *Die potemkinsche stadt* in «Ver Sacrum», July 1898.

3) A. LOOS, *Sämtliche Schriften*, Vienna 1962.

4) M. CACCIARI, *Oikos, da Loos a Wittgenstein*, op. cit., p. 24.

5) L. HEVESI, op. cit.

6) «Look at the Thonet chair! Wasn't this chair, which in its way of understanding its own function represents the *spirit of a time* that is hostile to ornaments, born out of the same sensibility that produced the shape of the back and the curved legs of the Greek chair? Look at the bicycle! Doesn't its shape remind you of the spirit of Athens and Pericles?» And he goes on to say «It is not *Greek* to want to express your own individuality in the utilitarian objects that surround you». A. LOOS, *Sämtliche Schriften*.

7) A. LOOS, *Sämtliche Schriften*.

8) The «play of mirrors», which hints of the unpredictability of perception, will become a recurrent theme in Loos' work and is one of the most elegant features of his design.

BIBLIOGRAPHY

L. HEVESI, «Kunst auf der Strasse», in «Fremden-Blatt», Vienna, 30 May 1899.
H. KULKA, *Adolf Loos*, op. cit., figs. 7-8 with comment.
L. MÜNZ, *Adolf Loos*, Milan 1956, p. 28.
L. MÜNZ, G. KÜNSTLER, *Der Architekt Adolf Loos*, op. cit., pp. 35-40, figs. 15-16.

APARTMENT FOR HUGO HABERFELD
Alserstrasse 53, Vienna 9

1899

The documentation on this work is limited to a few photographs (already published in H. Kulka's monograph), a pastel drawing of the corner of the living room cum studio cum bedroom and, finally, a pencil sketch of the corner of the drawing room.

Two features of this pastel drawing should be pointed out. On the one hand, there is the search for an intelligent and total utilization of space made necessary by the integration of several functions (those of leisure, work and rest): hence the idea of fusing the stove and the clock into a single block. On the other hand, there is the liveliness of the chromatic mixture made up of the blue of the flooring, the salmon pink of the upholstered bench, the band of dark green on the walls (above a frieze of light-colored wood) and finally the soft colors of the walls and furniture.

The way in which Loos relies on the use of colors for his «component of gaiety» is an important attribute of his language, allowing him to introduce the multicolored quality of daily life into the inside of the house. It is no coincidence that we find the same liveliness of hue in both the «interior design» of the same year and the apartment decorated for Willy Hirsch in Pilsen in 1929.

BIBLIOGRAPHY

«Das Interieur», vol. IV, Vienna 1903, figs. pp. 11-16.
A. LOOS, *Wohnungswanderungen*, op. cit.
L. HEVESI, *Adolf Loos*, in «Fremden-Blatt», Vienna 22 November 1907.
H. KULKA, *Adolf Loos*, op. cit., figs. 9-10 with captions.
L. MÜNZ, G. KÜNSTLER, *Der Architekt Adolf Loos*, op. cit., section n. 7, p. 183.

INTERIOR DESIGNS

This large drawing colored in pastel and a pencil sketch were found among Loos' papers. The dating is uncertain, however, and we owe the attribution of both drawings to Ludwig Münz. It has already been pointed out, in fact, that the errors of perspective to be seen in the pastel drawing suggest its more likely attribution to one of Loos' pupils. [1]

Despite this, the possibility that the sketches are indeed the work of Loos should not be excluded entirely, if only because they are an exceptionally effective synthesis of certain ideas of spatial design that are subsequently repeated many times. One thinks of the interpenetration of spaces of different heights (in relation to both functional and psychological dictates) as well as the typical elements of his «American» interiors: brick hearths, visible beams, alcoves and the use of various colors.

As Richard Neutra has remarked, in that period Loos had transplanted to Vienna «the characteristics of H.H. Richardson, that is, false beams in light oak placed there for their beauty and fireplaces of unplastered brick. But apart from these superficial things, it is the first time that a creative and capable European has adopted elements typical of the

1899

American style and used them as a starting point for his own schemes». [2]

Apart from a few understandable anachronisms, all the innovative significance of this method of spatial design remains intact, a design which was polemically introduced into the central European environment at the end of the 19th century. But what matters more is the extraordinary repetitiveness of some elements of interior design that crop up again and again and again over the entire span of his works: from the furnishings of the living room of his own house (1903) to the Khuner Country House (1930).

NOTES

1) Cf. B. RUKSCHCIO, *Studien zu Entwürfen, Projekten und ausgeführten Bauten von Adolf Loos, 1870-1930*, op. cit., p. 8.

2) R. NEUTRA, *Neues Bauen in der Welt*, vol. II, *Amerika*, Vienna 1930, p. 44.

BIBLIOGRAPHY

L. MÜNZ, G. KÜNSTLER, *Der Architekt Adolf Loos*, op. cit., p. 42-44, figs. 20-21.

APARTMENT FOR EUGEN STOESSLER
Landesgerichtsstrasse 18, Vienna 8

«Journalists, over the last few years, have sought to push us towards the bad taste of the modern artists. I would like to push you towards your own personal bad taste...

«Your house grows up with you and you grow up with your house...

«About your house, you are always right. No one else...

«Anyone who wants to fence must take the foil in his hand. And if he wants to learn to fight he needs a good fencing master as well. He must know how to do it. I want to be your master for your houses. Your house is full of mistakes.» [1]

These aphorisms — taken from a short article published in the paper *Das andere* (1903) — provide us with a key to interpreting the logic of Loos' interior design. His ultimate objective is to give back the joy of «feeling at home» to the person who lives in the house, freeing him from the oppression of the «bad taste of modern artists». Hence the discretion

1899

with which Loos intervenes inside these apartments on the basis of criteria of the highest rationality, simplicity and good taste, as is demonstrated by the polished maple furniture in the bedroom and the table and chairs (with brass feet) and the wardrobes with rounded corners (and brass frames) in the dining room. The furnishings are just a backdrop on which each person can superimpose his own «libido» of form.

NOTES

1) A. LOOS, in *Das andere* (1903).

BIBLIOGRAPHY

«*Das Interieur*», Vienna 1900, figs. on pp. 95-96.
H. KULKA, *Adolf Loos*, op. cit., figs. 3-4 with captions.

PROJECT FOR THE CHURCH COMMEMORATING KAISER FRANZ JOSEPH'S JUBILEE

(drawings in the Loos-Archiv at the Albertina, Vienna)

1899

It is significant that a project which tackles an urban theme should be among Loos' early architectural drawings. The relationship between architecture and city that is the unmistakable mark of this project is a central theme of Loos' architectural thought. This project is of particular relevance in relation to his subsequent development of the urban theme.

Only three drawings have survived from Loos' entry for a competition held in Vienna in 1899 for the design of a church to be built near Reichsbrücke, on the Danube, in memory of the fiftieth jubilee of the reign of Franz Joseph (celebrated the year before). [1] The competition was won by the architect Viktor Luntz with a plan in an academic and historicist style, built around 1912.

Loos' project, on the contrary, is distinguished by the clear elaboration of certain architectonic theses. The first is the close relationship between the form of the church and the urban morphology. The church complex is made up of two distinct architectural pieces, even though they are closely connected and complementary to each other: the church proper on an elliptical plan and the obelisk-tower. When the structure of the composition is analyzed, the clear intention emerges of restoring to the exterior an articulate image of the architectural object acting on different scales of perception.

On the urban scale, the pivotal element of the composition is the 49-meter-high tower that, standing out as it does against the visual backdrop of an important traffic artery (leading directly to the Cathedral of St. Stephen in the center of Vienna), would have accentuated by the isolation of its pure obelisk-like form its role as symbolic image of the whole organism. Lined up in perspective with the spire of St. Stephen's, the obelisk-tower would have marked that particular place in Vienna on the urban skyline.

Historical precedents exist for this idea of urban architecture. It has been pointed out that the Eiffel Tower has undoubted similarities of form in its external profile. [2] But an only slightly deeper analysis makes clear the conceptual difference between this monument of brick and the metallic tower of Paris, left ostentatiously unclad as a celebration of 19th-century technological optimism. It is a more likely hypothesis that what we see here is a reworking of memories from his stay in America (1893-1896) and in particular the influence of the monumental giganticism of some American object-symbols. [3]

One historical reference that cannot be ignored appears like a watermark to the drawing of the church with obelisk for Franz Joseph's Jubilee. This is the work of Johann Bernhard Fischer von Erlach. One thinks of the gigantic columns surmounted by a small temple that separate themselves from the classicized façade of the Karlskirche (1715) or again of the wooden column for Joseph I (1706), reconstructed in stone by his son Joseph Emmanuel. And how can one miss a subtle allusion to the two famous triumphal arches (1690) built by Fischer von Erlach at the entrance to Vienna for the coronation of Emperor Joseph I, in the arch that passes beneath the obelisk? It should not be forgotten that with his *Entwurf einer historischen Architektur* (the first history of architecture told in pictures) Fischer von Erlach introduced the eclectic revival of the great linguistic repertory of classical antiquity to Viennese architectural culture. [4] But what lies behind Loos' revival of the technique of linguistic montage tried out by the great Viennese master is, above all, the recovery of that particular technique of intervention in the city based on the insertion of disruptive architectural markers into the urban fabric.

In describing the tower, the allusions of its form as a whole to the obelisk and of the perfect semicircle underneath to the triumphal arches

Perspective sketch of the church with the base of the tower on the left.

have already been emphasized. Still to be analyzed is the terminal section in the shape of a stepped pyramid topped by a statue. Here the architectural journey into the past seems to be headed back toward the most ancient of mausoleums: the monumental tomb for Mausolus, satrap of Caria, built at Halicarnassus around the middle of the fourth century B.C.

Why? Apart from his game of learned quotations, there is a desire in Loos to go back to the essential purity of archaic forms. It is no coincidence that the stepped pyramid will be used again for the compositional layout of the large Department Store in Alexandria (1910), for the Grand Hotel Babylon (1923), for the Mausoleum of Max Dvořák (1921) and yet again for the base of the Chicago Tribune Column (1922). Thus architecture on the drawing board plays a fundamental role in Loos' design strategy: it represents an ideal laboratory for research into elements of language that may be reused, on a larger or smaller scale, in the diverse expressions of an essentially unitary process. Passing on to an analysis of the compositional structure of the church, the reflection of the past appears with equal clarity. The reference to the Pantheon is clearly recognizable in the mounting of a colonnaded pronaos at the ogival nucleus of the church. But the undogmatic and deliberately ungrammatical use of historical codes is also immediately obvious. Moreover, there are four pronaoi, not one, in homage perhaps to Palladio's famous Rotunda, and the cross section of the church is ellipsoidal rather than perfectly circular as in the case of the Pantheon. All this translates into a centrality and dynamism of unprejudiced modernity. And this is exactly the point. Loos rummages open-mindedly and cynically in the attic of history. He quotes words and fragments of ready-made sentences, but uses new syntactic patterns to say new things.

NOTES

1) This project, which is not illustrated in H. Kulka's monograph, has been published with a full critical commentary by Ludwig Münz in an essay entitled: *Über die Grundlagen des Baustils von Adolf Loos*. The facts related in this essay have been taken into account in the compilation of this section. See also: L. MÜNZ, G. KÜNSTLER, *Der Architekt Adolf Loos*, op. cit., in which this essay is quoted.

2) L. MÜNZ, G. KÜNSTLER, op. cit.

3) As L. Münz has brought to light: «Among Loos' papers was found an illustrated postcard of the monument at Bunker Hill, designed in 1825 and completed in 1843: a very tall and imposing obelisk, that is to say, a monument inspired by the ancient Egyptian tradition, that stands by the side of a low classical building. The juxtaposition of these two structures, so different in scale and in articulation, is typically American». Ibid.

4) Cf. J.B. FISCHER VON ERLACH, *Entwurf einer historischen Architektur*, Vienna 1721, Leipzig 1725. The original is in the Albertina of Vienna.

BIBLIOGRAPHY

L. MÜNZ, *Adolf Loos*, Milan 1956, p. 29 et seq.
L. MÜNZ, *Über die Grundlagen des Baustils von Adolf Loos*, in «Aufbau», n. 10, Vienna 1958, pp. 393-395.
L. MÜNZ, G. KÜNSTLER, *Der Architekt Adolf Loos*, op. cit., pp. 154-159, figs. 217-219.

Sketches of the tower.

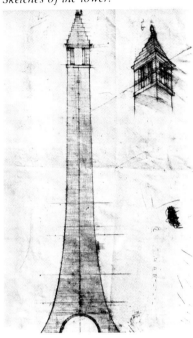

APARTMENT FOR GUSTAV TURNOWSKY
Wohllebengasse 19, Vienna 4

Among the many apartments decorated by Loos, the one for Gustav **1900** Turnowsky will stand out for one thing in particular: a simple wooden wardrobe. Reproduced in a photograph, it is one of the few pieces of furniture specifically built to the design of the architect.

The quality of this object is a matter of centimeters, or rather, of that centimeter by which the panel is recessed from the frame, creating a subtle chiaroscuro. Without ornaments, without molding, the wardrobe is made out of light-colored wood and stands on a base that is dark like the border of the doors. One detail of great refinement is provided by the diagonal joints of the boards that make up the frame — made in such a way that the pattern of crossed grains creates a visual effect of indentation similar to the one old furniture-makers obtained by beveling the corners. Other interesting features of this apartment include the way that the irregularity of an oblique wall in the dining room is visually annulled by the multiplication of the corners of the cupboards, and the decoration of the studio with its elegant mahogany furniture.

BIBLIOGRAPHY

A. LOOS, *Wohnungswanderungen*, op. cit.
H. KULKA, *Adolf Loos*, op. cit., figs. 5-6 with captions.
L. MÜNZ, G. KÜNSTLER, *Der Architekt Adolf Loos*, op. cit., p. 34, fig. 14.
F. KURRENT, J. SPALT, *Unbekanntes von Adolf Loos*, in «Bauforum», n. 21, 1970, pp. 32-34.
B. RUKSCHCIO, *Adolf Loos zum 110. Geburtstag*, in «Bauforum», n. 81, pp. 6-8.

1900 - APARTMENT OF OTTO STOESSL
Auhofstrasse 235, Vienna 13

A photograph of the dining room is preserved in the Loos archives. Some of the furniture constructed for this aparment was later moved to the house renovated for the same writer in 1911-1912 at Matrasgasse, 20.

BIBLIOGRAPHY

L. MÜNZ, G. KÜNSTLER, *Der Architekt Adolf Loos*, op. cit., section n. 10, p. 183.
F. KURRENT, J. SPALT, *Unbekanntes von Adolf Loos*, «Bauforum», n. 21, 1970, p. 33.
B. RUKSCHCIO, *Adolf Loos zum 110. Geburtstag*, in «Bauforum», n. 81, p. 6.

1900 - APARTMENT OF HUGO STEINER
Gumpendorferstrasse 22, Vienna 6

BIBLIOGRAPHY

B. RUKSCHCIO, *Studien zu Entwürfen, Projekten und ausgeführten Bauten von Adolf Loos 1870-1930*, op. cit. WV. W. 12.00.

1900 - DECORATION OF THE ROOMS OF THE FRAUEN-KLUB
Alter Trattnerhof, Vienna 1

Nothing remains to document the interior design of the reading room of this club but a graphic illustration in Loos' archives.

BIBLIOGRAPHY

L. MÜNZ, G. KÜNSTLER, *Der Architekt Adolf Loos*, op. cit., section n. 9, p. 183.

1900 - REDESIGNED FAÇADE FOR A BUILDING
Tivoli Jiraskova 26, Brno, Czechoslovakia

As well as the façade Loos designed a new entrance to the stairs.

BIBLIOGRAPHY

B. RUKSCHCIO, *Studien zu Entwürfen, Projekten und ausgeführten Bauten von Adolf Loos 1870-1930*, op. cit., WV. H. 09.00.

1900 - DRAWING OF A THEATER WITH TYMPANUM

BIBLIOGRAPHY

B. RUKSCHCIO, *Studien zu Entwürfen, Projekten und ausgeführten Bauten von Adolf Loos 1870-1930*, op. cit. WV. G. 03.98.P.

1902 - APARTMENT FOR ALFRED SOBOTKA
Elisabethstrasse 15, Vienna 1

In this apartment Loos decorated the lobby (white-painted wood), the bedroom (with built-in cupboards) and the studio (the walls lined in natural wood: oak).

BIBLIOGRAPHY

A. LOOS, *Wohnungswanderungen*, op. cit.
H. KULKA, *Adolf Loos*, op. cit., figs. 13-14 with captions.
L. MÜNZ, G. KÜNSTLER, *Der Architekt Adolf Loos*, op. cit., section n. 12, p. 184.

1903 - APARTMENT OF REITLER
Walfischgasse 7, Vienna 1

The date is assigned by L. Münz and G. Künstler. A photograph of the bedroom and of a corner of the sitting room is preserved in the Loos archives.

BIBLIOGRAPHY

L. MÜNZ, G. KÜNSTLER, *Der Architekt Adolf Loos*, op. cit., section n. 16, p. 184.

1903 - APARTMENT OF CLOTHILDE BRILL
Hinterbrühl, near Vienna

BIBLIOGRAPHY

B. RUKSCHCIO, *Studien zu Entwürfen, Projekten und ausgeführten Bauten von Adolf Loos 1870-1930*, op. cit., WV. W. 20.03.

1903 - APARTMENT OF JAKOB LANGER
Lodkowitzplatz 1, Vienna 1

BIBLIOGRAPHY

B. RUKSCHCIO, *Studien zu Entwürfen, Projekten und ausgeführten Bauten von Adolf Loos 1870-1930*, op. cit., WV. W. 20.03.

1903 - APARTMENT OF MICHAEL LEISS
Reichgasse (today Beckgasse) 16, Vienna 13

BIBLIOGRAPHY

B. RUKSCHCIO, *Studien zu Entwürfen, Projekten und ausgeführten Bauten von Adolf Loos 1870-1930*, op. cit., WV. W. 24.03.

1903 - APARTMENT OF FERDINAND REINER
Schwindgasse 13, Vienna 4

BIBLIOGRAPHY

B. RUKSCHCIO, *Studien zu Entwürfen, Projekten und ausgeführten Bauten von Adolf Loos 1870-1930*, op. cit., WV. W. 26.03.

1903 - APARTMENT OF GUSTAV ROSENBERG
Schottenbastei 11, Vienna 1

BIBLIOGRAPHY

B. RUKSCHCIO, *Studien zu Entwürfen, Projekten und ausgeführten Bauten von Adolf Loos 1870-1930*, op. cit., WV. W. 28.03.

1903 - MONEY-CHANGING COUNTER FOR LEOPOLD LANGER
Kärntnerring 1, Vienna 1

BIBLIOGRAPHY

B. RUKSCHCIO, *Studien zu Entwürfen, Projekten und ausgeführten Bauten von Adolf Loos 1870-1930*, op. cit., WV. L. 19.03.

APARTMENT FOR LEOPOLD LANGER

Opernring 13, Vienna 1

This is one of the first alterations to an interior carried out by Loos, although it should be pointed out that only the large living cum dining room is directly his work. The most interesting features of this decoration derive from the presence of the following recurrent solutions to problems of design: **1901 1903**

a) *the search for spatial continuum*, achieved in this case by the unification of two rooms through the removal of a dividing wall. For structural reasons, however, a high main beam remains visible that connects the two extremes of the previous load-bearing wall. This structural necessity suggests the solution to the problem of lowering the ceiling of the alcove thus formed. In other words, the false ceiling is constructed on a level with the lowest part of the beam, obtaining a balanced spatial design;

b) *the combination of materials*, wood (the open beams on the ceiling and the wall paneling; in this case, mahogany), marble (the lining of the splay of the three big windows; here, Paonazzo marble of Italian origin) and white plaster (covering the ceiling and the upper part of the walls; here with a rough finish);

c) *the principle of symmetry*, or rather of geometric equivalence between the different parts of the visual pattern. This is demonstrated by the design of the ceiling, which is based on the modular character of the beams. These subdivide the surface in such a way as to subdue the irregularity of the basic cross section. It is important to note here that Loos, infringing the rules of banal functionalism, breaks up the continuity of the ceiling rafters by introducing — in correspondence with the space linking the two previously separate rooms — a false main beam, which has no structural function but plays a visual role in the composition. The principle of geometric equivalence is still more clearly demonstrated by the marvelous solution for the corner between the lowered niche and the living room. Loos places a wooden molding on the rear wall of the living room (above the paneling) that has a similar length to that of the alcove area, creating in this way a subtle play of mathematical responses which enriches the articulation of space by defining what are in fact areas of equivalence. So a symmetry of *individual* parts is achieved in the dissymmetry of the pattern as a whole.

BIBLIOGRAPHY

A. LOOS, *Wohnungswanderungen*, op. cit.
H. KULKA, *Adolf Loos*, op. cit., figs. 11-12 with captions.
L. MÜNZ, G. KÜNSTLER, *Der Architekt Adolf Loos*, op. cit., pp. 43-46, figs. 22-23.

Bed-room.

APARTMENT FOR ADOLF LOOS

Giselastrasse 3, Vienna 1
(the living room was reconstructed in 1961 in the Historisches Museum der Stadt Wien)

1903

Peter Altenberg published two photographs of Loos' apartment in the first issue of the review «Kunst»: *«Halbmonatsschrift für Kunst und alles Andere»* (Fortnightly review of art and everything else, Vienna 1903). The text accompanying the pictures ran as follows: *«Adolf Loos, my wife's bedroom, white walls, white curtains, white Angora sheepskin.»*

The laconic nature of this comment lends itself well to clarifying the meaning of the abstract elegance of this room, whose conceptual allure derives precisely from this reduction of all objects to the same color. *White* as absence, as chromatic vacuum, as an allusion to a mythical classicity; the «air of the sacred» reserved for the bedroom (*Schlafzimmer*), for the most intimate, most private place in the house. This is unambiguously confirmed in the apartment that the architect decorated for himself. [1]

The bedroom is an *other* setting, simple, familiar and set apart from the living room by its materials. Here the materials have an unusual semantic clarity. They hark back to that American style of living so highly praised — in the very same year — in the review *Das andere*. The unplastered brick fireplace, the open beams on the ceiling, the wood panels that line the walls, the varying heights of the rooms communicate all that is «sayable». It is the *Sachlichkeit*, both in a functional and a psychological sense, that governs the design, that gauges the experience. But the living room is also the public part of the house: it is here that the person living in the house presents his own social image. The media for carrying this message are the materials and the dimensions of the space.

A wide opening (2.50×2.16 m.) places two rooms of different height and size in communication: the first is approximately 5.50×4.80×3 m. and the second about 5.50×2.20×2.35 m. As a consequence a semantic

Four views of the living room.

hierarchy is created within the living room itself. The large drop in height tends to create the impression of the latter space being *inside* the former. The relatively more cosy and intimate character of this second ambience is reinforced by the presence of the fireplace and of divans set against the wall. Even the direction of the beams on the ceiling (one perpendicular to the other) underlines a psychological and functional difference between the two spaces, which are at the same time united by their materials.

In conclusion we meet up in this house with two cultures, with two unmitigated civilizations: Europe and America, the silence of classical culture and the expressiveness of everyday culture, the cold fascination of extreme abstraction (in the *Schlafzimmer*) and the warm welcome of extreme realism (in the *Wohnzimmer*). As we shall see, all of Loos' work shuttles back and forth between these two poles.

NOTES

1) In this context Massimo Cacciari's comments on certain statements made by Claire Loos in *Adolf Loos privat*, Vienna 1936, are of interest: «'The owner of the house has his whole life in front of him,' (Cf. Loos, op. cit., p. 45), to grow into and up with the house — and he must have a place to arrange the things that please him, that are suitable to the house, which can only be shown, but never dictated, by the architect, never be 'worked out' — for which composition is impotence, and the skill of the 'artist' silence. 'The bedroom, Lerle, is the most private, most sacred thing - no stranger may profane it'. (Cf. Loos, op. cit., p. 42)». M. CACCIARI, *La Vienna di Wittgenstein*, in «Nuova Corrente», 72-73, Milan 1977.

BIBLIOGRAPHY

«Kunst», Vienna 1903, first issue, pp. XII-XII.
H. KULKA, *A. Loos*, op. cit., fig. 15 with caption.
L. MÜNZ, *Adolf Loos*, op. cit., fig. on p. 69.
L. MÜNZ, G. KÜNSTLER, *Der Architekt Adolf Loos*, op. cit., pp. 46-47, illustrations 24 and 25.

A corner of the living room.

Lina Loos' bedroom in the original apartment.

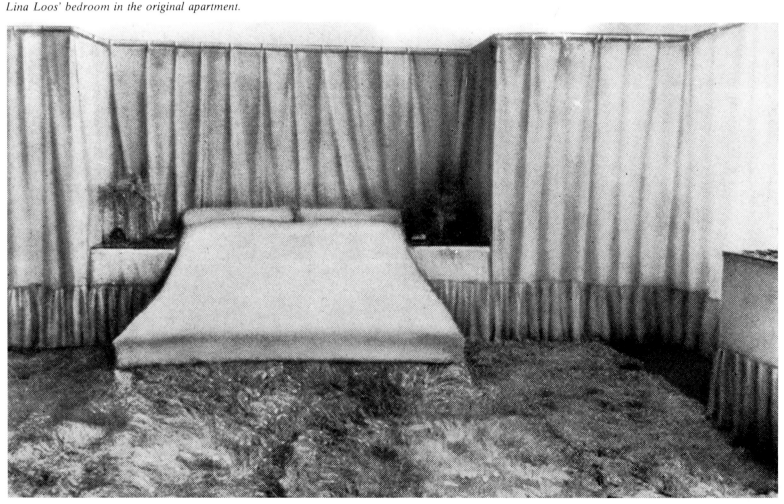

1904 - APARTMENT OF ELSA GALL
Gumpendorferstrasse 21, Vienna 6

BIBLIOGRAPHY

B. RUKSCHCIO, *Studien zu Entwürfen, Projekten und ausgeführten Bauten von Adolf Loos 1870-1930*, op. cit., W.V.W. 35.04.

1904 - APARTMENT OF WAGNER-WÜNSCH
Schleifmühlgasse 2, Vienna 4

BIBLIOGRAPHY

B. RUKSCHCIO, *Studien zu Entwürfen, Projekten und ausgeführten Bauten von Adolf Loos 1870-1930*, op. cit., W.V.W. 37.04.

1904 - APARTMENT OF GEORG WEISS
Falkenstrasse 6, Vienna 1

BIBLIOGRAPHY

B. RUKSCHCIO, *Studien zu Entwürfen, Projekten und ausgeführten Bauten von Adolf Loos 1870-1930*, op. cit., W.V.W. 38.04.

1904 - BANK IN MARIAHILFERSTRASSE
Mariahilferstrasse 122, Vienna 7

BIBLIOGRAPHY

B. RUKSCHCIO, *Studien zu Entwürfen, Projekten und ausgeführten Bauten von Adolf Loos 1870-1930*, op. cit., W.V.L. 34.04.

1904 - STEINER STORE
Mariahilferstrasse 56, Vienna 7

BIBLIOGRAPHY

B. RUKSCHCIO, *Studien zu Entwürfen, Projekten und ausgeführten Bauten von Adolf Loos 1870-1930*, op. cit., W.V.L. 32.04.

1904-1905 - APARTMENT OF EMMANUEL AUFRICHT
Naglergasse 1, Vienna 1

A photograph of the dining room with fireplace and wooden wall paneling is preserved in the Loos archives.

BIBLIOGRAPHY

A. LOOS, *Wohnungswanderungen*, op. cit.
L. MÜNZ, G. KÜNSTLER, *Der Architekt Adolf Loos*, section no. 14, p. 184.

1905 - APARTMENT OF HERMANN SCHWARZWALD
Josefstädterstrasse 68, Vienna 8

The ceiling of the dining room was lowered by the construction of a false ceiling with rafters and enlarged by the incorporation of a small room adjoining it at an angle. The walls were lined with panels of white-painted wood, leaving an upper strip of green plaster. The furniture was made out of cherry wood. These furnishings exemplify — as Kulka has pointed out — an approach to the decoration of houses intended for the middle classes, based on a criterion of economy.

BIBLIOGRAPHY

A. LOOS, *Wohnungswanderungen*, op. cit.
H. KULKA, *Adolf Loos*, op. cit., fig. 22 with caption.
L. MÜNZ, G. KÜNSTLER, *Der Architekt Adolf Loos*, op. cit., section 18, p. 184 with illustration.

1905 - APARTMENT OF HEDWIG KANNER
Untere Augartenstrasse 36, Vienna 2

BIBLIOGRAPHY

B. RUKSCHCIO, *Studien zu Entwürfen, Projekten und ausgeführten Bauten von Adolf Loos 1870-1930*, op. cit., W.V.W. 41.05.

1905 - APARTMENT OF CARL REININGHAUS
Brahmsplatz 4, Vienna 4

BIBLIOGRAPHY

B. RUKSCHCIO, *Studien zu Entwürfen, Projekten und ausgeführten Bauten von Adolf Loos 1870-1930*, op. cit., W.V.W. 43.05.

1905 - APARTMENT OF LUDWIG SCHWEIGER
Alserstrasse 68, Vienna 9

BIBLIOGRAPHY

B. RUKSCHCIO, *Studien zu Entwürfen, Projekten und ausgeführten Bauten von Adolf Loos 1870-1930*, op. cit., W.V.W. 45.05.

1905 - APARTMENT OF JOSEF WERTHEIMER
Marc-Aurelstrasse 8, Vienna 1

BIBLIOGRAPHY

B. RUKSCHCIO, *Studien zu Entwürfen, Projekten und ausgeführten Bauten von Adolf Loos 1870-1930*, op. cit., W.V.W. 46.05.

1906 - APARTMENT OF V. GROSER
Josefstädterstrasse 73, Vienna 8

BIBLIOGRAPHY

B. RUKSCHCIO, *Studien zu Entwürfen, Projekten und ausgeführten Bauten von Adolf Loos 1870-1930*, op. cit., W.V.W. 53.06.

1906 - APARTMENT OF EMMY PIRINGER
Nibelungengasse 13, Vienna 1

BIBLIOGRAPHY

B. RUKSCHCIO, *Studien zu Entwürfen, Projekten und ausgeführten Bauten von Adolf Loos 1870-1930*, op. cit., W.V.W. 54.06.

1906 - APARTMENT OF RUDOLF TÜRKEL
Wickenburggasse 24, Vienna 8

BIBLIOGRAPHY

B. RUKSCHCIO, *Studien zu Entwürfen, Projekten und ausgeführten Bauten von Adolf Loos 1870-1930*, op. cit., W.V.W. 55.06.

1906 - OFFICE OF ARTHUR FRIEDMANN
Schottenring 31, Vienna 1

BIBLIOGRAPHY

B. RUKSCHCIO, *Studien zu Entwürfen, Projekten und ausgeführten Bauten von Adolf Loos 1870-1930*, op. cit., W.V.L. 49.06.

1906 - EXHIBITION PAVILION OF THE SIEMENS COMPANY
Reichenberg, Czechoslovakia

BIBLIOGRAPHY

B. RUKSCHCIO, *Studien zu Entwürfen, Projekten und ausgeführten Bauten von Adolf Loos 1870-1930*, W.V.L. 47.06.

1908-1909 APARTMENT OF R. FISCHL
Mariahilferstrasse 97, Vienna 7

BIBLIOGRAPHY

B. RUKSCHCIO, *Studien zu Entwürfen, Projekten und ausgeführten Bauten von Adolf Loos 1870-1930*, op. cit., W.V.W. 65.08.

1908 - APARTMENT OF ARTHUR FRIEDMANN
Sternberg, Mähren, Czechoslovakia

BIBLIOGRAPHY

B. RUKSCHCIO, *Studien zu Entwürfen, Projekten und ausgeführten Bauten von Adolf Loos 1870-1930*, op. cit., W.V.W. 217.08.

VILLA KARMA
rue St. Moritz 352, between Clarens and Vevey, Switzerland

This is the first building constructed by Loos. It is not an entirely new structure, but a large-scale and radical rebuilding of an existing house, Maladaire, belonging to the psychiatrist Theodor Beer. Although the work was finished by the architect Hugo Erlich (who made some modifications to the original plan), [1] the villa is still recognizable not only as the work of Loos but also as a paradigm of his aesthetic sensibility. A large number of the techniques that later form a constant part of Loos' language are tried out here as if in a laboratory experiment. The foundation on which the project is based is extremely clear. Having eliminated the wide pitched roof of the old Maladaire house, the existing nucleus is «immersed» in the new shell which enwraps it on three sides, ending up with an almost square plan which by vertical extension tends towards a largely cubic composition.

1904
1906

Although it is essentially a unitary work, the clear-cut difference between outside and inside is nevertheless evident, to such an extent that it may be seen as an assembly of two superimposed shells, each of which is relatively autonomous. The external shell is designed to fit perfectly into nature, and the internal shell is completely consistent with the intimate scene of the architecture of living space.

Outside is the site that dictates the rules of the game. The house is deeply rooted in the building culture of the environment in which it is set, not only in its forms but also in its use of material. This tradition is interpreted by carrying out a genuine simplification, a process involving stripping off ornamental dross on the basis of a modern logic of construction. By this method the house attains an *individuality* — already recognized by P. Bournoud [2] — that is also the consequence of its perfect

South-east façade.

West façade.

North-west façade.

East façade.

Open veranda on the western side of the ground floor.

Portico on the north side.

topological relationship with the natural elements (the Lake of Geneva, the Dent du Midi, the grass that surrounds the house). It is worth quoting here what Loos himself has to say on the subject: «I had been given the enticing task of building at Montreux on the beautiful shores of the Lake of Geneva. There used to be a lot of stone on the shore and as the ancient inhabitants of the place had built all their houses out of these stones, I wanted to do the same. As for the rest I did not intend to do anything harmful. Who could describe my amazement then, when I was requested to present myself to the police and was asked how I, a foreigner, dared to make such an attack on the beauty of the Lake of Geneva? The building was too simple. What had happened to the ornaments? My timid objection that the lake too, when it is calm, is flat and absolutely void of ornament, and yet people find it really quite passable, fell on deaf ears. An injunction was obtained that forbade construction of such a house on the grounds of its simplicity and therefore of its ugliness. I went home happy and contented.... How many architects in the world have been recognized as an artist in black and white by the police?... Everyone had to believe in me, even I had to believe it. Because I was banned, banned by the police like Arnold Schoenberg or Frank Wedekind. Or rather, like Arnold Schoenberg would be banned if the police were capable of reading the thoughts behind the notes of his music.»[3]

So *simplicity* is the cause of the hostility that Loos encounters in the cultural climate of the period, hostility that had already been shown in the Vienna of the Secession and that would be met with again at the time of the construction of the building on the Michaelerplatz (1909-1911). Nor is it coincidental that he did not receive a commission to build a house until seven years after his final move to Vienna on returning from America. It is significant, too, that his client should be a prominent intellectual with an unusual personality like Theodor Beer. The then thirty-seven year old teacher at the Faculty of Medicine in Vienna had a vast store of learning to draw on, having written essays on art and epistemology as well as on psychology, including a critical reinterpretation of the analysis of perception made by Ernst Mach (the well-known Austrian physicist and philosopher). He had, in short, a progressive turn of mind that predisposed him for an encounter with the radical and unconventional architecture of the Viennese architect, as is shown by a letter written to Loos following their first meetings in 1903. «I take little notice of what they tell me, but much of my experience.... First I must see if my taste matches yours. And also disprove your reputation for intolerance and not finishing the job.»

It is always difficult to ascertain how much influence a client may have had on the final shape of a work, and it becomes even more so in a case like this where the client openly declares his intention of collaborating on the project: «I hope that you are going to tackle this unusual, unitary work with joy and love and that I may be able to provide something of real worth by my collaboration.»

Beer did not confine himself to making clear his desire that the house should take on the appearance of a kind of protective shelter for his and his wife's private life, but also made sketches of certain special features such as the entrance to the house. This was designed with an entrance way closed by a dazzling gate of chromed brass that stood out against the dark background of a wall concealed behind outward-facing pillars of marble. A short double flight of stairs led up to the door. It is a solution in which scenographic effects are mixed up with motifs that emerge from the unconscious, a solution, in short, a long way from the lucid rationality of the Viennese architect. Loos probably took the psychological needs of the client into account to some extent as is shown by the symbolic character of the architecture. On the outside the artifice of the corner cylinder and of the pure prisms which extend to the ends of the terrace pergolas give this villa the appearance of a bare and compact tower. In a sense, Loos reinterprets the psychological and physical needs of the person who has to live in the house, translating them into his own language, merging them into the architecture. And today we can reread those needs on the walls of the house and in their forms.

Let us make our way into the house.

A flight of stone steps is lined by four Doric columns, surmounted by a simple architrave, against the solid background of the wall connecting the passage leading from the outside to the inside. Stamped in bronze on the polished leaves of the entrance door are the esoteric symbols of Yin and Yang, a significant reference to oriental philosophy.

On crossing the threshold we find ourselves in the enclosing space of the two-story high oval hall. We have by now entered the *other* dimension of the internal space. The change in language is abrupt, radical and immediately perceptible.

Each room is distinguished by the specific qualities of the materials used. Only through the materials can Loos' architecture say all that is «sayable.» The intensity of natural light marks in turn the greater or lesser degree of intimacy of the room. The private rooms, intended for meditation, make use of indirect lighting.

In this sense the ground-floor plan may be broken up into four sectors: the L-shaped service space formed by the corridor and by the cloakroom; the ell of the library, which is on the outer perimeter of the square, facing the road; the ell of the dining room and of the veranda which closes the other two sides of the square nearest the lake; and finally the smoking room and the reading room, placed at the center of the house.

The axis of penetration into the house follows the long white corridor, as is emphasized by the direction of the dark oak beams that pattern the ceiling. The same dichromicity based on the contrast between white plaster and dark wood is used again in the cloakroom. Here an unadorned wall cupboard relies for its beauty on the wood of which it is made, while the elegant geometric lattice of the glass wall in the background gives the impression of an exotic quotation from Japanese figurative vocabulary.[4]

At the opposite extreme of the ell of the service area, the corridor separates two rooms that are the fulcrum of the living area on the ground

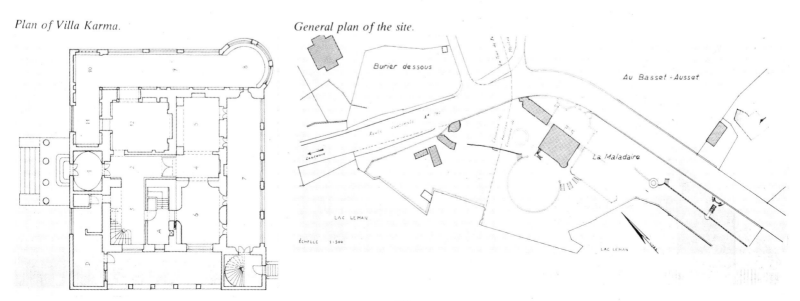

Plan of Villa Karma.   *General plan of the site.*

Detail of the staircase in the wardrobe passage.

floor: the dining room and the smoking room. The dining room is distinguished by the dominance of marble, the noble material that not only covers the floor in a black-and-white checkerboard pattern, but also the walls that curve towards the door. The use of curvilinear plastic shapes is very rare in Loos' interiors and is adopted here to emphasize the thickness of the existing walls. Marble is the basic material of the veranda overlooking the lake that communicates directly with the dining room. On the opposite side to the dining room, the smoking room reaches the highest degree of intimacy in its delicate harmony of chromatic tonalities that range from the pale blue of the walls, to the soft tints of the majolica lining of the fireplace, to the warm colors of the carpets; indirect light filters through colored glass to blend with the light from the fire and candles.

The most modern setting on the ground — and the one which has attracted the most attention from critics as a consequence — is the L-shaped library. As one crosses the room, four separate functions may be discerned, one after the other: *rest*, to which one is invited by the ample, encircling divan of the round hall; *research*, into books on the walls

lined with simple shelving built out of mahogany and interrupted by strips of veined marble that are echoed on the wall in front by mirrors that break up the large windows rhythmically; *writing*, to which is dedicated the corner space equipped with a specially designed writing desk; *intellectual work* for which the final space is intended. This last space communicates with the most secluded room on this floor: the reading room where, seated by a fireplace topped by three niches, it is possible to abandon oneself to calm reflection on one's own thoughts.

The difficult relationship between reception areas and intimate spaces (in a sense, between the public sphere and the private one) is resumed but staggered between the first and second floor, between the music room and the bedroom. Almost the entire first floor (which is also to some extent a mediating strip between the daytime zone on the ground floor and the nighttime zone on the second) is given over to a large room for music. The predominant material is the wood used for the walls and the lacunar ceiling that seems to project its own pattern onto that of the parquet flooring. All the elements of the furnishings betray the discreet charm of

Detail of external door.

The wardrobe passage.

The entrance hall.

Veranda on the first floor.

The library.

Detail of the library.

Vaulted ceiling of the entrance hall.

Oval balustrade of the gallery above the entrance hall.

The reading corner of the library.

Inner doors on the ground floor.

Design of bookcase for the library.

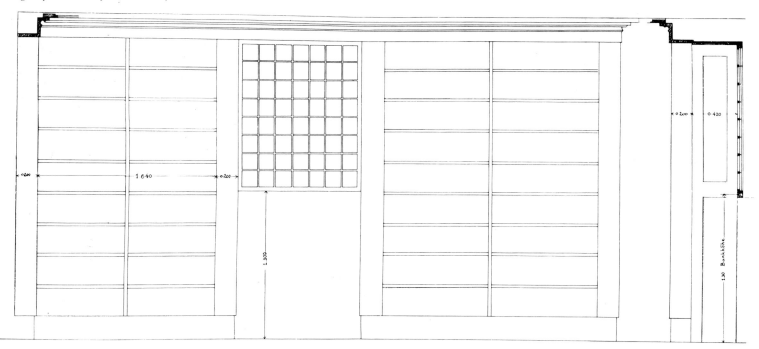

the «learned» atmosphere that one breathed in central European circles at the turn of the century.

On the second floor the bedroom is centrally situated and without direct openings to the outside. It is the most secret place in the whole house. Indirect natural light is barely able to filter in through a narrow window covered by a curtain. Apart from this the room is illuminated by artificial light that reflects off the nacreous ceiling and is uniformly diffused as if from a gigantic lampshade. The modern technical conquest of electricity allows perfect control over the quality of the environment, making indiscreet external openings superfluous. Here, one may choose to rest in the room cum verandah with a fireplace next to the bedroom or go on up to the roof garden with its pergolas from where the whole panoramic view may be enjoyed. But inside, the bedroom is hermetically sealed. Here Eros rules. The alcove is built into a niche carved out of the wall. The blue curtains and the cupboards made out of light ash that run the length of the wall complete the suffused sense of intimacy.

An extension of the zone of pleasure is the bathroom on the first floor. As Vera Behalova [5] recalls: «For Beer — as for the ancients — the body with all its physical needs was not something to be ashamed of but something to be taken care of.» So the bathroom takes on something of a pagan value and elegance. The two sunken bathtubs are surrounded by marble columns and are reached by descending four steps, while adjoining the room at a higher level is a space for gymnastics provided with a fireplace and illuminated from above. The evocation of the Roman spirit is obvious. Finally, Loos took care of the external arrangements; a tennis pavilion and the walls encircling the villa.

But, as has already been pointed out, it was not Loos who completed the work. The reason for him giving up on the job prematurely is obscure. It is probable that the strange personal fortunes of Theodor Beer that are closely bound up with the vicissitudes in the construction of the villa had something to do with it. Accused of a sexual offence, he had to break off his «collaboration on the project» until March 1904 in order to take refuge in America. [6] So we do not know if that contribution, that «something of real worth» that Beer offered towards the design of the house, is to be sought in a thin vein of irrationalism that slips through the highly controlled mesh of this architecture—an architecture that in other ways testifies to the consummate *craftsmanship* of the Viennese architect, who tries out many of the formulas of his linguistic repertory here and demonstrates an unrepeatable mastery of materials and lighting. There is something in this juvenile production that makes it one of the most fascinating of his architectural works.

NOTES

1) It is in the monograph on Adolf Loos by Heinrich Kulka (op. cit.) that we are told of the completion of the work by Hugo Erlich, a contemporary of Loos who had studied at the Technischen Hochschule in Vienna and practiced his profession mainly in Yugoslavia.

2) P. BOURNOUD, *Une construction d'Adolphe Loos en Suisse*; in «Formes et Couleurs», no. 4; Lausanne 1944. «The first thing that strikes one about this building is its individuality and particular elegance.»

3) ADOLF LOOS, *Sämtliche Schriften*.

4) On this subject see a significant passage written by Loos himself: «The East has always been the great reservoir of seeds of life for the West. It almost seems as though Asia has given us, today, the last residues of its own primordial energy. In fact we are forced to turn to the most remote part of the Orient, to Japan and to Polynesia. Thus we have reached the end. Even the masters of the Renaissance had to stretch far. They were the ones who conquered Persia and India. One thinks of the Persian carpets always to be found in the Madonnas of the period, of German inlay-work and of damasking. The rococo period had to turn to China, while only Japan is left for us.» A. LOOS, *Sämtliche Schriften*.

5) Quoted in VERA BEHALOVA, *Die Villa Karma von Adolf Loos*, in «Alte und moderne Kunst», no. 113, 1970, year XV.

6) Ibid.

BIBLIOGRAPHY

H. KULKA, *Adolf Loos*, op. cit., figs. 16-20.
P. BOURNOUD, *Une construction d'Adolphe Loos en Suisse*, in «Formes et Couleurs», p. 4. Lausanne 1944, pp. 40-47, with illustrations.
L. MÜNZ, *Adolf Loos*, op. cit., p. 35.
L. MÜNZ, G. KÜNSTLER, *Der Architekt Adolf Loos*, op. cit., pp. 61-70, figs. 48-61.
VERA BEHALOVA, *Die Villa Karma von Adolf Loos*, in «Alte und moderne Kunst», no. 113, 1970, year XV, p. 11-19.
VERA BEHALOVA, *Adolf Loos: Villa Karma*, unv. Dissertation an der Universität Wien. 1974.
J. GUBLER, G. BARLEY, *Loos' Villa Karma*, in «Architectural Review», London, no. 865, March 1969, pp. 115-116.

The bathroom on the first floor of Villa Karma.

Bathroom on the first floor.

Detail of the bathroom.

General view of the dining room on the ground floor.

Detail of the dining room.

APARTMENT FOR ALFRED KRAUS
Mohsgasse 2, Vienna 3

1905

Contemporary to the Villa Karma, this decoration undertaken for Alfred Kraus fully expresses the maturity that Loos' techniques for redesigning the interiors of existing apartments had achieved. The already tried and tested solutions — of using varying heights to differentiate rooms within a fluid, unitary space — of a measured balancing of the material qualities of wood, marble and the mirror — of the search for equilibrium in the composition of different parts; all these are used here at a level of extreme refinement, bordering on excess. This excess may probably be ascribed to the social standing of the client.

An example of this is the decoration of the dining room where the fireplace — a typically invariant element of Loos' interiors — is replaced by an elegant gas stove. The doors and the high (slanting) frieze on the ceiling are made out of carved mahogany, the panels lining the walls are of costly veined Cipolin marble, and a large mirror dominates the setting, creating illusory images of virtual space.

Trompe l'oeil is also the distinguishing feature of the refined ceiling of specular glass in the polygonal alcove that opens directly onto the dining room. As in the Langer apartment (1901), the ceiling of the alcove is set at exactly the same level as the lower edge of the wooden frieze, with the aim of lending visual emphasis to the deliberate continuity of space. The encircling seat — similar in some ways to that of the Villa Karma library — stands on a base of white-painted pine. The same material is used for the window frame that divides the large windows into small squares. This results in a crystalline fusion of soft tints and refractive materials that emphasizes the luminosity of the alcove, turning it into an effective «lantern» of natural light for the whole room.

BIBLIOGRAPHY

H. KULKA, *Adolf Loos*, op. cit., figs. 21-23 with captions.
L. MÜNZ, G. KÜNSTLER, *Der Architekt Adolf Loos*, op. cit., pp. 47-48, figs. 26-27.

APARTMENT OF ARTHUR FRIEDMANN
Bellariastrasse 4, Vienna 1

1906
1907

In this large apartment that occupied an entire floor, we again find many recurrent elements of Loos' interior design, including the entrance hall painted in white, the studio with an alcove, square panels on a light-colored ceiling, a fireplace of veined marble, the inevitable mirrors and even the surprising anticipation of a solution adopted for the Moller house in 1930: the shelves for holding the violins are built into the walls and closed by glass doors. Photographs of the living room, the studio and the dining room are preserved in the Loos archives.

BIBLIOGRAPHY

A. LOOS, *Wohnungswanderungen*, op. cit.
L. MÜNZ, G. KÜNSTLER, *Der Architekt Adolf Loos*, op. cit., section no. 19, p. 184.
F. KURRENT, J. SPALT, *Unbekanntes von Adolf Loos*, in «Bauforum» no. 21, 1970, pp. 29-48.

KÄRNTNER BAR

Kärntner Durchgang 10, Vienna 1
(the outside has undergone alterations)

The Kärntner Bar represents an experiment at the limits of an architecture that entrusts all that is «sayable» to its materials. Paraphrasing Loos, it could be said that this small-sized bar (3.50×7.00×3.50 m.) is a «little jewel», a jewel that concentrates «the greatest value possible into the smallest of volumes.» [1]

With the rigor of a theorem, the Kärntner Bar demonstrates the uselessness of ornament, the theme that Loos will hammer home in *Ornament und verbrechen* the following year (1908). Ornament is indecent because it overlays the material with a grotesque mask, compelling it to «lie». This interior is, instead, a masterpiece of skillful manipulation of classical materials: marble, onyx, wood and the mirror. As if writing a symphony, Loos confines himself to controlling their relationships in composition. The final result of this carefully measured splicing is a spectacular chromatic and visual pattern. The checkered floor, the lacunar ceiling of veined marble, the very thin panels of onyx on the upper part of the entrance wall, the dark mahogany facing of the walls, the black leather of the *separés*, the shiny, polished brass on the table edges, the warm, suffused and discreet light that is reflected by the crystal of the glasses and the glass of the shelves behind the counter; all this is blended in the intimate theatricality of the room. The ends of the walls are faced with mirrors, the alchemical material of Loos' language, reflecting the marble ceiling and multiplying its image to infinity.

The conceptual message underlying this optical illusion should not be undervalued. As. M. Tafuri has written: «In the Kärntner, as well as in the marvelous hall of the Kniže store on the Graben, the mirrors introduce the 'image' of precariousness: any completeness may be reflected, split up infinitely. The device functions as a kind of refractivity in Loos' work: turning the processes of the 'applied arts' upside down, it keeps the language immobile. Loos would be able to go along with Mach when he says: 'one must not think that everything that is true about a symbol is necessarily true of what is expressed by that symbol.'» [2]

In short, the subtle play of the Kärntner Bar moves between two opposite poles: optical deception and technical certainty. Trickery with mirrors introduces doubt into the confines of the *form* that technique allows one to realize in all its peremptory palpability. But there is no spectacle without technique. It is the structure that props the scenery up. An anecdote related by Claire Loos bears witness to the importance Loos attached to problems of structural engineering, and above all to the competence shown in solving them. «Mounting the heavy marble panels on the ceiling gave rise to quite a few difficulties and above all a great deal of skepticism on the part of the workmen. But when one Italian worker revealed his perplexity about putting the plan into effect, Loos replied calmly 'Put up the ceiling.' and the ceiling is still there, more than twenty years later.» [3] In the perfect execution of a complex way of thinking in a simple form, the Kärntner Bar achieves a distilled preciousness, a model for the extreme synthesis of language. It is significant that Loos wanted to dedicate this interior to his friend Peter Altenberg, the author of poetry «turning» on strict syntactic purity and on the laconic quality of the words. Making use of photomontage, Loos in fact placed a portrait of Altenberg, made by Jägerspacher, on the rear wall of the bar. [4]

But in contrast to the lyricism of the interior is the irony of the exterior. A large American flag dominates the original composition of the facade of this «American bar». The gaudiness of the colors, which erupt into the tranquil Viennese scene of the Kärntner Durchgang, reminds one of the sacrilegious sarcasm of his controversial writings in «Das andere» (1903). In fact, an *other* element, alien to Viennese culture, is deliberately and provocatively introduced.

The ostentatious foreignness has a theoretical matrix. Not incidentally, Loos wrote in an essay from the same year that the most beautiful palace in Vienna is the Liechtensteinpalast in the Bankgasse. «It is so little Viennese and has nothing of the shabby Viennese baroque about it.» [5] The strong link that Loos feels with the tradition of the site never turns into an uncritical copy of the stylistic features of the past, but involves the conscious and selective choice of a line of constructive research that leads to a genuine modernity.

The flag of the American bar is waved with deliberate insolence, in order to promote a process of liberation from nostalgic attachment to the ornaments of the past in Austrian culture. In the contrast between the monolithic pillars of Skyros marble and the colored-glass tesserae of the flag on the façade of the Kärntner Bar, two civilizations meet and coexist: the German culture and the Anglo-Saxon culture — or in Loos' words, the «civilization of the cat» and the «civilization of the pig.» [6] But what takes place behind the curtain is the authentic representation of modernity.

NOTES

1) A. LOOS, *Sämtliche Schriften*.

2) M. TAFURI, F. DAL CO, *Architettura contemporanea*, Milan 1976, p. 115.

3) C. LOOS, *Adolf Loos privat*, Vienna 1936, p. 14.

4) The photomontage is at present preserved in the Photo Gerlach archive in Vienna and has been reproduced in the monograph by L. Münz and G. Künstler.

5) A. LOOS, *Sämtliche Schriften*.

6) A. LOOS, *Sämtliche Schriften*.

BIBLIOGRAPHY

H. KULKA, *Adolf Loos*, op. cit., fig. 28-30 with captions.
L. MÜNZ, G. KÜNSTLER, *Der Architekt Adolf Loos*, op. cit., p. 40, figs. 17-19.
L. MÜNZ, *Adolf Loos*, op. cit., p. 23 with illustration.
H. CZECH, *Kärntner - American - Loos Bar*, in «Lotus» n. 29, p. 103-107, with illustrations

Interior of the bar — note Altenberg's portrait, photo-montage by Loos.

Original façade of the Bar.

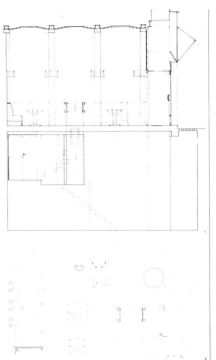

Interior sections.

The ceiling reflecting in the mirror-paneled wall.

Interior of the Kärntner Bar as it is today.

APARTMENT FOR WILLY HIRSCH

Plachygasse 6, Pilsen, Czechoslovakia

The alterations carried out involve the creation of a spatial continuity by **1907** the reunification of the living room, dining room and music room, producing an interesting play of transparencies and introspection between rooms that do not lose their specific functions. So the music room is distinguished from the remaining mahogany-paneled areas by the use of cherry wood, while Skyros marble is used as a unifying element in the decoration. Sketches and watercolors testifying to some of the phases in the evolution of the project are preserved in the Loos archives.

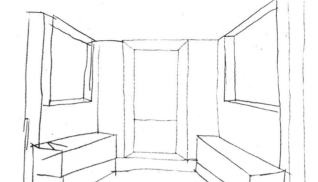

BIBLIOGRAPHY

H. KULKA, *Adolf Loos*, op. cit., figs. 26-27 with captions.
L. MÜNZ, G. KÜNSTLER, *Der Architekt Adolf Loos*, op. cit., section no. 23, p. 185 with illustration.
V. BEHALOVA, *Pilsner Wohnungen von Adolf Loos*, in «Bauforum» no. 21, 1970, p. 51.

APARTMENT FOR PAUL KHUNER

Möllwaldplatz 4, Vienna 4

The aspiration towards equilibrium — a constant feature of Loos' re- **1907** search into interior design — is fully satisfied in this apartment. The clean and regular pattern of the beams (made out of satined oak, crossing one another on the white ceiling) imparts geometric and spatial order to the entire setting. It is the most distinctive feature of the dining room and seems to project a principle of elementary geometric clarity onto the parallel frame of the wooden folding door (which takes up the whole width of the wall). A typical suspended lamp hangs from the ceiling, set at the barycentric point of the volume. One detail that should not be neglected is the floor-to-ceiling curtain that occupies the rear wall, anticipating a type of solution that only became a common feature of domestic furnishings many years afterwards. Yet in this setting it is the logical conclusion of research aimed at reducing the elements of decoration to geometric surfaces of clearly defined outline. If we try to mentally separate the furniture and fittings from the room, the up-to-dateness of the strict spatial grid becomes apparent, barely concealed as it is by the overlay of very dated chairs, carpets and hangings.

BIBLIOGRAPHY

H. KULKA, *Adolf Loos*, op. cit., figs. 24-25 with captions.
L. MÜNZ, G. KÜNSTLER, *Der Architekt Adolf Loos*, op. cit., p. 50, fig. 28.

APARTMENT FOR RUDOLF KRAUS

Nibelungengasse 13, Vienna 1

The application of geometric rules drawn from a «banal» code marks the **1907** design of the living area, obtained by enlarging the dining room by the addition of an adjacent low room. The added space — apart from the need for a visual expansion of the existing dining room — serves specifically as a winter garden.

The junction of pure prismatic volumes — lined with strongly veined Skyros marble — outlines the niches, the flower-holders and the benches covered with green leather cushions. In one of the niches, at the point where the walls join up with the ceiling, is placed a bronze copy of a frieze by Donatello.

As well as the living room, Loos decorated the entrance hall, the studio and the dining room — as may be seen from the photographic records collected in the Loos archives.

BIBLIOGRAPHY

A. LOOS, *Wohnungswanderungen*, op. cit., mentioned by L. HEVESI, *Adolf Loos*, «Fremden-Blatt», Vienna, 22 November 1907.
H. KULKA, *Adolf Loos*, op. cit., fig. 38, with caption.
L. MÜNZ, G. KÜNSTLER, *Der Architekt Adolf Loos*, op. cit., pp. 53-54, fig. 30.
F. KURRENT, J. SPALT, *Unbekanntes von Adolf Loos*, in «Bauforum» no. 21, 1970, p. 36.

SIGMUND STEINER PLUME AND FEATHER STORE

Kärntnerstrasse 33, Vienna 1 (no longer in existence)

1907

Unfortunately this very elegant Feather Store built on the Kärntnerstrasse has been completely demolished and replaced. In order to reconstruct its appearance, we must refer to the plans and to the few photographs of the period, as well as to an intelligent analytical description, not without accents of subtle irony, by the Viennese art critic Ludwig Hevesi. It is worthwhile quoting verbatim and at length from his long and witty article in the «Fremden-Blatt»: «A new plume and feather shop in Kärntnerstrasse arouses pleasant sensations. Ground floor and first floor are both set into a recess in the wall, with wide jambs, fascia and intrados in Skyros marble with its highly colored sheen, gold script and engraved ostrich feathers, sheets of glass curved towards the entrance, glass framed in brass. Inside, white plaster, including the ceiling with open beams faced with varnished wood. The counters are made of this wood too, with diamond-shaped inlays, producing an effect that is simultaneously more luminous and darker, with the upper part made from glass. The cupboards are framed in brass. Everything is rectangular, with straight lines and no trace of decoration. And the room seems to be doubled in size by the mirrors on the rear wall. An interior of geometric elegance and of very high precision, as if the whole thing was a steel safe.» [1]

Earlier on, Hevesi, who even in the years of triumph of the *Wiener Secession* had expressed his appreciation for the farsighted reserve of the *Café Nihilismus* (1899), stresses the innovative importance of the heresy introduced by Loos: «The era of triviality is over and this irreverent man Loos can already consider himself from a historic perspective to have been the outrider of new and sensible developments.» [2]

But he concludes contentiously by hinting at the presence of two functional errors: «And now I am sorry that I will be at loggerheads with him for ever because of this article, even though I have refrained so far from saying that I couldn't get through the door of his new shop in Kärntnerstrasse with my overcoat on and that I don't understand the structural significance of beams made out of soft wood.» [3]

One cannot ignore Hevesi's implicit objection to the lack of congruence between Loos' theory and his architecture.

In contrast to the appeals for absolute logical and functional rigor and for the elimination of any sort of «lying» with materials that occur over and over again in his theoretical writings, his design in practice often turns on structural pretences and on *trompe l'oeil*. Not only the beams on the ceiling (obviously «false» from the point of view of statics) but also the mirrors on the wall (that reflect and multiply the image of the tiny shop) produce a deception, an illusion. What is more, Loos will make use of similar optical trickery with the «useless» (in a structural sense) columns of the arcade in the Michaelerplatz (1910), a much more compelling lie, given the importance of the work.

This manifest incongruence can help us to comprehend a more intimate and deeper theoretical consistency. His radical condemnation of ornament should not be taken for a demand for the total abolition of pretence from the erudite game of architecture. Loos denies ornamentation only in so far as it is a «private mode of thought.» Besides, he makes the fullest use of the potentialities of the materials in order to produce pleasing visual effects. This is demostrated by the highly refined way in which he combines colors like the delicate pink shades of the Skyros marble on the façade with the shiny brass frames of the window, with the subtle flowing script of the sign and with the light pattern of ostrich feathers engraved above it. But, once again, at the bottom of this offhand elegance lie not only aesthetic motivations but also shrewd statements about the techniques of communication.

To the obvious objection about the illegibility of the sign Loos responded — as Kulka recalls — as follows: «It is not a question of making signs legible but of projecting an image characterized by the materials and the symbols. Illegibility is often a device.» [4] Technique, rather than function, is the categorical imperative of his research into design. For this reason the other criticism made by Hevesi about the narrow dimensions of the door, reduced to the minimal width of 67 cm., is much less tenable. The shrinking of the doorway to a minimum was a deliberate attempt to expand the dimensions of the curved shop windows to the maximum, «the biggest curved windows in Vienna at that time.» [5]

NOTES

1) L. HEVESI, «Fremden-Blatt» (Newspaper for tourists), Vienna, 22 November 1907, quoted in G. Künstler and L. Münz, *Der Architekt Adolf Loos*, op. cit., p. 24.

2) Ibid.

3) Ibid.

4) H. KULKA, *Adolf Loos*, op. cit., p. 29.

5) Cf. L. MÜNZ, G. KÜNSTLER, *Der Architekt Adolf Loos*, op. cit., p. 27.

BIBLIOGRAPHY

L. HEVESI, *Adolf Loos*, «Fremden-Blatt», Vienna, 22 November 1907.
H. KULKA, *Adolf Loos*, op. cit., fig. 31 with caption.
L. MÜNZ, *Adolf Loos*, op. cit., figs. 75-77.
L. MÜNZ, G. KÜNSTLER, *Der Architekt Adolf Loos*, op. cit., pp. 24-29, illustratopms 7-9.

PROJECT FOR THE WAR MINISTRY

Vienna

«The most beautiful palace that is dying: the War Ministry in the am Hof square. Ah, you Viennese, look at it closely because soon it will no longer exist. Everyone knows that it will shortly be destroyed, but no voice is raised to stop this crime. Well, look at it while you can and engrave it well on your minds until you hold it in your hearts. This building is the dominant chord of the square. Without this building the am Hof square would no longer exist.» [1]

In the same year (1907) it had been decided to transfer the administrative offices of the Ministry to a new building to be built on the Ringstrasse. For the occasion a public competition was announced (won by Ludwig Baumann, whose plan was carried out between 1909 and 1913) in which Otto Wagner (under the pseudonym Pallas) and Loos himself (under the pseudonym Homo) were among those who took part. But the projects of both Wagner and Loos were excluded from the running for not having fully respected the rules of the competition. And yet Loos' whole plan is centered on a scrupulous response to the basic requirement of the competition: to set into the façade of the new building the bronze equestrian statue designed in 1891 by Kaspar von Zumbusch in memory of Field Marshal Radetzky. The statue had stood until then in front of the neoclassical façade of the old War Ministry in the am Hof square, built in 1775 by Franz Hildebrand.

These facts, together with the words quoted, help to reconstruct the cultural background against which the project is set. The underlying significance of the proposal cannot be grasped, in fact, without investigating the intricate mesh — of references, allusions and links to a slice of the history of Vienna — that enfolds the design.

First of all, there is the imposing scenery of the volumetric scheme. Its massive bulk was imposed by the conditions of the competition. Yet Loos articulates the façade on the Ringstrasse by imparting a slight movement of protuberances and indentations that is based on a very simple pattern. Four prismatic blocks (an allusive reference to towers), set a constant distance apart, define an approximate symmetry between the two sides (of different lengths) into which the façade is subdivided. In fact, a kind of niche is carved out at the center of the façade to create a theatrical setting for the equestrian statue. The fact that this recess is not placed perfectly at the center is dictated by factors of urban planning. It is placed in line with the Georg Coch-Platz which opens in the direction of the famous Post-

1907

sparkasse designed by Otto Wagner (1903-1907). In this sense, at the bottom of Loos' plan there is an unconfessed desire for comparison at a distance with one of the buildings emblematic of the *Secessionstil*. Against Wagner's calligraphic decorative treatment of the stone wall, he sets a severe return to the classical, detectable not only in the use of the twin columns that dominate the rear of the niche but also, and especially, in the explicit use of symmetry. The rhythmic regularity of the turreted elements has no other aim than optical compensation for the differences in length between the sides of the Ringstrasse. Nor should one dismiss the possibility that the classicism is a nostalgic homage paid to Hildebrand's shortly-to-disappear building. But there are at least two other components in this project that, going beyond the confines of classicity, enter into dialectical relationship with the problems posed by the *Secession*. These are symbolism and color. Yet the problem of making the architecture semantically familiar, intuitively grasped by the *Wagnerschule*, finds an unsatisfactory response in a stylistic and decorative search that is as feverish as it is pointless. Loos' proposal, on the contrary, is based on a clear-cut separation between the form of the architecture and the symbolic possibilities that may be associated with it.

While it is true that the front elevation of the War Ministry is, at intervals, marked by decorations, they have no monumental function. They are, rather, genuine symbols (the two-headed eagle for instance). Besides, more than anything else in the building under discussion, it is the use of color that has a symbolic intention.

Loos had in fact envisaged the Ministry in terms of strongly colored architecture — as he makes clear in his typewritten report on the project: «The façade is heavily ashlar on the ground floor... in limestone. The upper stories are clad in yellow terra-cotta, with a strip of shiny black Belgian (calcareous) granite or Matscheko of the same color, that [would have] projected out towards the Ring. The main cornice is richly finished in yellow terra-cotta.» [2]

The contrast between the yellow of the brick facing and the black of the columns of shiny granite would have made possible a dichromatism that cannot be accidental. It is not difficult to detect an allusion to the symbolic colors of the Hapsburg Empire.

In this way the problem of representation is solved through the intrinsic chromatic value of the materials adopted, without recourse to coats of

paint. The symbolic quality is closely blended with the specific language of architecture. The project appears to be trying to show that popular recognition of an urban object does not necessarily imply the superimposition of an ornamental mask. This is the fundamental argument that Loos sets up opposite the façade of the Postsparkasse. Only it is a pity that the development of the theme then falls into the trap of semantic redundancy because of certain «unusual» features of Loos' silent poetics.

NOTES

1) A. LOOS, *Sämtliche Schriften.*

2) Cf. the descriptive report for the War Ministry competition — pseudonym Homo, in the Loos Archiv, quoted in L. Münz, G. Künstler, *Der Architekt Adolf Loos*, op. cit., p. 168.

BIBLIOGRAPHY

L. HEVESI, «*Der Neubau des Kriegsministeriums*» in «Fremden-Blatt», Vienna 21st May 1908.
H. KULKA, *Adolf Loos*, op. cit., figs. 32-34.
L. MÜNZ, G. KÜNSTLER, *Der Architekt Adolf Loos*, op. cit., pp. 167-170, figs. 227-231.

DRAWINGS OF A TOWER BLOCK
Vienna

1907

A poorly gauged monumental emphasis is the first fact that emerges from an examination of these two sketches for a tower building whose site is uncertain. It is an imposing complex that stands on four corner pillars, enclosing a system of roads that pass beneath on various levels: thus it is a genuine «urban fragment» both because of its bulk and because of the complexity of its volumetric articulation. Yet it is unlikely that we are dealing with utopian designs here since Loos refused to make the formulation of abstract hypotheses of urban planning a part of his working method. The attention paid to the site as a component that is closely linked to the shape of the architecture is a constant of which we find further evidence in these two sketches. As G. Künstler and L. Münz point out, the presence of a watercourse (visible in the drawings) makes it likely that the building was intended for a site on the bank of the river Wien.

«A building of such massive proportions needs to be viewed from a distance. The only suitable place for a project of this nature at the time — and up until recently — was at the end of Stadt park, where the road continues in the direction of the Wollzeile, crosses the Wien and joins up with the Landstrasser Hauptstrasse.»

The observation about the perceptual relationship between architecture and landscape catches the chief characteristic of this building-on-paper, that is, the specific way in which it emerges on the urban skyline. This is the motivation behind formal solutions like the pyramidal crown that is topped by a triumphal sculptural feature. The semantic excess is thus dictated by the role of place marker played by the architecture. But there is more. This design is also an analytical reflection on the composition of historical elements of urban design. More than anything else it demonstrates the way the ideas evolve in the transition from the first to the second drawing which depicts a square closed on three sides and opening onto the river on the fourth.

The square, the arcade, the tower building... are elements drawn from the collective memory of the European city. Their association seems to be a response to the desire to give back a recognizable center, an identity to the urban site.

BIBLIOGRAPHY

L. MÜNZ, G. KÜNSTLER, *Der Architekt Adolf Loos*, op. cit., pp. 162-163, figs. 222-223.

APARTMENT OF OTTO BECK

Klattaurxerstrasse 12, Pilsen, Czechoslovakia

Otto Beck was a gratings manufacturer and partner of Willy Hirsch for whom Loos had decorated an apartment two years earlier. In Beck's apartment Loos was limited to making alterations to just three rooms: the living room, dining room and bedroom.

1908
1909

The living and dining areas were connected by a wide opening but were at the same time distinguished by the different materials used for the wall paneling. In the living room these were made from white-painted soft wood; in the dining room the panels were of highly polished oak. The large bedroom was lined with panels bearing floral designs.

It would be as well to point out that we find the typical elements that recur in Loos' interiors in this apartment, too, such as the fireplace built from unplastered red bricks in the living room and the lacunar ceiling of the dining room.

BIBLIOGRAPHY

L. MÜNZ, G. KÜNSTLER, *Der Architekt Adolf Loos*, op. cit., section no. 29.
V. BEHALOVA, *Pilsner Wohnungen von Adolf Loos*, in «Bauforum» no. 21, 1970, p. 51 with illustration.

DESIGNS FOR THE TECHNICAL MUSEUM

Vienna

The drawings kept in the Technical Museum were put on show in 1964 at the exhibition dedicated to Loos at the Museum of the 20th Century in Vienna. Loos was appointed consultant for the competition along with Professor Victor Loos, his cousin. From an architectural point of view the sketch presents certain thematic starting points that seem to anticipate morphological aspects of the Looshaus in the Michaelerplatz of 1910.

1908
1909

BIBLIOGRAPHY

L. MÜNZ, G. KÜNSTLER, *Der Architekt Adolf Loos*, op. cit., section no. 27, p. 185.
A. LOOS, *Austellung des Museum des 20. Jahrhunderts*, Vienna 1964.
F. KURRENT, J. SPALT, *Unbekanntes von Adolf Loos*, in «Bauforum» no. 21, 1970, p. 44.

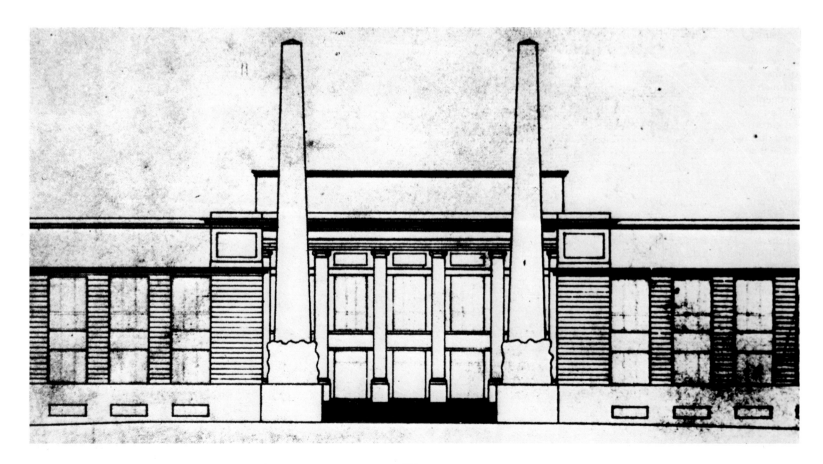

THE LOOSHAUS IN THE MICHAELERPLATZ

Michaelerplatz 3, Vienna 1

1909
1911

«The architectural character of a city is a very special kind of problem. *Each city possesses an individual character*. What seems beautiful and lovable in one city may be ugly and detestable in another.... Not just the materials but the forms as well are bound up with the place, with the nature of the earth and of the air.... I accuse our contemporary architects of consciously setting out to ignore particular architectural character.... The Hofburg! Everything around us can serve as a touchstone to distinguish the true from the false. A new building was to be constructed in the vicinity of the Hofburg, a *modern commercial building*. It involved creating a link between the imperial seat and the noble palace of the most exclusive commercial street in Vienna, the Kohlmarkt.... An attempt has been made to do this. An attempt to harmonize the building with the Hofburg, with the square and with the city» (my italics). [1]

These words outline the logical route that must be followed in order to decipher the meaning of the best-known and most complex of all Loos' works. So the fundamental character of the house in the Michaelerplatz derives from its quality as an element of urban design consciously placed in critical continuity with the historical process of construction of the city. Hence the extreme interest of this modern work of architecture, built in the ancient heart of a metropolis, enunciating as it does certain theorems on the relationship, or rather on the dialectic, between building tradition and the formalization of modern typology, between the memory of a great city and the invention of the new, between the historic past and the future of architecture. In the end this house shows how it is possible to immerse oneself totally in the history of a city without drowning in vulgar mimicry of anachronistic forms. Tradition, adopted as method, permits one to take up the interrupted thread of a search that follows a process of constant renewal of the urban image of a metropolis. [2] And yet, through a real irony of history, this architecture — so deeply rooted in the place, in the Viennese soil and air and today so well accepted by people as to be known simply as the Looshaus — was the subject, during its construction, of a blazing controversy that involved, on one side, municipal councillors like Rykl, Scheider and Neumayer and newspapers such as the «Neue Freie Presse», the «Extrablatt», the «Kikeriki» and on the other, intellectuals like Karl Kraus, poets like Georg Trakl and architects like Paul Engelmann and Otto Wagner. On 21 October 1910, at a meeting of the Municipal Council, the Christian-Socialist Rykl (sculptor, dealer in stone and head of a deputation opposed to the «too simple way of building») opened the hostilities against the «monstrous house», that, in his opinion, disfigured the face of Vienna-capital-of-the-Arts. [3] The true target of the virulent criticism directed against the Looshaus was the simplicity of its architecture without ornament. Before embarking on a critical analysis of the work, it is worth picking out the salient events of the tormented ups and downs in the construction of the Looshaus, as they reveal some largely unknown features that are helpful in understanding the stages in the elaboration of the project. [4]

It was in 1909 that Loos received a commission from the firm of Goldman & Salatsch and from the contractors L. Goldman and E. Aufricht to draw up plans for a commercial building in the Michaelerplatz to replace the previous Dreilauferhaus (1797) that was demolished the same year. [5] The plan was approved and a building permit granted on 11 March 1910. However, the plan was signed not by Loos but by the architect Ernst

Wien in der Karikatur.

XXXVI.

Das Loos-Haus auf dem Michaelerplatz.

Der selige Fischer v. Erlach: Schade, daß ich diesen Stil nicht schon gekannt hab', dann hätt' ich den schönen Platz nicht mit meiner dalkerten Ornamentik verschandelt!»

A contemporary cartoon from "Der Morgen". Fischer von Erlach, the original creator of the Michaelerplatz, in the foreground.

Epstein, director of the works. It should be noted that this first plan differed from the final one by two not insignificant factors: by the presence of a high roof and, above all, by the design of the ornate façade with moldings and friezes. It may be asked if the architect had not fallen into a glaring contradiction, seeing that only two years had passed since he had written the iconoclastic essay *Ornament and Crime*. In the absence of any evidence as to the genuineness of his intentions, it seems a credible hypothesis that this was solely a tactical expedient to accelerate the approval of the plans by the licensing authority. In fact, on 25 July of the same year a modified plan was presented in which all the ornamental plastic shapes had disappeared from the façade to be replaced by a pattern of horizontal lines that calls to mind the technique of calligraphic wall decoration introduced by the Wagnerschule (one thinks of Otto Wagner's Postsparkasse, 1903-1907, or Haus in der Neustiftgasse,1909-1910). In any case, his antiornamental intentions were confirmed by the fact that at the end of September 1910 the building was finished off with smooth surfaces of white plaster, with no sign of the horizontal lines or still less the decorative squares of the first plan. This is why the Municipal Council ordered work suspended, as may be gathered from the newspaper reports of 29 and 30 September 1910. Events entered a heated phase that would end with an obligation to insert «flowers on the windowsills» of this house that wanted to be «mute» on the outside in order to speak the language without qualities of the metropolis. The theme of architecture of the metropolis is the true key to understanding Loos' stubborn determination not to put any ornaments on the white walls pierced at regular intervals by windows of identical shape. [6] «My building in the Michaelerplatz», Loos would write in his essay, *Heimatkunst*, «may be beautiful or ugly, but one characteristic even its detractors must recognize: it is not provincial. It is a building that can stand only in a metropolis (*in einer millionenstadt*).» [7] In the same essay Loos attacks the anachronistic formalism of the *Heimatkünstler* who, seeing the link with the history of a nation in terms of nostalgia for the values of a peasant culture, «wishes to reduce metropolises to small towns and small towns to villages.» [8] For Loos the language of the metropolis is the total absence of ornament. In this sense the final compromise solution —proposed and accepted by Loos himself — of superimposing window boxes in the shape of bronze baskets on the walls does violence to the meaning of the work and should be interpreted as a yielding to the nostalgia for the past. It is an attempt to countrify and make familiar the building of the metropolis. But it is a forced choice imposed by economic reasons that should not be underestimated. In November 1910 — following the denial of a permit of habitability that cost the contractors 18,000 crowns — Ernst Epstein had to design a new façade for the building on the lines of a pencil drawing suggested by the councillor Hans Schneider, the architect of the Technical Museum. The permit was then granted against a caution of 4,000 crowns and the obligation to carry out the modification mentioned above by June 1911. Only the arrival of unforeseen events prevented this «ornamental crime» from being carried out. In fact just before the end of the time limit imposed, that is on 6 May 1911, the contractors announced a competition to find ideas for the façade, a competition that was boycotted by the«Gesellschaft Österreichischer Architekten» (Austrian Association of Architects) on the magnanimous grounds that they considered it «irreconcilable with their view of art to deform the work of a living artist with external tinsel.» This judgment exerted an indirect influence over the attitude of the Municipal Council, marking a turning point in events. In fact, when the agreed period ran out (June 1911) the Council did not go ahead with the realization of the Epstein-Schneider façade but invited the contractors to come up with a new solution. The new plan, probably suggested by Loos himself, was presented on 14 July. On the plan appeared a watercolor representation of the window boxes in the shape of bronze baskets. The proposal was rejected, but on 24 October Loos — watched with great general curiosity — had five flower-holders mounted on the windowsills of the Looshaus and let it be known that approval had not been obtained for such a thoughtful solution.

The attack on the councillors and hostile newspapers was resumed with renewed ardor on 11 December 1911, at a public meeting held in the packed hall of the Sophiensaal, in front of a crowd of more than 2000 people. A few months later (29 March 1912) the Council decided, without debate, to renounce the imposition of the façade designed by Epstein and Schneider, but ordered the placing of similar bronze window boxes on the lateral faces of the building. So comes to an end the difficult battle fought by Loos for the affirmation of a new language against the cultural backwardness of the time; a battle that could be used as a metaphor for the more general difficulties encountered by the modern architect on the threshold of a new era. But it would be grossly oversimplifying matters to interpret the Looshaus solely in terms of the extent to which it anticipated the later movement of Rationalism. The work develops a complexity of themes and of aims in an architecture that in many ways represents an advanced alternative to Rationalism itself.

The first theme is the relation to history. The above-mentioned dialectical relationship between the dimension of memory and the invention of the new is in many ways the main axis of the compositional articulation of the Looshaus. The roots of these dialectics go down into the specific urban site on which the Looshaus stands. In conceiving a commercial building to replace the 18th-century Dreilauferhaus, Loos was faced with a dual problem: to intervene in the process of historical stratification of the design of the city and, at the same time, to give shape to the modern typology of the commercial building. The Michaelerplatz, the point where the original Roman layout of the Augustiner Strasse-Herrengasse axis crosses the Kohlmarkt-Burgtor, had undergone constant historical transformation and only settled into the definitive form, in which it presented itself to Loos in 1909, towards the end of the 19th century (with the demolition of the Burgtheater, 1888, and the construction of the Burgtor, 1890-95, architect F. Kirschner, and of the Herberstein palace, 1897-1898, architect K. Könia). [9] In that period the outstanding architectural elements were essentially three in number: the Hofburg, the Herberstein palace and the Michaelerkirche. Loos adopted a severely critical attitude towards the existing buildings. He clearly refused the late historicism of the Herberstein palace, while accepting the «invitation» of the Hofburg to a curvilinear development of the square by extending this geometric matrix within the arcade of the Looshaus. At the same time he draws a morphological parallel with the neoclassical façade of the Michaelerkirche articulated in a colonnaded pronaos and in smooth white-plastered walls. [10] The columns of the Looshaus therefore play a dual role: they close the volume of the building on a single story of the façade, but at the same time they allow the curved geometry of the windows (now destroyed) to appear on the background (recessed by 3.50 meters). These enwrapping glass sheets reflected the curve of the Hofburg in an almost mirror-like manner. In this way the Looshaus completes the design of the square by setting itself up as a virtual synthesis of the existing buildings.

But the deepest ties of this architecture are to be looked for not only in this relationship with the Hofburg and the square but also with the history of the city of Vienna as a whole. It is no accident that the four stories intended for lodgings are finished with «good old limewash» like the old Viennese houses. In fact, the identity of a city can be recognized by a particular way of paving the streets, as in Berlin, or by the characteristic

shape of the windows, as in Paris, or by the height of the roofs and the color of the unplastered brick, as in Danzig, or again by the nature of the plaster, as in Vienna. Loos demonstrates a conception of a close relationship between architecture and location where by *location* is meant something that goes beyond the simple environmental setting that surrounds it,[11] location understood as memory of a city, as a projection of the evolution of forms in the long history of a city onto an imaginary screen. «And I saw how the ancients had built, and I saw how they, century after century, year after year, had freed themselves from ornament. Therefore I had to take up again from the point at which the chain of development had been broken. One thing I knew: to stay on the track of this development I had to become much more simple.... The house must not hit you in the eye.»[12] In this sense the Looshaus expresses in a new way what we might define — paraphrasing Christian Norberg-Schulz — as the «genius loci.»[13] But whereas the house is the interrupted tradition that dictates the rules of the game, no historical chain exists to which the modern commercial undertaking can be attached. «The old masters could not leave us any model for the modern commercial enter-

model of the «commercial houses» (*Geschäftshäuser*), a pattern typical of large central European cities in which the ground floor and the mezzanine were traditionally intended for commercial activities. In those selfsame years, on the crest of the new technological innovations, a prototype was being established with large plate-glass walls on the bottom stories. In Vienna, Otto Wagner had confirmed this trend with the Ankerhaus (1894-1895) and especially with the Neuman warehouses (1894), giving shape to a new pattern characterized by a design based on, so to speak, an upturned pyramid. This resulted in a sort of semantic distortion, in the sense that the upper floors, less easily noticed, had the greatest richness of form while the lower floors, in direct visual contact, bore a minimum of architectural signs.

Loos turned this model upside down. The memory of his experience of the American metropolis told him that perception of the lower floors of a building is favored by anyone moving along the streets of a big city.[16] An undifferentiated and apparently unlimited grill extends above the «base» of a skyscraper precisely because it is hidden from the distracted perception of the metropolis. This is why Loos adopts the model of the sky-

prise. Just as they could not do so for electric systems. But if they were to come out from their graves, they would certainly know how to find a solution. And not in the sense of the upholsterers who imitate the antique, but new, modern and completely different solutions...»[14] Loos knows well that the «modern bad» is only the mirror image of the «antique bad.» Both these ways of making architecture are vitiated by the absence of thought. Ornament is only the symptom of a sickness of the intelligence that renounces thinking in order merely to «make up» objects.

On the contrary, it is the desire to give form to the modern typology of the commercial house which spurs Loos on to the invention of a new model of architecture. In this invention the memory of classical antiquity and the evocation of the great masters of central European architecture (Fischer von Erlach, Schlüter, Schinkel)[15] are blended with the need for modernity and with his own memories of the American metropolis, the Chicago of L. Sullivan and D.H. Burnham.

The typology to be reinvented for the Michaelerplatz was not that of the large warehouses, the *Warenhäuser* (a typology that evolved in the German cultural setting from the model introduced by Alfred Hessel in the Wertheim warehouses, 1896-1904, in Berlin and reworked with extreme elegance by Joseph Maria Olbrich in the Tietz warehouses, 1906-1908 in Düsseldorf). It was a question, rather, of redesigning the

scraper in its tripartite form of the column (which he will use again in his 1922 project for the «Chicago Tribune») as a pattern for the Haus am Michaelerplatz. The Looshaus may in fact be broken down into three distinct parts:

1) the base, or the first two levels intended for commercial activities, to which corresponds the maximum of semantic expressiveness;

2) the shaft, or the four stories intended for lodgings, whose external surface is scored by window holes at regular intervals;

3) the capital, or the roof set above a strongly jutting cornice which crowns the composition.

An awareness of this division into three parts is a starting point for the architectural analysis of the work. But it is not enough. There is a great deal more! The idea of tripartition is enriched by at least three more architectural intentions which it is useful to draw attention to before starting on an interpretation of the building itself.

a) Otherness. This means the difference between outside and inside — elsewhere expressed in the Steiner House of 1910. Here, however, the diversity is not just between interior and exterior but is projected in an

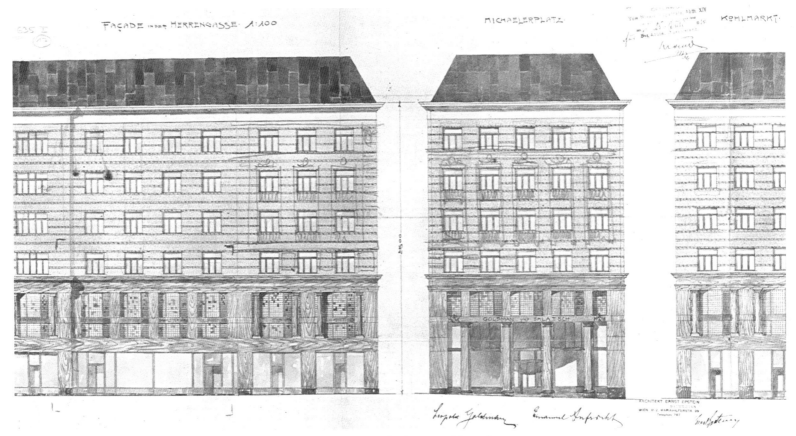

FAÇADE in der HERRENGASSE · 1:100   MICHAELERPLATZ ·   KOHLMARKT ·

Watercolor proposing a brick decoration on the façade (Plan- und Schriftenkammer, Vienna).

The entrance to the apartments.

The stairway to the apartments.

explicit manner (on the inside of the outside itself) onto the screen of the façade, where the materials make a clear distinction between the *ancient* function of the house and the *modern* function of the commercial premises.

b) *Dissociation*, or a lack of congruity between the structural skeleton and the shape of the architecture. Loos hides the supporting structure of reinforced concrete inside an envelope of walls that is given absolute autonomy. In this way the coherence between form and function proper to the idea of *Sachlichkeit* is denied. On the contrary, the form adheres strictly to the character of the architecture of the city of Vienna. The windows of the apartments, for example, mimic the design of old Viennese houses so as to strike deeper roots in the nature of the location. We meet here with an idea that is an alternative to the later theory of *reine Zweckkunst* (pure functional art) and denies, in particular, the fundamental presuppositions of the *moderner Zweckbau* on which Adolf Behne will later base his theories. [17]

c) *Transgression* of the rules of the game. An unexpected component is introduced into Loos' language here: pretence. The columns of the arcade on the ground floor are not load-bearing but only pretend to hold up the mezzanine floor. [18] This is proved by the fact that they were the last part to be assembled and that there is no correspondence of the gaps between the columns with those of the windows on the floors above. Why this apparent «lie»? The most likely answer is that the arcade fulfills a much more important function than one of statics: it realizes architecture as representation of architecture, meaning as a staging of the urban spectacle.

We shall try to look closely at the fundamental stages through which passes the disenchanted game which Loos uses to manipulate the formal materials he has available to him. We will take this toy apart into three pieces. Let us start with the base. The materials that make up the external image of the Goldman & Salatsch Company are marble, bow windows and columns. Cipolin marble from Euboea covers all three faces of the trapezoidal base, wrapping it in a unitary mantle. Loos makes constant external use of marble to denote commercial premises. In this sense it is an unvarying feature of his language. But within the openings in the walls, in the holes that are almost carved out of the stone, the other two recurrent elements mentioned above are joined. The bow window [19] is an explicit quotation from English architecture — introduced into Vienna, consistently with the arguments of the review «Das andere» (1903), as a synonym for civilization and for modernity. This element had already been revived in the architecture of the Chicago skyscrapers (one thinks of D.H. Burnham and J. Root's Reliance Building (1890-95). But it should not be forgotten that it was the *Art Nouveau* movement that brought it back in a modern key to Europe. Examples of this are the bow window used by Victor Horta in the Tassel House in Brussels (1893) and again the one adopted by Max Fabiani in the Artaria House in Vienna (1901), an example which bears closer resemblance to Loos' model.

In a way, the elegant chromatic fusion between the marble of the walls or columns and the glittering brass of the dense squares of the bow window frames still belongs (in spite of all) to the realm of *Art Nouveau*, which developed refined techniques for the assembly of diverse materials that have never been surpassed. Moreover, as in the Villa Karma, the lattice of frames lends an air of intimacy and of protectiveness to the interior — that is to say, the sensation of being inside that derives directly from the pattern — by designing the glass wall as a lattice that closes off the outside. But the architectural element that plays the major part in determining the external image is the column.

The improper use that is made of this archetype here has already been mentioned. Not only are the columns (made of blocks of Cipolin marble) not structural but they do not even respect the syntax of the classical code from which they are drawn. We are faced here with a free and unbiased use of the ready-made object, a use that is closer to the American one (one thinks of the Guaranty Building designed by D. Adler and L.

Plans and section of the Looshaus (Plan- und Schriftenkammer, Vienna).

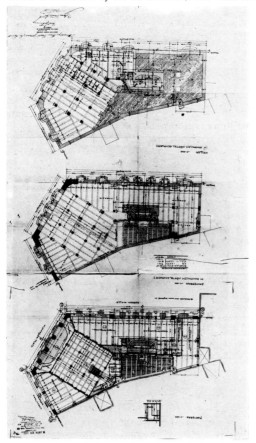
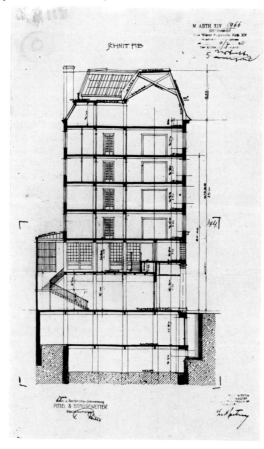
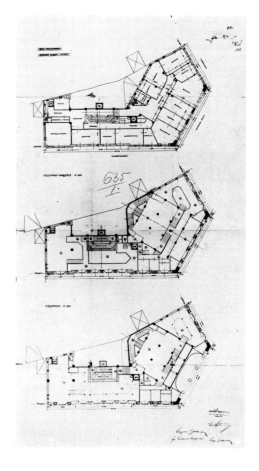

Interiors destroyed in 1938 of Looshaus: Goldman & Salatsch store.

Waiting room of the tailoring department.

Tailors' workshop.

Tailoring school.

Sullivan in Buffalo, 1894-1895) than to the classical German one of Schinkel (in the Altes Museum, 1824-1828, in Berlin, for example). So the theoretical question of the inconsistency of the author of *Ornament and Crime* raises its head again. Is the column of the Looshaus an ornament? Once more the answer is in the negative. The column, here, is not a decorative form, but a symbolic one. It is a symbol of the architecture of the metropolis and it is no coincidence that it will be reproposed for the «Chicago Tribune.» [20] The transgression of the rational rules concerning the perfect congruence of form, function and structure is made here in the name of a desire for a form that transcends banal functionalism in order to acknowledge architecture as a «representation» of the urban scene. This pretence is not a lie in Loos' sense of the word. [21] It is only a use of the symbolic as far away from the later esthetics of the *Neue Sachlichkeit* as it is close to recent trends in American poparchitecture. The journey into the past leads to the future! But if the outside belongs to the city (becomes a part of the agelong stratification of the urban image), the inside belongs to those who live and work there. The independence of the interior from the exterior in the Looshaus reproposes, and takes much further, the *otherness* of inside and outside in the Steiner House.

Yet it is not the private, ancient and conservative function of the house that dictates the shape of the space here, but the modern, public and innovative function of commerce. The plan aims at the commensurability of space. The large panels of the ceiling allow one to see the geometrical matrix of the square plan (subdivided by sixteen regularly spaced pillars) whose upward extension allows a virtual caging of the space within a cubical logico-mathematical lattice. The costly woods which are used to cover the pillars attain to a material elegance that has the abstract quality of geometry. This cubic space is anticipated in the convex space of the flight of stairs. The stairs are a masterpiece of skilled craftsmanship (in the perfection of detail and the elegance of the woods which line the sinusoidal parapet), but they are also an exceptional intrusion of the plastic. The reworked model is typical of Viennese baroque castles (that is, a single flight at the bottom which separates into two lateral branches forming a well of light). But at the rear of the first flight there is a mirror — a constant feature of Loos' vocabulary. Here the mirror plays more than one rôle: not only does it multiply the space — as in the Kärntner Bar — but it also diffuses the light that shines down from a skylight on the ceiling, filtered through a sheet of colored glass that attenuates and softens the intensity of natural light. In order to capture the light from above, the walls enveloping the staircase penetrate the perimeter wall, emerging like a spur into the courtyard behind. The stairs lead to the upper area intended for the workshops, the changing booths and the waiting room for customers. The spatial articulation of this section on three levels is extremely interesting, developing as completely as it does the concept of the *Raumplan*. The height of each room is proportional to its cross section and to its function, but in the end the whole thing is reformed into a unitary shell.

The large workshops are arranged along the side walls (to take advantage of the greater height permitted by the lowering of the floors above the secondary windows) while the fitting rooms, not so high, are situated above the high arcade of the main entrance.

The change in syntax in the second part of the Looshaus intended for living quarters is abrupt, radical and completely without mediation. The difference between the first and the second section is clearly legible in the clean-cut separation of the white shell of the apartments from the marble-clad base of the commercial premises. Loos writes: «White plaster is a skin. Stone is structure. Despite the similarities in their chemical composition, there is a great difference in the way the two materials are used.... When plaster shows itself candidly as a covering for a brick wall, it has as little to be ashamed of in its humble origin as a Tyrolese with his leather trousers in the Hofburg.» [22] So the humble plaster denotes the archaic function of the house. The real reason for the use of this material should be looked for in its ties with tradition rather than in any foretaste of Rationalism. [23] Besides, the Looshaus' links with the history of the city are so strong as to manifest themselves in the very design of the façade where the elementary holes of the windows seem to be a quotation from the «minor» architecture of village houses. Even in the second part of the building the load-bearing structure (with its reinforced concrete frame) could have permitted a freer shape to be given to the windows, arranging them in strips perhaps. Once again, then, there is a dissociation between the traditional form of the exterior and the technical possibilities offered by the reinforced concrete frame.

«Tradition revisited» is visible inside as well, from the very first steps of the flight of stairs leading to the floors intended for apartments. And the reason that it is possible to read his architectural thought in the materials is that everything sayable in the architecture is entrusted to these materials. It is no accident that the steps are of stone (as in old flights of stairs) and the walls of speckled Skyros marble. The continuous and linear serpentine of the banisters made from horizontal tubing emphasizes the fluid canal of the stairs. The multiplicity of materials is in the end fused into a synthesis of opposites. It would be superfluous to comment on the detailed craftsmanship of the work.

Finally, Loos' lack of interest in a rigid typological distribution of the apartments is not a casual one. Each person may arrange his own house as he thinks best. This confirms the otherness of the interior with respect to the exterior. His long experience as an interior designer leads Loos to leave the person who lives there with the freedom to shape his living space according to his own needs. It is obvious that this freedom is linked to the economic status of the well-to-do class for whom the lodgings are intended and that it is not viable in mass-produced housing for workers (where typological study of the apartment plays a fundamental role as the subsequent rationalist experience of the *Existenzminimum* shows). But we do know that Loos will succeed in obtaining a flexible distribution in workers' housing as well in the Siedlung am Heuberg (1920-22), making use of very plain techniques. Distributive freedom in the house is, for Loos, a requirement that can find simple and extremely economical solutions.

The third piece of the Looshaus is the roof. A projecting cornice tops the four white-washed stories. Loos declares on this subject: «It is the Viennese custom to finish off the building with a horizontal line marked by the cornice, without roofs, cupolas, bow windows or other superstructures.... But the roof must be made use of and therefore must house the ateliers and other rentable rooms. Because land is very expensive and taxes are very high. The old architectural character of Vienna has been lost because of these financial problems.» [24] This passage should not be interpreted too literally. Apparently the roof is an unwanted feature forced on him by economic reasons; and to a certain extent this is true as it contradicts the modern character of this house that can only stand in a metropolis. But in this particular case the architectural element of the roof acquires the dignity of a genuine concluding third part. At times it is necessary to take a skeptical attitude towards the architect's words in order to interpret correctly what the architecture itself says. Even if one desires to stick to a faithful interpretation of the written text, one cannot avoid noticing the way it is contradicted by a subsequent paragraph of the same passage in which Loos praises the beauty of this copper roof «which will very soon turn black and will be noticed only on St. John's night by the nightbirds around.» [25] Apart from its external charm it is the very quality of the rooms inside (used as ateliers and covered on the courtyard side by a large area of cascading glass) that puts any doubts to rest about the architectural value of this third and conclusive part of the building.

The tripartite division that is so clearly marked on the façades overlooking the Michaelerplatz is only recomposed into a unitary design in the façades looking out onto the inner courtyard. Here the load-bearing structure remains visible and gives pattern to the dense and strictly

Pastel drawing showing the flower-boxes demanded by the city authorities. (Plan- und Schriftenkammer, Vienna).

functional composition of this wall.

A new inversion of language, then. The dominant element is the reticular cage of the lift whose square lattice extends along the glazed sides of the corridors. The parapet walls are clad in white bricks like those of the courtyard, onto which the window spaces open freely in unconstrained adherence to their function.

It should come as no surprise that this severely functional design contradicts the scenic quality of the walls facing the Michaelerplatz. Otherness, dissociation, transgression, in short, the ambiguous relationship between interior and exterior and between form and structure, are the basic ingredients of this architecture which speaks in a variety of languages. Nothing could be further from the ideology of functionalism, from the *reine Zweckkunst*.

But the most profound quality of the Looshaus lies in its links to the individual character of the architecture of the city. And this is why, if one wants to attempt a conclusive summation of the value of this work, there can be no more fitting words than those that Loos himself wrote in a letter: «Any words that one may happen to read in praise of our old city,

Corner resolve.

Detail of columns.

Inner courtyard.

Detail of front façade.

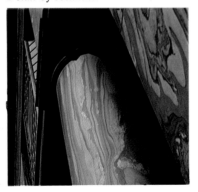

advocating the preservation of its rapidly disappearing image, find a considerably deeper echo in me than in many others. If indeed I had ever been found guilty of a crime perpetrated against this ancient image of the city, such a rebuke would strike me harder than many think. And yet I have designed the house to fit into the square as well as possible.... I have always been under the illusion of having solved this problem in the manner of the old Viennese masters. And this illusion has been confirmed in me by what a modern artist-enemy of mine has said: he wants to be a modern artist and builds a house like the old Viennese houses!» [26]

NOTES

1) A. LOOS, *Sämtliche Schriften*.

2) In numerous essays Loos stresses the important role played by tradition in his method of design, even going so far as to adopt it as a supporting pillar for his architectural «lesson». «So the Adolf Loos school of architecture was born. Instead of the kind of architecture taught at our universities, which consists in part in adapting architectonic styles of the past to the exigencies of present-day life, and in part in the search for a new style, I want to base my teaching on tradition... *The present is built on the past just as the past was built on the times that preceded it*» (my italics), A. LOOS, *Sämtliche Schriften.*.

3) It is worth quoting part of Rykl's statement to the mayor, the rare idiocy of which needs no further comment: «None of the many private buildings that have gone up in recent times has aroused so much scandal and disapproval as the new construction, not yet completed, in the inner city, on the corner of Kohlmarkt and Herrengasse. It is an outrage and an insult to Fischer von Erlach's masterpiece to erect such a construction, shamelessly and in full view, that is void of taste, of architectural sense and of artistic feeling. It is necessary to take a stand and make the strongest protest against architects like this who build without architecture and without ornaments». Cf. typewritten report of the public session of the Municipal Council on 21 October 1910, in «Amtsblatt» Jg. XIX, no. 85.

4) On this subject see the richly documented philological reconstruction made by Hermann Czech and Wolfgang Mistelbauer in the essay *Das Looshaus*, Vienna 1976, from which a great number of the facts reported here are taken.

5) «Well now, one day an unfortunate soul came to me and commissioned me to draw up plans for a house. He was my tailor. This worthy person, though there were in fact two worthy people, had made my clothes for years and had patiently sent me his bill on the first of each year, a bill which, I cannot deny, never got any smaller. I have never been and still am not able to escape the suspicion that I was entrusted with this flattering commission in the hope that my bill would, at least to some extent, be met.... I told these two honest men to beware of me. In vain. They wanted at all costs to get their bill paid — pardon, to entrust the costruction to an artist with the official stamp of approval. I told them: do you really want to bring down the police on people who have had a clean record up till now? They said they did.» A. LOOS, *Sämtliche Schriften*.
   Do not be deceived by the self-mockery of these words. Loos had already carried out one of his first and most famous projects for Goldman and Salatsch, the men's clothing store of 1898. In fact, the esteem in which he was held by these two clients is shown to have been very great indeed by this difficult test. Moreover he received the commission following a competition held by the building contractors Leopold Goldman and Emanuel Aufricht that had not yielded any positive result. Loos had not taken part in this competition — notwithstanding Kulka's statement to the contrary, op. cit., p. 30.

6) «The task of the modern architect is the Metropolis». It is significant that Otto Wagner's important essay entitled «Moderne Architektur» (in three successive editions of 1895, 1899 and 1901, and a fourth in 1914 under the title *Die Baukunst unserer Zeit*) turns on this statement. This is the essay which introduced the theme of modern architecture to Vienna. As is known Loos took a critical attitude towards Wagner's architectural theory and, in opposition to the «new style», set up America as an alternative tabula rasa to the decadent formalism of the *Secession*. But this very attack (one thinks of the essay *Die potemkinsche stadt* 1898, published in the review «Ver Sacrum», organ of the *Secession*) provides further confirmation of the central importance the theme of architecture in the metropolis assumes, not only in Loos' theoretical reflections, but also more generally for the intellectual architects who worked in the Vienna of the *finis Austriae*.

7) A. LOOS, *Sämtliche Schriften*.

8) Ibid.

9) In particular the Burgtheater was demolished in 1888 and the construction of the Burgtor (the work of the architect F. Kirschner) was completed in 1890 and that of the Herberstein palace (work of the architect K. Könia) between that of 1897 and 1898. Yet the first works involving radical alterations to the fortified Burg that was built in the 13th century date back to the beginning of the 18th century as may be seen from the projects of Joseph Emanuel Fischer von Erlach (son of Johann Bernhard), of Balthasar Neuman, of Jadot de Vilce-Issey, of Nicolaus Pacassi. Between 1723 and 1725 J.E. Fischer von Erlach (known as the younger) built the riding school in the Michaelerplatz that was to make up the left flank of the façade of the Burg. Cf. H. Czech, W. Mistelbauer, op. cit., pp. 9-17.

10) Loos himself made this clear when he wrote: «The style of the church which formed the *pendant* of the new construction was the decisive factor for me.» A. LOOS, *Sämtliche Schriften*.

11) I refer in particular to the definition of «location» or «place» given by Christian Norberg-Schulz in *Il concetto di luogo*, «Controspazio», no. 1, 1969. By the same author see also *Intentions in Architecture*, Cambridge, Mass., 1965.

12) A. LOOS, in *Sämtliche Schriften*.

13) Christian Norberg-Schulz, «Genius Loci», in «Lotus» no. 13, 1976.

14) A. LOOS, *Sämtliche Schriften*.

15) «But every time architecture strays from its model at the prompting of the minor architects, the decorativists, the great architect appears to lead it back to antiquity». The reference to the «grandeur of classical antiquity» and to the above-mentioned masters of European architecture is made in the final part of the essay *Architektur*, op. cit., p. 256.

16) Cf. the chapter of this book entitled *America*.

17) The theory of «pure functional art» (*reine Zweckkunst*) was formulated in those same years within the *Werkbund* (an association of artists, architects and industrialists founded in 1907). It will undergo further critical developments until it becomes a fundamental current in German Rationalism as may be evinced from the volume compiled by A. BEHNE, *Der moderne Zweckbau* (1923).

18) It is interesting to note that Loos never refers to these columns' lack of any structural function.

19) I use the more common term of bow windows (as used by Loos) to indicate the glazed projecting balcony typical of English architecture. In more technical terms the form used by Loos in the Michaelerplatz would be called a bay window, and not bow window, as it is not curved in shape but angular. Nevertheless the word bow window, because of its common use in ordinary language, may be used in a wider sense, and I saw no reason to modify the term used by Loos himself.

20) On this subject see the report on the project for the «Chicago Tribune». A. LOOS, *Die «Chicago Tribune» Column* in «Zeitschrift des Österr. Ingenieur- und Architekten-Vereines», 1923, vol. 75, no. 34.

21) «Art has nothing to do with falsification, with the *lie*». A. LOOS, *Sämtliche Schriften*.

22) A. LOOS, *Sämtliche Schriften*.

23) Besides, even J. Hoffmann in the Purkersdorf Sanatorium (1903) had reduced the walls to simple planes of white plaster. But there, the rows of bricks in blue white squares (that emphasize the borders of the planes) reveal an architectonic intention that is a forerunner of the neoplastic decomposition of volumes into planes, an intention that has nothing to do with Loos' love for the tradition of simplicity, of the right to be obvious.

24) A. LOOS, *Sämtliche Schriften*.

25) Ibid.

26) A. LOOS, *Sämtliche Schriften*.

BIBLIOGRAPHY

H. WITTMANN, *Das Haus gegenüber der Burg*, in «Neue Freie Presse», Vienna 4 December 1910.
K. MARILAUN, *Das Haus auf dem Michaelerplatz*, in «Reichspost», Vienna 15 December 1910.
O. STOESSL, *Das Haus auf dem Michaelerplatz*, in «Die Fackel», Vienna, no. 317-318, 3 March 1911.
H. KULKA, *Adolf Loos*, op. cit., figs. 44-50 with captions.
F. GLÜCK, *Die Gefährdung des Loos-Hauses auf dem Michaelerplatz*, in «Wiener Zeitung» 19 January 1936.
L. MÜNZ, *Adolf Loos*, op. cit., p. 37 et seq.
A. ROSSI, *Adolf Loos, 1870-1933*, in «Casabella», no. 233, November 1959, p. 8.
H. LORENZ, *Adolf Loos: Das Haus am Michaelerplatz; Aufnahmearbeit am Kunsthistorischen Institut der Universität Wien*, op. cit., Manuscript, 1963.
L. MÜNZ, G. KÜNSTLER, *Der Architekt Adolf Loos*, op. cit., pp. 93-108, figs. 98-112.
H. CZECH, W. MISTELBAUER, *Das Looshaus*, in «Der Aufbau», Vienna 1964, pp. 172-176.
H. CZECH, W. MISTELBAUER, *Das Looshaus*, in «Bau», Vienna, 1 September 1970, pp. 8-11.
B. SCHOCK-WERNER, *Das Loos-Haus am Michaelerplatz und andere Grossprojekte von Adolf Loos*; Seminarreferat am Kunsthistorischen Institut der Universität Wien, 1974.
H. CZECH, W. MISTELBAUER, *Das Looshaus*, Vienna 1976 (contains an ample bibliography of the newspapers and reviews involved in the story of the Looshaus).

KNIŽE STORE

Graben 13, Vienna 1 (the store has remained substantially in its original form)

1909
1913

«I am all for traditional architecture. A building typical of the Graben is that of the Savings Bank. After the construction of this building tradition has been abandoned. And at what point should we take it up again? Have there been any changes? Oh, yes! The same changes that have created the new culture. No one can repeat a work. Every day, man creates something new and the new man is not capable of repeating what has been created by his predecessor. He thinks he is repeating the same work, but it turns out to be something new. Perhaps something imperceptibly new, but from the distance of a century one can tell.» [1]

Loos wrote this in 1914 (the year after the construction of the Kniže Store on the Graben), propounding the links with the «memory of the city» as a parameter and guide for a modern method of planning. Although Loos never formulated an abstract and comprehensive model for intervention in the city, he always showed a strong interest in the network of urban relationships in his actual practice of planning and in his essays. In this sense, the work may be seen as a fragment of an articulate and integral urban plan aimed at a continuity in progress of the collective culture of building.

The still up-to-date elegance of the external and internal articulation of the Kniže Store is based on a deep intuition: the overthrow of the myth of modernity as a shiny novelty, as the fashion of the moment, and therefore, recognition of invention as an imperceptible work, as a discreet manipulation of new techniques of construction, a work that is detectable only at a distance in time.

The first thing to be noticed is the containment or, if you prefer, the «freezing» of invention within the balanced play of the masses of shiny black Swedish granite that make up the façade. Along with this goes the refinement of recessing slightly the panes of the shop windows accompanied by the plastic rounding of the pillars that leaves it up to their sharply edged shadows to mark the geometrical distances between the surfaces of the composition. In their turn the very slender frames of reddish cherry wood (that support the sheets of glass) clearly outline the transparent planes within the dark space of the entrance.

The use of granite also throws light on an invariant of Loos' language of materials: the theory of design through repetition, based on the economy of architectural work which tends towards the perfecting of techniques from an essentially unitary point of view. The reproposition of the «ready-made» should not be understood in a historical sense alone — as the passage quoted above explains — but should also be extended to the internal interpretation of all of Loos' work.

On the other hand it is not a question of simple repetition but of continual progress in a fully conscious evolutionary process, free from the prejudices of creative narcissism. For example, the technique of rounding the stone pillars had already been tried out in the dining room of the Karma (1904-1906). But for Loos, self-quotation is never self-congratulation. The repetition of this element produces something substantially new in the *other* context, in this case external, of the Kniže Store. It is no accident that the external image of all Loos' stores is represented by semiprecious stone, a material that is by definition immutable. This is a constant factor that should not be underestimated.

Loos recognizes the city to be the preferred center for the exchange and distribution of goods, and the store, to an even greater extent, to be the place fixed for consumption. But in Loos' eyes the rapid consumption of goods is only the negative result of the new *Zeitgeist*. His criticism of the way that *Zivilisation* turns the utilitarian value of goods into their value as goods of exchange is unequivocal on this point. The heavy sarcasm with which he attack the fashion of the fop as well as the decoration of utilitarian objects undoubtedly arises out of a desire to preserve the long-lasting quality of objects.

Hence the challenge of this solid architecture of stone, of this elegant, blasé architecture that is indifferent to rapid fluctuations of taste and that contrasts the permanency of its forms with the disintegration of the goods that it houses.

This aspiration to the immutability of forms is at the same time the matrix that gives shape to the internal space. Here it is oak (the material chosen for all the wooden accessories) that imposes the solidity of the forms. One detail that should not be left out is that of the capitals of the wooden columns, columns which cannot be seen as mere decorative elements since they have a clear symbolic function. They denote the *Klassizismus* at which the entire composition of the interior is aimed. A modern, not a nostalgic classicism, as is demonstrated by the magnificent helical staircase that leads to the back of the shop on the upper sales floor.

Façade today.

First floor today.

Four views of the interior today.

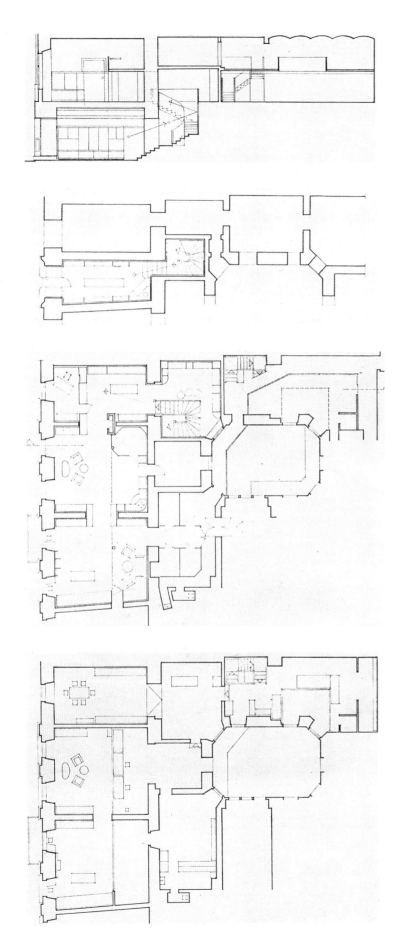

In this case it is cherry, a softer wood, that covers the plastic shape of the solid railing. Seen from above, the image of the stairs plunges, so to speak, into the mirror on the wall of the landing that optically prolongs the descent into infinity. Thus the mirror is a destabilizing element. It insinuates the doubt of «pretence», that is to say, of visual show. But to be sure, all the architecture of the Kniže Store plays on contradictions in the materials, blending the transparency of sheets of glass with the rigidity of black granite on the façade, just as it blends the solidity of the wooden structure with the unpredictability of mirrored reflections on the inside.

NOTES

1) A. LOOS, *Sämtliche Schriften.*

BIBLIOGRAPHY

H. KULKA, *Adolf Loos*, op. cit., figs. 58-61 with captions.
L. MÜNZ, G. KÜNSTLER, *Der Architekt Adolf Loos*, op. cit., pp. 29-30, figs. 9-11.
D. WORBS, *Kniže — Beschreibung und Analyse eines Herrenmodengeschäftes von A. Loos* (1909), in «Bauforum», no. 21, 1970, pp. 26-28.

Left: section and plans of three different levels.
Below: an early photograph of the façade.

DESIGNS FOR THE REORGANIZATION OF THE KARLSPLATZ

Vienna

Although they are only rapid pencil sketches, drawn untidily on loose sheets, these two designs for the reorganisation of the Karlsplatz are of considerable importance. They are evidence of Loos' interest in architectural planning on an urban scale and, above all, an indication of the method involved in his technique of intervention in the historic city.

The occasion probably arose out of a Competition of Ideas for the construction of the Kaiser Franz Josef-Stadt-Museum which brought up again the problem of redesigning the entire Karlsplatz, an action that had been favored for some time by the mayor of Vienna, Karl Lueger. Among those who took part was Otto Wagner, who had already built the famous underground railway station in the Karlsplatz. He presented a model as well as technical studies. Loos abstained from the competition, but not from drawing up design proposals — as these sketches show; sketches which, if you overlook the fragmentary nature of the graphics, demonstrate a rare lucidity of design.

There are two fundamental methodological principles that may be deduced from them:
1) the use of the existing historic material to generate the morphological structure in which the new links up with the old;
2) the definition of a precise hierarchy of form between the elements to be combined, on the basis of a judgment of their value.

The Karlskirche — built between 1717 and 1739 by J.B. Fischer von Erlach — is adopted as the focal point for a new perspective given by two parallel blocks of buildings with plain façades. In reality one of the two blocks represented the mirror image of the other, already in existence, that included the neoclassical façade of the *Technische Hochschule*. The semantic neutralization of the façades (designed with simple arcades that hollow out their volumes at the base) serves to give the greatest possible formal value to the church. But to favor the dominance of a monument over the urban fabric and to define a syntactic order in the town-planning «discourse» is perhaps the modern translation of a late-baroque technique of designing the city.

The reference to an idea of Charles VI is explicit. The modern variant consists in the acceptance of the constructed, i.e. of the historical stratification laid down by earlier building along the Ringstrasse. This clarifies

1909

the «Proclamation to the citizens of Vienna» written by Loos on the occasion of the death of Karl Lueger (10 March 1910).

«The guardian of the Karlskirche will be buried today in the person of Dr. Lueger. He revived Charles VI's idea of making the church the terminal point of a wide avenue that would go from the Schottentor to the Wieden, passing through the Josefplatz.

«The building in the Ringstrasse put an end to his idea.

«The original grandiose plan can no longer be realized. We have very little right to disapprove of the builders of the Ringstrasse. After all, we ourselves have abandoned the idea of Maria Teresa, who wanted her descendants to have the possibility of following the Praterstrasse right into the heart of the city center, by putting up blocks of buildings.

«Lueger and all those who have judgment wished to give the Karlskirche what it deserved and what it needed.

«The Karlskirche needs to be set between horizontal surfaces and long lines. These could only be provided by a public building.» [1]

From this passage we can deduce three further guiding principles that regulate Loos' method of urban intervention. These are the evolutionistic conception of the process of historical construction of the city, the equal value of green areas and built-up areas as elements of urban architecture and the restriction of imaginative display on the façades of individual buildings in favor of the more ambitious creation of new, wide urbanistic gestures.

NOTES

1) A. LOOS, *Aufruf an die Wiener*, in *Trotzdem* in *Sämtliche Schriften I*, p. 291; L. MÜNZ, G. KÜNSTLER, *Der Architekt Adolf Loos*, op. cit., p. 160.

BIBLIOGRAPHY

Catalog of the Würthle Galerie, Vienna 1961, fig. 3.
L. MÜNZ, G. KÜNSTLER, *Der Architekt Adolf Loos*, op. cit., pp. 159-163, figs. 220-221.

PROJECT FOR A HOTEL
Vienna 1

The dominant theme of the composition is the contrast between the **1909** volumetric mass in the background and the emptying of it made possible by the neoclassical expedient of the twin column. In this sense it expands on a compositional starting point taken from the project for the War Ministry of 1907. It should be noted finally that, with provision made for shops on the ground floor and for a wide rooftop terrace with pergolas, the project prefigures a typological scheme developed further by Loos in his later hotel designs.

BIBLIOGRAPHY

L. MÜNZ, G. KÜNSTLER, *Der Architekt Adolf Loos*, op. cit., section no. 30, p. 186 with illustrations.

APARTMENT OF JULIUS BELLAK
Kohlmessergasse 8, Vienna 1

A step backward, as far as the control over materials shown in previous **1909** works is concerned, is what marks this decoration of questionable taste. **1913** Even the use of the veining of Cipolin marble to obtain a design on the walls — a decorative technique widely used by Loos — achieves in this case effects that are almost grotesque. The horizontal positioning of the veining in the architrave, for example (above a picture of a Dutch landscape built into a wall of the same size), is on the borderline of kitsch if it is true — as has been claimed — that it hints at a visual continuity with the cloudy sky of the painting.

The juncture between walls and ceiling is closed by a fake frieze in an imitation late-Roman style — an anachronistic «tattoo» — and small bronze lions' heads spurt thin jets of water from their mouths into a marble basin sunk into the floor and surrounded by flowerpots. The furniture completes the pathetically luxurious image of the room.

BIBLIOGRAPHY

H. KULKA, *Adolf Loos*, op. cit., fig. 37 with caption.
L. MÜNZ, G. KÜNSTLER, *Der Architekt Adolf Loos*, op. cit., p. 55, fig. 31.

PROJECT FOR AN ESTATE OF TERRACED HOUSING
Vienna

The location is uncertain. This is a recently discovered project, where **1909** blocks of houses are set around the edges of a square at the center of which stands an equestrian statue. It was probably intended for a Jewish quarter. The most interesting feature of this project is the building pattern of terraced houses, a typology that Loos returns to and develops with greater architectural force in the Scheu House of 1912.

BIBLIOGRAPHY

B. RUKSCHCIO, *Studien zu Entwürfen, Projekten und ausgeführten Bauten von Adolf Loos, 1870-1930*, op. cit., WH.H. 67.09. P.
B. RUKSCHCIO, *Adolf Loos zum 110. Geburtstag* in «Bauforum» 81, 1980, p. 11.

STEINER HOUSE

St. Veitgasse 10, Vienna 13

(the façade on St. Veitgasse has been so radically tampered with, the original curved and plated roof having been replaced by a pitched roof, that it is almost unrecognizable. The interior has also been subjected to substantial alterations)

1910

Built in the same year as the essay *Architektur* was published (1910), Hugo Steiner's house is one of Loos' most significant and well-known works. Because of its severe and advanced modernity of form it has been adopted in the histories of contemporary architecture as an example of the phase of transition and an anticipation of the language of Rationalism.

In this view certain aspects have been stressed, such as functional coherence, the absence of ornaments, spatial economy, use of the flat roof on the garden side, the reduction of the external image to a pure white shell. All these aspects are undoubtedly present in the work and, moreover, exerted an unquestionable influence on the stylistic revolution of the postwar years. But, in emphasizing the elements of anticipation, the evolutionistic interpretation has shown its limits, leaving unexplored the theoretical weight and specifics of methodology of Loos' design, which it reduces to a trivial search for functional solutions. One far from negligible fact that it fails to grasp is that the surprising modernity of the Steiner House is the result not so much of a process of abstraction as of an updated reproposition of building techniques that have been tested out by a long tradition. Proof of this is afforded by just those elements that appear to be the newest ones, such as the total absence of decoration on the outside walls (in fact, plastered with simple lime mortar like the old Viennese houses) or the use of the curved sheet-metal roof (in its turn drawn from the local historical building culture).

In short, the disruptive and innovative character of this work derives from an analytical and selective reflection on history, and not yet from the desire for the denial of history on which the Bauhaus will build its theories after the war, and still less from an adherence to functionalism.

Instead, the curved sheet-metal roof — the most marked architectural feature of the St. Veitgasse façade — has more often than not been interpreted as a simple expedient made necessary by the constraints of the building regulations then in force in the residential district of Hietzing. These regulations — as recorded by L. Münz and G. Künstler — laid down that the height of the street façade should not exceed one story (to be exact: one story plus the elevation of the ground floor), while those relating to the side overlooking the garden were less restrictive. [1] Wishing to make the greatest possible use of the legally permitted dimensions, Loos had, in the authors' opinion, «split» the building into two sections of different heights creating three stories on the side of the garden. As a consequence, the curve of the attic represents the link between the two heights of the building. This interpretation could be developed further along these lines, taking in other elements attesting to the functional severity of the work. But there would not be much point to this.

Behind its apparent coherence, the Steiner House develops a linked series of conceptual antinomies to such a degree that it could be taken as a complete manifestation of the language of difference, Loos' technique of architectural expression that will never fit neatly into the methodological confines of the *reiner Zweckbau* or, in a broader sense, of the postwar architectural trend that has been given the name Rationalism. Following the theoretical guidelines laid down in his essay *Architektur*, this work, in fact, shows the unmitigated presence of antitheses such as those between private and public, inside and outside, rational and irrational.

The most obvious architectural translation of these problems is that of the high degree of *otherness* between the interior (so to speak, positive) and the exterior (so to speak, negative). «On the outside the building must remain dumb and reveal all its richness only on the inside,» Loos will write in an essay of 1914. [2]

In line with this assumption, the exterior of the Steiner House undergoes a sort of semantic annihilation. This results in an unusual linguistic separation between the silent coolness of the shell and the warm welcome of the space it encloses. The exterior does not say, on the contrary it conceals, contradicts what it contains within it. The motivation for this reticence lies in the theoretical need to distinguish, to separate the public sphere cleanly from the private one.

The exterior belongs to the city, to civilization. The interior belongs to the private individual.

The nudity «without qualities» of the façade marks out the house as a purely utilitarian object immersed in the anonymous flow of the tools of collective existence. If civilization «is synonymous with liberation from ornament,» then the self-censorship of any erotic and decorative excess on the external walls, the public walls, becomes necessary. The choice of materials and forms must answer to strictly logical reasons here. Outside, in fact, rules technique, understood as the historical consequence of an age-old collective culture.

The very syntactic inconsistency of design between the various faces of the house enters into this logic. The exterior is marked, in its turn, by a contradictory variety of design schemes. One notes the pronounced diversity of codes of composition between the face looking onto the garden (*classical* in its perfect balance between voids and solids with respect to an axis of bilateral symmetry), the two lateral faces (*ungrammatical* in their openings empirically arranged in correspondence with the interior) and the façade overlooking the St. Veitgasse (*dissymmetrical* in the measured play between openings of different sizes).

Symmetry and asymmetry: here is another conceptual dichotomy developed by the Steiner House, the equilibrium between a return to the «unsurpassable grandeur of classical antiquity» and transparent adherence to the empirical quality of Anglo-Saxon culture.

But *Nihilismus* comes to a halt at the threshold of the house. Inside, the dialogue is turned completely on its head. The statement «The room must appear welcoming, the house livable-in» [3] finds a clear architectural demonstration here. The wall separates the individual from the social, sheltering his own experience and the memory of his values within the intimacy of the room. The aspiration to habitability is the secret of Loos' interiors.

And the adjective *welcoming* is what best describes the character of the large family living room on the ground floor. This is a single room that occupies the entire raised ground floor and that sums up in itself the main functions of domestic living: eating, talking and playing and listening to music. The oak of the beams left visible on the ceiling and of the high paneling that lines the walls gives something of a monochromatic cast to the setting that is broken only by the red of the unplastered brick that appears at intervals between the wooden panels and by the white of the strip of plaster that separates them from the ceiling.

It is true, however, that the image of the room as a whole is not typical of central European residences of the period. An influence that derives from cultures outside Europe may be detected. Expressive of this is a statement made by Loos himself and quoted by Kulka: «The plan of a room, nowadays, is centrifugal under the influence of the Japanese. The furniture is arranged at the corners of the room, not at an angle, but straight. The center is empty, a space for movement.» [4] A careful morphological analysis lays bare the signs of an acceptance of the American influence of H.H. Richardson. Even more than the details (such as the open brickwork and rafters, the lights hung from the ceiling, the rough look to the design of the furniture), it is the architectonic concept of spatial continuum that attests to the refined evocation of the house of the American pioneer.

It is only in this sense, that is to say, only on the strength of a common matrix in Richardson's work, that certain analogies can be found with the interiors of the contemporary houses of Frank Lloyd Wright. But these similarities do not go beyond a few superficial features. Wright's organic projection of space outward in many directions constrasts strongly with Loos' conception of centrifugal space deliberately contained within a rigidly stereometrical box of walls. In short, the hint of foreign cultures is passed through a filter of European tradition. This results in an original line of research that seems instead to prefigure the idea of the *free plan*. An example of this is provided by the generative geometry of the space that is clearly legible in the plan. It is a cross section with a severely geometric perimeter, where the distributive subdivision of the rooms relies on functional elements like staircases, service blocks or structural pillars.

One last aspect that should be pointed out is the standard of spatial economy adhered to by making an intensive use of the tiny rooms carved out of the space beneath the roof and others between the main two rooms of the house, which are intended for sleeping quarters.

In conclusion, a further thematic motif of this «architecture of difference» is developed in the way that the complexity of the internal articulation of space is in deliberate contrast to the external volumetric distribution, a contrast that is profoundly alien to the linear coherence of naive Rationalism.

NOTES

1) Cf. L. MÜNZ, G. KÜNSTLER, *Der Architekt Adolf Loos*, op. cit., pp. 72-73.

2) A. LOOS, *Sämtliche Schriften*.

3) A. LOOS, *Sämtliche Schriften*.

4) H. KULKA, *Adolf Loos*, op. cit., p. 28.

BIBLIOGRAPHY

H. KULKA, *Adolf Loos*, op. cit., figs. 39-43 with captions.
L. MÜNZ, *Adolf Loos*, op. cit., p. 37.
L. MÜNZ, G. KÜNSTLER, *Der Architekt Adolf Loos*, op. cit., pp. 72-79, figs 64-70.
G.C. ARGAN, *L'arte moderna 1770-1970*, Florence 1970, pp. 267-270.
R. DE FUSCO, *Storia dell'architettura contemporanea*, Bari 1974, pp. 174-175.

Side and back elevations (Plan- und Schriftenkammer, Vienna).

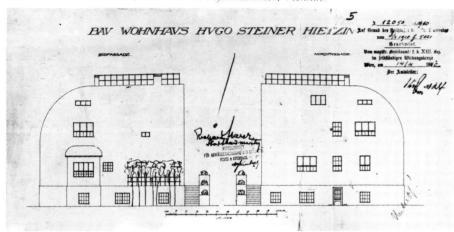

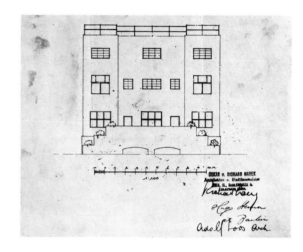

An early picture of the house from the garden.

Ground floor stairway.

Study.

Rear elevation.

141

PROJECT FOR A DEPARTMENT STORE

Alexandria, Egypt

An unusual project, this, for a department store in Alexandria, but one so dear to Loos that he kept it jealously in his house right up to his death. It is represented by a watercolor made by his pupil R. Wells that is kept today in the Adolf Loos room of the Historical Museum of Vienna.

From a strictly typological point of view it has nothing essentially new to offer nor does it present any motifs of special interest. In some ways it is even a step backward with respect to the innovative process set in motion in this planning sector by the Warenhaus Wertheim (Berlin 1896) designed by Alfred Messel.

The line of research does in fact get sidetracked from the technical problem to the definition of form. This is probably also due to the limits of a rough design. But the whole thing seems to come down to a simple substitution of the neo-gothic stylistic features of the new «cathedrals of consumption» by a classicist *bricolage* in which Hellenistic reminiscences are mixed up with allusions to Pharaonic architecture. Revisiting the past seems — in this case — not to result in an updating of history, but in the mere salvage of a heap of archaeological exhibits.

And yet this building at Alexandria merits special critical attention fot two main reasons. First because it is a prototype — the paradigm of the compositional scheme for terraced buildings — reused many times in different versions from the Scheu House in 1912 to the Fleischner House

1910

in 1931. It shows the unconfessed origin of a constantly reproposed idea of architecture to have been the influence of the ancient Orient.

Second, because it is an architectural work that inquires into the role and the meaning of monumentality. Its closed, monolithic form condenses, increasing or reducing the scale, several archetypal models (the column, the pyramid, the peristyle) saturated, as such, in atemporal symbolic values. In this sense, it is a kind of «archive of symbols» which we will find again, expressed in different syntactic combinations and also isolated in their own semantic autonomy, every time that symbolic representation is required by a monumental theme.

This happens, for example, in the Mausoleum for Max Dvořák (1921, in which it is the pure compositional block that is revived) or in the «Chicago Tribune» Column (which typifies the process of extrapolation and expansion in size of single elements).

BIBLIOGRAPHY

Der Architekt, Vol. XIX, Vienna 1913.
L. MÜNZ, *Adolf Loos*, op. cit., p. 38 and illustrations.
L. MÜNZ, G. KÜNSTLER, *Der Architekt Adolf Loos*, op. cit., pp. 111-112, fig. 130.

ALTERATIONS TO GOLDMAN HOUSE

Hardtgasse 27-29, Vienna 19

As well as decorating Leopold Goldman's apartment Loos also carried out some alterations to his mansion. The plans drawn up for these alterations are on file to this day at the *Plan- und Schriftenkammer des Magistrats der Stadt Wien*. There are, to be exact, two projects, one dated 1909 and the other, the final version, dated 1910. The extent of the alterations may be deduced from these. Loos was responsible for the helical flight of stairs and, in all likelihood, for the redesigning of the entrance, marked by Tuscan columns that have obvious similarities in shape to those used for the arcade of the Looshaus in the Michaelerplatz, built over the same period.

As far as the decorations are concerned, at least the quality of the materials should be mentioned. Cipolin marble was used to line the walls of the dining room and mahogany coupled with white-painted wood for the living room.

1910
1911

Main portico now.

BIBLIOGRAPHY

H. KULKA, *Adolf Loos*, op. cit., figs. 35-36 with captions.
L. MÜNZ, G. KÜNSTLER, *Der Architekt Adolf Loos*, op. cit., section no. 28, p. 186.
B. RUKSCHCIO, *Studien zu Entwürfen, Projekten und ausgeführten Bauten von Adolf Loos 1870-1933*, op. cit., p. 79, W.V. H. 73.10, W.V. W.81.11.

Plan of the alteration.

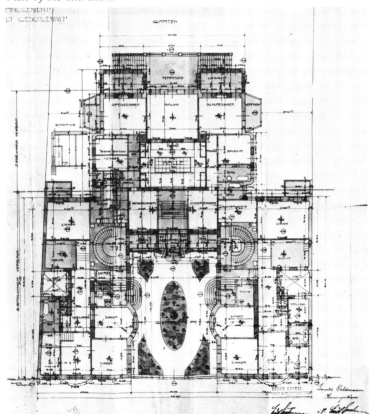

The stairwell today.

ALTERATIONS TO EPSTEIN HOUSE

Hardtgasse 25, Vienna 19

In the same year as the alterations to Goldman House, Loos redesigned **1910** the staircase and the front door of the Epstein mansion, situated only a few meters away along the Hardtgasse. The work was. therefore, of limited extent, but clearly recognizable all the same by its quality and its characteristics as a *gestalt*.

The large «English» front door is characteristic, with its oak-paneled frame, cut-glass windows and brass handrails. So are the stone steps of the flight of stairs whose outline faithfully imitates the form used in the Looshaus in the Michaelerplatz. The design of the banisters is of great refinement in its simplicity, where the curve of the brass handrails emphasizes the curvilinear matrix of the stairs. The finishing touches to the flooring of the entrance, playing on the contrast between black and white marble, and the brass lamps complete the tone of sober quality that he has given to the environment.

It should be pointed out, finally, that the plan of the alterations, still kept in the archives of the *Plan- und Schriftenkammer des Magistrats der Stadt Wien*, is signed by the architect Ernst Epstein. This does not belie its attribution to Loos, however; on the contrary it backs it up to some extent, since Epstein is known to have signed the plans for the Looshaus in the Michaelerplatz that were drawn up in the same year.

BIBLIOGRAPHY

B. RUKSCHCIO, *Studien zu Entwürfen, Projekten und ausgeführten Bauten von Adolf Loos 1870-1930*, op. cit., WV. H. 72.10.

Original plans for the alteration (Plan- und Schriftenkammer, Vienna).

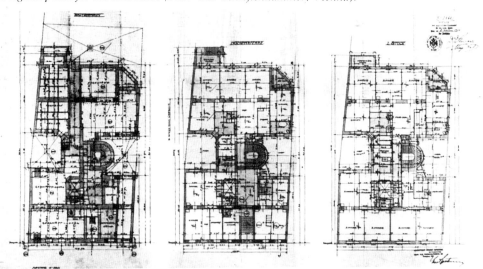

Groundfloor staircase.

Stairwell.

ALTERATIONS TO STOESSL HOUSE

Matrasgasse 20, Vienna 13

Only a few of the original elements of Loos' work remain on the outside, such as the door space hollowed out diagonally from the wall.

1911
1912

This design may be considered a genuine anticipation of the one used in 1928 for the front door of Moller House. So we find the principle of *repetition* of elements of composition confirmed yet again as an «unvarying» method of design in Loos' work.

All that can be said about the interior is that it has been substantially transformed in the course of subsequent redecorations.

BIBLIOGRAPHY

B. RUKSCHCIO, *Studien zu Entwürfen, Projekten und ausgeführten Bauten von Adolf Loos 1870-1933*, op. cit., pp. 84-87, W.V. H.78.11.

North façade today.

Original proposals for the alteration (Plan- und Schriftenkammer, Vienna).

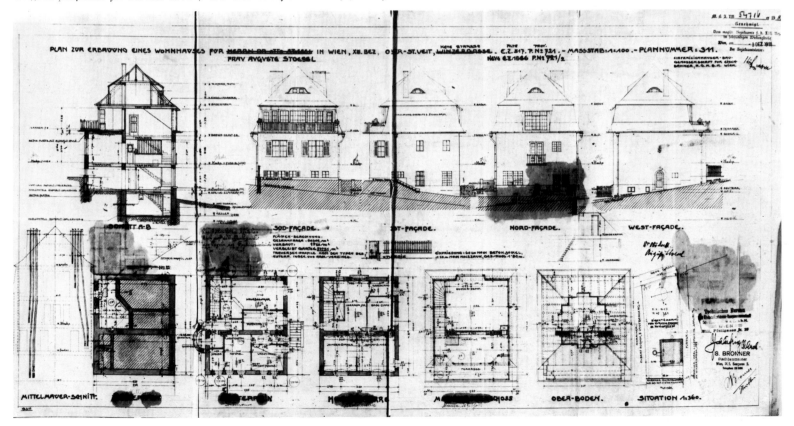

SCHEU HOUSE

Larochegasse 3, Hietzing, Vienna 13

1912

«Years ago I built the house of Dr. Gustav Scheu in Hietzing, Vienna. It aroused general disapproval. It was thought that this type of building would have been fine in Algiers, but not in Vienna. I had not even thought of the East when I built this house. I just thought that it would be pleasant to be able to step out onto a large common terrace from the bedrooms located on the first floor. In Vienna just as much as in Algiers. So this terrace, repeated on the second floor (a rented apartment), represented something unusual, abnormal even. One person went to the Municipal Council to ask if this type of building was permitted by the law.» [1]

In this passage Loos clearly picks out the central factor of the revolution in technique and form that the Scheu House introduces into the architectural culture of the time. To build a terraced house, and moreover one with a flat roof, in a central European setting meant to go against the conventional image of local architecture. Hence the extreme interest shown in this first terraced building built by Loos, a building that consciously sets out to create a foreign air in the urban context in which it is located. As is well-known the «question of the flat roof», for reasons that went well beyond the merely technical aspect, became one of the most hard-fought battle lines in the struggle of Rationalist architects for the achievement of a modern language. [2] But what matters more is that this work is a practical demonstration of Loos' technique for intervention in the city. In fact, on one hand the Scheu House confirms in the bareness of its walls the argument already expressed in the Steiner House that the exterior of the architectural work belongs to the city-Nihilismus, to the universe of objects without qualities: the asymmetrical composition of the opening in the façade is dictated strictly by the functional *logos*, although an extreme refinement is retained in the very careful design of the frames. On the other, this house interprets and expresses in modern language the critical link with tradition, thus resuming the polemic against the *Heimat-Künstler*.

For Loos, tradition is not a stock of embalmed forms but an active memory that selects from the past, linking it up again with a long and hard

Original plans and elevations (Plan- und Schriftenkammer, Vienna).

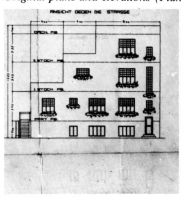
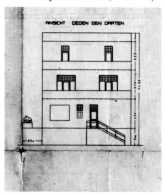
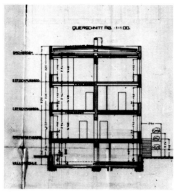
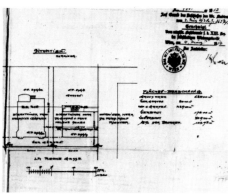
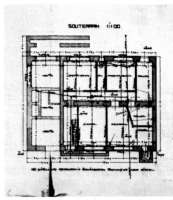
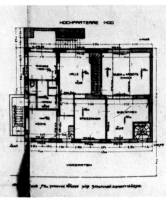
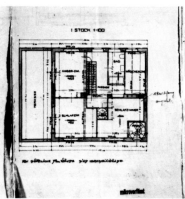
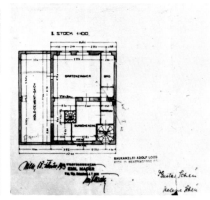

Street façade.

View from the garden.

Hall.

Dining room.

"View from the gate".

Four views of Loos' model currently in the Albertina Museum.

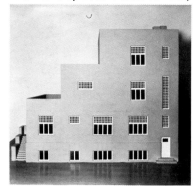  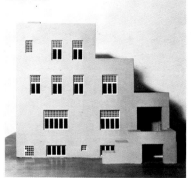 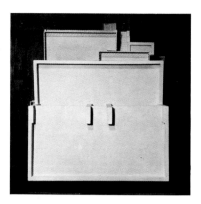

Scheu House as seen from Larochegasse.

evolutionary process, a process that does not exclude, indeed implies, new concepts of space and form deriving from a deep and critical awareness of new construction processes. In this sense Loos interprets the flat roof as an architectural trend already present in history, although it is only with the technological invention of the roof made out of Holzzement that this tendency could be fully expressed. He wrote about this in 1926: «I don't know what happened elsewhere. But I know that in Austria, Renaissance façades were being built everywhere that gave the impression of a flat roof; but it was only an illusion in which the façade hid the pitched roof behind it. The windows on the top floor were false; only here and there was a window that corresponded with a tympanum; if the Holzzement roof had been known then!» [3]

So the foreignness provokes a break, but at the same time — once over the initial shock — it is of help in a critical reconsideration of a process founded on the logic of building. The ultimate form of the Scheu house is only the final outcome of a linked series of reasoned choices.

More than anything else it is the deliberate refusal to make any concessions to current taste and to the conventional image of the Austrian house that leads to the pure, radical and extremely modern shape of this stepped white shell immersed in greenery. Once again Loos methodically favors the needs of living over stereotypes of form. The logical sequence of choices may be reduced to a bare outline of extreme simplicity: if «it is pleasant to be able to step out onto a large terrace» and this is technically possible, then there is no reason to deny this pleasure of the sake of an attachment to the distorted image of national art. This simple way of thinking gives rise to the invention of a new typological model for extensive residential building outside the geographical confines of the Mediterranean. In fact, despite his declaration to the contrary, it should be remembered that Loos had devoted a great deal of attention to

Mediterranean residential models in those very years. The watercolor of a *Department Store in Alexandria* of 1910 may be considered as a sort of preface to the Scheu House, that in its turn anticipates some important projects of 1923 such as the Grand Hotel Babylon and the unit of very small apartments for the Municipality of Vienna, which extends the typological scheme of the Scheu House to working-class housing. The supranational character of the architecture is another modern category of Loos' work that stands out in all its significance when compared with the contemporary architectural production of Viennese villas by Otto Wagner and Josef Hoffmann, still crammed with decorative elements drawn from the historicist repertory of forms.

It remains, finally, to analyze the articulation and quality of the internal settings. The layout is typical of highly residential building schemes of the time: the first floor is assigned to the reception area and contains a library cum living room and a dining room; the services are located in the basement, while the bedrooms are situated on the second and third floors. The peculiar quality of the interior lies in the welcoming character of the whole that is obtained by the reutilization of certain invariants of Loosian decoration: the wooden beams in full view on the ceiling, the almost architectural predominance of built-in furniture, the use of junctional spaces (the cupboards under the stairs, for instance), the vaguely Richardson-like flavor of the chairs and tables. All this confirms the disjunction between exterior and interior, that is to say the *otherness* of private and public, of individual and collective, that had already been taken to an extreme in the Steiner House of 1910.

NOTES

1) A. LOOS, *Das Grand-Hotel Babylon*, in «Die Neue Wirtschaft», Jahrg. I, Vienna, 20 December 1923.

2) After the war «Das Neue Frankfurt», a review in the foreground of cultural debate under the Weimar Republic, devoted many pages to this «question» involving, among others, architects and theoreticians of the intelligence of E$_t$ May, A. Behne, P. Oud and H. Tessenow. Cf. «Das Neue Frankfurt», no. 7, October-December 1927.

3) A. LOOS, *Sämtliche Schriften*.

BIBLIOGRAPHY

H. KULKA, *Adolf Loos*, op. cit., figs. 51-53, with caption.
L. MÜNZ, *Adolf Loos*, op. cit., p. 37.
L. MÜNZ, G. KÜNSTLER, *Der Architekt Adolf Loos*, op. cit., pp. 113-115, figs. 131-133.

MANZ BOOKSHOP
Kohlmarkt 16, Vienna 1

1912

This is one of the works that remained unknown for a long time. Its recent rediscovery and attribution to Loos was made by F. Kurrent and J. Spalt who drew attention to it in their essay *Unbekanntes von Adolf Loos* (1970, listed in the bibliography) that has ample documentation of the subject.

Those elements of the original version that are still recognizable are the marble doorway of the façade and the manager's office on the first floor. The striped gray marble that covers the façade confirms his repeated use of this material to denote the exteriors of commercial architecture. In this case the marble covering shows signs of being reduced to a pure slab. Apart from certain soft light-and-shade effects obtained by a slight staggering of the stone panels, the whole is reduced to a flat surface, like a sheet of cardboard pierced by those openings that cannot be dispensed with. It should be noted, however, that in a sketch for the projeck, kept in the Loos-Archiv (Inv. 0322), lateral insignia appear stamped with the Hapsburgian symbol of the double-faced eagle, intended to be used for publicity notices but not included in the final work.

Inside, the rooms used for offices are in a good state of preservation and may be used to evaluate the material quality of Loos' original decorations. What stands out is the severe geometrical pattern of the expensive oak paneling that brings every element of the surroundings back to a unitary module, from the door to the bookshop itself. Loos loved to congratulate himself sarcastically on having taken the inspiration for his modern and very elegant system of wood paneling from the cisterns of water closets. Further, the elegant hellenized design of the frieze that closes the *boiserie* should be noted, a design adopted, in the same period, in the interiors of the Kniže Store. It should finally be pointed out that the small room of the office contains a few objects of very fine craftsmanship designed by Loos, including a small table on classical lines with columnshaped legs and a marble base.

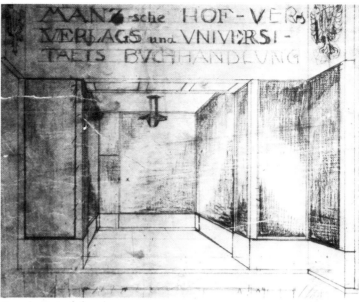

Loos' original drawing.

BIBLIOGRAPHY

F. KURRENT, J. SPALT, *Unbekanntes von Adolf Loos*, in «Bauforum» no. 21, Vienna 1970, p. 43.
B. RUKSCHCIO, *Studien zu Entwürfen, Projekten und ausgeführten Bauten von Adolf Loos 1870-1933*, op. cit., p. 100, œW.V. L.84.12.
B. RUKSCHCIO, *Adolf Loos zum 110. Geburtstag*, in «Bauforum» no. 81, 1980, p. 10.

Façade today.

Manager's Office.

PROJECT FOR THE SCHWARZWALD SCHOOL
Vienna

Not only the date but also the location of this project is uncertain. Copies **1912** of the original drawings (elevations, plans and a perspective drawing) are preserved in the Loos archives. It is a multifunctional building that integrates a school with a cinema, a café and wide, well-equipped terraces. The plans were probably intended — as Künstler and Münz point out — for the Schwarzwald School in Vienna.

BIBLIOGRAPHY

L. MÜNZ, G. KÜNSTLER, *Der Architekt Adolf Loos*, op. cit., section no. 38, p. 186.

SKETCH OF A THEATER
Märzpark, Vienna 15

The subject of a 4000 - seat theater, already tackled by Loos in 1898, and **1912** returned to in 1905, is further developed in this graphic work. Worthy of note are the designs for the blocks that enclose the egg-shaped area of the stalls. In the first, upper design, simple monolithic volumes are employed, while in the second one, below, the blocks are crowned by a stepped, pyramid-shaped top that recalls the project for a Department Store in Alexandria in 1910. The sketch (recently discovered and dating in all probability from 1912) attests in any case to the interest shown by Loos in settling the problem of theatre typology.

BIBLIOGRAPHY

B. RUKSCHCIO, *Studien zu Entwürfen, Projekten und ausgeführten Bauten von Adolf Loos 1870-1930*, op. cit., W.V. 89.12.P.
B. RUKSCHCIO, *Adolf Loos zum 110. Geburtstag*, in «Bauforum» no. 81, 1980, p. 18.

PLAN FOR AN ALTERATION TO THE HISTORIC CITY CENTER
Innere Stadt, Vienna 1

A drawing entitled *Plan einer Erweiterung und Regulierung der inneren* **1912** *Stadt Wien — àuf Grund des Bestandes vom Jahre 1859* (Inv. 403) is preserved in the Loos-Archiv of the Albertina in Vienna. The drawing is signed by Paul Engelmann and dated 1912, but it very probably dates back to 1909. It is a «school» project carried out under the direct guidance of Loos. Although not strictly attributable to the Viennese master, it may nevertheless be taken as deriving substantially from his thought. For this reason it represents a rare document that is important to any evaluation of the guiding principle underlying Loos' urban planning.

The subject of the exercise is the proposal of a planning variation theoretically intended for the Competition for the Design of the Kärntnertor Platz of 1859. The idea developed is based on the creation of a large semicircular piazza where Augustinerstrasse crosses Mariahilferstrasse and Verlaugerterstrasse. The hypothetical form evidently aims to emphasize the view of the two opposite monuments of the Oper and the Burgtheater, while creating gaps that open onto the Stadtpark behind.

Although it deliberately keeps to the limits of a «backdated» academic exercise, the drawing shows, in its attempt to turn back history, an unmistakable desire to make a critical reassimilation of 19th-century techniques. It is on this principle of critical continuity with the past that Loos' *architecture of memory* is based, a principle which, as such, never translates into a nostalgic regression.

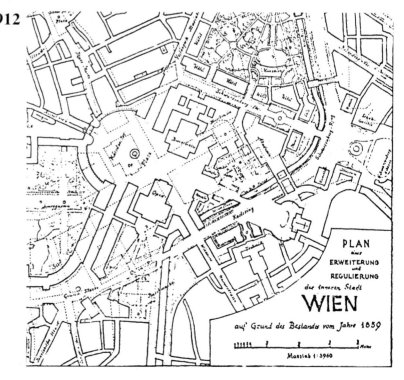

BIBLIOGRAPHY

B. RUKSCHCIO, *Studien zu Entwürfen, Projekten und ausgeführten Bauten von Adolf Loos 1870-1930*, op. cit., WV. G. 88. 12. P.

HORNER HOUSE

Nothartgasse 7, Vienna 13

This work is of two fold interest. On the one hand it represents a kind of **1913** reassembly of proven elements of Loos' language, creating an opportunity to make a rigorous check on his technique of *repetition*. On the other it takes the «game of fitting together spaces», on whose board Loos moves with such skill, to new levels of perfection.

The data and rules which form the starting point for the project posed a problem of far from easy solution. The cross-sectional area available was quite small (about 10×10 m.) and located, moreover, at a crossroads (the point at which Sauraugasse and Nothartgasse meet) in a suburban residential district. This meant that the conditions imposed by the same building regulations in force for the Steiner House (1910), permitting a maximum height of one story plus the basement, applied this time to two sides of the building.

Taking the greatest advantage of the possibilities, including a natural slope to the ground, Loos produced a building on a more or less cubical pattern (the height from the floor of the basement to the garret on the top floor is also 10 meters) topped by an original, wagon-like roof covered, flouting the aesthetic conventions of the time, with simple sheet metal. It is true that this roof is only a logical extension of that idea of architecture already tried out in the façade of the Steiner House overlooking St. Veitgasse. But the repetition of an already tested solution is never a pure and simple mechanical reproduction. Once again the radical formal innovation expressed by this roof is closely tied to the technical problem of having to create another habitable floor inside the roof.

Another element easily recognizable as one of Loos' linguistic invariants is the way that the windows are built up from modular squares. Then there is the terrace (set above the wide porch) that represents an element drawn from the Mediterranean model of housing and one that crops up frequently in his prewar works, like the Scheu House (1912) and the Steiner House (1910) itself.

Of further interest is the distributive layout of the interior that, exploiting the possibility of using the whole wall of the house for openings to the outside, subdivides the plan into four sectors, giving rise to an extremely simple typology in which the rooms are rotated around a single area of disengagement. The plan includes a clearly legible vertical section showing the way the spaces fit together. The servants quarters are located in the basement while beneath the roof there is yet another room of about 2 meters in height at the center, as well as the regular floor.

In conclusion, what makes this work stand out is the unconstrained logic on which Loos' method of design is based, a logic that is visible even from the outside in the dry design of the walls.

BIBLIOGRAPHY

H. KULKA, *Adolf Loos*, op. cit., fig. 56.
L. MÜNZ, G. KÜNSTLER, *Der Architekt Adolf Loos*, op. cit., pp. 79-82, figs. 71-73.

Early photograph of garden façade.

Four elevations of the original project (Plan- und Schriftenkammer, Vienna).

151

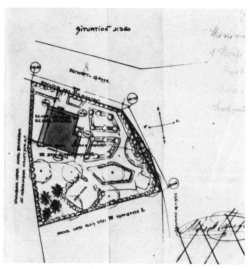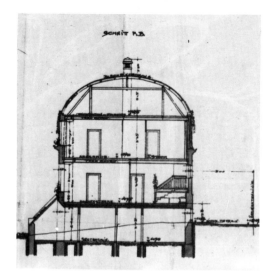

Site plan and section as originally drawn (Plan- und Schriftenkammer, Vienna).

Two present-day views.

PROJECT FOR A GRAND HOTEL
Semmering, Austria

1913

Even more than his other hotels this one planned at about 60 kilometers to the south of Vienna demonstrates the originality of the typological conception developed by Loos in this sector. The hotel is a genuinely autonomous urban fragment, condensing lodging, parks and leisure facilities. Judging by what Kulka says, this center would have been provided with many of the requisites for relaxation: games, music, dance halls, gymnasiums, baths, a nightclub and a theater — a sort of phalanstery of pleasure. The model is preserved in the Loos archives.

BIBLIOGRAPHY

H. KULKA, *Adolf Loos*, op. cit., figs. 62-72, with captions.
L. MÜNZ, G. KÜNSTLER, *Der Architekt Adolf Loos*, op. cit., section no. 43, p. 187.

PROJECT FOR THE JANITOR'S HOUSE
OF THE SCHWARZWALD SCHOOL
Semmering, Austria

1913

This house designed for the janitor of the Schwarzwald School in the Semmering can be seen as one of the first planning applications of the principle of the *Raumplan*. It is a very simple, rural construction, built entirely from wood with a wide pitched roof only 6.40 meters above the ground. The plans clearly show the variation in height of the floors (in relation to the slope of the roof), the extremely functional nature of the internal distribution (with a sharp distinction between daytime and night-time areas), the spatial economy (the alcoves and the entrance are located in the lowest parts of the building) and the cruciform cross section (more obvious on the second floor, but still detectable in the design of the ceiling on the ground floor). The elementary nature of the system of construction reminds one of the well-known American system of the *Balloon Frame*. This throws light on one of the matrices of the principle of staggering floors (*Raumplan*) whose roots are to be found in a careful consideration of the empirical tradition of American pioneering architecture. From rural architecture Loos extracts a few logical procedures that may be extended, on the level of method, to the entire sphere of construction. In this sense, rather than a late-romantic exploration of the Germanic spirituality of construction, this project seems to fit onto a purely rational level that is similar in many ways to the imaginary projection of America (just as it is described by Loos in his critical essays).

BIBLIOGRAPHY

L. MÜNZ, G. KÜNSTLER, *Der Architekt Adolf Loos*, op. cit., p. 122, figs. 148-150.

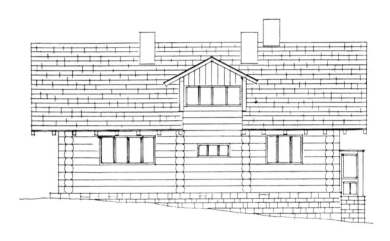

CAFÉ CAPUA
Johannesgasse 3, Vienna 1 (no longer in existence)

1913

Nothing remains today of Loos' refined furnishings. We can, however, reconstruct their appearance from photographs of the period (one of which has already been published in H. Kulka's monograph) and the drafts of the project (the plans and a few drawings of details) preserved in the Loos-Archiv at the Albertina in Vienna. The walls of the Café were lined with typical panels of veined marble. In this case, however, a very advanced technique was applied to economize on the material by reducing the thickness of the panels to a very considerable degree.

The furniture consisted of small tables with round marble tops and a single central cylindrical leg, comfortable chairs and small divans of a traditional shape placed against the walls. Along the line where walls and ceiling meet ran a frieze of questionable taste, but one frequently to be found in the interiors designed by Loos at that period, the Bellak apartment (Vienna 1912), for instance. Last, the large mirror at the center of the rear wall merits particular attention as it introduces once again the play of optical illusion.

BIBLIOGRAPHY

P. ALTENBERG, *Fechsung*, Berlin 1915, pp. 61-62.
H. KULKA, *Adolf Loos*, op. cit., fig. 57 with caption.
L. MÜNZ, G. KÜNSTLER, *Der Architekt Adolf Loos*, op. cit., section no. 41, p. 187.
B. BREHM, *Erinnerung an Georg Trakl*, in «Wiener Neueste Nachrichten» 19 November 1933.

ALTERATIONS TO THE ZENTRALSPARKASSE
Mariahilferstrasse 70, Vienna 7

It is undeniable that the grand doorway of polished black granite, on which the words *Zentralsparkasse der Gemeinde Wien* stand out in shiny brass, attracts the attention of anyone passing, even absentmindedly, along the Mariahilferstrasse.[1]

And this, at a distance in time, is the best proof of the validity of Loos' intuition of design: to impose an image of architecture along the great commercial arteries of the metropolis, an absolute, severe classicity was necessary.

In fact, the atemporal immutability of the classical is set up as a contrast to the speedy obsolescence of commercial products and the change of public taste. In this sense, in its deliberate opposition to the unending flow of perishable goods, the classical operates as a kind of clearing of the stage that translates into a progressive, modern communi-

1914

«The bank must say: here your money is safe and well looked after by wonderful people. Adolf Loos». So it «must say»; the semantic intention of this architecture is beyond argument.

All that remains is to evaluate the means by which the message is transmitted. It is interesting to note that this is one of the very few works in which Loos makes recourse to fluting on the pillars (widely used by the *Wagnerschule* and by Hoffmann in particular). Fluting, in this case, represents more a simple way of patterning the material with shadows than an allusion to the column. Once again, in fact, the language of materials is entrusted with the most important semantic task.

One should note, besides, the relative autonomy of the interior, where the monumental tension of the doorway dies down into a serene simplicity of line. Even the materials emphasize this jump. From black granite, one

Bank entrance today.

Early sketch of the entrance.

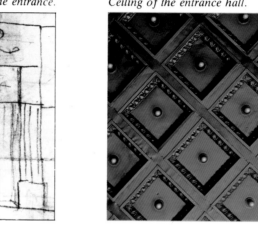
Ceiling of the entrance hall.

Interior.

cation technique. This idea will be developed further, and perhaps even more suggestively, in the unrealized project for a gigantic column (also of polished black granite), entered for the international competition held in 1922 for the construction of the *Chicago Tribune* skyscraper.

But the classicity of the doorway to the Zentralsparkasse has another specific purpose: it sets out to communicate a sense of security and trustworthiness. The inscription cut into the marble at the entrance throws light on this.

passes through the copper of the lacunar ceiling in the entrance to the white-striated marble that lines the walls of the large hall, lending a tone of sobriety and calm to the whole setting. The light from above, filtered through opaque panes of glass set in the ceiling, completes the warm and welcoming atmosphere of the room.

It should be made clear, finally, that the hall as it presents itself today is only a reconstruction, though a reliable and carefully documented one, of the original *Schalterhalle* of the Anglo-Österreichische Bank designed by Loos.[2]

NOTES

1) It should be noted, however, that in an early sketch plan the Habsburgian symbol of the double-faced eagle was mounted high on the facade of the *Anglo-Österreichische Bank* (which was the original name of the present *Zentralsparkasse*) in place of the brass script put up later by the Municipality of Vienna. Cf. the drawing Inv. 0421, today kept in the Loos-Archiv at the Albertina.

2) A photograph of the original version published in the volume *Das neue Wien* (Bd IV, Vienna 1928, p. 171) has been opportunely reproduced in the essay by Roland L. Schachel (cited in the bibliography).

On the basis of this and other documents of the period it has been possible for a team of experts coordinated by Hermann Czech to go ahead with a rigorous restoration project. The oak benches of excellent craftsmanship, set against the wall, are authentic while the lamps are only reproductions, though faithful ones, of Loos' originals. While recognizing the great merit of having salvaged what could be saved, conserving the surviving elements, one cannot but point out the inevitable loss of quality in the present reconstruction as compared with Loos' original version.

BIBLIOGRAPHY

F.KURRENT, J. SPALT, *Unbekanntes von Adolf Loos*, in «Bauforum» no. 21, Vienna 1970, pp. 29-48.

R.L. SACHEL, *Loos-Hoffmann: 1870-1970* in «Steine sprechen» nos. 31-32, Vienna 1970, p. 7.

RUKSCHCIO, *Studien zu Entwürfen, Projekten und ausgeführten Bauten von Adolf Loos 1870-1933*, op. cit., p. 100; WV. L.96.14.

R.L. SCHACHEL, *Eine Bank von Adolf Loos - Analyse eines Un-Glücksfalles*, in «Steine sprechen», Vienna, nos. 43-44, 1973, pp. 7-9.

H. CZECH, *Zentralsparkasse der Gemeinde Wien*, in «Architektur aktuell», no. VI, 1975, pp. 31-33.

H. CZECH, *A newly discovered bank by Adolf Loos restored in Vienna*, in «A+U», no. 68, 1976, pp. 17-20.

B. RUKSCHCIO, *Adolf Loos zum 110. Geburtstag*, in «Bauforum» no. 81, p. 11.

Interior today after restoration.

1910 - APARTMENT OF ARMIN HOROWITZ
Frankgasse 1, Vienna 9

BIBLIOGRAPHY

B. RUKSCHCIO, *Studien zu Entwürfen, Projekten und ausgeführten Bauten von Adolf Loos 1870-1930*, W.V. W.77.10.

1912 - PLANS FOR VILLAS IN THE MOUNTAINS

Here the date has been determined with fair probability by Künstler and Münz. The drawings are preserved in the Loos archives.

BIBLIOGRAPHY

L. MÜNZ, G. KÜNSTLER, *Der Architekt Adolf Loos*, op. cit., section no. 39, p. 186.

1912 - APARTMENT OF VALENTIN ROSENFELD
Wattmanngasse 11, Vienna 13

Loos decorated the dining room, making use of compositional modules that had already been tried out.

BIBLIOGRAPHY

H. KULKA, *Adolf Loos*, op. cit., fig. 55.
L. MÜNZ, G. KÜNSTLER, *Der Architekt Adolf Loos*, op. cit., section no. 37, p. 186.
F. KURRENT, J. SPALT, *Unbekanntes von Adolf Loos*, in «Bauforum» no. 21, 1970, p. 33.

1913 - APARTMENT OF ROBERT STEIN
Pfarrhofgasse 16, Vienna 3

BIBLIOGRAPHY

B. RUKSCHCIO, *Studien zu Entwürfen, Projekten und ausgeführten Bauten von Adolf Loos 1870-1930*, op. cit., WV: W.218.13.

1913 - APARTMENT OF JOSEF HALBAN-SELMA KURZ
Löwelstrasse 8, Vienna 1

BIBLIOGRAPHY

B. RUKSCHCIO, *Studien zu Entwürfen, Projekten und ausgeführten Bauten von Adolf Loos 1870-1930*, op. cit., WV. W.219.13.

1913 - PROJECT FOR THE SCHWARZWALD-ANSTALTEN SCHOOL
Semmering, Austria

The project was probably never carried out because of the outbreak of war and was left at a very rough stage.

BIBLIOGRAPHY

H. KULKA, *Adolf Loos*, op. cit., figs. 73-75.
L. MÜNZ, G. KÜNSTLER, *Der Architekt Adolf Loos*, op. cit., section no. 44, p. 187.

1913 - PROJECT FOR ALTERATIONS TO THE ANGLO-ÖSTERREICHISCHE BANK
Mariahilferstrasse 13, Vienna 6

The drafts of the plan for the alterations and the design of the façade are preserved in the Loos-Archiv at the Albertina.

BIBLIOGRAPHY

B. RUKSCHCIO, *Studien zu Entwürfen, Projekten und ausgeführten Bauten von Adolf Loos 1870-1930*, op. cit., WV. L.92.13.

1914 - APARTMENT OF PAUL MAYER
Prinz Eugenstrasse 80, Vienna 4

Photographs of the dining room and the living room are preserved, along with the original plans of the other rooms, in the Loos archives.

BIBLIOGRAPHY

L. MÜNZ, G. KÜNSTLER, *Der Architekt Adolf Loos*, op. cit., section no. 42, p. 187.

1914 - APARTMENT AND WORKSHOP OF THE G. HENTSCHEL FASHION HOUSE
Karl Schweighoferstrasse 7, Vienna 7

BIBLIOGRAPHY

«Neue Freie Presse», 9 January 1917, p. 19.
B. RUKSCHCIO, *Studien zu Entwürfen, Projekten und ausgeführten Bauten von Adolf Loos 1870-1930*, op. cit., W.V. L.98.14.

1918 - CANTEEN OF THE ALT-BRÜNNER ZUCKERFABRIK
Brno, Czechoslovakia

A few snapshots are preserved in the Loos archives.

BIBLIOGRAPHY

L. MÜNZ, G. KÜNSTLER, *Der Architekt Adolf Loos*, op. cit., section no. 51, p. 188.

1918 - PLAN FOR ADAPTATION AND RENOVATION OF THE KRASICYN PALACE
near Przemyśl, Poland

BIBLIOGRAPHY

B. RUKSCHCIO, *Studien zu Entwürfen, Projekten und ausgeführten Bauten von Adolf Loos 1870-1930*, op. cit., W.V. H.111.18.P.

1919 - PLAN OF KONSTANDT HOUSE
Olomuc, Czechoslovakia

This project that was never carried out was drawn up in collaboration with Paul Engelmann, who would collaborate with Ludwig Wittgenstein a few years later on the plans of the house for his sister Margarethe Stoneborough (1926).

BIBLIOGRAPHY

L. MÜNZ, G. KÜNSTLER, *Der Architekt Adolf Loos*, op. cit., (mentioned) p. 188.

1919 - DESIGN FOR ALTERATIONS TO THE STATE BANK
Vienna

The date of this hurried sketch was assigned by Künstler and Münz, taking into account the similarities of form shown by the high corner tower to those designed a short time before for the monument to Franz Joseph. There is no evidence of a commission from the bank and so this drawing just represents an idea of urban planning.

BIBLIOGRAPHY

L. MÜNZ, G. KÜNSTLER, *Der Architekt Adolf Loos*, op. cit., p. 188, with illustration.

APARTMENT OF EMIL LÖWENBACH

Schallauterstrasse 4, Vienna 1

1914

These furnishings seem to support a well-known claim of Loos that «the house is conservative.» Alongside unvarying elements of Loos' language, traditional motifs of interior design resurface here in a mixture that has broadly conventional results.

An example of this is the decorated parquet floor of the dining room (probably already in existence). The lacunar ceiling (with the introduction of modern lamps within an imitation Renaissance pattern) and the frieze below are made from dark wood. This contrasts with the luminosity of the walls of light, veined marble, which collect and diffuse the light that filters through curtains draped over the large windows. Apart from the marble, Loos' hand may be recognized in the space built into the end wall, the back of which is lined with mirrors. This confirms the repetitive nature of the use of the mirror as a material cum symbol, indeed, as the magic material of architecture. But apart from a few expressive linguistic innovations, the overall image of this room keeps to the familiar tracks of conventional domestic propriety.

BIBLIOGRAPHY

H. KULKA, *Adolf Loos*, op. cit., figs. 80-82 with caption.
L. MÜNZ, G. KÜNSTLER, *Der Architekt Adolf Loos*, op. cit., p. 50, fig. 29.

ALTERATIONS TO DUSCHNITZ HOUSE

Weimarerstrasse 87, Vienna 19

1915
1916

The alterations to the house belonging to the collector of antique art Willibald Duschnitz were carried out in two stages, as may be seen from the plans signed by Adolf Loos and the *Baumeister* Adolf Micheroli (who also directed work on the Mandl House), plans that are still on file today in the relevant section of the *Plan- und Schriftenkammer des Magistrats der Stadt Wien*. In the first stage (based on the plan dated 1 December 1915) Loos made alterations to the interior and the entrance to the villa. Worthy of special mention is the beautiful music room, dominated by the large organ which covered the entire rear wall (unfortunately removed today, but documented in a photograph reproduced in H. Kulka's monograph). The dining room is still in an excellent state of preservation, distinguished by a lining of single slabs of veined marble of about three meters in height that cover the entire wall surface: this is proof of the high degree of technical skill attained. The office with its large glass walls, the marble bathroom on the floor above and the entrance with its black-and-white marble floor are also well preserved. The design of the latter seems to mirror the checkerboard pattern of rafters on the ceiling. Outside Loos confined himself to designing an entrance porch supported by unusually shaped pillars and a simple flight of steps classically closed on one side by a wall of the same height as the threshold. In the second stage (represented by the plan dated 29 January 1916) the characteristic tower-shaped form was raised (made still more striking by a postwar elevation).

BIBLIOGRAPHY

H. KULKA, *Adolf Loos*, op. cit., figs. 77-79, with caption.
L. MÜNZ, G. KÜNSTLER, *Der Architekt Adolf Loos*, op. cit., section no. 49, p. 188.
K. SCHWANZER, *Wiener Bauten 1900 bis heute*, Vienna 1964.
B. RUKSCHCIO, *Studien zu Entwürfen, Projekten und ausgeführten Bauten von Adolf Loos 1870-1930*, op. cit., p. 104, W.V. H.101.15.

Door reflected in a mirror to the right.

Inner door of the hall.

Library.

View through the dining room.

Duschnitz House: the dining room.

Music room.

SCHWARZWALD SCHOOL GYMNASIUM

Herrengasse 10, Vienna 1 (no longer in existence)

1915

It is interesting to note that this building was conceived as a multifunctional setting that could be used, at times when no sports are taking place, for theatrical performances (thanks to the incorporation of a small stage), receptions or festivals.

BIBLIOGRAPHY

P. STEFAN, *Frau Doktor*, Vienna 1922, p. 8
L. MÜNZ, G. KÜNSTLER, *Der Architekt Adolf Loos*, op. cit., section no. 48, p. 188.
F. KURRENT, J. SPALT, *Unbekanntes von Adolf Loos*, in «Bauforum» no. 21, 1970, p. 39.

SUGAR REFINERY
Rohrbach, near Brno, Czechoslovakia

This is one of the few cases in which Loos tackles the problem of designing a factory. The imposing industrial plant was built during the war and its labor was provided by prisoners of war. **1916 1919**

What stands out on the level of composition is its unadorned, almost sacred, monumental character that, seen from a distance, gives the impression of a sort of «cathedral of work» which surfaces from the village and stands over the civilian buildings that surround it.

The industrial complex is made up of two sections located on staggered levels: a large parallelepiped block (of four stories) and a tower surmounted by a tall chimney. The two buildings are linked by the volume containing the stairs, marked by long diagonal openings whose angle places an optical emphasis on the difference in height of the sections.

From close up, the element of composition that draws one's attention is the high pillar (with rounded corners in the fashion of a column) that rhythmically punctuates the facade with the structural magnificence of a giant order. One may recall the lesson of Schinkel from whose architecture, crowded with allusions to Greek and Roman classicity, Loos often took his inspiration. But there is a closer precedent which this factory, consciously or unconsciously, calls to mind. This is the façade overlooking Voltasstrasse in Berlin of the A.E.G. *Kleinmotorenfabrik* (1910-1913) built by Peter Behrens. The link between these two works probably goes much deeper than their obvious similarities of form and should be sought in an affinity of ideological attitude towards the unbiased acceptance of and tendency to glorify the new *Industriekultur*.

It shoud be stressed, finally, that the greatest fascination of the construction lies in the severe, almost obsessive, uniformity of the openings which gave it the appearance of a gigantic and exaggeratedly realistic grill.

BIBLIOGRAPHY

L. MÜNZ, *Adolf Loos*, op. cit., fig. a., p. 105.
L. MÜNZ, G. KÜNSTLER, *Der Architekt Adolf Loos*, op. cit., section no. 53, p. 188.
H. CZECH, *Fabriksgebäude und Villa in Hrusovany bei Brünn*, in «Bau», Vienna, no. 1, 1970, pp. 12-15.

Three views of the sugar refinery today.

HOUSE OF THE SUGAR-REFINERY MANAGER
near Brno, Czechoslovakia

1918
1919

What stands out in this composition is the strict bilateral symmetry that dominates the design of the façades, measured by the even and regular succession of the windows (predominantly square in shape).

Extremely simple, too, is the play of volumes. The layout of the architecture tends, in fact, toward an elementary prismatic shape (of 29×15×11 m.), accentuated by the flat roofing and, only in part, scored by two terrace cum pergolas on the first floor. The slope of the site itself is compensated by uniform levelings of the ground to form three steps. We are faced here, then, with an unmistakable return to the classical, in those very years when, on the crest of the avant-garde, the modern language of architecture seems destined for a triumph of dissymetry. In this sense, the villa is a portent of the controversial claim to the right not to be up-to-date that recurs in Loos' architecture during the twenties.

It is also interesting to note that the layout (repeated on both upper floors as well as in the basement) presents an obvious anomaly with respect to Loos' usual method of interior design. Not only is there a complete absence of interpenetrations of space and the staggering of floors onto more than one level, but the most conventional of arrangements has been adopted — a central corridor with the rooms opening off on both sides.

The absence of the original drafts of the plan prevents us from identifying exactly the initial functional location of the rooms. (At present, in fact, the house has been adapted as a workshop for a shoe factory and has undergone quite a few alterations). Yet it is possible to make a reliable reconstruction by referring to the plans produced on the basis of careful research with this aim in mind by Dietrich Worbs. Judging by these indications the ground floor (raised about 1.80 meters from the ground, as may be seen clearly from the outside by the 10 centimeter protrusion that demarcates — at its base — the level of the floor) was intended for the day-time zone and comprised a library, three reception rooms, a dining room, a kitchen and other adjoining rooms. The entrance was on the northern side, facing the sugar refinery. A central room gave access to a loggia cum portico hollowed out, so to speak, of the solid volume.

This void, that breaks up the peremptory box-like layout, is one of the most important elements since it introduces a compositional feature reused subsequently in other monolithic works such as the Rufer House in Vienna (1922) and the house of Tristan Tzara in Paris (1926). One notes, besides, the stepped block of the parapet of the flights of steps that led to the garden, whose form recalls from close up the one used at the back of Scheu House (1912): in one way it represents a development of this, a kind of bilateral duplication.

The basement floor is reached by a staircase on the south side, while from the vestibule on the ground floor a helical staircase led to the first floor (intended for the bedrooms), which narrowed along the north-south axis to make room for two terraces each of 5 meters in length. (One of these is at present walled up following an extension of the construction). Here too we find a feature that is recurrent in Loos' work, the structural pillar that acts as a support for the pergola. It is an element that had already been used in the terrace of Villa Karma at Clarens (1904) and will be used again in the project for the Moissi House at the Venice Lido (1923). The terrace represents, in its turn, a repeated theme of composition in his design of residential buildings from the first models of the second decade of the century onward.

Because of its repetitiveness and at the same time its anticipation of certain constant themes of composition, this villa should be considered a significant experimental stage in an essentially consistent course of design.

BIBLIOGRAPHY

H. KULKA, *Adolf Loos*, op. cit., fig. 94.
L. MÜNZ, G. KÜNSTLER, *Der Architekt Adolf Loos*, op. cit., section no. 52, p. 188.
D. WORBS, «*Unbekannte*» *Bauten und Projekte von Adolf Loos in der C.S.S.R.*, in Alte und moderne Kunst», Vienna, no. 144, 1976, pp. 16-18.

Four elevation drawings.

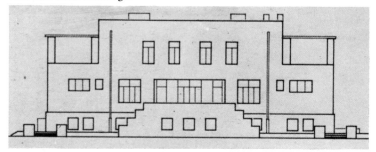

FAÇADE OF THE HUGO & ALFRED SPITZ STORE

Kärntnerstrasse 39, Vienna 1 (no longer in existence)

The most interesting thing about this elegantly classical composition was **1918**
the reutilization of the column, already seen in the Looshaus in the
Michaelerplatz (1909-11).

The façade, in white marble, was broken up by the pattern of these
columns that defined three visual divisions. A further morphological
similarity to the solution tried out in the Michaelerplatz was the superimposition of a prismatic module on top of the capitals, meaning a fragment
of pillar interposed between the column and the architrave. This departure from the classical code from which it was drawn brought about an
accentuation of the vertical lines without altering the traditional proportions of the archetypal column.

BIBLIOGRAPHY

F. OTTMAN, *Adolf Loos* in *Der Architekt*, Vienna 1919, p. 168.
L. MÜNZ, G. KÜNSTLER, *Der Architekt Adolf Loos*, op. cit., section no. 57, p. 188.

PLAN OF A COUNTRY HOUSE FOR LEO SAPIEHA

This is the design of a country house which is a variation on the rural **1918**
model of the pitched roof house, a typology already proposed in 1913 for
the project for the Janitor's House of the Schwarzwald School, put forward again in 1922 for the country house in Gastein and realized in 1930
in the Khuner Country House.

BIBLIOGRAPHY

B. RUKSCHCIO, *Studien zu Entwürfen, Projekten und ausgeführten Bauten von Adolf Loos,
1870-1930*, op. cit., W.V.H. 112.18.P.
B. RUKSCHCIO, *Adolf Loos zum 110. Geburtstag*, «Bauforum» no. 81, 1980, p. 13.

ALTERATIONS TO STRASSER HOUSE

Kupelwiesergasse 28, Vienna 13

These are radical alterations made to an existing house. Yet, both for the **1919** scale and for the method of operation, Strasser House represents an important stage in the development of Loos' design, since it is one of the first applications of the *Raumplan*. Loos works, one could say excavates, within the building, reorganizing the articulation of space, creating, for example, rooms on different levels in the basement. All the spaces that emerge from this staggering of levels play a dual functional and psychological role. This is why the main interest in the Strasser House lies in its interior.

But before going into this aspect it is necessary to take a look at the most important external features of the architecture. In the first place, there is the free and sober composition of the façade, which shows once again one of Loos' syntactic invariants — the reticence of his architecture in the urban and public context. Second, there is the idea of the habitable roof (that is a new version of the wagon-like solution for the roof of Horner House, see here, p. 151). Adjoining this is another element worthy of attention: the terrace that is provided with its own living area, creating a further elevation. Once more the terrace is proposed as a constant element of residential architecture but this time with the additional function of a roof terrace, allowing its own roofing to be used to the fullest advantage.

However, Strasser House — in line with Loos' most authentic research — is above all an introverted architectural work. The documentation of the original interiors is interesting in that it offers considerable material for a reconstruction of the entire range of pieces of furnishing used by Loos. We shall try to decipher the language of materials from these. One repeated element is the white-painted wood that is as much a feature of the entrance, divided into two by a low and transparent *séparé* as it is of the living room, made up from a number of intercommunicating spaces. There is also a flight of stairs leading to a room above that should be considered an extension of the living room itself; a fireplace is fitted

beneath the stairs whose design echoes the diagonal of the stairs and develops it into a triangular shape.

It is more difficult to evaluate the dining room. Here the walls are lined with panels of onyx marble, cut and assembled with a typically Loosian technique that tends to underline the continuity of the pattern of veining. This confirms his desire to let the materials speak by themselves. But the end result, in this case, is somewhat debatable, just because of an excess of preciosity. An anecdote recounted by H. Kulka may help to show up the timeless aristocratic atmosphere of this room: the wall panels were cut from a single block of stone that had been a gift to the emperor of Austria from the khedive of Egypt and cunningly acquired by the owner after the fall of the empire.

This reveals the indifference that Loos felt towards the evolution of external conditions, an indifference that translates into a kind of disciplinary conservatism, even though on a high level of quality. This interior could date back to a prewar phase. Confirmation of this is provided by the music room itself, on two levels, with a *Musikpodium* raised by several steps and ideally separated from the listening area by a symbolic element: the column. It is not hard to detect a subtle reference to the arcade of the Looshaus that seems to hint at the listening area being «outside» with respect to the *Musikpodium*. But the most outstanding feature, in conclusion, is the logic of an architecture that develops independently «within» itself, through a refined intellectual game of self-quotation that runs the risk of turning into a pure disciplinary tautology.

BIBLIOGRAPHY

H. KULKA, *Adolf Loos*, op. cit., figs. 85-91.
L. MÜNZ, G. KÜNSTLER, *Der Architekt Adolf Loos*, op. cit., pp. 82-83, figs. 74-82.
F. KURRENT, J. SPALT, *Unbekanntes von Adolf Loos*, in «Bauforum» no. 21, 1970, p. 36.

Side view today.

ALTERATIONS TO MANDL HOUSE

Blaasstrasse 8, Vienna 19

The first thing that strikes one about the reorganization of the interior of **1916** this 19th-century house is the intelligent use made of space in the large living room, where rooms of different heights fit together, among which the projecting space of the studio «suspended» on the level of the first landing of the stairs is worthy of special mention. But its strong visual allure derives principally from the gradual material reduction of each element of the surroundings to the simple tonal contrast between the darkened ash and the white plaster of the walls.

Along with the living room, Loos redesigned the dining room, introducing dark veined marble into the play of precious materials. Some rooms on the upper floors restructured by Loos can still be seen, including the children's room (with a raised wooden landing intended as a games area) and the bathroom (where the tubes of the hot-water system, designed to be used as racks for drying towels, show how much attention was paid to the smallest details of the project).

The drafts of the project for alterations to the house of Mrs. Anna Mandl — filed in the offices of the *Plan- und Schriftenkammer des Magistrats der Stadt Wien* — are dated 16 July 1916. The date suggested by Kulka (1914) and backed up by L. Münz and G. Künstler should be revised in view of this fact. Finally it should be pointed out that the plan does not bear the signature of Loos, but of the *Baumeister* Adolf Micheroli, who directed the work on Duschnitz House in the same year.

BIBLIOGRAPHY

H. KULKA, *Adolf Loos*, op. cit., fig. 76, with caption.
L. MÜNZ, G. KÜNSTLER, *Der Architekt Adolf Loos*, op. cit., section no. 47, p. 188.
F. KURRENT, J. SPALT, *Unbekanntes von Adolf Loos*, in «Bauforum» no. 21, Vienna 1970, p. 40.
B. RUKSCHCIO, *Studien zu Entwürfen, Projekten und ausgeführten Bauten von Adolf Loos 1870-1930*, op. cit., p. 105 W.V. H.102.16.

Early photograph and original drawings of exterior.

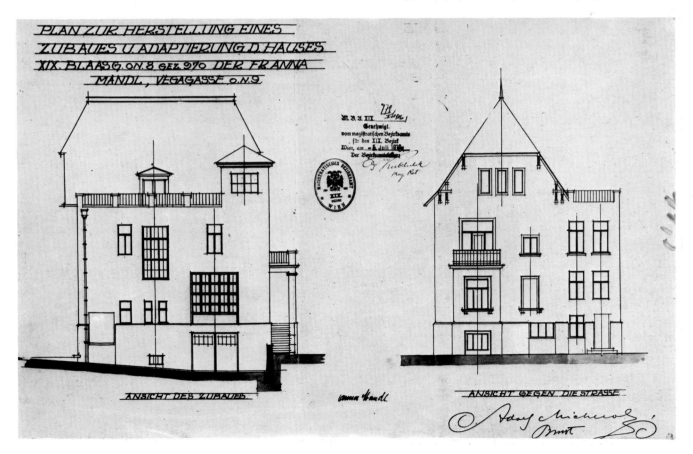

PROJECT FOR THE MONUMENT TO FRANZ JOSEPH

Vienna

1917

This monument — designed in memory of the emperor of Musil's *Kakania* — lies decidedly out side of the Modern Movement, showing no fear of not being up-to-date. The renunciation of any kind of linguistic innovation — through a radical use of historical quotation in the design — is the outstanding feature of this project that gets uncomfortably close to revivalist temptations. Two wide, colonnaded arms outline a monumental square that is closed on three sides and open towards the Ringstrasse. It is not difficult to detect, in the haunting presence of the *stoa*, an allusion to the propylaea of Athens — seen, however, through the interpretative filter of the Altes Museum (Berlin, 1824-1828) or Karl Friedrich von Schinkel (of whom — it should not be forgotten — Loos expressed a high opinion in his essay *Architektur*). [1]

Moreover — like Schinkel's masterpiece, and perhaps even more so — Loos' project sets out to be an urbanistic gesture linking the architectural images which are protagonists of the urban scene. To be sure, the Franz Josefs-Denkmal is only a curtain that frames in perspective, on the backdrop defined by the high prismatic towers, the neoclassical Coburg Palace (1864, situated in the Seilerstätte). These same towers, however, contend — with discretion — for dominance of the Viennese skyline with the spires of Saint Stephen's Cathedral — as is unequivocally demonstrated by a sketch plan in which the height of the towers is calibrated against that of the cathedral. (It should be noted, by the way, that in this sketch the towers are surmounted by the typical stepped pyramid, a feature which is abandoned in the final drawing). All this confirms the attention to topology that is a methodological constant in Loos' urban planning. But there is an undoubtedly rhetorical theatricality in this compositional scheme. A monumental flight of steps — in line with the park envisaged as a replacement for the existing Gardens of the Horticultural Association — would have led solemnly to an open atrium enclosed by propylaea, at the center of which would have been placed the statue of the emperor, seated on a throne, against a background of ten-meter high columns. We are at the heights of transgression of the ethical principles of the Modern Movement (especially of their functionalistic conclusions). From this angle the desire for form (that is to say the need — felt by Loos — for the architecture to be directed towards designing the city) does not justify, cannot justify, the reuse of historically superseded models. Nor does the stated monumental intent serve to legitimize a return to antiquity in search of the sublime, a goal attained through the contemplative fixity of the volumes. Apparently, then, the explicit antimodernism of this work makes it belong to the reactionary category of the *rappels à l'ordre* so frequent in those years. Yet it is precisely in this amorality, this demolition of the idols of his own time, that Loos' architecture seems to reunite itself with the ultimate meaning of Nietzschean negation. Beyond Dada, beyond the «break» of the avant-garde, there is the extreme negation of the «already said», of imaginative tautology. Without any nostalgia for lost order, the reconstruction of the past takes place by means of a radically destructive operation. Even from a strictly syntactic point of view the monument to Franz Joseph shatters the rules of coherence. As in one of Mahler's symphonies, different languages are mixed together in a composition that is lacerated at intervals by unexpected dissonances. If the leitmotiv of the composition really is a sort of clever montage of classical quotations then, despite this, two gigantic vertical towers leap up unpredictably onto the perspective drawing, towers that are completely foreign to the basic linguistic code. Their formal matrix is abstract, original, elementary, almost metaphysical. They are monolithic blocks resembling tombstones, standing in the open, immobile, outside time. This is how the Dionysian creeps through the chinks in the Apollonian. And the result of this duplicity opposed to classical realism and to metaphysical unreality alike, without mediation, without synthesis, is an uncommon pathos of form that tends to the tragic.

The Kaiser Franz Josefs-Denkmal is, in the end, an architecture of struggle: for its contradictions, for its unresolved crisis, for its ambivalence of broken threads, it is involuntarily a monument to the *finis Austriae*, the swan song at the sunset of an age. [2]

NOTES

1) «Ever since humanity grasped the grandeur of classical antiquity, one single thought has united the great architects. They think: I am building how the ancient Romans would have built. We know that they are wrong. Time, purpose, climate, environment, all conspire to make this impossible. But every time architecture strays from its model at the prompting of the lesser, decorative architects, the great architect reappears to lead it back to antiquity. Fischer von Erlach in the south, Schlüter in the north, were rightly the great masters of the eighteenth century. And on the threshold of the nineteenth century there was Schinkel. We have forgotten him. If only the light of this extraordinary figure would illuminate our future generation of architects.» A. LOOS, *Architektur*, in *Sämtliche Schriften*.

2) It is probably only a coincidence, but it was in this very garden belonging to the Horticultural Association, in the cabaret Der Gartenbau, that the scene was set for the prelude to the Habsburg tragedy portrayed by Karl Kraus in *Die letzten Tage der Menschheit* (The last days of humanity).

BIBLIOGRAPHY

H. KULKA, *Adolf Loos*, op. cit., figs. 83-84 with captions.
L. MÜNZ, *Adolf Loos, und sein Franz Josephs-Denkmal*, in «Wiener Zeitung», 16 May 1937.
L. MÜNZ, *Adolf Loos*, op. cit., pp. 27-30, illustrations.
Catalog of the exhibition at the Galerie Würthle, Vienna.
L. MÜNZ, G. KÜNSTLER, *Der Architekt Adolf Loos*, op. cit., pp. 170-175, figs, 232-234.

TOMBSTONE FOR PETER ALTENBERG
Zentralfriedhof, Vienna 11

1919

«He loved and he saw» is the aphorism placed as an epigraph on the tomb of his writer-friend to whom Loos dedicated a sorrowful *Leave-Taking* the same year. Like this commemoration made up of words, the monument made of stone is at the same time without solemnity and intimately heroic in tone. A sober lyricism is achieved in the extreme simplicity of the slab of granite — engraved with his name — surmounted by a block of rough stone in which a tall wooden cross is fixed. The tombstone is in the central cemetery of Vienna.

BIBLIOGRAPHY

L. MÜNZ, G. KÜNSTLER, *Der Architekt Adolf Loos*, op. cit., section no. 55, p. 188.

PROJECTS FOR SIEDLUNGEN (LAINZ, HEUBERG, HIRSCHSTETTEN)
Vienna

1920
1922

In 1920, the year that the Social-Democratic party gained a majority in the municipal elections for Vienna, Adolf Loos was taken on as chief architect of the city of Vienna's housing department (*Chefarchitekt des Siedlungsamtes der Stadt Wien*). Over the brief period in which he held this position (1920-1922) he drew up a program that envisaged the construction of several rural districts for workers. These were the Siedlung am Heuberg (1922-1923) and the Gartenstadt-Siedlung Friedensstadt (1921-1922), both only partially built on the basis of Loos' plans, and the Kriegbeschädigten in Hirschstetten (Housing for war invalids), which remained on the drawing board.

It can only come as a surprise that there is a great lack of documentation of this work and that such an important experience should have been left out of the monographs on Loos. The only one dealt with in the volumes by H. Kulka and L. Münz is the Siedlung am Heuberg. [1]

Moreover, the relevant housing department of Vienna has no documents on the Siedlungen Lainz and Hirschstetten, and for information on this sector of residential building financed by the Municipality of Vienna during the years from 1920 to 1922 it is necessary to refer to the *Verwaltungsbericht* 1919-22 (administration report) in «Neues Wien» of 1927, and to the *Sozialer Wohnbau der Stadt Wien*.

Other sources worthy of special mention are the model plan of a housing terrace signed «Adolf Loos» that has been discovered recently at the Kriegerheimstätten of Hirschstetten and the unique testimony to be found in Elsie Altmann Loos' biography *Adolf Loos, Der Mensch* on the subject of the *Siedlung* built to the south of Hermesstrasse, near the Lainz zoo. It is worth quoting at length from E. Altmann Loos' description of the Siedlung Lainz.

«Finally the land necessary for the construction of the houses was handed over to the department. It was an extensive site, situated close to the entrance of the Lainz zoological gardens. Loos was to construct the first houses, for which eight long and narrow plots with space for a small vegetable garden were made available. Other architects were also assigned plots, but only one or two. The only one to start work on building was Loos.

«But it was not a simple task. Loos wanted to build his eight houses in a row, one next to the other. The houses were to be similar to each other, so that no one would feel privileged. Then each person would have been able to express his own personality inside the house and, not incidentally,

a great deal of money would be saved, as in this way each house had a fireproof dividing wall in common with another.

«The day of the opening we all went to Lainz. I remember the plan of the house exactly. It was a miracle of exploitation of space.

«On crossing the threshold one found oneself in a long and narrow corridor that divided the ground floor into two parts. At the end of the corridor a door opened onto the vegetable garden through which shone light reflected off the greenery outside. On the left were two rooms, completed and provided with beautiful windows, but unfurnished, so that each tenant could arrange things to his own satisfaction.

«To the right of the front door was the door of the kitchen. Loos had had a corner bench and a fine table built. The windows were large and hung with light-colored curtains through which a pleasant light filtered. Under the windows were shelves for plates and crockery. On this side of the house there was no partition wall and one passed straight from the kitchen into the livingroom. A fine bench was set beneath the quite large window, bookshelves were fixed to the wall, and at the back of the room, near the door leading to the vegetable garden and the sink, a flight of stairs led up to the garret. Here two bedrooms were located, one large and the other smaller. The stairs, together with a protrusion of the wall, formed a niche facing the kitchen in which the cooking range was placed.

«The furniture was made from soft, white-painted wood and provision was made for separating the kitchen and living room by a cretonne curtain. Yes, it's true that the staircase was narrow and inconvenient, with very high stairs, yet it was the only kind of staircase that could have fitted into that space and the steepness of the stairs allowed the builders to economize on wood.»

If we make a comparison of the description of the rows of houses built in Lainz with the drafts of the plans for the Siedlung am Heuberg and with the indications Loos himself gave about his method at the conference *Die moderne siedlung* (held in Stuttgart on 12 November 1926), we can deduce the basic typological scheme that underlies his design of rural districts. [3] We are dealing here with rows of two-story houses built to extremely economical standards. In fact, a simple technology is used that involves laying wooden beams of a standard length across the two lateral structural walls. The use of such elementary techniques to keep construction costs to a minimum may raise a smile when compared, for example, with the advanced experiments in large-scale prefabrication of compo-

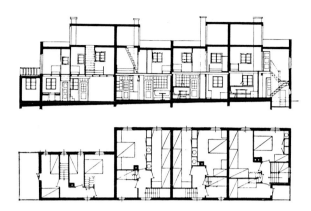

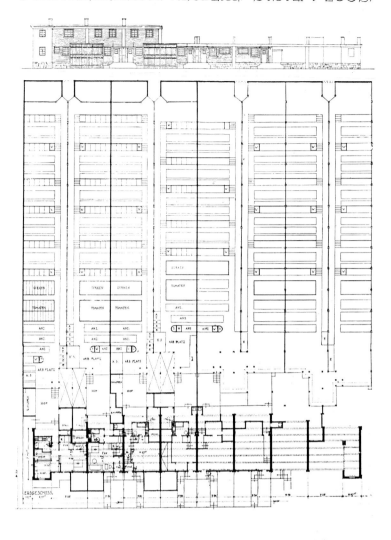

nents carried out not many years afterwards by Ernst May or with the studies made by Le Corbusier over the same period on the adaption of Taylor's methods to the building industry. But above and beyond the obvious differences in cultural setting, the difference in Loos' attitude towards manufacturing needs stressing. Without putting an emphasis on its rational significance Loos sets himself the problem of making an impartial use of primitive construction techniques that are not up-to-date and have been excluded from official research into a language for the new world. Technological and artisan tradition is subjected to a rigorously selective sifting according to critical and logical criteria. Making no concession to romantic yearnings, the pitched roof, so firmly rooted in the landscape painter's image of the peasant house, is replaced in the *Siedlungen* by the flat Holzzement roof. This was a very progressive choice if one bears in mind the strong resistance to and harsh attacks on the new flat-roofed building model that were rife at the time in the German-speaking cultural area. [4] And again the criteria of distribution and division of the rooms in the rural house were based on a logic of simplification. There is a clear distinction between the daytime zone located on the first floor (living room cum kitchen to the south, services to the north) and the night time zone on the upper floor (three bedrooms). Internal subdivision aims at a maximum of flexibility, relying on furnishings of domestic simplicity (such as cupboards, curtains and wooden partitions) rather than on sophisticated systems of removable walls. There is one last feature to be emphasized. The houses are provided with a vegetable garden of about 200 square meters. It is significant that Loos should give such importance to the vegetable garden, going so far as to turn the logical priority of the planning method on its head. «What should a building of the *Siedlungen* look like then?» he wrote in *Die moderne siedlung*. «We need to start with the garden. The garden is of primary importance and the house secondary.» [5]

It should come as no surprise then that the drawings for the Siedlung am Heuberg meticulously trace out how the land should be divided up into separate cultivations or that, at the conference mentioned above, much more attention was paid to the choice of the best place to store potatoes, to keep casks of cider and to situate the latrine than was devoted to strictly architectural problems. Once again Loos starts out from the way of life in order to arrive at the form of the architecture. Although it must be admitted that his vision of the life of the *Siedler*, filtered by his mythical memory of the American peasant, is very rough, simplistic and not without ambiguities and anachronisms that lead him to theorize on working both in factory and field and the elimination of modern water closets in order to replace them by the latrine that would permit people to collect manure for the fields. Besides, on his own admission, Loos never managed to take an organic view of housing policy, which is one of the reasons for the rapid end to his career as chief architect for the Municipality of Vienna. In fact, as is well-known, the five year plan of the Municipality of Vienna was launched the year after his resignation as *Chefarchitekt*. This plan envisaged the construction of 5000 lodgings a year and the building scheme adopted was that of the *Höfe*, that is of the superblocks built around internal courtyards provided with areas of grass, playgrounds and spaces for communal social services. This choice marked the political and cultural defeat of the model of the *Siedlung* supported not only by Loos, but also by Frank and Schuster. [6]

NOTES

1) Cf. H. KULKA, *Adolf Loos*, op. cit., and L. MÜNZ, G. KÜNSTLER, *Der Architekt Adolf Loos*, op. cit.

2) E. ALTMANN-LOOS, *Adolf Loos, der Mensch*, Vienna-Munich 1968, pp. 102-108.

3) A. LOOS, *Die moderne siedlung*, in *Sämtliche Schriften*.

4) The question of the superiority of the pitched roof or the flat roof is a purely technical question today. But in the twenties it was so charged with cultural, social and political connotations that in Germany the flat roof became the favorite object of attacks by right-wing architectural journalists, opposed to «functional» architecture. The roof was defined as the most fundamental part of the German «rational appearance» by figures like Hans F.K. Gunther (*Rasse und Stil*, Munich 1926), Paul Schultze-Naumburg (*Zur Frage... des flachen Daches*), Albrecht Haupt (*Rasse und Bau Kunst*, «Deutsche Bauhütte, 1926).

5) A. LOOS, *Die moderne siedlung*, in *Sämtliche Schriften*.

6) On the theoretical implications of this fundamental planning experience for Loos see the chapter *Architecture or Proletarischer Stil* in this book.

BIBLIOGRAPHY

VV. AA. *Verwaltungsbericht 1919-22*, in «Neues Wien», Vienna 1927.
H.J. ZECHLIN, *Siedlungen von Adolf Loos und Leopold Fischer* in «Wasmuths Monatshefte für Baukunst», vol. XIII, Berlin 1929, pp. 70-78, with illustrations.
H. KULKA, *Adolf Loos*, op. cit., fig. 110-112, with caption.
L. MÜNZ, *Adolf Loos*, op. cit., p. 38.
L. MÜNZ, G. KÜNSTLER, *Der Architekt Adolf Loos*, pp. 145-153, figs. 195-208.
H. KREBITZ, *Adolf Loos, unbekannte Bauten*, in «Bau» no. 1, 1966, pp. 24-25.
E. ALTMANN LOOS, *Adolf Loos, der Mensch*, Vienna-Munich 1968, pp. 102-108.
C. AYMONINO, *L'abitazione razionale*, Padua 1971, pp. 13-34.
M. TAFURI, *Austromarxismo e città. Das Rote Wien*, «Contropiano» no. 2, 1971, pp. 285-311.

PROJECT FOR A MAUSOLEUM FOR MAX DVŎRÁK

Vienna

1921

This mausoleum is of twofold interest: on the one hand it bears witness to a search for monumental form that attains here to a contained, sober and in some ways unrepeatable pathos. On the other it is a homage paid to a celebrated art historian whose influence on Loos' architectural research is subtle but tangible. The model of the project was made in the same year as Dvŏrák's death. It is a massive block of black granite, crowned by a stepped pyramid, with a total height of about seven meters. The interior was to have been decorated with frescoes by Oskar Kokoschka. In fact this project turns on a complex three-way game between architect, painter and art critic, whose prize is the acknowledgment of art as an expression of human spirituality and as an existential problem.[1] This sharp-edged and massive black tomb calls to mind Loos' well-known argument confining the possibility of belonging to the realm of art to only two architectural genera: the tomb and the monument. But the mausoleum is a synthesis of both of these. In it the desire for form is expressed in lyrical purity, without functional reservations. If art is a private experience of the artist, here it becomes a design for an unconscious archetype in which personal memory is blended with the collective one. The inevitable expressionism which imbues the subject of death is caught by Loos in the primitive simplicity of the pyramid-shaped block, punctured only by the dark door in the base and by the perfectly square window. On the other hand, the invitation to Kokoschka to depict the emotion aroused by the commemoration *inside* the tomb denotes the fact that Loos restricts the exhibition of intimate feelings to enclosed space. Outside, the tomb *keeps silent*, in dignified reserve. «Our silence is a black cavern.» Without intending to, the verses of Georg Trakl seem to be written as a commentary on this lyrical but never realized monument.

NOTES

1) The overall message of this *monumentum*, of this object dedicated to memory, may be summed up in the words used by Dvŏrák himself at a celebrated conference «On El Greco and Mannerism» in 1920: «What Michelangelo painted and sculpted in his last years seems to belong to another world... having reached the limits of art he set about the deeper problems of existence: what does man live for and what is the relationship between the transitory, earthly and material posessions of humanity and eternity, the spirit and the supernatural?» MAX DVŎRÁK, *Über Greco und den Manierismus*, in «Repertorium für Kunstwissenschaft», 1925. These words may serve just as well as an epigraph for Dvŏrák's critical idealism as they may, for other reasons, for Kokoschka's poetic expressionism and for Loos' architectonic existentialism (in the borderline experience of architecture that becomes art).

BIBLIOGRAPHY

H. KULKA, *Adolf Loos*, op. cit., fig. 134.
L. MÜNZ, G. KÜNSTLER, *Der Architekt Adolf Loos*, section no. 61, p. 189.

PROJECT FOR VILLA BRONNER

Grimmelshausengasse, Vienna 3

1921

The severe symmetry and the application of the classical code — with revivalist echoes of arcades with a giant order of columns — make this work into an important text for the understanding of the whole range of analytical reflection on history carried out by Loos during those years. Certain unadmitted points of contact with the research of the *Wagnerschule* are visible here which bear witness to the presence of a common current in Viennese architectural culture at the beginning of the century. Yet the externally static construction is dynamically overturned by the complex articulation of staggered floors in the interior. So we encounter once again a semantic implosion of the play of spaces contained within a volume that is rigidly isolated from the outside.

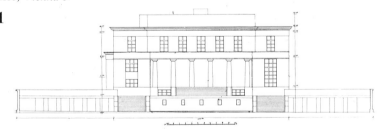

Front elevation.

BIBLIOGRAPHY

H. KULKA, *Adolf Loos*, op. cit. figs. 113-117.
L. MÜNZ, G. KÜNSTLER, *Der Architekt Adolf Loos*, op. cit., section no. 62, p. 189.

PATENT FOR A CONSTRUCTION SCHEME

1921

Patent no. 84.460, dated 2 December 1921, on file at the Patents Office in Vienna, describes a *Konstruktionsschema* invented by Loos in February of the same year, for the construction of «houses with only one wall» (*Haus mit einer Mauer*). The underlying motivations for this invention, conceived while he was still employed by the housing department of the Municipality of Vienna, are unmistakably dictated by the need to keep building costs to a minimum in order to increase the amount of housing that could be built. In appraising this scheme it is as well to bear in mind the historical background to the invention, a situation characterized by heavy demand for working-class housing offset by a grave economic crisis brought about by inflation of the Austrian economy.

«The invention,» as Loos himself explains, «serves for the production of economical residential buildings or of other buildings for offices, shops and factories or for military, agricultural and other uses. The high prices paid for building materials and the high cost of labor, along with the necessity to build because of the great shortage of housing, make it urgent to keep the costs of construction as low as possible, especially in the case of buildings for which a speedy and economic production is an essential condition, and the length of time they will last seems to be of secondary importance. If the cost of land, of building materials and of labor remain constant, economical construction is only possible through a saving on materials and labor. There are well-known methods of doing this, such as doing away with attics and cellars. The invention we are examining here permits yet further economies, this time with the foundations which are always relatively expensive. In this system they are limited to the foundations of the fire-breaking walls that enclose the building. So, in the construction system for which a patent is registered here, the foundations of two external walls are dispensed with. This is done by suspending them from, rather than basing them on, the foundation that supports them.»

The method, illustrated by an elevation and two sections, was tried out in part in the construction of the *Siedlungen*.

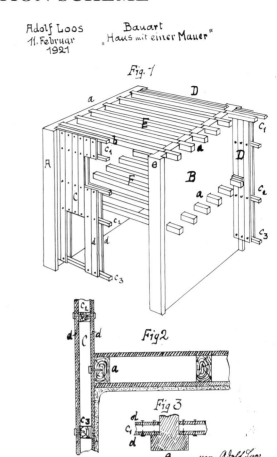

BIBLIOGRAPHY

H. KULKA, *Adolf Loos*, op. cit., fig. 111, with caption.
L. MÜNZ, G. KÜNSTLER, *Der Architekt Adolf Loos*, op. cit., pp. 149-152, fig. 209.

PLAN OF THE HABERFELD COUNTRY HOUSE
Bad Gastein, Austria

1922

Interest in this project derives largely from the attempt to apply the typological scheme of the house with terraces to rural building. In this way an expressive fusion of the stepped model of Scheu House (1912) with the compositional modules of the roofed peasant house is achieved. The chalet is in fact crowned by a wooden structure of sloping pitch, standing on a base of severely geometrical design. One feature that should not be left out is the flight of steps giving access to the house, an element of very similar shape to the one used for the façade overlooking the garden of the Rufer House, built in Vienna in the same year. The final thing to be noted is the fluid arrangement of internal space (visible in section) that bears witness to the degree of maturity reached by the principle of the *Raumplan*. Although the chalet was never built, it is an important experiment that anticipates many solutions subsequently put into practise and in particular many of those used in the Khuner Country House in 1930.

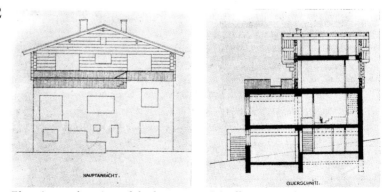

Elevation and section of the house as originally proposed.

BIBLIOGRAPHY

H. KULKA, *Adolf Loos*, op. cit., figs. 118-123, with caption.
L. MÜNZ, G. KÜNSTLER, *Der Architekt Adolf Loos*, op. cit., section no. 64, p. 190, with illustrations.

RUFER HOUSE

Schliessmanngasse 11, Vienna 13 (the original layout of the interior has been modified in recent alterations)

This work is the first complete construction generated entirely by the principle of the *Raumplan*. [1] Here Loos takes the principle to its limit: a limit attained by an elaboration of the form generated by a rigorously logical process that moves from the interior to the exterior.

Outside, the house has the appearance of a pure prism. The walls are smooth, solid and without protrusions. Only the windows break up this pattern arhythmically, appearing where they are required by the internal distribution. The roof is of the flat, Holzzement type. The house takes on the shape of a box (10 × 10 × 12 m.).

If it was not for the *lapsus* of the cornice (that forms the anachronistic crown to the cube) Rufer House would represent an extreme radicalization of Loos' logic. But the cornice neutralizes the «abstract» perception of the cubic object by introducing a recognizable feature that brings the image back onto the familiar tracks of realism. One must ask the reason for this. Once again this lapse reveals the deep-rooted motivations of a conception of architecture that is linked to an evolutionistic interpretation of history. Had not Loos seen the Holzzement roof as the modern technical realization of an idea of architecture already deliberately expressed by Viennese neoclassical architects in the horizontal closure of buildings where cornices were used as a device to conceal the roofs behind them? [2] So this is no casual quotation but denotes the interlacing of tradition and innovation constantly to be found in Loos' work.

But despite this anachronistic element the gradual nullification of the exterior remains evident. And this is the significant factor. By freezing the semantic dimension of the exterior, the syntactic articulation of the internal space takes on unusual importance. In this way the architectonic medium — traditionally given preference — remains exposed, offering a starting point for the development of a theory that adopts the section (and no longer the façade) as the geometrical structure of the composition.

Confirmation of this is to be found in the way the plans are drawn up. Loos had a dismantleable model made with the express purpose of making it possible to view simultaneously the internal distribution and the external one subordinate to it. The perspective drawings show how an analytical study has been made of the window openings in strict relation to the vertical positioning of the floors, so that they are almost visible on the façade itself; the elements are made to interact, as in a chemical compound, with the same analytical detachment as in a laboratory experiment. So let us try taking the walls off the box and looking at the way in which the spaces fit together. The house has four floors, plus a basement where the janitor's lodging and services are located. The living area is on the first floor while the upper floor are used for the nighttime zone. The whole is concluded by a garret (with various service rooms and a terrace). The pivot of the composition is the single central pillar that serves both a structural function and to conduct the electrial, water and heating systems. The structural scheme is in fact extremely simple, made up of the

1922

load-bearing external walls and the above-mentioned single pillar. This has the advantage of reducing internal dividing walls to a minimum, and they are largely replaced by thin wooden partitions or by pieces of furniture. Right from the entrance, the way the steps cross over and lead off in several directions hints at the multileveled dynamics of the interior, which receive a growing emphasis until the living room (Musikzimmer) is reached, the true center of the life of the house. This is conceived as a fluid space communicating directly with the dining room and the veranda facing onto the garden. Nor is it an accident that this more hidden side is where one encounters the most marked play of forms on the outside. The way in which the volume is hollowed out in correspondence with the veranda is of great expressive effectiveness, balanced as it is by the plastic mass of the steps. Thus we find confirmation of the logical priority of an internal planning that projects an indirect, involuntary semantics onto the exterior, producing an impression of transparency.

NOTES

1) As is well-known, the *Raumplan* is more a way of thinking in three dimensions than a principle of spatial economy, and is a method that passed through a long period of gestation. Partial applications of it are discernible in works like the Looshaus in the Michaelerplatz (1909-11) and Strasser House (1919) or in drawings like that of the House with patio of 1912 and the Janitor's House of the Schwarzwald-School of 1913.

2) Cf. A. LOOS, *Sämtliche Schriften.*

BIBLIOGRAPHY

H. KULKA, *Adolf Loos*, op. cit., figs. 124-133, with caption.
L. MÜNZ, *Adolf Loos*, op. cit., p. 36 with illustration.
L. MÜNZ, G. KÜNSTLER, *Der Architekt Adolf Loos*, op. cit., pp. 125-128, figs. 151-160.

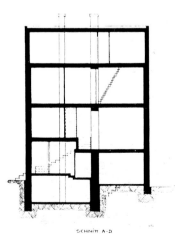

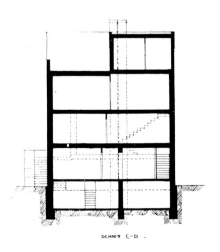

THE «CHICAGO TRIBUNE» COLUMN
Chicago, Illinois.

When, on 10 June 1922, the management of the American newspaper **1922** *The Chicago Tribune* announced a far-reaching international competition for the construction of its new head office, Loos sent a design proposal from Paris that is one of the most enigmatic of all his works, a gigantic Doric column of polished black granite.

The theme proposed in the announcement unequivocally aims at quality: it is stressed more than once that the objective is to build the «most beautiful skyscraper in the world.» And it is on the typological and formal definition of an urban object capable of imposing itself on the absent-minded perception of the metropolis that a great deal of attention is concentrated in the designs submitted by one hundred and forty-five American architects and by highly qualified European architects, including the Germans Walter Gropius, Adolf Meyer, Ludwig Hilberseimer, Bruno and Max Taut, Hans and Wassili Luckhardt; the Dutchmen A. van Baalen and D. A. van Zanten and the Finn Eliel Saarinen; who received second prize. [1] The award of the first prize to the neo-gothic proposal by the Americans J.M. Howells and R.H. Hood is not entirely free from chauvinistic motives and even Louis H. Sullivan in the essay *The «Chicago Tribune» Competition* published in «The Architectural Record» (February 1923) stresses the negative features of the winning project. [2] Leaving aside the questionable nature of the criteria of judgment adopted by the jury (underlined by the fact that Loos' project — like that of Ludwig Hilberseimer — was not even given a place in the short list of the first fifty works), it remains true that this competition is of great interest, not only because of the cross section it offers of an important phase in the historical evolution of the skyscraper and of the differing ways in which the European and American cultures tackled the theme, but above all because it permits — and this concerns us more closely — an evaluation of the evolution of Loos' attitude towards America. [3] To the America that he has built into a myth in the pages of «Das andere» as the land of modernity achieved, Loos proposes — at just the moment when the greatest efforts were being made to establish the Modern Movement — an out-of-date object drawn from historical memory. Hence the enigma met with in any attempt at an interpretation of the meaning of the project. Certain facts lead one to suppose an ironic intent, others the exact opposite.

It should not be forgotten that 1922 was a critical year of reflection for Loos that coincided with his resignation as chief architect of the Socialist administration of Vienna and with his subsequent move to France, where he resumed his links with the avant-garde (forged years before, through the mediation of Schoenberg, with the radical intelligentsia of Berlin), becoming soon afterwards a member of the Parisian Dadaist circle of Tristan Tzara. On the other hand, the great attention paid in his design to solving the functional problems of making a column habitable and the report on the project itself (published in an illustrated pamphlet entitled *The Chicago Tribune Column*) seem to leave little doubt as to the seriousness of his architectural intentions. [4]

«The fact is,» writes Manfredo Tafuri, «that in 1922 Loos seemed to have lost touch with the clarity of his prewar attitudes. His column is not symbolic; it is only a polemical stand against the metropolis seen as a world of change. But a single column, taken out of the context of its order, is not strictly speaking even an allegory: rather it is a phantom. As a paradoxical specter of a code outside time it is blown up to enormous proportions in a last attempt to get across an appeal for the interchangeability of values; but like Kandinsky's giants in *Der gelbe Klang*, Loos' gigantic phantom only succeeds in communicating its own pathetic will to exist. Pathetic because it is expressed in front of the metropolis, in front of the very world of change, of the eclipse of values, of the 'decline of mystique,' that makes that column and that desire to communicate absolute values so tragically out-of-date». [5]

And yet — leaving aside any judgment of the work's merit — Loos had been talking of values ever since the years prior to the *finis Austriae* to the extent that the idea of the Column is so consistent with the theoretic principles formulated in his essay *Architektur* of 1910 as to appear backdated. Had not Loos drawn a radical distinction between the *house* and the *monument*, that is to say, the logic of building housing in response to the wide need for architecture as representation of architecture, which answers to a more intimate desire for form? And yet when faced with the explicit call for a monument («the most beautiful skyscraper in the world»), his consistent response turns out to be an objet d'art. But architecture that wants to be art cannot but be serious; it must speak of values outside those of historical becoming. «Art wants to be the image of death» Bruno Taut will say later. In his essay *Architektur* Loos seems to anticipate this: «Only a very small part of architecture belongs to art: the tomb and the monument. The rest, everything that serves a purpose, should be excluded from the realm of art.... If in a wood we come across a tumulus, six feet long and three feet wide, shaped by the spade into a pyramid, we become serious and something within us says: here someone is buried. This is architecture.» [6]

Loos' imaginative contribution to theory lies in having proposed (provocatively) the coexistence of historically produced architectural forms. One cannot grasp the real polemical significance of Loos' Column without taking into account the methodological antihistoricism that had grown up in the European architectural culture of that time. Faced with the removal of history — which emerges from the heated phase of the war over language in the Modern Movement — Loos demonstrates the limits

of the linguistic game: to speak and to say new things with words that have already been said. It is no accident — he remarks in his report — that the most successful models of «skyscraper architecture» derive from monuments that were never meant to be lived in: the Metropolitan Building from the tomb of King Mausolus at Halicarnassus; the Woolworth Building from the gothic tower. If an imaginary traveler were to traverse the historical labyrinth of architecture, he would discover after all those centuries that the infinite number of compositions are only patient assemblies of a few similar forms. The combinations within the limits of the game are unlimited. Loos seems to transcribe the principle of the *eternal return* into architecture. In this way Loos leads us, keys in hand, to the door of the enigma. He wrote in his report «The basic idea of this project is naturally the one laid down in the program of the *Chicago Tribune*, i.e., to build something that, whether seen in reproduction or in reality, will leave an indelible mark on the person who looks at it, and that will be connected in the minds of all intellectuals with the city of Chicago, in the same way as St. Peter's is linked with Rome and the Leaning Tower with Pisa; a monument that intellectuals will immediately associate with the

Plan showing division of offices.

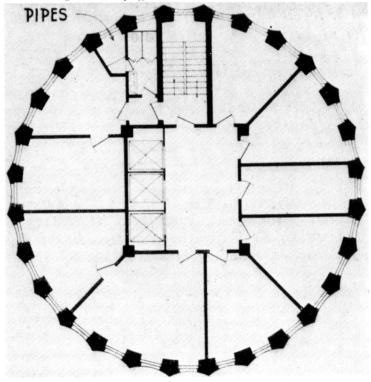

Chicago Tribune newspaper. And how may this result be obtained? By increasing the height of the skyscraper until it is taller than the Woolworth building or by copying the new ideas introduced in the New York Herald Building or in the Morgan Building, which are lower than the surrounding structures? «The first idea is in any case unattainable because of the limitation of the height of the building to 120 meters, and the second, being no longer original, would be contrary to the intentions of the *Chicago Tribune*. There remains yet another idea, that of adopting the new architectural forms without any traditional basis, such as those now proposed by artist-architects in Germany, Austria and France, that derive from Berlinese cubism or from the Belgian revival of 1848. However, these nontraditional forms are rapidly supplanted by others, or the proprietors complain that they are out of fashion, since the fashion in forms changes very frequently, just like that of clothing. This being how things stand, can we perhaps build another of the skyscrapers so characteristic of the American way of seeing life, but so numerous today that even an expert would have difficulty in distinguishing those of San Francisco from those of Detroit? After examining all these possibilities, I have chosen the column as the best solution of the problem. The isolated column is a

tradition. The model for the huge and massive column in Place Vendôme was Trajanus' column.» [7]

Recycling an element — cutting it out of the syntactical system in which it is traditionally set — is inevitably accompanied by the repetition of an already familiar symbol, but its novelty lies in just this operation of shattering, of semantic destructuring, of isolation, in other words reduction to repetition. If we try to analyze the meaning of this «abbreviated repetition», of this detachment of a fragment, the irony of the project that comes close to Duchamp's device of *displacing* ready-made objects will become clear. But irony is not always (or not only) irreverent. At times (as in this case) the irony can be a serious one, which reaches «the point where *yes* and *no* meet.» The column is taken out of the context of its function and out of its dimensional scale and set down in the *autre* reality of the metropolis. But, just as a «urinal» — stripped of its function and placed in a museum, in the sacred temple of values — becomes a «fountain» and acquires the positive status of art, the column, at the same time as it desecrates the image without qualities of the metropolis (where the interminable transformation and exchange of goods takes place), turns its function of a radical negative criticism to positive effect. [8]

But whatever the biographical data and whatever Loos himself may have said, the Chicago Tribune Column is Dada. In fact, it is not necessary to interpret his declared intentions to the letter since, while offering us a clue with which to solve the riddle Loos subtly introduces a second enigma. Moreover, it is in the very years between 1920 and 1922 that Paris becomes the favored workshop for an advanced research into language carried out by *Dada, Société Anonyme pour l'exploitation du vocabulaire*. Had not Tristan Tzara himself explained that «To make a Dadaist poem» it is enough to take a pair of scissors and cut out «every word» from a newspaper article and, after having shaken them up in a bag, take them out and arrange them in the desired order? [9] It is not necessary to invent new terms if, by picking out a worn-out word (but doesn't this argument apply to architectural language as well?) and extrapolating it from its customary syntax, one gives it a new «virginity of meaning». All that remains to be asked is why the extracted word should be a column?

The answer to this question is probably twofold. One answer may come from a perusal of the essay *Architektur* where Loos offers an interesting interpretation of the secret of the Romans' greatness: «From the Romans we have derived the very technique of our thought.... It is no accident that the Romans did not invent a new order of columns. They were too advanced for this. They derived it all from the Greeks and adapted it to their own purposes.» [10] So Roman construction is an anticipatory technique of the ready-made object; Riegl has nothing to do with this. Against *Expressionismus*, against the theory of *Kunstwollen* that reappraises the *Spätrömische Kunstindustrie* as decadence, Loos sets up a Semperian *Können*, the technique of a thought that reflects on the possibilities. [11] The explicit reference to Trajanus' Column offers us cultural parameters ideal for discerning the idea of architecture that underlies Loos' Column — an idea that is a long way from the previous historicist retrievals of someone like J.B. Fischer von Erlach (who, for instance, inserts the gigantic columns that stand out from the façade of the Karlskirche in a new syntactic context) and even more so from the naïve revival of the Egyptian column proposed for the *Chicago Tribune* by the American Paul Gerhardt (in which, if anything, a sort of caricature of the tripartition of the skyscraper introduced by Post and Sullivan is recognizable). The similarities between the two columns are only superficial and, however paradoxical it may seem, the only project for the *Chicago Tribune* Competition that is comparable in cultural attitude to Loos' proposal is the abstract and elementary spatial grid of Ludwig Hilberseimer. Extreme abstraction is the mirror image of extreme realism. The two proposals represent the far edges of avant-garde thought, of extreme renunciation and the refusal of mediation.

But a second answer to this question may be sought in the role played by the «symbolic» in architecture. Loos sees the *Großstadt* as the «scene» for architecture. The dual relationship between urban context and architectural object is never lacking in his work. If, in late-imperial Vienna crammed with nostalgic repression and false modernity, Loos had proposed the extreme negation of his façades «without qualities» and of his *Nihilismus* houses, here in Chicago, the metropolis realized, in the universe of pure quality, he contrasts the absolute quality of a symbolic object, symbolic inasmuch as it is an allusive fragment of a wider, obsolete code. This apparent contradiction in Loos' attitude towards the urbanized situation is, in reality, completely consistent with his poetics of «difference.» The plurality of languages is inherent in his method of design, as a comparison between different works designed in the same year makes apparent (one thinks of Rufer House or the country house at Gastein). The conceptual content hinted at by the column as symbolic object is the squeezing of the entire history of architecture onto a contemporary plane. In as much as it is a conscious attempt to pour the history of the past into the future, the Column is, strictly speaking, a *modern* work. Loos is well aware that his proposal is an advanced one, a prototype, and that its realization is therefore unlikely in the short run. This awareness is what lies behind the ambiguously prophetic tone of the closing words of his report: «The Big Greek Column will be built / if not in Chicago elsewhere / If not for the Chicago Tribune for someone else / If not by me by some other architect.» [12].

NOTES

1) About 260 projects from 32 different countries were entered. The final result of the competition was made known on 3 December 1922: the first prize of $ 50,000 was given to Howells and Hood, the second $ 20,000 to Eliel Saarinen, and the third of $ 10,000 to Holabird and Roche. Eleven Italians also took part in the competition, including the academic Marcello Piacentini.

2) L. SULLIVAN, *The «Chicago Tribune» Competition*, «The Architectural Record», February 1923, in *The Literature of Architecture*, New York 1966, pp. 624-631.

3) A lucid and well-documented critical analysis of the historical and cultural implications of the competition for the «Chicago Tribune» may be found in Manfredo Tafuri, *La montagna dinsincantata*, in (VV. AA.) *La città americana, dalla guerra civile al «New Deal»*, Bari, 1973 (pp. 418-453). On this subject see also: T.E. TALLMADGE, *A Critique of the «Chicago Tribune» Building Competition*, in «The Western Architect», 1923, vol. 32, no. 1, pp. 7-8; R. NEUTRA, *Die ältesten Hochhäuser und der jüngste Turm*, in «Die Baugilde», 1924, no. 21.

4) It is in fact on the basis of a re-reading of this report that as informed a critic as Manfredo Tafuri has, in his essay *La montagna disincantata*, overturned the arguments he previously sustained in *Teoria e Storia dell'Architettura* (about a presumed ironic intent prophetic of pop-art) in a harsh attack on the «pathetic desire» of the Viennese master «to speak of Values.» Cf. M. TAFURI, *Teoria e Storia dell'Architettura*, Bari, 1968, p. 101.

5) M. TAFURI, *La montagna disincantata*, op. cit., p. 432.

6) A. LOOS, *Architektur, Sämtliche Schriften*.

7) Translated from: *Der internationale Wettbewerb für den neuen Zeitungspalast der «Chicago Tribune»*, in «Zeitschrift des Österr. Ingenieur- und Architekten-Vereines», Vienna, Jahrg. 75, 1923.

8) I am refering to the celebrated *urinoir* that Marcel Duchamp sent to the exhibition of independents in New York under the title *Fountain* and signed R. Mutt.

9) «To make a Dadaist poem: Take a newspaper / Take a pair of scissors / Choose an article in the newspaper that is the same length as you want your poem to be / Cut out the article / Cut out carefully each word of this article / and put all the words in a bag / Shake gently / Take out the words one after the other, arranging them in the order that they are extracted / Copy them faithfully / The poetry will resemble you / And here you are, an infinitely original writer and endowed with charming sensitivity, although, to be sure, not understood by vulgar people. /» The *Manifesto on weak love and bitter love*, from which the passage «To make a Dadaist poem» is drawn, was read by Tristan Tzara in Paris on 22 December 1920 at the Galerie Povolozky and then published in issue no. 4 of *La vie des lettres*.

10) A. LOOS, *Architektur, Sämtliche Schriften*.

11) A. RIEGL, *Spätrömische Kunstindustrie*, Vienna 1901; G. SEMPER, *Der Stil in den technischen und architektonischen Künsten*, Munich 1878.

12) Translated from: *Zeitschrift des Österr. Ingenieur- und Architekten-Vereines*, op. cit.

BIBLIOGRAPHY

A. LOOS, *The Chicago Tribune Column* (illustrated pamphlet, presented as a report on the project); *Der internationale Wettbewerb für den neuen Zeitungspalast der Chicago Tribune*, in «Zeitschrift des Österr. Ingenieur- und Architekten- Vereines», vol. 75, nos. 3/4, dated 26 January 1923, page 16 et seq. The English version of the text in *The International Competition for a new Administration Building for the Chicago Tribune MCMXXXII*, Chicago 1923, fig. 196 (the book contains reproductions of all the drawings).
H. KULKA, *Adolf Loos*, op. cit., fig. 156 with caption.
L. MÜNZ, *Adolf Loos*, op. cit., p. 26 et seq. and an illustration.
L. MÜNZ, G. KÜNSTLER, *Der Architekt Adolf Loos*, op. cit., pp. 175-177, figs. 235-236.
M. TAFURI, *La montagna disincantata*, in VV. AA. *La città americana, dalla guerra civile al «New Deal»*, Bari 1973, pp. 430-434.
A. SIEGEL, *Chicago's Famous Buildings*, Chicago-London 1965; second edition 1969.
VV.AA., *Tribune Tower Competition*, New York 1980 (reprint of *The International competition for a new Administration Building for The Chicago Tribune*, New York 1923).

PROJECT FOR BUILDINGS WITH COURTYARDS NEAR THE MODENA-GRÜNDE
Vienna 3

1922

There is an archaic, medieval flavor to this plan of buildings with courtyards for the completion of the Modena gardens in Vienna, drawn on thirteen loose sheets (scattered among Loos' papers) and dating in all probability from 1922. [1] According to H. Kulka's account, Loos intended the complex as a center for leisure facilities (with a hotel, theater, casino, swimming pool, ice rink and even a miniature train in a tunnel). But the basic objective of the plan was to redesign the northern section of the Modena-Gründe by defining a regular mesh of architecture that would have enclosed part of the green area laid out in direct continuity with an existing park to the south. The project never not got beyond the embryonic stage. Despite this, certain morphological characteristics are clearly distinguishable. The most outstanding architectural feature among these is the use of the colonnade to define a complicated network of sheltered pedestrian routes, around which the whole complex is arranged. In this sense, traces of the Roman forums are mixed up with the medieval patterns of monastery cloisters in this typological model. The medieval character in still more evident in the design of an orthogonal courtyard open on only one side through a narrow passage delimited by two imposing square towers (surmounted by high sloping roofs, in the shape of a pyramid). The modernity of the procedure of composition is only recognizable in this design in the clearly legible way the elements are assembled. And it is certainly surprising to note that this archaism of form is proposed for a project that aims to provide facilities for the great urban masses, that is to say, for an object derived directly from modern mass culture. This contrast should make us pause for reflection. It shows that Loos recognizes a relative independence of form and function: a contemporary function can be fulfilled by a historic form.

NOTES

1) The original drawings and the numerous sketches relating to this project are kept in the Loos-Archiv. The date, 1922, is attributed by Heinrich Kulka, op. cit.

BIBLIOGRAPHY

H. KULKA, *Adolf Loos*, op. cit., p. 26.
L. MÜNZ, G. KÜNSTLER, *Der Architekt Adolf Loos*, op. cit., pp. 163-166, figs. 224, 226.

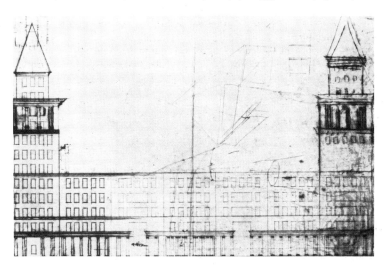

SPANNER COUNTRY HOUSE
near Gumpoldskirchen, in Lower Austria

1923

«How should the architect of the metropolis build when he is called on to build in the country? The supporters of the national heritage say: like a peasant!... But the architect doesn't work like that. He works according to a preestablished plan. And if he wanted to copy the ingenuousness of the peasant he would annoy all the cultivated people, as happens with the ladies who wear Saltzburger costumes at Ischl.... This affected taste for the *naïf*, this deliberate regression to a different cultural level is ridiculous and lacking in dignity, and was in fact unknown to the old masters who were not lacking in dignity and were still less ridiculous.

«We are more advanced than the peasant. But he should not only take advantage of our threshing machines, but also be able to share in our achievements and experiments in the building field. We must be his guide, not imitate him.» [1]

The Spanner Country House is a development in architecture that parallels this cultural stand taken in 1914, in his polemical essay attacking the *Heimatkünst*. The building was constructed in an evocative rural setting to the south of Vienna, during a troubling period of economic inflation. In an attempt to reduce costs an experiment was made in the advanced application of «poor technologies.» The load-bearing structure is made of wood and fixed on a stone base. But neither ingenuousness nor regression nor naive imitation can be detected in this technological choice. On the contrary, we know that as far back as 1921, Loos had patented a construction scheme in wood and stone that proposed an intelligent updating of the structural logic of such a scheme.

So the attention given to poor technologies is aimed at a modern recovery of an obsolete technical heritage that, without yielding to nostalgia, picks out all its potentialities for renovation and reuse.

This is demonstrated by the introduction of a flat roof in the Spanner country house, upsetting the conventional image of the rural house. For Loos, unlike the *Heimatkünstler*, the flat Holzzement roof is a modern technical achievement that fulfills an age-old aspiration of Austrian architecture.

«The roof in Austria should be flat. The inhabitants of the Alps, because of the wind and snow, give the roof the least slope possible: so it is obvious that our nationalistic artists would build roofs for them with the steepest pitch possible, so that at every snowfall they represent a danger for all the inhabitants. The flat roof adds an element of beauty to our alpine landscape, the pitched roof deadens. This is a clear example of how the most profound truth also produces aesthetic perfection.» [2]

Technical motivations, then, are closely interwoven with formal ones. Despite this there remains a field of specific relevance to composition. From this point of view two facts should be emphasized: the use of color on the external walls and the reduction of volumetric play to two prismatic elements.

The contrast between the white and green vertical stripes adds an unusual optical quality that dissolves the box-like appearance of the building, immersing it in the landscape. But the basic composition remains extremely simple: a horizontal prism and a vertical one. In the lowest part of the building the roof terrace is used as a solarium.

NOTES

1) A. LOOS, *Sämtliche Schriften*.

2) Idem, p. 281.

BIBLIOGRAPHY

H. KULKA, *Adolf Loos*, op. cit., figs. 146-148, with caption.
F. GLÜCK, *Der Aufbau*, Vienna 1958, p. 396 with illustrations.
L. MÜNZ, G. KÜNSTLER, *Der Architekt Adolf Loos*, op. cit., p. 70-72, figs. 62-63.

P. C. LESCHKA & CO. MEN'S OUTFITTING STORE
Spiegelgasse 13, Vienna 1 (radically modified today)

1923
1924

The basic problem was a rather complex one: to transform two adjacent rooms, simultaneously very narrow and very tall, into an elegant fashion store. Moreover, the second of the two rooms completely lacked openings to admit natural light.

The connection between the two rooms is made by means of a wide trabeated space that contains (in the extension of the structural pillars) four steps: the raising of the floor optically reduces the abnormal height of the store. For the second room a highly luminous lacunar ceiling is constructed within the breadth of the architrave, hung with forty lamps. This room in its turn communicates, by means of a smaller architrave, with a further storage space hollowed out at the rear, producing an almost kaleidoscopic effect. The rhythmic scansion of the rooms that fit one into the other is emphasized by elegant frames painted in lively colors and set into the ceiling and walls.

But the overall visual effect of the store relies on the contrast between the white of the ceiling and the glossy black of the wood from which the cupboards lining the walls and the sales counters are made. There is nothing left but to regret the destruction of such a modern, simple and refined decoration.

BIBLIOGRAPHY

H. KULKA, *Adolf Loos*, op. cit., fig. 155, with caption.
L. MÜNZ, G. KÜNSTLER, *Der Architekt Adolf Loos*, op. cit., p. 30, fig. 13.

HOUSING UNIT FOR THE MUNICIPALITY OF VIENNA

Inzersdorferstrasse - Staudiglgasse, Vienna 10

1923

At the time Loos designed this Housing Unit he had already resigned from his post as chief architect of the housing department of the Municipality of Vienna. Despite this the proposal may be considered a logical and consistent extension of his stubborn and controversial search for new building patterns for working-class housing.

The plan was not approved by the Social-Democratic administration of *Rote Wien*. One wonders why. It describes a stepped residential complex, with wide terraces with pergolas and genuine galleries giving direct access to the duplex flats. It is, then, a wholly original compositional scheme. Unlike the *Höfe* — that rework and update the model of the monasteries that are to be found all over Vienna — the scheme worked out by Loos is an authentic invention without historical precedent.

Loos' design proposal is based on simple ethical and social motivations dictated by an empirical common sense rather than on complex political evaluations. But it is this very apolitical skepticism that determines the distance he consciously puts between himself and the heart of the Social-Democratic debate as far as public intervention in the building industry is concerned and the inevitable failure of his urban plan. He says about this in his essay *Die moderne siedlung* (1926): «I imagine these houses made up of two stories, each with its own entrance from the street. I have in mind a plan for a building that would in fact be a house with terraces, access to which would be by an external staircase. We can also look on these terraces as a raised street; each with its own entrance, its own pergola where one may linger of an evening to take a breath of fresh air. Children can play on the terrace without the danger of being run over by a car, etc. This was my idea, because I was aware that one often reads in the newspaper of children, left unattended by their parents who were too busy with something else, climbing onto the window sill and then falling into the street or courtyard. This would be a cruel end for the children of the poor. This safe and quiet street of terraces gives them the chance to pass the whole day in the open, near their house and under the eye of the neighbors. This was my idea as far as the children were concerned.» [1]

It is true that this residential complex is only the result of an ingenious assembly of the living cells of the Siedlung am Heuberg where the vegetable garden — impossible in the heart of the *Großstadt* — is replaced by the terrace. Yet the primary function of the terrace is as a social meeting-place for the neighborhood group rather than a covered walk. Collective housing as *Gemeinschaft*, then: this is the controversial aim of Loos' project.

The architecture translates this intention into the formal strength of its image. The massive building block is bent along Inzersdorferstrasse, following the curve of the street. The pattern of volumes derives from the system of open staircases and long terraces. The opposite face, looking onto Staudiglgasse, is dominated by the vertical bulk of the wall, pierced by regular square windows and broken at two points by wide terraced walks. The stepped layout of the structure is clearly visible on the smaller lateral façades.

Elsewhere in the above-mentioned essay Loos declares: «Up to now I have only designed one multifamily building, that was, however, rejected by the Municipal Council. In it I had envisaged only apartments arranged on two floors. This is no discovery of mine. The English and the Americans have apartments that take up two floors in buildings that are ten or even twenty stories high. People attach very great importance to the rooms of the living area not being close to the bedrooms, preferring that they remain separated by the stairs.» [2]

There is a deliberate rhetorical deceit in this passage in its attempt to make his own proposal convincing by putting it across as a widely used model in Anglo-Saxon culture, adopted once again as an imaginary projection of his own aspiration to modernity. In reality this stepped residential complex is the end point of a rigorous disciplinary research, whose development was self-contained.

The most obvious antecedent is Scheu House (1912), whose façade overlooking La-Roche-Gasse presents unmistakable similarities of form to the lateral faces of the Housing Unit looking onto the Bürgergasse. A similar compositional theme of terraced architecture is further developed the same year in the contemporaneous plans for the Grand Hotel Babylon and for the House at the Venice Lido, and in a sketch for the Otto Haas-Hof. The novelty of the project lies in, if anything, the application of high levels of quality, of comfort and a feeling of airiness to mass working-class housing.

NOTES

1) A. LOOS, *Die moderne siedlung*, in *Sämtliche Schriften*.

2) Ibid., p. 362.

BIBLIOGRAPHY

H. KULKA, *Adolf Loos*, op. cit., figs. 95-103 with caption.
L. MÜNZ, G. KÜNSTLER, *Der Architekt Adolf Loos*, op. cit., pp. 152-154, figs. 210-216.

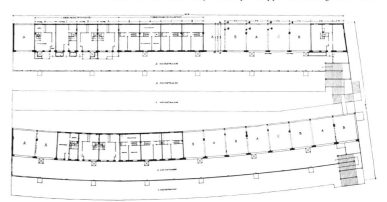

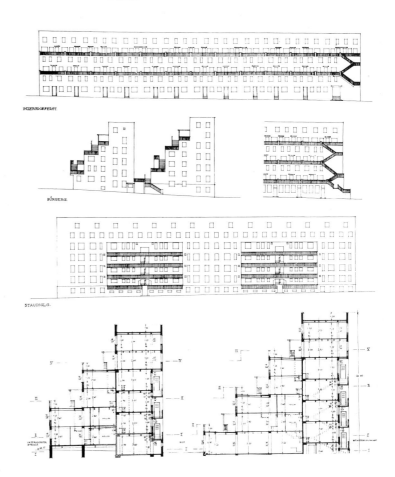

PROJECT FOR A GROUP OF TWENTY HOUSES WITH TERRACES

Côte d'Azur, France

1923

With systematic perseverance, Loos carries on with his analytical investigation of terraced apartments, assembling and reassembling the typological model until it attains in this project to a refined, complex and articulate compositional pattern. The twenty houses are set on the French Riviera and are designed to furnish a view of the landscape and the pleasure of sitting on the terrace, all within very narrow limits of space (a building area of only 850 square meters). It is, in short, a high quality and potentially repeatable prototype for intensive residential building.

It is not difficult to make out, behind the tight orchestration of volumes, the pyramidal scheme of composition worked out the same year for the Grand Hotel Babylon. More exactly, a scheme based on an upturned pyramid is clearly visible in the volumetric plan. Three blocks of apartments that become progressively narrower at both top and bottom extend along southward-pointing axes from a lamellar block exposed to the north. Each apartment, provided with a separate entrance, uses the roof of the apartment below as a terrace (except the last, smaller one, that has a panoramic view on three sides instead). The prismatic building in the rear is intended for offices, apart from the top floor which is used as an apartment (making use of the roof of the office below as a terrace, on the same principle).

What emerges from a comparative analysis of the plans is the repetitiveness of the distributive layout, in an attempt to preserve the logical and functional *organigramme* despite the increase in scale.

Of great interest is the vertical section that reveals the principle behind the articulation of internal space: the *Raumplan*. In this case, staggering takes place not only between the floors of each single apartment, but also between the floors belonging to different apartments (with the aim of facilitating the panoramic view as in a theater). This results in a complex structure, but a closely linked and united one.

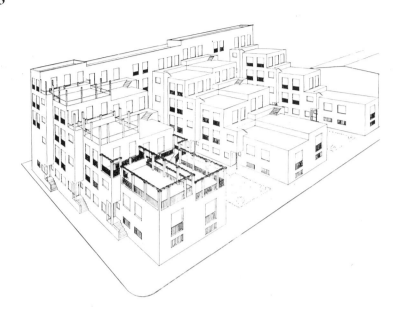

BIBLIOGRAPHY

H. KULKA, *Eine neue Bauform an der Riviera*, in «Die Riviera-Wochenschau», Jahr II, no. 30, 29 May 1931.
H. KULKA, *Adolf Loos*, op. cit., figs. 157-159 with captions.
L. MÜNZ, G. KÜNSTLER, *Der Architekt Adolf Loos*, op. cit., p. 120, figs. 143-145.

PROJECT FOR THE GRAND HOTEL BABYLON

Nice, France

1923

Babylon, the mythical city of gardens: this is the poetical phantasm evoked by this project (for a hotel of 700 rooms and 1000 beds) selected for the exhibition held in 1923 at the Salon d'Automne in Paris. But there is a more precise literary reference, as Loos himself suggests:

«I got the name from a popular novel by Arnold Bennett, *The Grand Babylon Hotel*. Every hotel should be planned so as to answer to the requirements of its setting. I decided on the Riviera, which I know well.»[1]

Apart from allegories, the project has a precise objective: the invention of a model for a hotel in which all the rooms are arranged along terraces, each room having all the necessary facilities.

«Dark rooms giving onto the courtyard have to be cheap even in luxury hotels. But a hotel arranged around terraces has none of these rooms: it only has front rooms. Moreover, with girder construction, that is, with the use of steel structures, it is possible to extend the sides exposed to the sun, to the east and to the west. The main thing is that each room should have its own terrace. They are only absent on the north face.»[2]

In the planning estimates the Pharaonic complex was to have included shops and sports and leisure facilities as well. But the fundamental question does not so much concern functional and typological aspects — which are well-handled — as the choice of form. Why the pyramid?

We can attempt to answer this question by reconstructing the evolution of the idea from the original early sketches, in which some alternative possibilities can be made out, such as the adoption of a scheme (with steps on only one side) similar to that of the Scheu House. It is clear that the extension of a solution of this kind to the enormous scale of the hotel would have created grotesquely rhetorical effects. The pyramid shape, on the contrary, with its gradual shrinking from base to vertex, offered the

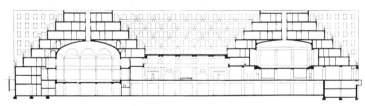

Elevation of the south side and section of the two pyramids.

dual advantage of attenuating the mass of the building on an oblique triangular plane and of making its appearance in perspective identical on all sides. Despite the archaic, almost ancestral, nature of the model, the pyramid represented the most advanced, the most «modern» solution to the problem of blending an architectural object of huge dimensions into the landscape. «The best form,» Loos had already made clear, «is always already available.»[3] It is no coincidence, besides, that Le Corbusier will make use of the same elementary model for the Mundaneum project in Geneva (1929). What seems less convincing — as far as what has been said up to now goes — is the grafting of a large box-like block onto the rear that neutralizes the lucidly radical appearance of the pure pyramidal shape (evident in the early sketches). But once again the articulation of space inside this block demonstrates an intuition that is extraordinary to say the least: two large vaulted rooms illuminated from above by a deep *oculus* are connected by a rectangular space, roofed by a tank of glass and steel that would have filtered the light, modulating it by the movement of the water contained therein.

It is worth looking at Loos' description again: «We may liken the design of two linked pyramids to two enormous sepulchral vaults. One of these will be used as an ice palace, the other as a large dance hall. Between the two is a large room illuminated from above that — instead of a glass roof, which would not look good from the internal terraces — will have a tank of water with its bottom made from Luxfer.» [4]

NOTES

1) A. LOOS, *Das Grand Hotel Babylon*, 1923, in «Die neue Wirtschaft», Jahr I, Vienna, 20 December 1923, p. 113.

2) Ibid.

3) A. LOOS, *Sämtliche Schriften*.

4) A. LOOS, *Das Grand Hotel Babylon*, op. cit.

BIBLIOGRAPHY

H. KULKA, *Aldolf Loos*, op. cit., figs. 160-169 with caption.
L. MÜNZ, *Adolf Loos*, op. cit., p. 38, illustrations.
Catalog of the Galerie Würthle, Vienna 1961, fig. 7.
L. MÜNZ, G. KÜSTLER, *Der Architekt Adolf Loos*, op. cit., pp. 116-120, figs. 139-142.

PROJECT FOR A TOWN HALL
Mexico City

1923

This is a monumental stepped building, with a hint of the Aztec pyramid, already published in the monograph by L. Münz and G. Künstler (fig. 142, p. 117) but incorrectly labeled as a sketch for the Grand Hotel Babylon project.

BIBLIOGRAPHY

B. RUKSCHCIO, *Studien zu Entwürfen, Projekten und ausgeführten Bauten von Adolf Loos. 1870-1930*, op. cit., WV. H.155.23.P.

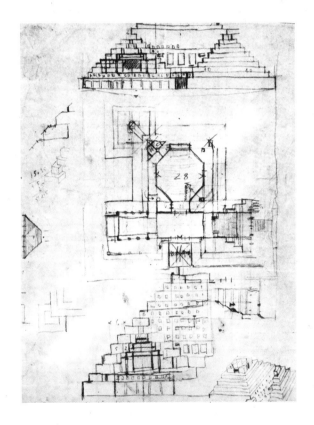

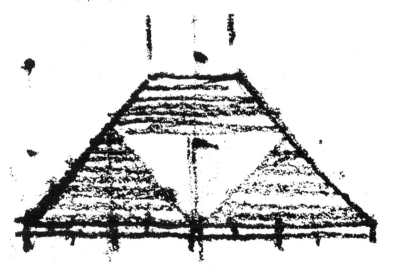

PROJECT FOR THE VILLA SIMON
Vienna

1923

The project was never carried out. The drafts (plans and elevations) are kept in the Loos-Archiv at the Albertina. It is interesting to note the rigorously classical formulation of the composition. Symmetry is, in fact, the governing factor in the design. On the outside the two columns of the entrance hall are worthy of special mention as they are an explicit sign of the way the architecture harks back to an unmistakable linguistic code.

Inside, the large living and music room communicates with two adja-cent areas (dining room and studio) through wide openings, thereby creating a visual and spatial continuum.

BIBLIOGRAPHY

H. KULKA, *Adolf Loos*, op. cit., figs. 153-154.
L. MÜNZ, G. KÜNSTLER, *Der Architekt Adolf Loos*, op. cit., section no. 78, p. 191.
B. RUKSCHCIO, *Studien zu Entwürfen, Projekten und ausgeführten Bauten von Adolf Loos 1870-1930*, op. cit., WV. H.158.23.P.

1920 - COMMUNITY KITCHEN OF THE LAINZER-SIEDLUNG

Nothing now remains of the original work.

BIBLIOGRAPHY

P. STEFAN, *Frau Doktor*, Vienna 1922, p. 27.
B. RUKSCHCIO, *Studien zu Entwürfen, Projekten und ausgeführten Bauten von Adolf Loos 1870-1930*. op. cit., WV. L.120.20.

1922 - ALTERATIONS TO STEINER HOUSE
Chimanistrasse 26, Vienna 19

Colored copies of the final drafts of the project (plans, elevations and sections) are preserved in the Loos-Archiv. The colors indicate where modifications have been made.

BIBLIOGRAPHY

L. MÜNZ, G. KÜNSTLER, *Der Architekt Adolf Loos*, op. cit., section no. 70, p. 191.
B. RUKSCHCIO, *Studien zu Entwürfen, Projekten und ausgeführten Bauten von Adolf Loos 1870-1930*, op. cit., WV. H.142.22.P.

1922 - ALTERATIONS TO VILLA REITLER
Elsslergasse 9, Vienna 13

Nothing remains of the alterations that were originally carried out.

BIBLIOGRAPHY

B. RUKSCHCIO, *Studien zu Entwürfen, Projekten und ausgeführten Bauten von Adolf Loos 1870-1930*, op. cit., WV. H.134.22.

1922 - PLAN OF STROSS HOUSE
Vienna

A fadel copy of the plan and elevations dated Vienna, April 1922 is in the Loos archives.

BIBLIOGRAPHY

L. MÜNZ, G. KÜNSTLER, *Der Architekt Adolf Loos*, op. cit., section no. 66, p. 190 with illustrations.

1922 - DRAWING OF A MULTIFUNCTIONAL BUILDING

This attempt at reorganizing his ideas about a typological model that is used again in his projects is not linked to any one site. It recalls the complex of leisure facilities near the Modena gardens designed in the same year.

BIBLIOGRAPHY

L. MÜNZ, G. KÜNSTLER, *Der Architekt Adolf Loos*, op. cit., section no. 68, p. 190 with illustrations.

1922 - APARTMENT OF HUGO KALLBERG
Freiheitsplatz 10, Vienna 9

BIBLIOGRAPHY

B. RUKSCHCIO, *Studien zu Entwürfen, Projekten und ausgeführten Bauten von Adolf Loos 1870-1930*, op. cit., WV. W. 147.22.

1922 - ALTERATIONS TO THE MERKURBANK
F. Schmidtplatz 6, Vienna 8

BIBLIOGRAPHY

B. RUKSCHCIO, *Studien zu Entwürfen, Projekten und ausgführten Bauten von Adolf Loos 1870-1930*, op. cit., WV. L.137.22.

1922 - ALTERATIONS TO THE ARBEITERBANK
Praterstrasse 8, Vienna 2

BIBLIOGRAPHY

B. RUKSCHCIO, *Studien zu Entwürfern, Projekten und ausgeführten Bauten von Adolf Loos 1870-1930*, op. cit., WV. L. 138.22.

1922-1923 - PROJECT FOR THE SIEDLUNG SÜDOST
Laaerbergstrasse, Vienna 10

BIBLIOGRAPHY

B. RUKSCHCIO, *Studien zu Entwürfern, Projekten und ausgeführten Bauten von Adolf Loos 1870-1930*, op. cit., WV. H. 136.22.

1923 - DECORATIONS CARRIED OUT FOR ERICH MANDL
Rotenturmstrasse 2/4, Vienna 1

Only a few photographs and original designs kept in the Loos-Archiv remain to document the interior decoration of the ground floor and first floor of the building in which the firm was located. The firm, in fact, no longer exists.

BIBLIOGRAPHY

H. KULKA, *Adolf Loos*, op. cit., figs. 92-93.
L. MÜNZ, G. KÜNSTLER, *Der Architekt Adolf Loos*, op. cit., section no. 59, p. 189.
F. KURRENT, J. SPALT, *Unbekanntes von Adolf Loos*, in «Bauforum» no. 21, 1970, p. 39.

1923 - PROJECT FOR THE VILLA VERDIER
Le Lavandou (Var), France

The distribution of volumes is based on the deep recession of sections of the building. The large central living room on two levels is of great interest. Facing onto one side of this room are galleries giving access to the sleeping area and on the other side, that of the terrace, a curvilinear matrix is introduced.

BIBLIOGRAPHY

J. GANTNER, *Adolf Loös, zum 60. Geburtstag* in «Das neue Frankfurt», Jahr V, 1931, no. I, fig. 8.
H. KULKA, *Adolf Loos*, op. cit., figs. 139-145 with captions.
L. MÜNZ, G. KÜNSTLER, *Der Architekt Adolf Loos*, op. cit., section no. 74, p. 190.

1923 - PROJECT FOR THE SPORT-HOTEL
Bois de Boulogne, Paris

BIBLIOGRAPHY

B. RUKSCHCIO, *Studien zu Entwürfen, Projekten und ausgeführten Bauten von Adolf Loos 1870-1930*, op. cit., WV. H.160.23.P.

1923 - PLAN OF A HOUSE WITH COURTYARD

Already published in the monograph by L. Münz and G. Künstler as a project by the «school of Loos» (*Schülerarbeit*).

BIBLIOGRAPHY

L. MÜNZ, G. KÜNSTLER, *Der Architekt Adolf Loos*, op. cit., figs. 146-147.
B. RUKSCHCIO, *Studien zu Entwürfen, Projekten und ausgeführten Bauten von Adolf Loos 1870-1930*, op. cit., WV. H.159.23.P.

PROJECT FOR MOISSI HOUSE
The Lido of Venice

1923

This house, designed for the actor Alexander Moissi, develops the analytical bias of Loos' architecture, as the drafts of the project clearly show (these are more than sufficient to permit a reliable interpretation of the underlying architectural intention: a model was made as well as the drawings). It is, in effect, a transcription into modern language of the typological model of the Mediterranean house. And this is exactly where his analytical grasp of a minor language, that is to say of Italian rural architecture, shows itself, not in the imitative terms of the pseudopopular, but in the selective ones of a reinterpretation. There are, in this case, few derivative features: the compositional scheme of the terrace that acts as a pivot for the arrangement of the living areas, the open flight of stairs, the pure volumes, the flat roof and the openings cut straight through the wall.

It is interesting to note that, apart from the first two, these elements of composition already form an integral part of the consolidated repertory of forms in the twenties (a sign of the assimilation that had taken place of the functional patterns of minor architecture favored by the convergent analytical introspection of masters of such diverse cultural origins as Wright and Le Corbusier, not to mention Loos). But in the Lido house these take on an unusual, extreme and conscious neatness, as is demonstrated by the severely geometrical, in some ways *classical* design of the façades.

On the lower part of the western face, to the left, are two rows of windows that break up the terse rectangular plane of the wall with their close and regular pattern. On the eastern face the wide balcony is the modular element that, repeated, marks the *leitmotiv* of the composition, while the open flight of stairs dominates the design of the south face, contrasting with the closed composition of the northern one, where the wall is barely pierced by small openings for ventilation.

The *otherness* of the design of the façades is not casual. It is dictated by the position of the natural elements: the light and the sea. This house is designed in rapport with the place. Taking climatic conditions into account, Loos confines the openings essentially to the east and west faces (to catch the morning and afternoon sun), avoiding exposure to the south (too hot) and utilizing the small openings to the north to ensure perfect ventilation (favored by the difference in temperature between the north and south sides). The large size of the balconies derives in turn from the presence of the sea to the east, onto which faces the terrace itself, destined to be used as a solarium.

The terrace (sheltered by a pergola that rests on simple square pillars) is the true pivot of the house, and is also the element of composition that most clearly derives from the Mediterranean model of the house.

Like the atrium of the ancient *domus italica*, the terrace gives direct access onto the rooms intended for sitting and relaxation. On the first floor of the house is, in fact, located the large dining and music room that communicates, across a gradient of two steps, with a living room given a welcoming atmosphere by the presence of a fireplace and alcove. The latter is formed out of the space beneath the stairs that lead from the terrace to the roof. The way in which the open stairs are situated above the internal ones is very ingenious, leaving gaps between the treads that serve to illuminate the corridors and rooms below. The distribution of internal space is based on a complex application of the *Raumplan*. On the two lower floors are located, on staggered levels, the sleeping quarters of the owners of the house, those for guests and the service rooms. The access corridors are internal and Loos devises advanced technical solutions for their lighting and ventilation (such as the skylight set in the floor of the terrace that indirectly illuminates the corridor of the guests' sleeping quarters below).

BIBLIOGRAPHY

Le Salon d'Automne, in «L'Amour de l'Art», vol. IV, Paris 1923.
H. KULKA, *Adolf Loos*, op. cit., figs. 170-181 with captions.
L. MÜNZ, G. KÜNSTLER, *Der Architekt Adolf Loos*, op. cit., figs. 184-194, pp. 143-144.

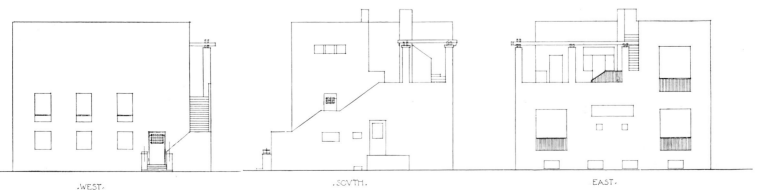

.WEST.   .SOVTH.   .EAST.

OTTO HAAS-HOF

Durchlaufstrasse - Pasettistrasse, Vienna 22 (with Karl Dirnhuber, Franz Schuster, Grete Schütte Lihotzky)

Although it remained for a long time «unpublished», this work constitutes a document of exceptional value to an understanding of the meaning and quality of the work he carried out for the municipal council of «Red Vienna.» [1] With the construction of the block of about 50 apartments in the Otto Haas-Hof (containing 273 apartments in all) Loos had the chance to give a practical demonstration of his architectural polemics against the *Proletarischer Stil*. This opposition to any style that claimed to represent working-class culture by populist rhetoric was already evident, in its basic theoretical presuppositions, in the work he carried out as chief

1924

architect of the housing department of the Municipality of Vienna, which had led to the limited and partial realization of the *Siedlungen* at Lainz and at Heuberg. But the particular urban location of the property (a short distance from the Winarskyhof, a building emblematic of the first phase in the fulfillment of the housing policy of Red Vienna) gave this project quite another strategic importance.

The fact that the project is for a *Wohnhof* is already significant in itself. The *Wohnhof* is a superblock of apartments arranged around a closed inner court where communal facilities are situated (in this case, a nursery

Original plans (Plan- und Schriftenkammer, Vienna).

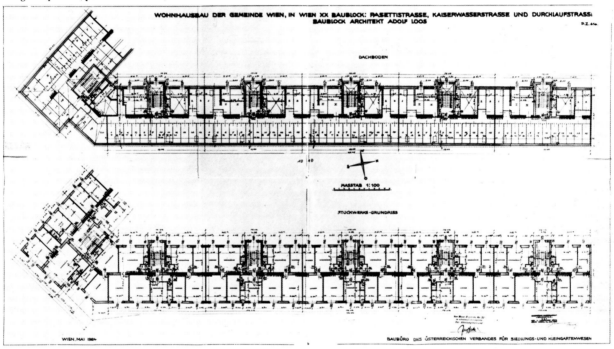

Two views of Otto Haas-Hof today.

school, a pharmacy, and various workshops). This type of scheme (that took its inspiration from the monastery buildings that have such deep and widespread roots in the urban history of Vienna) is known to have been adopted as the building pattern of the *Wohnungspolitik der Gemeinde Wien* launched in 1923 with the approval of the first «five year plan» for housing. The fact that Loos should have made a far from negligible contribution to one of the first superblocks constructed by the Municipality of Vienna demonstrates the unreliability of those interprétations that tend to reduce Loos' dissent from the architectural choices made by Red Vienna to a pure and simple conflict over the type of models to be adopted (in short, the *Siedlungen* versus the *Höfe*). Nor should it be forgotten that the year before Loos had designed a housing unit for the same municipal administration, with raised walkways and duplex apartments. Although it represented an alternative design to the canonical model of the *Höfe*, it should, strictly speaking, be placed in the category of the superblock. So the deep motivations for the dissonance of aims should be sought elsewhere, and more specifically, in questions of architecture.

Loos received the commission for the Otto Haas-Hof project — to be drawn up in collaboration with Karl Dirnhuber, Franz Schuster and Grete Schütte Lihotzky — before his move to Paris. The *Wohnhof* was part of a wider plan of development that included the Winarskyhof itself (planned by J. Hoffmann, P. Behrens, J. Frank and others) and was financed as a single operation. Despite the intention of fostering an «encounter» in order to produce a group design, the complex looks like a puzzle in which the «pieces» designed by each architect are distinguishable.

The plan of the Otto Haas-Hof is essentially triangular in shape, following the boundary of the building plot.

An unadorned austerity is the unmistakable characteristic that marks out the block designed by Loos (the side along Durchlaufstrasse) from those built to the designs of Dirnhuber (the corner opposite the Winarskyhof), of Schuster (the side facing Pasettistrasse) and of Schütte Lihotzky (the side facing Kaiserwasserstrasse, today Winarskystrasse).

The polemical intent behind Loos' severe geometrical purism is particularly evident when compared with the plastic and linear excess of Dirnhuber's solution, which echoes the semantic expressionism of the doorway to the Winarskyhof designed by Peter Behrens. The Durchlaufstrasse façade has, in fact, the appearance of a pure, smooth surface, pierced by four kinds of regular, more or less square windows. To sum up, it is a neutral screen of large dimensions that renounces any form of «tattooing», any deliberately semantic, decorative show. The roof itself,

with a single pitch, is recessed so that the skyline is a pure horizontal line. Only within the court do the high towers of the staircases (that allude on a larger scale to the ones that dominate the composition of the façades of the Siedlung am Heuberg) and the projecting volume of the Kindergarten break up the deliberate monotony of the layout.

This last prismatic block that projects into the court and is pierced by three high and imposing windows is particularly fascinating. Perhaps only the central block of the Klosehof, designed the same year by Josef Hoffmann, achieves a comparable sobriety and elegance of line. A final mention should be made of Dietrich Worb's recent attribution to Loos of a different idea for an initial design for the Otto Haas-Hof, on the basis of an interpretation of a draft discovered in the Loos-Archiv (Graph. Slg. Albertina, A.L. Archiv, Inv. n. 0459). According to this hypothesis Loos had envisaged at an early stage (in 1923) a terraced building that sloped down toward the courtyard. But leaving aside the unending search for the «original idea», it remains a fact that Loos' nucleus is, just as it was built, an unequivocally polemical manifesto for architecture without ornaments. In other words, Loos puts forward the absence of tattos as the only decent possibility for architecture intended for the proletariat. This is the real dividing line that marks the great theoretical difference between the architecture proposed by Loos and the new *Baustil* manufactured for Red Vienna by the pupils of the *Wagnerschule*.

NOTES

1) The first mention of this work, inexplicably left out of the monographs by Kulka and Münz, is to be found in the essay by Hans Krebitz listed in the bibliography.

BIBLIOGRAPHY

H. KREBITZ, *Adolf Loos, unbekannte Bauten*, in «Bau», Vienna nos. I-2, 1966, pp. 24-25.
B. RUKSCHCIO, *Studien zu Entwürfen, Projekten und ausgeführten Bauten von Adolf Loos 1870-1930*, op. cit., WV. H.152.23.P.
D. WORBS, *Die Wiener Arbeiterterrassenhäuser von Adolf Loos 1923*, in VV. AA., *Architektur, Stadt und Politik*, Giessen, 1979, pp. 118-134.
M. TAFURI, (editor), *Vienna Rossa*, Milan 1980, pp. 176-177.

Elevations of the original project (Plan- und Schriftenkammer, Vienna).

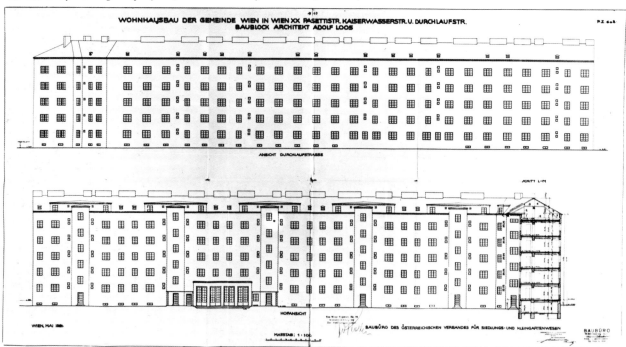

PROJECT FOR A HOTEL
Avenue des Champs-Elysées, Paris

1924

This is a project, never carried out, for a large block construction that would have covered the entire area between rue de la Boëtie and rue du Colisée. The hotel would have been provided with a large swimming pool, a dance hall, shops, commercial offices, a roof garden, etc. In this sense it is something more than a hotel: it is an urban concentration of public functions and leisure facilities. Loos' treatment of the project was probably influenced by literary accounts of a large building, called «le Colisée», that had been the center for entertainment, amusements and cultural activity in the quarter up until the 18th century. But what matters more is the definition of a model that evokes the large blocks built around courts typical of the Viennese monasteries: a massive closed exterior and concentration of communal activities in the *Hof* (court).

The roof garden, set on the first floor roof, would have been enclosed in a triangle open to the sky and sheltered on three sides by the eight-story-high construction. At the point where the two roads mentioned above intersect at an oblique angle, a cylindrical tower rises that is repeated at the other extreme of the side facing the rue du Colisée. The two towers have an important function in the composition: they are the hinge elements around which the building blocks are articulated, blocks which are set at different angles. Only at the opposite point to the rue du Colisée façade do the wings of the construction meet at a right angle. [1]

The equilibrium between plastic masses is the dominant factor in Loos' design, not the dynamism. Rather it is within his own research, between the cylindrical towers of Villa Karma (1904-1906) and those of the house for Josephine Baker (1928), that elements of anticipation and growth may be detected. The trend towards terraces that reappears in the top three stories was consistent with a constantly proposed idea of architecture (in the Grand Hotel Babylon of 1923, for instance). Particular attention should be paid to the arrangement of internal spaces. A precise axis of penetration can be discerned on the ground floor leading from the arcade (concave in shape) through the rectangular entrance hall to the *salle de fêtes* (in the form of a semicircular amphitheater). The outside of the building, along the streets, is lined with shops. These have no back rooms but are provided instead with rooms of a similar size in the basement. Light enters through full-length slits set into the pavement. The basement section is on two levels. On the first level are the garages; the second is taken up by the large indoor swimming pool, whose shape echoes that of the *salle de fêtes* fused with that of the entrance hall. The first floor, which holds the dining room and administrative offices, concludes the *public* zone of the building. On the upper floors are the bedrooms of the hotel proper, which face onto the inner courtyard.

The most interesting feature of the project lies in the response to the urban theme proposed by such a pattern: isolation from the streets, and the creation of a protected nucleus of public activities on the inside.

NOTES

1) If it was not so reckless, and indefensible from a critical viewpoint, one might speak of the formal analogies between these towers and the cylindrical elements in certain drawings by Sant'Elia and to an even greater degree with those of Mario Chiattone (his 1914 block of apartments for instance). The similarities would seem to be strengthened by the reappearance of a stepped outline in the top three floors of the hotel, revealing the circular shape of the towers to an ever greater extent. Although this is not impossible — given the widespread influence of futurist designs in Europe — the analogy should in the end be excluded because of the profound conceptual differences in the use of these elements of composition.

BIBLIOGRAPHY

H. KULKA, *Adolf Loos*, op. cit., figs. 182-188.
L. MÜNZ, G. KÜNSTLER, *Der Architekt Adolf Loos*, op. cit., pp. 108-110, figs. 113-119.

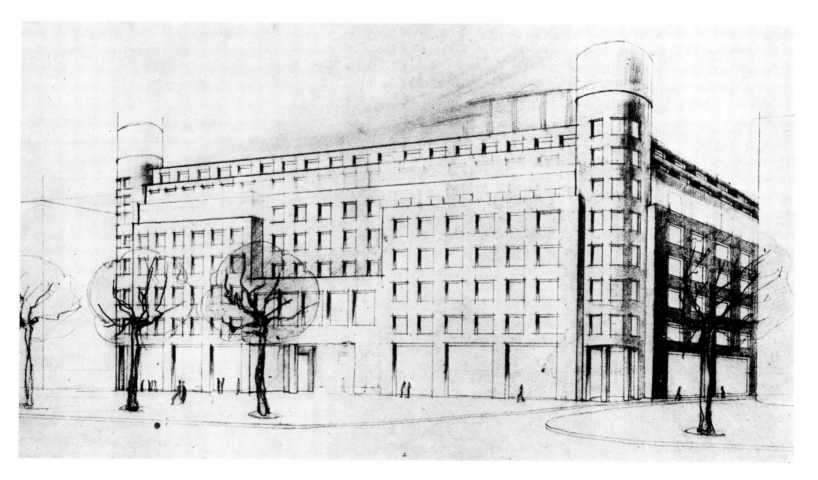

PROJECT FOR AN EXHIBITION BUILDING
Tientsin, China

1925

Not many facts are available for an evaluation of this project which is only drawn up on the most general lines. The drafts, kept today in the Loos-Archiv at the Albertina, do, however, give us some indications that are not without interest as to the architecture, such as the idea of creating a theater on the top floors of the building set in the foreground of the perspective drawing. This produces an external image of great effectiveness, as a result of the total lack of openings in the upper part of the monolithic block. This monolithic quality (extended over the entire building) is the other clearly visible element of design. A predominance of solids over voids, an almost obsessive regularity in the pattern and geometry of the openings and stereometric purity of the volumes are the chief ingredients in the composition. This large-scale complex was intended as a multifunctional community center for a city in north China that was very active in international trade at the time.

Apart from a center for exhibitions, with large rooms suitable for displaying a wide variety of merchandise, a hotel was envisaged together with a large garden, equipped for outdoor events (open to the sky and situated in a wedge of the building where it would have been sheltered by the wings of the U-shaped building).

BIBLIOGRAPHY

H. KULKA, *Adolf Loos*, op. cit., fig. 189, with caption.
L. MÜNZ, G. KÜNSTLER, *Der Architekt Adolf Loos*, op. cit., p. 110, figs. 126-129.

PROJECT FOR AN OFFICE BUILDING
Boulevard des Italiens, Paris

1925

«Mankind seems to have returned to its senses: classicism in France». These words from Loos' essay *Ornament und erziehung* written in 1924 offer us a clue to the interpretation of this project for a building that was to have included a cinema, a restaurant and other public facilities as well as offices. Judging from the drafts, the project never went beyond a rough outline of the complex that — in any case — represents one of the least convincing works he ever produced. It is marred by the heavy classicist lines. Classicist and not classical, in the sense that the hint of the Roman spirit and the use of columns have a reactionary flavor here, a long way from the refined conception of works like the Column for the «Chicago Tribune».

The site, which is bounded by rue de la Michodière, rue du Hanovre, rue Louis Le Grand and Boulevard des Italiens, was in the shape of an irregular trapezoid. The proposal involves placing a vertical tower block on the side facing the Boulevard des Italiens. The block is fifty meters high with a restaurant on the top two floors, surrounded by a wide colonnaded loggia (a kind of Ionic pronaos).

The lowest sides (still nine stories high) are patterned by the regular sequence of square windows and completed by sloping terraces on the Louis Le Grand façade. A large cinema, with an entrance on the Boulevard des Italiens, would have taken up almost the entire area of the building on the first five floors. The cross section of the cinema is interesting in that it shows the excavation of the ground and the way in which the spaces determined by the parabolic shape of the roof of the stage and by the office block fit together. A closed triangular court with rounded corners is set above the roof of the stalls, level with the fifth floor.

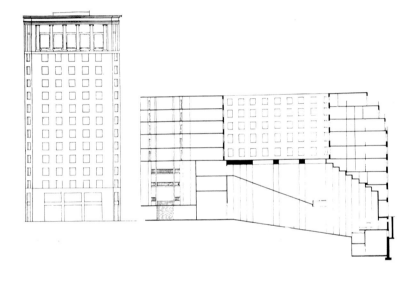

BIBLIOGRAPHY

H. KULKA, *Adolf Loos*, op. cit., figs. 230-217 with captions.
L. MÜNZ, G. KÜNSTLER, *Der Architekt Adolf Loos*, op. cit., p. 110, figs. 120-125.

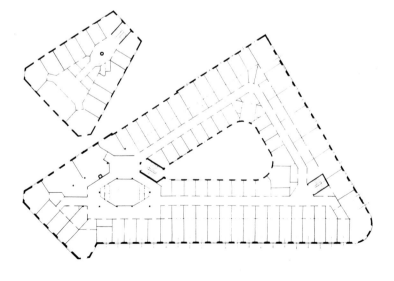

1924 - PROJECT FOR THE STABLES OF COUNT SANGUSKO
South Africa

This drawing confirms Loos' tendency towards theatrical solutions in urban planning. As in the monument for Franz Joseph two high towers frame the view of a neoclassical building set at the focal point of the background.

BIBLIOGRAPHY

L. MÜNZ, *Adolf Loos*, op. cit., p. 34, fig. on p. 127.
L. MÜNZ, G. KÜNSTLER, *Der Architekt Adolf Loos*, op.-cit., section no. 81, p. 191.

1924 - PROJECT FOR FLESCH HOUSE
Croissy (Seine-et-Marne), France

One encounters in this project an emphatic *difference* between the symmetrical and axial monumental character of the exterior and the complex asymmetrical articulation of the interior (which is an advanced attempt at application of the *Raumplan*).

BIBLIOGRAPHY

H. KULKA, *Adolf Loos*, op. cit., figs. 190-195 with captions.
L. MÜNZ, G. KÜNSTLER, *Der Architekt Adolf Loos*, op. cit., section no. 82, p. 182.

1924 - KNIŻE STORE
Neue Wilhelmstrasse 9-11, Berlin

BIBLIOGRAPHY

B. RUKSCHCIO, *Studien zu Entwürfen, Projekten und ausgeführten Bauten von Adolf Loos 1870-1930*, op. cit., WV. L.162.24.

1924 - PROJECT FOR THE RUBINSTEIN HOUSE
rue du Faubourg St. Honoré, Paris

BIBLIOGRAPHY

B. RUKSCHCIO, *Studien zu Entwürfen, Projekten und ausgeführten Bauten von Adolf Loos 1870-1930*, WV. H.165.24.P.

1924-1925 - PROJECT FOR AN EXHIBITION PAVILION
Paris

BIBLIOGRAPHY

B. RUKSCHCIO, *Studien zu Entwürfen, Projekten und ausgeführten Bauten von Adolf Loos 1870-1930*, op. cit., WV. H. 168.24.P.

1925 - PROJECT FOR AN APARTMENT FOR ADOLF LOOS
Paris

Only two sketch plans remain that are preserved in the Loos archives.

BIBLIOGRAPHY

L. MÜNZ, G. KÜNSTLER, *Der Architekt Adolf Loos*, op. cit., section no. 85, p. 192.

1925 - DECORATION OF THE DINING ROOM OF VON BAUER'S APARTMENT
Vystaviste I, Brno, Czechoslovakia

BIBLIOGRAPHY

VV. AA., *Modern architektura v Brno 1900-1965*, Brno, 1968, p. 12.
B. RUKSCHCIO, *Studien zu Entwürfen, Projekten und ausgeführten Bauten von Adolf Loos 1870-1930*, op. cit., WV. L.170.25.

1926 - STAGING OF AN OPERA BY ARNOLD SCHOENBERG
Paris

BIBLIOGRAPHY

B. RUKSCHCIO, *Studien zu Entwürfen, Projekten und ausgeführten Bauten von Adolf Loos 1870-1930*, op. cit., WV. G.146.26.P.

1928 - ALTERATIONS TO THE ZELENKA TRADING HOUSE
Kärntnerstrasse, Vienna 1

This is a project for the alteration and redesign of the façade.

BIBLIOGRAPHY

B. RUKSCHCIO, *Studien zu Entwürfen, Projekten und ausgeführten Bauten von Adolf Loos 1870-1930*, op. cit., WV. H.181.28.P.

1929 - APARTMENT FOR JOSEF VOGL
Trida-Legionaru 12, Pilsen, Czechoslovakia

The walls of the dining room were lined with panels of travertine marble arranged horizontally; while cherry wood and green hangings were chosen for the living room. The photographs of these two rooms and of the children's room are in the Loos archives.

BIBLIOGRAPHY

H. KULKA, *Adolf Loos*, op. cit., figs. 234-235 with caption.
L. MÜNZ, G. KÜNSTLER, *Der Architekt Adolf Loos*, op. cit., section no. 91, p. 192.
V. BEHALOVA, *Pilsner Wohnungen von Adolf Loos*, in «Bauforum» no. 21, 1970, p. 51.

1929 - ALTERATIONS TO VILLA KAPSA
Dejirce Na Présypce 7, Prague

Nothing remains of the original work.

BIBLIOGRAPHY

B. RUKSCHCIO, *Studien zu Entwürfen, Projekten und ausgeführten Bauten von Adolf Loos 1870-1930*, op. cit., WV. H.185.29.

THE HOUSE OF TRISTAN TZARA

Avenue Junot 15, Paris (the interior has been altered)

The Parisian house of the Dadaist poet Tristan Tzara marks a fundamental stage in Loos' architectural journey. In a way it is a work of transition, a threshold over which a new technique of expression, based on the triplication of meaning, is introduced.

1926
1927

We know that the *poetics of difference* has for long been an invariant of Loos' work, but the Tzara house offers an extraordinarily clear example of the simultaneous presence of three different syntaxes of composition within a single context: a model which — as we shall see — is propaedeutic to subsequent experiments and especially to the Moller House built in Vienna in 1928. In fact it is easy to distinguish here between an external mode of architectural expression (façade), an internal one (articulation of internal space) and a lateral one (the remaining external faces of the house). In this collusion of languages without mediation one may discern a subtle intellectual complicity (never completely demonstrable) between the poet-client and the architect. Loos seems to subscribe in his architecture to Tzara's well-known statement that «art is a continual procession of differences.» But this tangle of meanings, this semantic ambivalence can only be grasped by looking at the work as a whole since, in a precise analysis of the individual parts of the building, each of the three modes of expression, taken separately, shows itself to be relatively consistent.

The first — comparitively autonomous — level of expression may be detected in the façade on Avenue Junot. Here that «*volonté d'ordre, de clarté, de logique*» of which Lautremont spoke seems to prevail, indirectly producing an effect of estrangement. The geometrical composition is in fact extremely simple. The façade is materially divided into two: a rectangle of stone at the base and a white plaster square above.

Undoubtedly, this choice of mode of expression may have been influenced by some basic technical facts. The Avenue Junot — that climbs the hill of Montmartre — borders on very rugged terrain. As a consequence, extensive work has been necessary to contain the ground, involving the construction of large walls on solid foundations.

Yet anyone who recalls the Looshaus in the Michaelerplatz (Vienna 1910) knows well that the use of materials to divide a façade into two arises out of considerations which go well beyond simple technical and functional requirements. If, on the one hand, the separation denotes two different intended purposes (in this case distinguishing the house for rent on the first three levels and the poet's house on the upper floors), on the other, and more important, it traces two different geometries. In short, it is a tactical device that permits Loos to outline an almost perfect square. The square is a pure geometric figure that by its simplicity of design gives rise to the above-mentioned effect of estrangement. It is no coincidence that in *Rythmus 21* (1921) the Dadaist Hans Richter had repeated squares in an obsessive film sequence, producing one of the most advanced experiments with visual language. This alienating intention is more clearly visible in the sheet of sketches (dated 1 August 1925) than in the building itself (where the insertion of railings on the roof terrace makes the boundary of the square more vague).

Besides, the functions of living impose limits on abstraction in architecture. The only way Loos has left to fulfill this intention is to make radical use of symmetry. In this way an «outmoded» syntax is revived as an extreme expression of the architecture of reticence. On the blank page of the façade the openings are designed according to a rigorous order of communication.

The large central void of the balcony that looks onto Avenue Junot stands in contrast to the close rhythm of the three minor openings of the floor below, arranged in absolute bilateral symmetry about the vertical geometrical axis.

At the base, however, the entrance — sheltered by a wide balcony — is made by a diagonal cut, almost carved out of the stone. The emphasis given to the open concrete beam-architrave harks back to a more archaic, almost barbaric technique. So there is a close two-way relationship between material and design. Loos himself had explained that plaster is a skin and stone is a structure. The implications of this are obvious.

But the radical logic of the language used for the façade contrasts with the sequence of non-sense on the other faces of the building. There one finds a strictly neutral assembly of detached elements, bits that have no apparent syntactic connection with each other. Each element has its own value, its own functional clarity. This results in a disturbing dissonance and a degree of deliberate unpredictability, though clarity always remains. It is in this sense that one may speak of the *lateral quality* of an architectural style that is in its turn very different from the *internal quality* that shapes the articulation of space inside. Within the Tzara house Loos carries on with his fascinating chess game in space. The *interieur* is where his architectural thought reveals how vibrant it is with life. With the «patience of à alchemist» Loos carries out his work of excavation, fitting rooms of different heights within a unitary volume, rooms that — like Chinese boxes — get more secret as they grow smaller.

But it is not difficult to grasp — from the photographic images of the original decoration — the manifest *otherness* between the ratio of the architecture and the exotericism of the African masks that Tzara hangs on the walls, which is totally legitimate within the limits that Loos imposes on the project. «The wall and the furniture» is up to the architect. There remains a vacuum in the house that the person who lives there has the right to fill with his own (private) bad taste.

Drawing showing the original proposals of the façade.

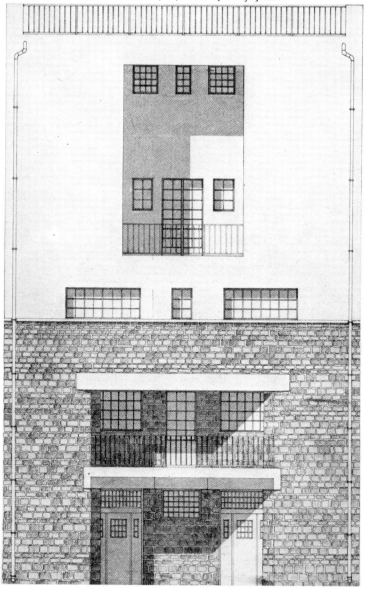

But there is one detail of the decoration of the living room that cannot escape our attention, a detail that is typical of Loos. Once again Loos sets the emptiness of his work in front of a mirror. «Just as the mirror reflects an image without effort and without asking why, material belongs to no one because it is only a physico-chemical product.» These are Tristan Tzara's words, taken from the preface to *Les champs délicieux* (1922), and they explain, without intending to, the ultimate meaning of the Loosian mirror.

NOTES

1) A. LOOS, *Sämtliche Schriften*.

2) For a description of the arrangement of rooms one may refer to Heinrich Kulka's *Führung durch das Haus* (A guided tour through the house): *First floor*: main entrance, hall, garage and central heating plant, main stairs leading to the apartment. *Second floor*: on this floor there is an apartment for rent, with a wide balcony overlooking Avenue Junot. Its entrance and kitchen are at the rear of third floor. The main staircase does not lead to the second floor, but arrives directly at the third. *Third floor*: here is the entrance hall to the owner's apartment, with access to the kitchen and cellars. From the third floor the stairs lead to the *fourth floor*: the lowest floor of the owner's apartment. It holds a sittingroom with a terrace in front, a diningroom on a slightly higher level, a balcony facing onto Avenue Junot and a library. There are also the ladies' sitting room and the larder; these are all lower that the big sitting room. On the *fifth floor* are the bedrooms with a terrace and on the *sixth floor* another large habitable floor is planned (see H. KULKA, *Adolf Loos*, op. cit., pp. 40-41).

BIBLIOGRAPHY

H. KULKA, *Adolf Loos*, op. cit., figs. 203-217 with caption.
L. MÜNZ, G. KÜNSTLER, *Der Architekt Adolf Loos*, op. cit., pp. 83-91, figs. 83-94.
W. SCHALLENBERG, *Loos Haus in Paris*, in «Die Presse», Vienna, January 1971.
J.P. FORTIN, M. PIETU, *Adolf Loos: Maison pour Tristan Tzara*, in «Architecture Mouvement Continuité», Paris 1976, no. 38, pp. 43-51.

Rear view.

Stairway.

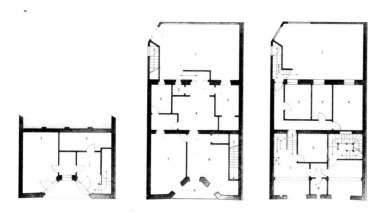
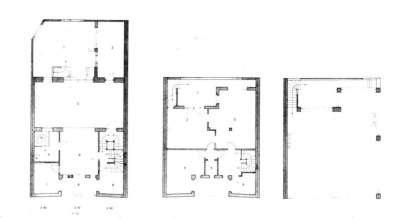

Plans of successive floors commencing with the basement on the left.

First floor with terrace.

General section.

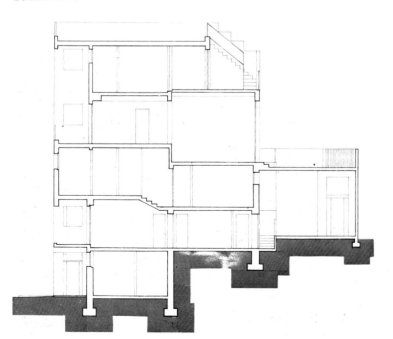

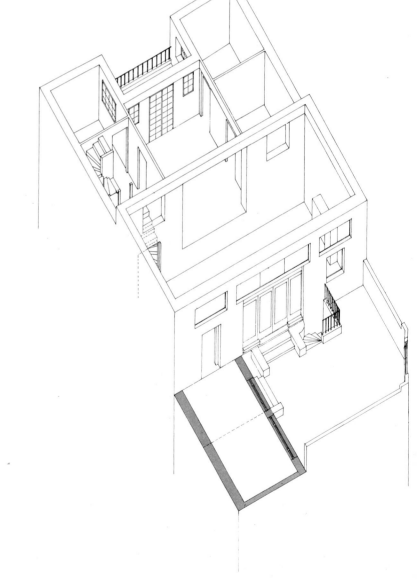

KNIŽE STORE

146, Avenue des Champs-Elysées, Paris (radically transformed)

1927

The most striking thing in this elegant Parisian store (that underwent radical alteration in the fifties after the premises changed hands) was a gigantic sculpture of a polo player, placed in the first-floor window facing the street. Recourse to such a publicity technique was motivated by the need to attract the attention of the absentminded metropolitan crowd to a sales point. And in a way this vaguely surreal object offers a clue to the interpretation of the design as a whole, based as it is on effects of surprise, of frivolity, of consumption, of chromatic contrast and, perhaps, of subtle irony. It is not difficult to imagine the carefully calculated emotions that must have assailed consumers on their arrival in the main rooms, flooded by natural light from the large windows opening onto the street, carpeted with black velvet, the walls lined with pale Cipolin marble, the white ceiling, bamboo chairs and tables lacquered in bright red — all this after having passed through the entrance lined with polished mahogany and furnished with elegant wardrobes with mirrored doors and shiny brass fittings. These singular rooms were created out of the reunification of many apartments: this explains the persistence of open beams that act as architraves for the communicating spaces cut out of structural walls.

Apart from the marble, the material most characteristic of Loos is the mirror that dominates the fireplace built into the wall of the fitting room.

BIBLIOGRAPHY

H. KULKA, *Adolf Loos*, op. cit., figs. 218-221 with captions.
L. MÜNZ, G. KÜNSTLER, *Der Architekt Adolf Loos*, op. cit., pp. 29-30, fig. 12.

PROJECT FOR THE HOUSE OF JOSEPHINE BAKER

Paris

1928

All that remains by which to evaluate the totally extraordinary idea of architecture shown by this project is a model, some colored copies of the drafts (plans, sections and elevations) and an analytical description by Kurt Unger. The plans are of a house for the famous ballerina and cabaret singer Josephine Baker, which was unfortunately never built. [1] Despite this the fundamental intentions of the design stand out clearly.

First there is the charm of this gay architecture. It is not just the dichromatism of the façades but — as we shall see — the spectacular nature of the internal articulation that determines its refined and seductive character. Rather than abandon oneself to the pleasure of suggestions, it is necessary to take this «toy» to pieces with analytical detachment if one wishes to understand the mechanism of composition.

Starting from the outside, what stands out most clearly is the Mediterranean appearance of the house which derives from a predominance of solids over voids, from the way the openings are reduced to holes (small in size and usually square in shape) and from the use of a flat roof — a Mediterranean quality that finds further confirmation in at least three other features:

a) *the architectural introversion*: in line with Loos' way of thinking, the exterior says nothing about the interior. Only by careful analysis is it possible to make out a close, though complex, two-way relationship between outside and inside. It is true, besides, that introversion, as well as being an invariant in Loos' design, ia a constant feature of Mediterranean housing models;

b) *the revival of dichromatism*: this is an *expressive technique* typical of medieval Tuscan language (one thinks of the exterior of the cathedral of San Giovanni in Pistoia or the interior of the cathedral of Siena), re-proposed here as a modern optical trick to extend the volume in the opposite direction to that of the alternate lines of black and white marble. In his ability to break down the stylistic stereotypes of the architecture of the twenties, disinterring and reworking formal materials drawn from neglected historical periods, Loos demonstrates an uncommonly farsighted and independent line of thought;

c) *the plastic arrangement*: the architectural composition comes down to a simple assembly of primary volumes — the prism and the cylinder. It is significant here that, in order to achieve his aim of making the volumes clearly legible, Loos introduces a split between the lower part of the building — which follows the acute-angled layout of the street — and the striped upper part — made up of a cylinder and a prism that project slightly on one side, as if they had slipped a little off the base on which they stand. That this slipping should produce a shelter for the entrance is only an incidental functional advantage. It is the play between plastic forms, that is to say, the pattern created by the volumes, that is more important than function.

If we go on to analyze the interior, we again find the independence from the exterior that was mentioned above; an autonomy that is the result of the complexity and richness of a junction of spaces on many levels that could not be imagined from the rigidly box-like exterior.

Yet the use made of the *Raumplan* gradually increases in complexity as one moves up from the lower floors (used for services) to the upper ones (intended for amusement). Reversing the usual criteria of structural economy, a large swimming pool, that would have taken up two floors (of about $4 \times 10 \times 2$ m.), is situated on the upper stories, implying the construction of robust pillars rising from the basement. The reason for this logical inversion of weight distribution should be sought in a highly suggestive architectural purpose: the swimming pool, enclosed in a pure prism without lateral openings, would have gathered light from above — through a skylight. Do we not detect here an allusion to the *oculus* of the Imperial Roman baths? On the other hand, the widespread use of overhead light as an architectural material brings to mind one of Loos' first works as well: the Villa Karma on the Lake of Geneva (1904-1906). The self-quotation is further confirmed by the cylindrical corner tower (that had also been reproposed in the project for a Hotel on the Avenue des Champs Élysées in Paris, 1924). But the mental link between the two works lies primarily in the «pagan» rediscovery of the cult of the body, expressed in the architecture by an allusion to the Roman spirit.

By Roman spirit, more an allusive reference than a slavish imitation, are intended the rooms that surround the swimming pool: on the first level a big hall intercommunicating with a large lobby illuminated from above. Only the semicircular iron staircase (that leads from the lobby to the access gallery, on the second level) breaks — by a deliberate contrast of materials — the chain of classical and literary metaphors, introducing an element that dates unmistakably from modern times; as modern as the entire spatial conception based on the *Raumplan* and as the idea of the gallery which runs around a great central «void» that has the dual function of allowing light to enter from above and of permitting a pan-optical view of the various levels of the house.

But the swimming pool is the real pleasure center and also the compositional pivot around which the spaces are fitted together. On the first level the tank of water is surrounded by two low corridors (2.20×1.30 m.) that connect the big hall (intercommunicating with the 7.50-meters-high lobby) to the small hall (that opens onto a circular bar room). On the second level (reached by means of the above-mentioned semicircular stairs in the lobby) the gallery links up not only the swimming pool floor, but also two bedrooms, a dining room and a small circular sitting room. In this way one passes abruptly from the cramped spaces of the corridors to spacious halls and lobbies. But this is not all! As Kurt Unger recalls, windows made of thick and transparent plates of glass were envisaged along the low corridors that would allow one to «watch people swimming and diving in the crystalline water, lit from above: an underwater 'revue,' so to speak.» [2]

The water flooded with light, the refreshing swim, the voyeuristic pleasure of underwater exploration — these are the carefully balanced ingredients of this gay architecture. But what matters more is that the invitation to the spectacular suggested by the theme of a house for a cabaret star is handled by Loos with discretion and intellectual detachment, more as a poetic game, involving the mnemonic pursuit of quotations and allusions to the Roman spirit, than as a vulgar surrender to the taste of Hollywood.

NOTES

1) The description of the layout of the Baker house by Kurt Unger (who collaborated with Loos in drawing up the plans) comes from a letter written on 23 July 1935 in response to a series of questions put to him by Ludwig Münz. The colored drawings and the model are kept today in the Loos-Archiv, Albertina, Vienna.

2) From the letter by Kurt Unger to Ludwig Münz, quoted in G. Künstler and L. Münz, *Der Architekt Adolf Loos*, op. cit., p. 178.

BIBLIOGRAPHY

H. KULKA, *Adolf Loos*, op. cit., fig. 222 with caption.
Exhibition catalog of the Galerie Würthle in Vienna.
L. MÜNZ, G. KÜNSTLER, *Der Architekt Adolf Loos*, op. cit., pp. 177-180, figs. 237-243.

HANS BRUMMEL HOUSE
Hussgasse 58, Pilsen, Czechoslovakia

These unusual alterations made to the apartment of Hans Brummel lie at **1928** the limits of conceptual abstraction, and perhaps form the best example of interior design realized by Loos.

The functional motivation for the operation is banal: it was a matter of extending the living room by the addition of a small adjoining space, difficult to make use of by itself. The resulting form is surprising: two pillars (replacing the previous structural wall and faced with poplar root) are duplicated on the back wall that is covered with mirrors. This simple device creates an alchemical, almost magical, multiplication of reflected images, producing an effect of surreal estrangement from everyday triviality; an effect that evokes the discreet charm of the Kärntner Bar (1907).

No less suggestive is the bedroom where a classical use is made of the bordering of dark wood (in this case, cherry) that outlines the light-colored planes of the composition. Geometric rationality dominates the whole design, from the grid of the large window to the cupboards built into a single wall. The articulation of space based on the difference in levels of the ceiling gives a «sacred» air of intimacy to the bedchamber. The tendency of the composition to avoid functional obviousness is also demonstrated by the hanging, over the dark wall of the bed, of a useless curtain whose only motivation is the formal one of analogy with the curtain hanging over the real window.

Rationality and make-believe, geometric severity and visual ambiguity: the architecture created adds an unexpected ingredient to the theoretical antidecorative nature of the design.

BIBLIOGRAPHY

H. KULKA, *Adolf Loos*, op. cit., figs. 236-237 with captions.
L. MÜNZ, G. KÜNSTLER, *Der Architekt Adolf Loos*, op. cit., pp. 50-53, figs. 32-33.
V. BEHALOVA, *Pilsner Wohnungen von Adolf Loos*, in «Bauforum», no. 21, 1970, pp. 19-56.

Combined dining and sitting room today.

MOLLER HOUSE
Starkfriedgasse 19, Vienna 18

1928

The Moller House is the end point of Loos' long intellectual journey and it would be a mistake to see it as a kind of linking up with the «destiny of the Modern Movement» as it is, on the contrary, wholly consistent with a *logos* that he had developed independently, so much so that this house may be regarded as a «manifesto» of Loos' aesthetics, as an emblematic testimony to a self-imposed code of syntax.

Evidence for this lies in the terse, axiomatic and in some ways out-of-date character of its form, resulting from the wholesale application of the principles informing Loos' theory of design.

In its polemical classicity, the Moller House, despite its date, might appear to be pre-Rationalist. But the distance of this work from contemporaneous European Rationalism shows up not so much in the ostentation of a *symmetry* that is indifferent to the «permanent revolution in language» carried out by the avant-garde, as in a different ideological standpoint. This attitude he makes clear in the commemorative passage he wrote the year after in memory of Josef Veillich; a passage that — because of his obvious identification with his carpenter friend («deaf like me») — may be taken as an architectonic testament. There one reads: «The real difference between me and the others is as follows: I maintain that use determines the forms of civilized life, the shape of objects; the others that a new form can have an influence on the forms of civilized life (the way of sitting, of living, of eating, etc.).» [1] And earlier: «There exists ... no progress for things that have already been solved. They have maintained the same form over centuries, until a new discovery caused them to fall into disuse or a new form of civilization radically transformed them.» [2]

So it is not a feverish search for new forms, for an idealized *neue Welt*, but a patient one that aims at results proven by the permanence of some modes of use: this is what lies behind Loos' message.

The logic of the slow transformation of language (which denies the ideology of continual revolution) leads to works like the Moller House that we could define more accurately as post-Rationalist than as pre-Rationalist.

Let us take a look at the way this architecture is articulated. What emerges and is confirmed here is the *poetics of difference* or the *otherness* of exterior and interior or even of the different faces of the exterior. The main factor in the composition of the façade overlooking Starkfriedgasse is the cutting edge of the white, perfectly rectangular wall that stresses by its geometric purity its nature as a wall separating private from public. This wall is like a gigantic screen on which (and from which) forms are projected.

In this sense it plays the same conceptual role as the Renaissance plane of perspective. But symmetry, in this case, is not a tardy adherence to classicism but the taking of a renunciation to an extreme, the extreme that is, of the *architecture of negation*. We are faced here with the arrival of nihilism in the abstract, mathematical, in a way unreal poetics of the pure gesture. The wall provides the conceptual grid that cages the whole composition: it is a compact, dense, solid presence, pierced only in a few places by the rectangular windows and scored only by the diagonal cuts that mark the entrance. The only element that projects, almost in opposition to the obsessively static quality of the wall, is the white parallelepiped suspended in an almost surrealistic manner above the entrance.

But if abstraction is the law that dominates the façade looking onto the street, it is, on the contrary, realism that dominates the one overlooking the garden. Here the choice falls on absolutely banal forms.

The windows, the balconies, the steps, the railings, in short, all the elements of composition, are reduced to pure tautology: the object stands only for itself without reference to anything else. For example, the shape of the window is reduced to the elementary role of answering to its function: the window is therefore simply a window.

View from the garden.

Street façade.

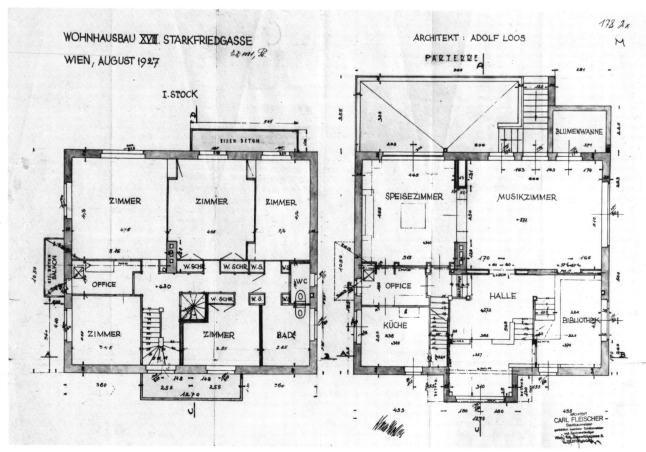

Original plans and section drawings (Plan- und Schriftenkammer, Vienna).

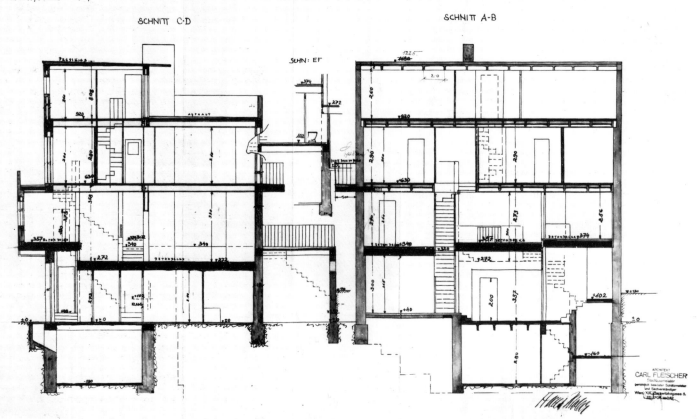

View of the raised sitting room.

To the *otherness* of the external façades of the Moller House may be added the *otherness* of interior and exterior. But it is interesting to note that for the first time the architecture of the interior, as well, is reduced to a pure geometrical simplicity, almost attaining to a unitary *Gesamtkunstwerk*.In other words, even the decoration becomes a pure play of architectural volumes and shapes. It would be difficult to deny the influence exerted over this work by the project drawn up by Ludwig Wittgenstein for his sister Margarethe Stoneborough (in 1926, with the collaboration of Loos' pupil, Paul Engelmann).

Quite a few formal analogies exist (such as the bareness of the rooms, the absolutely prismatic quality of the pillars, the beams, the volumes and such details as the right-angled internal staircase) that tend to confirm this hypothesis. But once again a profound difference in conceptual intent may be detected: where Wittgenstein turns the entire articulation of space into logico-philosophical calculation, Loos, on the contrary, proposes an emotive quality of «feeling oneself inside» that tends to give the interior an air of the sacred. The interior is the favored place, the sheltered place, the raison d'être of the house.

The transition from profane (public) space to sacred (interior) space occurs along a carefully planned route of penetration, that also becomes the perceptive axis of an articulate assembly of forms. The entrance hall is a compressed, low space that serves as a genuine clearing station, shunting one off in other directions. A few steps on the right lead up to the first stop, the brightly lit cloakroom (2.50 meters high). Continuing up the stairs (that turn through 90 degrees) the solemnity of the ascent is accentuated, revealed by the abstract play of volumes stripped to their geometrical essence and to the web of their reciprocal interrelationships and intro-spections. At the top of the stairs one enters the large space of the living

room that is set on several levels. We have penetrated to the heart of the house. The most intimate (most private) room is the alcove set five steps above the floor of the living room and enclosed by the white paral-lelepiped «suspended» on the outside of the house. The fact that the living room is higher (3.20 meters) than the alcove (2.50 meters) denotes the relatively more public character of the former with respect to the latter. This confirms that the *Raumplan* is a method of spatial design that is charged with psychological meanings.

The other characteristic peculiar to this floor of the house is the way spaces are linked up, each one communicating with the others. As in the Rufer House the dining room is connected with the music room by a large sliding door (2.50 meters wide). One not insignificant detail here is that the floor of the dining room is raised 70 centimers above that of the music room and that there is no visible way of getting from one to the other. In fact, the only way to get from the music room to the dining room is to take out a folding ladder well hidden in the base. This lack of visible connection serves to express the «foreignness» of the two rooms, which are only visually interrelated. It is no accident that the materials used to line them are distinct, though similar. The dining room — very well lit, thanks to the large French windows that open onto the terrace — is lined with panels of Okumé plywood interrupted at the corners by projecting pillars faced with travertine. Even the furnishings are reduced to architecture. The sideboard, for instance, is built into the wall and enclosed by plates of glass. The only movable objects are the table and the Thonet chairs. The Thonet chair is a genuine ready-made object. Loos explains: «The act of designing a new chair for the dining room seems a joke to me, and a pointless one at that, involving a waste of time and money.... The wooden chair has now been replaced by the Thonet chair that established itself as the only modern one some thirty years ago. Even Jeanneret (Le Corbusier) has understood this and has used it widely in his houses; unfortunately he has chosen the wrong model.... In the dining room of the last house I built — the one on Starkfriedgasse in Vienna that for the moment only dismays inoffensive winter sports enthusiasts — I used Thonet chairs.» [3]

The dark tints of the wall panels predominate in the *Musikzimmer*. These stretch right up to the ceiling and cover the beams themselves and, along with the polished ebony flooring (macassar), contribute to the creation of a warm, snug atmosphere, suitable for listening to good music. Here too the furnishings are built into the walls. One feature of great beauty is the glass-enclosed space that contains the musical equipment. But it is difficult to avoid noticing an extraordinary dominance of the «empty» over the «solid» in these rooms. The desire for emptiness is the most important feature of Loos' last phase of work.

NOTES

1) A. LOOS, *Josef Veillich, Sämtliche Schriften*.

2) Ibid.

3) Ibid., pp. 371-373.

BIBLIOGRAPHY

H. KULKA, *Adolf Loos*, op. cit., figs. 223-233, with caption.
L. MÜNZ, G. KÜNSTLER, *Der Architekt Adolf Loos*, op. cit., pp. 128-133, figs. 161-171.

Music and dining rooms.

APARTMENT OF WILLY HIRSCH

Plachygasse 6, Pilsen, Czechoslovakia

1929

Loos had decorated several rooms of Hirsch's apartment in Pilsen as far back as 1907, and in a way this work of 1929 is only a return to a previous one, interesting insofar as it constitutes a record of evolving or unvarying elements in his language of materials. In fact, the use of materials such as veined marble and wood remains unchanged, but what does change significantly is their material essence. For instance, the Skyros marble used in 1907 for the hall cum living room is replaced by more homogeneous travertine in the elegant garden room of 1929. In the same way, wood painted in pale tints is substituted for dark mahogany. This gives rise to a greater degree of modernity, of simplicity and of luminosity (emphasized further by the great increase in the area of glass used).

What stands out from this setting is its intimate relationship with the surrounding landscape. That this was intended in the design is demonstrated by the extent of the work of restructuring carried out in order to reduce the width of the pillars and even to get rid of them entirely on the shorter sides. But it is interesting to note how the rectangular division of the frames takes us back — in a sort of self-quotation — to the cloakroom of the Villa Karma (1904-1906). Then, as now, Loos seems to have been under the influence of exotic oriental cultures and in particular that of Japan. Even the bamboo chairs and the lacquered tables help to create a relaxing atmosphere of escape in this room where the landscape enters with its disturbing mass of greenery. The whole work merges together in a successful synthesis of architecture and nature.

BIBLIOGRAPHY

H. KULKA, *Adolf Loos*, op. cit., figs. 240-241 with caption.
L. MÜNZ, G. KÜNSTLER, *Der Architekt Adolf Loos*, op. cit., p. 56, fig. 35.
V. BEHALOVA, *Pilsner Wohnungen von Adolf Loos*, in «Bauforum», no. 21, 1970, p. 50.

APARTMENT OF LEOPOLD EISNER

Safarik Park 9, Pilsen, Czechoslovakia

1929

Kurt Unger, who collaborated on the project and directed the work, has stated that Loos' intention was to create a setting as simple and welcoming as a Spanish *bodega*. This effect was to be attained through the absolute dominance of a single material: the burnished oak of the wall paneling.

In its turn the symmetry of the composition contributed to the creation of a sober and cheering atmosphere.

The furniture consisted of a round table with Windsor chairs, much loved by Loos for their elegance of function. Worthy of special mention, as far as the fixed furnishings are concerned, are the large bench upholstered in pale leather, built into a niche below two English-style windows, and the fireplace (in black-and-white marble) surmounted by a mirror divided into squares. The latter represents a feature repeated so many times in Loos' last interiors that it becomes a sort of characteristic badge of the final phase of his work.

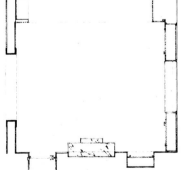

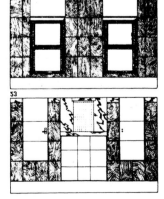

Interior drawing made in 1969.

BIBLIOGRAPHY

H. KULKA, *Adolf Loos*, op. cit., fig. 238, with caption.
L. MÜNZ, G. KÜNSTLER, *Der Architekt Adolf Loos*, op. cit., section no. 96, p. 193.
V. BEHALOVA, *Pilsner Wohnungen von Adolf Loos*, in «Bauforum», no. 37, 1973, Vienna, p. 35, figs. 22-25.
B. RUKSCHCIO, *Studien zu Entwürfen, Projekten und ausgeführten Bauten von Adolf Loos 1870-1930*, WV. W.190.29.

ENTRANCE OF THE ALBERT MATZNER TEXTILE FACTORY

Rotenturmstrasse-Kohmesser 8, Vienna 1 (no longer in existence)

The façade was of marble — the symbolic material constantly adopted by Loos as an external marker for commercial premises. Here it is used for the entrance to the Albert Matzner Textile Factory where the composition is based on the geometric elementarism of rectangles inscribed one within the other and on the combination of white — lightly veined — marble with wrought iron — painted green — and with the large — reflective — sheets of glass of the windows. Inside, curtains of yellow silk that act as a back-cloth to the windows emphasize liveliness of color as one of the principal thematic motifs of the composition. It should be noted,

1929
1930

finally, that the fitting out of the room under discussion (on which H. Kulka collaborated) required the removal of several cumbersome pillars with a structural function, making necessary the use of some advanced engineering techniques.

BIBLIOGRAPHY

H. KULKA, *Adolf Loos*, op. cit., figs. 242-243 with caption.
L. MÜNZ, G. KÜNSTLER, *Der Architekt Adolf Loos*, op. cit., section no. 93, p. 192.

APARTMENT OF LEO BRUMMEL

Friedrichsplatz 26, Pilsen, Czechoslovakia

The image of this airy living cum dining room in Leo Brummel's apartment, flooded with natural light, is dominated by the gaiety of the colors. So vivid is the contrast of pure, almost primary, tints that it calls to mind the neoplastic interiors of men like G. T. Rietveld or T. Van Doesburg: the green of the floor, the red of the baseboard, the black and red of the inner and outer faces of the bicolor door, the gray of the curtains, the silver dazzle of the panels, and so on. But we know that polychromy has long been a constant feature of Loos' design and also that it is largely entrusted to the intrinsic chromatic quality of the materials.

1929

Early photograph of the interior.

The other unvarying element — that attains to an absolute semantic autonomy in this context — is the large mirror (divided into sixteen squares and hung above the sideboard) that gathers and distorts fragments of images, in almost the same way as one of Kurt Schwitters' *Märzbilder* gathers rubbish. In this sense, freed from its usual function of optically expanding the space, it takes on the unequivocal autonomy of a piece of art, of a picture. Any shadow of a doubt about this is dismissed by the significant positioning of a large, late-impressionist painting at a similar point and with a similar intention in the same apartment.

On the threshold of the conclusion of his work, Loos seems to want to reveal all the conceptual mechanisms and double meanings so profuse in his long and patient work on material. This ironic collage of mirrored reflections amounts, in fact, to an explicit baring of the profound structure that governs his use of material, stripping it of the veils that cover it in «appearance».

BIBLIOGRAPHY

H. KULKA, *Adolf Loos*, op. cit., fig. 239.
L. MÜNZ, G. KÜNSTLER, *Der Architekt Adolf Loos*, op. cit., p. 56, fig. 34.
V. BEHALOVA, *Pilsner Wohnungen von Adolf Loos*, in «Bauforum», no. 21, 1970, p. 55.

Drawing of the cupboard with mirror.

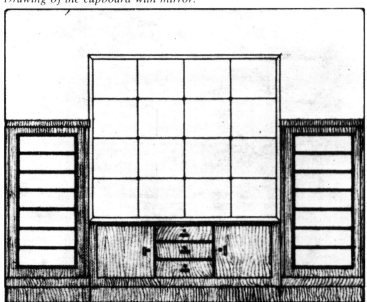

Drawing of the cupboard as proposed by Kurt Unger (Albertina).

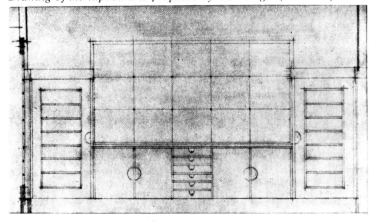

MÜLLER HOUSE

Stresovicka 33, Prague (Karel Lhota collaborated on the design of the structural elements)

His long intellectual journey through the maze of experimental architecture draws to a close in the Müller House, the last significant construction built by Loos. There can be no doubt that it is a work that synthesizes many of the ideas of design that had emerged in previous works.

Its predecessor, or rather its most immediate antecedent, is the Moller House built in Vienna two years earlier. The underlying basis to the whole construction derives from this model. Like Moller House, Müller House is a cubic house. There are so many unvarying elements that this project may be interpreted as a true reworking of an earlier work. Not only the white parallelepiped suspended from the lateral façade (seemingly borrowed from the Starkfriedgasse façade of the Moller House), but many other similarities of form (detectable, for example, in the way of cutting the windows directly into the wall, in the typological and distributive structure of the interior, in the use of solid parapets that extend the surfaces of the walls, in the roof terrace used to crown the house, and so on) support such an interpretation. Besides, the identification of an

1930

Two external views in the original state.

analogon makes it easier to understand those concepts that do vary and cannot be ignored. One substantial difference lies in the formal coherence of the outer shell. If it is true that a radical *otherness* between the different faces of the cube is a distinctive feature of the Moller House, here, on the contrary, an essential homologation prevails. The reason may be looked for in the difference between the sites on which the buildings are located. Perception of the exterior, that is to say, the indiscretion of the stranger's glance, is the variant which dictates the rules of the game.

In this case the house may be viewed from many different points, and for this reason the screen-like design of the façade — that marks the border between public and private sphere — is extended to all sides of the house and not limited to the main façade as in Moller House.

In this way a unitary treatment — closure — of the shell is attained, giving rise to an impression of estrangement. This is confirmed by the anecdote related by the architect Willy Hoffmann in which he recalls that «ten planning commissions rejected the project, because it did not take the rather mediocre neighboring houses into account, and only on the eleventh attempt did it receive official approval.» [1]

What evidently escaped the commissioners is that the Müller house represents a well thought out, careful, modern reinterpretation of a link with the history of dwelling that is much more profound than its superficial connection with the nearby houses.

Passing from an analysis of the exterior to one of the interior, the most prominent feature is the reproposition of the typological scheme of the private single-family house (already used for the Rufer and Moller houses, for example): a clear separation between the daytime zone — on the first floor — and the nighttime zone — on the second; location of services on the ground floor; conclusion of the house by two further bedrooms that face onto a wide terrace. Such a reproposition does not lessen, but increases, the chances of it responding to specific requirements, by adapting the shape of the spaces to particular functions, *function* being understood in the wider sense that includes the dialectics of psychological needs and desires.

Evidence for this is provided by the amount of attention paid in the design to the function of penetration from the outside to the inside. Once more the solution is provided by a calculated and scenic spatial sequence. The entrance is narrow and leads directly to a short spiral staircase that suddenly reveals a view of the living room. Eight more steps lead higher up to the dining room that is in visual contact with the same living room.

It is on this floor of the house, on the living floor, that his way of thinking about space achieves its most mature expression. The play of levels in space, in a word the *Raumplan*, is developed in the Müller house to its highest level of complexity and refinement. Had not Loos himself written, the year before, that the only «progress», the only «great revolu-

Exterior view today.

tion in the field of architecture [is] the solution of the plan in space»? [2] He goes on to say: «Before Kant, humanity could not yet think in space and architects were compelled to make the toilet as high as the hall. Only by dividing everything in two could they obtain lower rooms. As man will one day succeed in playing chess on a three-dimensional board, so too other architects will solve the problem of the three-dimensional plan.» [3]

So let us try to understand how this «game» is played. The basic principle is the *Raumdurchdringung*, that is to say, the spatial interpenetration that brings linked spaces into close visual contact. Two substantial associated spaces are easily recognizable on this floor of the Müller House: the coupling of the library with the lady's reading room and that of the living room with the dining room.

From the landing (next to the dining room) it is necessary to go down eight steps to reach the lady's reading room and then a further four steps to enter the library proper. The reading room is in its turn divided into two by a gradient of three steps that cleanly separates the writing area (lower

down, illuminated by a large window) from the conversation area, more intimate, more snug and therefore lower in height. One detail that should not be left out is the long internal window embrasure that has no other reason for existence than that of allowing one to see into the living room while relaxing in the conversation area. The light, glazed wood, with its clearly visible grain, differentiates this setting markedly from the adjacent library where the decoration depends on the classic contrast between elegant, dark mahogany and white walls. Thus we find reproposed here the artistic device of *symbolizing materially* the psycho-functional diversity of the rooms. But this is not the only invariant of design!

To comprehend fully the sense and the value of certain design choices it is, in fact, necessary to go back to work that he carried out a long time before. An example of this is the use of light from above — already used with extraordinary efficacy in the Villa Karma (1904-1906) — and used again here to illuminate the innermost sections of the house, like the area separating the library and the reading room. This is not just a simple

Interior views and project drawings.

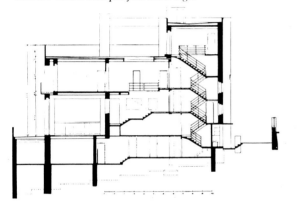

technical device (in any case both this area and the adjacent stairs have other sources of indirect lighting) but an authentic spatial invention: a void is created at the center of the house, a void around which runs the gallery that gives access to the bedrooms on the floor above.

Inside the library many other elements of the furnishings serve as reminders of previous work. The fireplace lined with majolica, the open beams on the ceiling and the shelving built into the walls evoke in a refined manner the Richardsonian taste of his early interiors. And then there is the large mirror divided into squares and reflecting the light from the only side window that serves as a trademark for Loos' entire body of work. Time has refined, but not changed, the essence of an architectural idea.

This is demonstrated by the marvelous space created by joining the living and dining rooms. The coupling of these two settings is not new (it was done in the Rufer and Moller houses, for instance). What is new is the form of this spatial interpenetration. The conceptual abstraction of the Moller House gives way to the material realism of the Cipolin marble of Sion, the precious green marble from the Rhône valley, mounted in panels whose pattern of veining creates a design over the entire wall of the staircase. The material here forms a block of stone that stands out against the white walls, allowing one to glimpse the entire junction of stairs that lead to the various levels of the house. It is perhaps the most beautiful «piece» in all of Loos' interiors.

The dining room, which faces onto the living room, extends beyond the wall, creating the projecting volume on the outside that has been spoken of. What strikes one about the inside is the extreme variety of colors that acts as a further link between this hall and the two-story-high living room below. The yellow curtains and red brick fire place of the living room are contrasted by the green curtains and the slab of sienite that is used as a table in the dining room. The emphasis on colors reveals the gay side of living to be an ultimate goal of Loos' design. But how can one forget his first highly colored pastel sketches of interiors (1899)? The permanence of this intention is surprising, to such an extent that the Müller House may be seen as the conclusion of a program of architecture that had been clearly expressed many years before. This is why one may concur with H. Kulka in his assessment of this work as the most complete expression of his conception of architecture. [4]

NOTES

1) WILLY HOFFMANN, «Prager Tagblatt», 22 February 1930; quoted in L. Münz, G. Künstler, *Der Architekt Adolf Loos*, op. cit., p. 135.

2) A. LOOS, *Sämtliche Schriften*.

3) Ibid.

4) H. KULKA, *Adolf Loos*, op. cit.

BIBLIOGRAPHY

W. HOFFMANN, *Eine Villa von Adolf Loos*, in «Prager Tagblatt», 22 February 1930.
H. KULKA, *Adolf Loos*, op. cit., figs. 257-270 with captions.
W. MRAZEK, *Das Haus Müller in Prag*, in «Alte und moderne Kunst», 1960, vol. V, nos. 11-12, pp. 2-5 with illustrations.
I MÜNZ, G. KÜNSTLER, *Der Architekt Adolf Loos*, op. cit., pp. 133-143, figs. 172-183.

KHUNER COUNTRY HOUSE
Kreuzberg, Payerbach, Austria

1930

Contemporary to the whitewashed masterpieces of his last phase (Moller House in Vienna, 1928, and Müller House in Prague, 1930), this country house that is so vernacular, so anachronistically alpine, so rustic, raises a theoretical question. It has to be asked if, or to what extent, this manifest contradiction of languages reveals a poetic dissociation, a sort of architectural schizophrenia.

How can the same architect, over the same period, carry out works that arrive at the extremes of formal and conceptual abstraction and others that make use of the most obvious and traditional processes of rural building? The answer brings us to the heart of a fundamental presupposition of Loos' theory of design — the *architecture of difference*.

The wooden Khuner House — set on a wide base of greenish stone and with a large pitched roof covered with laminated metal — is above all a reflection of the technique of building: it shows that in architecture no *Typisierung*, no a priori model outside the context, can exist. «Just as in no way can we conceive of spatial objects outside space, temporal objects outside time», Ludwig Wittgenstein explained in his *Tractatus logico-philosophicus*, «we cannot conceive of any object outside the possibilities of its connection with others. If I can conceive of the object in the context of the state of things, I cannot conceive of it outside the possibilities of this context.» [1] Loos' work seems to extend the search for the limits of thought into architecture. If, set in the world of the metropolis, Moller House shows the extreme reticence of *nihilismus*, Khuner Country House, situated on the slopes of the Semmering, speaks the dialect of the place. Loos substitutes the logical modesty of building works with deep roots in their site for the fetishism of the «grand form», of the narcissistic search for poetic consistency: «To bring material from far away is more a question of money than of architecture. In mountains rich in timber, one builds in wood; on a stony mountain, stones will be used.» [2]

In this sense the Khuner House has little in common with an earlier rural work by Walter Gropius, the Sommerfeld house, built near Berlin in 1921. Where Gropius looks *expressionistically* into the historical roots of Nordic spirituality in search of a synthesis of art, craftsmanship and architecture, [3] Loos, on the contrary, rationally explores the possibilities of artisan skill within the limits of an unbiased logic that is founded on the potential of the material. This detachment is corroborated by the introduction of significant technical innovations into the rural building pattern, such as the opening of large windows onto the lower floor, the strong

Two views from the garden today.

overhang of the roof and the use of sheet metal for the roofing itself.

But the Khuner House is, above all, an application of Loos' principle of planning «from the inside out.» Inside, rooms of different heights are merged in a basically unitary space that returns to patterns of composition that had been tried out many times. The large two-story-high living room — onto which faces the gallery, giving access to the nighttime zone on the second floor — confirms the aspiration to spatial fluidity visible from the

An early view of the sitting room opening onto the terrace.

first sketches and borrowed from the American pioneering tradition. It is no coincidence that a hint of Richardson may be detected in the green slate-lined fireplace, in the open beams of the roof (that have a structural load-bearing function) and in the abundant use of oak paneling.

Onto this trunk of youthful inspiration is grafted the original design method that Loos introduced in the mature phase of his work: the *Raumplan*. The rooms follow one another in a fascinating narrative

sequence of spaces that are shaped to the requirements of the activities they harbor: the entrance and the dining room — of reduced height (since the floor is at the same level as that of the living room, while the ceiling is set beneath the second floor), the living room — two stories high — and then the studio, the guest room and the kitchen section — of intermediate height (thanks to a lowering of the floor by several steps).

If one adds to this the principles of economy and flexibility of arrangement (deriving from the extreme simplicity of the wooden partitions), the liveliness of color (for instance, the red-painted balustrades) and the intimacy (of the fireside area and of the elegant bedrooms with alcoves), one can well understand how this represents a work of synthesis.

The *Grundbegriffe* (basic concept) is the priority of living over building, of *Erlebnis* as a genuine generatrix of architecture. «Only if we know how to live in a house can we build it.» [4] It would not be rash to take this statement by Martin Heidegger as the true key to the interpretation of this conclusive work by Adolf Loos.

NOTES

1) L. WITTGENSTEIN, *Tractatus logico-philosophicus*, Vienna 1921.

2) Statement by Adolf Loos quoted in H. Kulka, *Adolf Loos*, op. cit., p. 18.

3) Cf. G.C. ARGAN, *Walter Gropius e la Bauhaus*, Turin 1951, pp. 93-95.

4) M. HEIDEGGER, *Bauen, Wohnen, Denken*, 1954.

BIBLIOGRAPHY

H. KULKA, *Adolf Loos*, op. cit., figs. 244-256 with captions.
L. MÜNZ, *Adolf Loos*, op. cit., p. 39 and illustration.
L. MÜNZ, G. KÜNSTLER, *Der Architekt Adolf Loos*, op. cit., pp. 57-61, figs. 36-47.

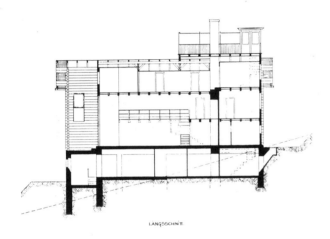

Section, plan and view of the gallery above the sitting room.

HOUSES FOR THE VIENNA WERKBUNDSIEDLUNG
Woinovichgasse, 13-15-17-19, Vienna 13

1930
1932

When Josef Frank, then vice-president of the *Österreichischer Werkbund*, was entrusted with the task of coordinating the construction of an experimental *Siedlung* (Public Housings) in Vienna, Adolf Loos was also invited to take part. This is significant in itself if one bears in mind the fact that Loos had never hidden his reservations about the theoretical and cultural program of this association, right from the moment of its foundation. [1]

All the more reason, then, for it to be taken as a public acknowledgment of the merit of Loos' architectural arguments that the chosen theme for the Viennese *Siedlung*, in imitation of the principle of the *Raumplan*, is expressly aimed at a quest «for the maximum exploitation of space, for the greatest comfort possible in accordance with a strict observance of the principle of minimum wastage of space.» [2] In other words, the viewpoint that prevailed in the Stuttgart *Siedlung* would be overturned in the Viennese one. In fact, methodological priority over the rationalization of the construction process, over the standardization of housing models and

monumentalism of the *Höfe* adopted as a residential paradigm in Vienna. Against the production-line lodging and the creation of little square boxes put together in blocks of architectural propaganda, it sets up a domestic pattern that aims at individuality. What this *Siedlung* sets out to demonstrate is the possibility of offering, within the limits imposed by the containment of costs, a vast range of different models and a balanced relationship with nature, extending the architectural and environmental requisites of the bourgeois residence to the lower middle and working classes. One may glimpse, behind this attempt to shift urban quality from the center to the periphery, Howard's utopia of garden cities. But rather than an antiurban model, the *Siedlung* offers a suburban one. On the periphery of the city, on the edges of the countryside, the urbanized individual can rediscover, in his house and his bit of land, his inner experience, his history and his role as «subject» (carrying out a highly humane work of construction and destruction). The *Siedlung*, then, as

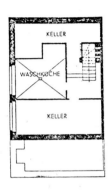

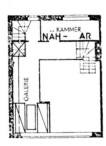
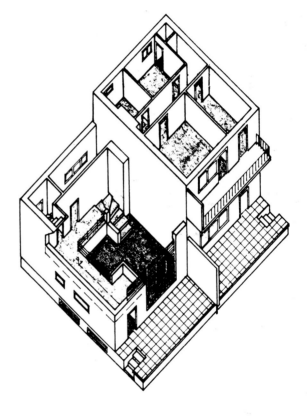

over the codification of an aesthetic syntax, as valid for the city as it is for furniture, is given to the search for a new standard of living.

On this occasion Loos built two pairs of semidetached houses (on whose plans Henry Kulka collaborated) that are a reworking of the model of working-class housing that he had already proposed in his capacity as chief architect of the Municipality of Vienna, in the *Siedlungen* at Heuberg and at Lainz. But it is worth pausing to take a look at the response to the urban problem suggested by the Werkbundsiedlung as a whole, a response that is consistent with Loos' arguments on the subject put forward at the conference on «The Modern *Siedlung*» held in 1926 and developed in his own way by Frank in *Architektur als Symbol*.

What stands out, in fact, in the clear demonstrative intent of the volumetric plan of the complex is the cultural battle over housing models fought by Loos, Frank, Schuster and Leopold Bauer within the debate on building policy that took place in «Red Vienna». In this sense the Viennese Werkbundsiedlung has a controversial dual objective: to oppose on the one hand — as has been pointed out — «the industrial ethics» of the *Maschinenstil* that Stuttgart made its own, and on the other, the symbolic

negation of the *Großstadt*: the *Erlebnis* of the semidetached house against the *Nervenleben* of the metropolis. In the controversial way that a precapitalist housing model is set up in opposition to *Zivilisation*, there is undoubtedly an appeal to «romantic» socialism. It is no coincidence that the only German architect to be invited was Hugo Häring (proponent of an *Organische Architektur*, aimed at molding plastic and spatial forms around human behavior); among the French, André Lurcat (engaged at that time in a Marxist redefinition of the role of the architect through his experience in planning for the socialist administration of Villejuif, and later choosing to move to the U.S.S.R.); and among the Dutch, Gerrit T. Rietveld (who had tried out an advanced application of neoplastic figurative models to residential building in his Schröder House).

But, despite its romantic limits, the hypothesis of overcoming the contradiction between center and periphery is formulated in socially progressive terms. So much so that, shortly afterward right-wing political forces launched a harsh attack on the «Semiticization» of the *Werkbund*, forcing the resignation of the Jewish Social-Democrat Josef Frank and the refoundation of the *Neuer Werkbund Österreichs* (1934, the presidency

Living room on two levels.

being given to Clemens Holzmeister, who became under Dollfuss «*Staats-rat für Kunst*» and the vice-presidencies to Josef Hoffmann and Peter Behrens). This is why it is more interesting to assess the comprehensive meaning of the Werkbundsiedlung as a whole than to look at individual houses. The *Siedlung* is the point of arrival of a cultural battle shared by

Frank and Loos and testimony to an alternative idea of urban development that was prematurely cut off by historical events.

NOTES

1) Born out of the «Third Exhibition of German Handicrafts» (Dresden 1906) and founded in 1907, the *Deutscher Werkbund* became within a few years a most important association that laid down the founding principles of modern industrial design (by 1910 there were already 731 members: 360 artists, 276 industrialists and 95 experts). The influence of the association gradually began to spread beyod the borders of Germany. Friedrich Achleitner, writing about the *Österreichischer Werkbund*, says: «The initially national purview of the *Deutscher Werkbund* raised echoes in those Austrian circles that had traditional ties of sympathy with Germany; but only very rarely did the wind that blew from the Reich succeed in reaching the capital of the Danubian monarchy; only twice, to be exact, in 1912 and in 1930, the two dates when meetings of the *Deutscher Werkbund* were held in Vienna. Moreover, the activity of the Austrian *Werkbund* was largely concentrated in two rather brief periods: from 1913, that is the year of its foundation, to the Cologne exhibition of 1914, and from 1929 to 1932, or until the opening of the Viennese *Siedlung* of the *Werkbund*.» Loos denigrates with a great deal of sarcasm the *Deutscher Werkbund's* search for a synthesis of art, industry and handicraft, aimed at an improvement of the industrial cycle. The ripples caused by Loos'attack were probably the reason behind his systematic exclusion from important works of the *Werkbund* such as the Weissenhofsiedlung in Stuttgart (co ordinated by Mies van der Rohe in 1927) and the Austrian Exhibition in Vienna (directed by Josef Hoffmann in 1930). Cf. A. LOOS, *Sämtliche Schriften*.

2) F. ACHLEITNER, op. cit., p. 110.

BIBLIOGRAPHY

Die Internationale Werkbundsiedlung, Vienna 1932, figs. 200-210 (*Neues Bauen in der Welt*, vol. VI, Vienna, 1932).
L. MÜNZ, G. KÜNSTLER, *Der Architekt Adolf Loos*, op. cit., section no. 101, p. 193.
W. DREIBHOLZ, *Die Internationale Werkbundsiedlung, Wien 1932*, in «Bauforum», n. 61, pp. 19-27.

APARTMENT OF WILLY KRAUS
Bendgasse 10, Pilsen, Czechoslovakia

These alterations made to a four-room apartment once again bear Loos' unmistakable stamp in the attempt to fuse different rooms into a spatial continuum. By knocking down a dividing wall the dining room is, in fact, integrated with the living room, creating a single large room. Only two massive pillars, faced with Cipolin marble, and a few low glass cupboards mark the original division of the two annexed spaces.

The wide use of reflective and refractive surfaces should also be emphasized. The use of mirrors is known to be a constant feature of Loos' interiors, but in this case it takes on a wholly exceptional prominence. As well as the ceiling made from mahogany, polished to a mirror, a determinant role in defining the image of the setting is played by two large mirrors fixed vis-à-vis on the two side walls. This results in an infinite reproduction of the marble elements, producing a highly suggestive optical illusion.

The decoration of the bedroom is dominated instead by a rigorous geometrical linearity. Another distinctive element of this room is the unusual luminosity and airiness that is particularly important in an intimate setting. The wall paneling and part of the furniture are made out of maple wood.

1930

Dining room.

BIBLIOGRAPHY

L. MÜNZ, G. KÜNSTLER, *Der Architekt Adolf Loos*, op. cit., section no. 103, P. 194.
V. BEHALOVA, *Pilsner Wohnungen von Adolf Loos*, in «Bauforum», no. 21, 1970, p. 54.

Drawing of the opened-up bedroom walls.

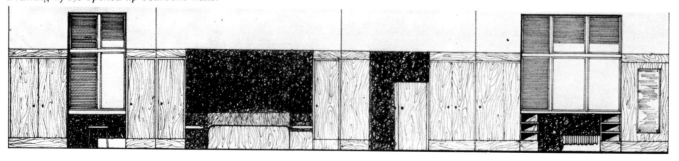

Detail showing materials used in the dining room.

1930 - APARTMENT FOR THE JANITOR OF KHUNER COUNTRY HOUSE
Kreuzberg, Payerbach, Austria

BIBLIOGRAPHY

L. MÜNZ, G. KÜNSTLER, *Der Architekt Adolf Loos*, op. cit., section no. 94, p. 193.

1930 - DECORATION OF THE SURGERY OF DR. TEICHNER
Republik-Platz 22, Pilsen, Czechoslovakia

The sketch-plan of this apartment, made up of two visiting rooms, one on each side of a central waiting room, a dental laboratory and a cloakroom, is kept in the Loos-Archiv. The waiting room was lined with burnished oak and furnished with benches and bookshelves on the wall. The visiting rooms were also fitted with built-in cupboards, but painted in different colors. The walls and ceiling were of white plaster. Only the wall paneling in the waiting room is still in a good state of preservation today.

BIBLIOGRAPHY

L. MÜNZ, G. KÜNSTLER, *Der Architekt Adolf Loos*, op. cit., section no. 102, p. 193.
V. BEHALOVA, *Pilsner Wohnungen von Adolf Loos*, in «Bauforum» no. 21, 1970, p. 56, with illustration.

1930 - APARTMENT OF VICTOR VON BAUER
Altellehmstatte 39-41, Brno, Czechoslovakia

BIBLIOGRAPHY

B. RUKSCHCIO, *Studien zu Entwürfen, Projekten und ausgeführten Bauten von Adolf Loos, 1870-1930*, op. cit., WV. W.199.30.

1930 - PROJECT FOR THE DANCE HALL OF THE AUTOMOBILE CLUB
Pilsen, Czechoslovakia

The original drawings of this project that was never carried out are in the Loos-Archiv. In particular the designs of the panels made for the carpenter are preserved, dated 22 July 1930.

BIBLIOGRAPHY

L. MÜNZ, G. KÜNSTLER, *Der Architekt Adolf Loos*, op. cit., section no. 97, p. 193.

1930 - PLAN FOR ALTERATIONS TO A LARGE WAREHOUSE

The date is uncertain. It should very probably be ascribed to 1930, as suggested by L. Münz and G. Künstler. It is a plan for the extension of an existing warehouse that envisages an expansion into the courtyard and four adjacent plots of land. The original drafts of the project (plans, sections, elevations) are preserved in the Loos-Archiv.

BIBLIOGRAPHY

L. MÜNZ, G. KÜNSTLER, *Der Architekt Adolf Loos*, op. cit., section no. 99, p. 193.

1930 - PROJECT FOR A SINGLE-FAMILY HOUSE
Paris

The Loos-Archiv holds colored copies of three plans and sections of this project signed «Adolf Loos, Paris, 1930».
Kurt Unger, who collaborated in drawing up the plans, has stated that Loos intended to apply the *Raumplan*, but that this was not possible owing to the advanced state of work.

BIBLIOGRAPHY

L. MÜNZ, G. KÜNSTLER, *Der Architekt Adolf Loos*, op. cit., section no. 100, p. 193.

1931 - PLAN FOR ALTERATIONS TO THE VILLA MERCEDES-JELLINEK
Promenade des Anglais, Nice, France

BIBLIOGRAPHY

B. RUKSCHCIO, *Studien zu Entwürfen, Projekten und ausgeführten Bauten von Adolf Loos 1870-1930*, op. cit., WV. H.210.31.P.

1931 - PROJECT FOR A MINI-APARTMENT BUILDING
Prague, Czechoslovakia

BIBLIOGRAPHY

B. RUKSCHCIO, *Studien zu Entwürfen, Projekten und ausgeführten Bauten von Adolf Loos 1870-1930*, op. cit., WV. H.210.31.P.

1931 - DINING ROOM FOR THE COLOGNE EXHIBITION
Cologne, Germany

The project, drawn up with the collaboration of Kurt Unger, received — predictably — considerable critical acclaim.

BIBLIOGRAPHY

Innendekoration, vol. XLIII, 1932, illustration p. 39.
C.A. PLATZ, *Wohnräume der Gegenwart*, Berlin 1933, fig. 347.
L. MÜNZ, G. KÜNSTLER, *Der Architekt Adolf Loos*, op. cit., section no. 110, p. 195.

1931-1937 - SINGLE-FAMILY HOUSE FOR MITZI SCHNABL
Flachsweg 27, Vienna 22

This a small wooden house designed for his housekeeper (dated «Prague, March 1931») and built after his death in 1937.

BIBLIOGRAPHY

L. MÜNZ, G. KÜNSTLER, *Der Architekt Adolf Loos*, op. cit., section no. 106, p. 195.

1932 - PROJECT FOR THE KLEIN COUNTRY HOUSE
Marienbad, Czechoslovakia

BIBLIOGRAPHY

B. RUKSCHCIO, *Studien zu Entwürfen, Projekten und ausgeführten Bauten von Adolf Loos 1870-1930*, op. cit., WV. H.216.32.P.

WINTERNITZ HOUSE
Na Cihlarce 10, Prague-Smichov

It can only come as a surprise to discover that a work of such high quality as this — a masterpiece of his final phase, so to speak — should have been ignored for such a long time in the monographic literature on Loos. [1]

1931
1932

The layout of the composition, of extraordinary effectiveness, increases the tension between volumes. Thanks to a simple bilateral projection of the first-floor section, the architecture takes on the appearance of a true junction of two upside-down L-shaped volumes. This results in an extreme dynamism of the external image that is deliberately counterbalanced, almost opposed, by the imposing monolithic quality of the solid masses. Further emphasis is given to the joining of volumes by the pergola on the terrace (of typical architraved pillars, made out of the same chimney pots as were used in the Müller House) that creates a structural cage linking the two L-shaped blocks, completing the essentially prismatic design on the lateral faces of the building.

The design of the exterior, then, is marked by a strong semantic expressivity that lets the spatial organization of the interior shine through. Expressive of this are the shapes and position of the openings, cut once again straight into the wall and surrounded by white frames divided into squares. An example of this is provided by the three high windows facing onto the terrace that indicate on the façade the presence of the large two-story-high hall cum living room that occupies the entire volume of the section projecting over the garden. And this is the true pivot of composition around which the spaces of the interior are articulated. Onto it face the dining room and the conversation room, set on a raised level as in the scheme tried out in the Müller House. The wide use of glass surfaces and the placing of mirrors at keypoints completes the strategy of introspection and visual linkage of the rooms, giving rise to a visual continuum that is of great charm but that does not interfere with the functional separateness of the different rooms. Moreover, a quick glance at the sections is sufficient to get an idea of how complex and animated is the fit of spaces within the rigid stereometric block. An analysis of the planimetric distribution offers a useful key to an understanding of the geometric matrix underlying the shape of the shell as well. The building has four stories, one of which is the basement (used for cellars and stores) that acts as a base and includes the room whose roof serves as the terrace giving access to the garden.

The ground floor (on two levels, including, as well as the living room and the dining room, the rooms associated with the entrance) is perfectly T-shaped. The upper floor (intended for nighttime use) undergoes a lateral expansion along one of the two axes of the tee, ending up in a purely rectangular shape with a wide adjoining terrace. On the top floor (intended for guests) the cross-sectional rectangle shrinks along both axes, lining up with the edge of the lower block of the tee of the ground floor. This results in the optical effect of interpenetration of the two L-shaped volumes that has been spoken of.

It is interesting to note, finally, how this house, in its skillful reproposition of the play between entire, closed, projecting sections, represents a thematic development of the compositional *leitmotiv* used earlier in Moller House in Vienna and in Müller House in Prague, attaining in this work to an unusual level of dynamic tension that is frozen in the plastic quality of the three-dimensional structure.

Detail of terrace mullion.

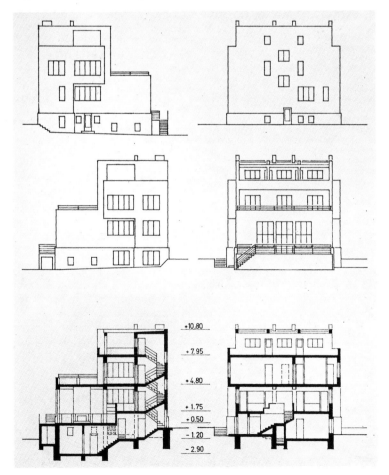

NOTES

1) If one excludes an essay of 1933 (illustrated by three plans and some photographs), devoted to it by K. Lhota, the professor of engineering who directed the work, the existing literature on the subject is so inappropriate to the importance of the work that it may be considered essentially «unpublished». The Winternitz villa is not mentioned in the monographs by H. Kulka and L. Münz. A reference to the work is contained in the recent monograph by M. Kubinsky, as well as in B. Rukschcio's *Dissertation*, but we owe the first careful analysis and graphic reconstruction of the work to D. Worbs. Cf. on this subject the works listed in the bibliography below.

The delay in its rediscovery was probably due to the difficulty of access to the original planning material that is kept in the private archives of the Winternitz family. At present the property is used as a Kindergarten and is still in a good state of preservation.

BIBLIOGRAPHY

K. LHOTA, *Architekt Adolf Loos*, in Architekt SIA, XXXII (1933), pp. 137-143.
M. KUBINSKY, *Adolf Loos*, Berlin 1970, fig. 39, p. 30.
B. RUKSCHCIO, *Studien zu Entwürfen, Projekten und ausgeführten Bauten von Adolf Loos, 1870-1930*, op. cit., p. 169, WV. H.204.31.
D. WORBS, «*Unbekannte» Bauten und Projekte von Adolf Loos in der Č.S.S.R.*, in «Alte und moderne Kunst», Vienna no. 144, 1976, pp. 19-23, figs. 11-14.

SIEDLUNG BABÍ
near Nachod, Czechoslovakia

Built at a time when Loos was already seriously ill, this *Arbeitersiedlung* **1931** offers a unique working verification of his long and patient research into models for working-class housing — a research, as is well-known, often frustrated by the difficulties encountered at the stage of its being put into effect. The compact block, made up of houses in rows (with flat roofs and terraces) in direct contact with the countryside, seems to be a variation on the scheme of composition adopted for the Siedlung am Heuberg. But the reworking of this pattern is translated into a more accentuatedly geometric reduction that gives rise to a construction that is massive, tomb-like, but at the same time extremely modern, in its severe simplicity. This worker's district is still lived in today and merits particular attention.

BIBLIOGRAPHY

L. MÜNZ, *Adolf Loos*, op. cit., pp. 34-39 with illustrations.
L. MÜNZ, G. KÜNSTLER, *Der Architekt Adolf Loos*, op. cit., section no. 103, p. 194.

Early view.

Present-day view.

Front façade of Siedlung Babí today.

ALTERATIONS TO THE ESPLANADE NURSING HOME

Karlsbad, Czechoslovakia

1931

The alteration were carried out — in collaboration with Kurt Unger — to several shops in order to adapt them for use as a dining room and a reading room for the clinic. The materials used are typical of his language: Cipolin marble and cherry wood to line the walls of the dining room; mahogany on the walls and ceiling of the reading room. The unusual combination of strong colors (green and blue) used for the floor is expressive. According to Unger this provoked unjustified reactions on the part of the owner (Dr. V. Simon) to whom Loos responded by pointing out that the beauty of the peacock is based on just this combination of colors.

BIBLIOGRAPHY

L. MÜNZ, G. KÜNSTLER, *Der Architekt Adolf Loos*, op. cit., section no. 104, p. 194.

PLAN FOR ALTERATIONS TO JORDAN HOUSE

Brno, Czechoslovakia

1931

This project is worthy of particular attention, if only for the unconventional idea of raising the building by three floors in order to create a penthouse-villa literally standing on the base of the existing four stories. [1]

Access to the penthouse-villa should have been by a lift as well as by stairs. The floor where one emerges from the lift cccupies the entire basal area (14 × 11 m.) of the existing property. On it are located the services (such as the kitchen and washroom) and various stores, as well as the dining room and entrance.

The second floor is shrunk by about 6 meters to make room for a wide garden terrace. The whole internal space is taken up by a single large living room on two levels, one about 75 centimeters higher than the other. This staggering derives from application of the *Raumplan*: the oft-repeated criterion of spatial economy. On the lower floor, in fact, the height of the service rooms (3 meters) differs from that of the storerooms (2.50 m.) Even the terrace is on two levels so as to remain level with the floor of the living room. A pergola supported by typical square pillars follows the perimeter of the terrace.

The third floor is used for sleeping, with two bedrooms provided with wide balconies facing onto the terrace, and served by a corridor illuminated by four windows.

The elevations, including an axonometric projection, make perfectly clear the intention in the design of concentrating the openings on only one of the four sides, that is, on the south one looking onto the terrace.

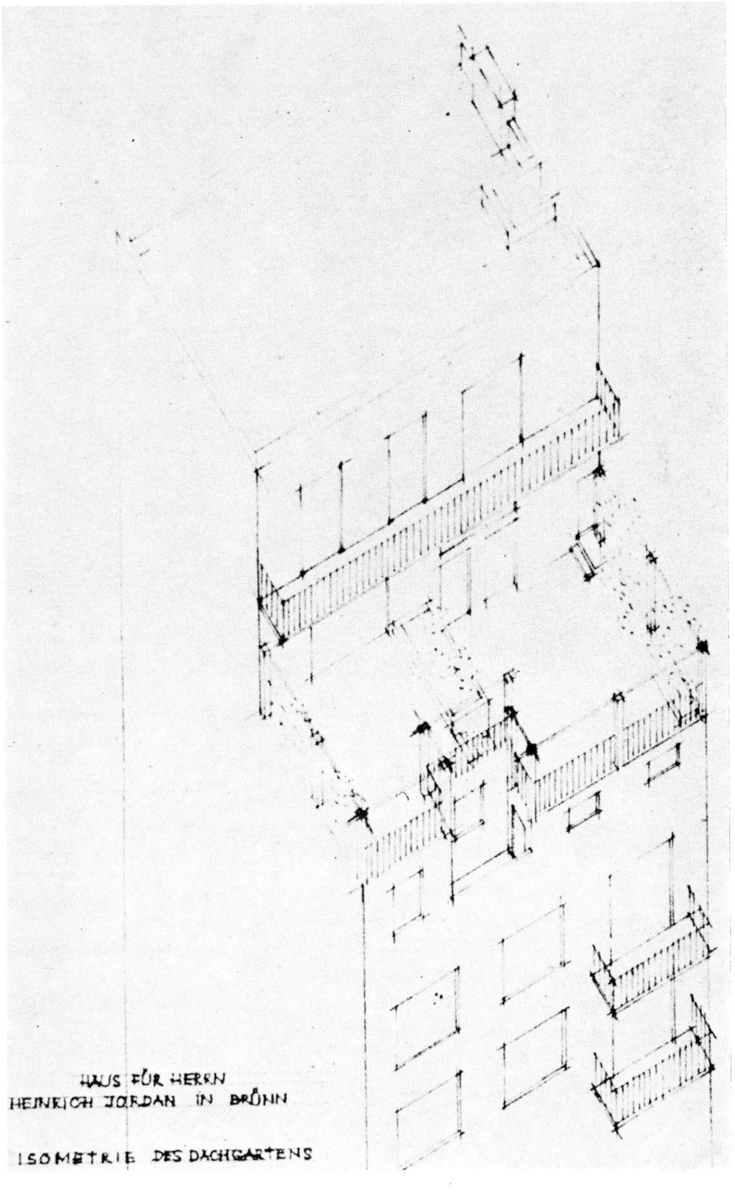

NOTES

1) The project, which was not approved by the competent Building Authority, was never carried out and remained unknown for a long time. The recent discovery of the original drawings was made by Dietrich Worbs, who published them in the pages of the review «Alte und moderne Kunst» listed in the bibliography.

BIBLIOGRAPHY

L. MÜNZ, G. KÜNSTLER, *Der Architekt Adolf Loos*, op. cit., section no. 107, p. 195.
D. WORBS, «*Unbekannte» Bauten und Projekte von A. Loos in der Č.S.S.R.*, in «Alte und moderne Kunst», Vienna, no. 114, pp. 18-19.

HAUS FÜR HERRN
HEINRICH JORDAN IN BRÜNN

ISOMETRIE DES DACHGARTENS

SET OF GLASSES

Made by the firm J. & L. Lobmeyr, this set of glasses — that can be seen today in the Museum des 20. Jahrhunderts in Vienna — is one of the rare examples of utilitarian objects specifically designed by Loos. By his own admission their elementary cylindrical shape was inspired by the rustic glasses he had seen in France. Here we find a firm confirmation of his well-known thesis on the superfluity of the inventive fantasy of the artists of the applied arts. The «best» form is always already there: to produce «modern» objects all that is needed is to discover it, take it up and recycle it. Loos confines himself to adding onto the basic model a *Steinl* cut on the base, drawn in its turn from the Napoleon service. In his opinion, in fact, the only innovation legitimate for utilitarian objects is one that arises out of technical research. The still up-to-date elegance of the shape of these glasses speaks for itself and is the best litmus test of the validity of his method.

1931

BIBLIOGRAPHY

L. MÜNZ, G. KÜNSTLER, *Der Architekt Adolf Loos*, op. cit., section no. 111, p. 195.
V. BEHALOVA, *Das Loos-Service von J. & L. Lobmeyr*, in «Bauforum», no. 39, 1973, pp. 48-49.

PROJECT FOR A HOTEL
Juan-les-Pins, near Cannes, France

This design for a multistory hotel that would have been built by the side of a large pinewoods on the French Riviera shows an extraordinary control over form. The project was drawn up as an alternative to an already existing one that envisaged cutting down about a third of the park. Loos, on the contrary, confines the construction to the edge of the Avenue du Littoral, with the dual aim of avoiding any kind of destruction of the pinewoods and at the same time of filtering the image of the greenery through a screen of architecture that is significantly hollowed out at the base by a gigantic round arch. From a typological point of view the addition of shops to the bottom floors and the conclusion of the block with

1931

sloping terraces should be noted; along with the location of the dance hall and the restaurant on the high panoramic floors. The pattern of the openings gives a clear indication of the internal distribution.

BIBLIOGRAPHY

A. LOOS, *Projet de Sauvetage d'une Pinède*, in «L'architecture d'aujourd'-hui», October 1931, no. 7. pp. 67-70.
L. MÜNZ, G. KÜNSTLER, *Der Architekt Adolf Loos*, op. cit., section no. 109, p. 195 with illustration.

PROJECT FOR FLEISCHNER HOUSE

on Mount Karmel, Haifa, Israel

This house that was never built is a variation on a theme of composition **1931** recurrent in Loos' work: the pattern of the house built on terraces. The stepped layout presents a number of similarities to that of the Scheu House, built in 1912 in Vienna, but the system of open stairs and the basis of distribution of the first two floors recall the solution adopted in the project for the country house at Gastein (1922). It is interesting to note, besides, how the same theme of composition is reproposed, that same year, in the plan for alterations to Jordan House.

At present the drafts (colored plans, elevations, sections and an axonometrical projection) are kept in the Loos-Archiv.

BIBLIOGRAPHY

L. MÜNZ, G. KÜNSTLER, *Der Architekt Adolf Loos*, op. cit., section no. 109, p. 194, with illustration.

HAUS D. FLEISCHNER
IN HAIFA
ISOMETRISCHE ANSICHT
M: 1:100

ARCH. ADOLF LOOS
PRAG, MÄRZ 1931

DESIGN FOR HIS OWN TOMBSTONE

1931

The theme of death — a frequent one in his work — finds an architectural sublimation in this self-commemorative tomb, drawn with an unsteady hand at a moment when he must have been aware of the imminence of his fate. Loos had been admitted to the Rosenhügel Hospital in Vienna with a serious illness that led to his death two years later in the clinic of Dr. Schwarzman in Kalksburg (23 August 1933). In 1958 a tomb was built along the lines of this drawing by the Municipal Council of Vienna and put up in section 32c of the graves of honor in the city cemetery.

Despite the sketchiness of the drawing, the deliberately extreme simplicity of the tomb is clearly visible: a pure cube of granite — with his name engraved in the center — standing on a flat slab. So his own tombstone — even more than the mausoleum for the art historian Max Dvořák (1921) and the gravestone for his friend Peter Altenberg (1919) — marks the experience of a limit. It is a silent return to the most elemental of forms, the final outcome of a long process involving the reduction of geometric construction to primary, almost ancestral, essentiality. Nor is it a coincidence that this limit should be reached in a tomb, that is to say, in a monumental object where architecture stands on the threshold of art. «Art sets out to be the image of death,» Bruno Taut had made clear. [1]

The contemplative geometric stability of the cube seems to want to cancel the flow of time. Symbolically marking the point where the life of forms has its beginning and end, the cube becomes a metaphor for the circular nature of existence. But it is also Loos' poetic testament, his prophecy of a (cyclic) return to «mineral architecture» as the vanishing point where the past and the future are irresistibly joined.

NOTES

1) B. TAUT, *Der Weltbaumeister*, Berlin 1920.

BIBLIOGRAPHY

L. MÜNZ, G. KÜNSTLER, *Der Architekt Adolf Loos*, op. cit., section no. 112, p. 195.

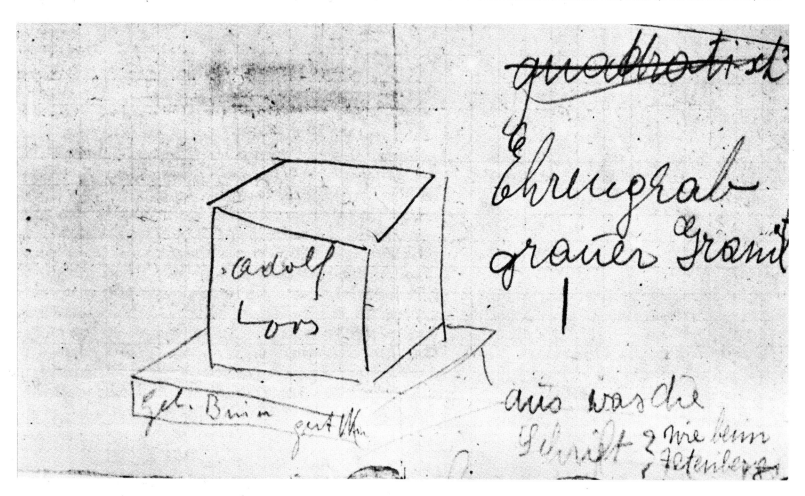

APARTMENT OF OLLY NASCHAUER
Hussgasse 20, Pilsen, Czechoslovakia

1931
1932

Loos was responsible for the decoration of the living room carried out in collaboration with N. Krieger. The furniture was largely of burnished and polished oak. Unusual features included the U-shaped corner divan upholstered in pale leather and the «Egyptian» stools painted in different colors (blue, green, red, yellow).

The furnishings underwent radical changes in 1938 following alterations carried out by N. Krieger himself.

BIBLIOGRAPHY

V. BEHALOVA, *Pilsner Wohnungen von Adolf Loos*, in «Bauforum» no. 21, 1970, Vienna, p. 56.
B. RUKSCHCIO, *Studien zu Entwürfen, Projekten und ausgeführten Bauten von Adolf Loos, 1870-1930*, op. cit., WV. W.211.31.

APARTMENT OF HUGO SEMMLER

1st May St., 19 (formerly Klattauerstrasse) Pilsen, Czechoslovakia

A rigorous symmetry dominated the composition of this elegant music room where the floor-to-ceiling marble lining of the walls was concluded by a double strip of classically molded dark wood. Interesting use was made of the play of visual correspondences between different elements, such as the two doors of polished white sheet metal placed in line with the two windows of the facing hall so as to reflect the light.

. Exactly at the center of the wall opposite the large opening giving access to the adjacent hall, there was a niche which enclosed a typical red brick chimney surmounted by a mirror divided into squares. So once again Loos made use of a deliberate «optical splitting» of the image reflected in the segmented mirror surface. Similar effects of reflection, both of light and of images, were produced by the mirrors set above the glass book-

1931
1932

cases, resulting in an intense luminosity in the room, accentuated by the predominant light and shade contrast of black and white.

The original wall paneling and fixed furnishings of the apartment are still in existence today, though it has been adapted for use as a military headquarters.

BIBLIOGRAPHY

V. BEHALOVA, *Pilsner Wohnungen von Adolf Loos*, in «Bauforum» no. 21, 1970, Vienna, p. 55, fig. 26.
B. RUKSCHCIO, *Studien zu Entwürfen, Projekten und ausgeführten Bauten von Adolf Loos, 1870-1930*, op. cit., WV. W.212.31.

Music room shown in an early photograph.

THE LAST HOUSE
Prague

1933

An extreme geometric purity distinguishes this cubic house ($8 \times 9 \times 9$ m.) designed for the daughter of Dr. F. Müller at a time when Loos was already gravely ill. He was probably asked to draw up the plans during one of his frequent stays in Prague to follow the progress of work on Müller House and the Workers' Estate at Babì, as well as various alterations being carried out, such as the ones to Jordan House. It was Dietrich Worbs who discovered a handwritten report on a project in the library of Müller House, a report whose description corresponds exactly to the drawings (plans and elevations, some of which are signed by Dr. Müller and dated 1 June 1933) found in the same house. This throws doubt on the authenticity of the drawings attributed as das «letzte» Haus von Adolf Loos by Jilka Klingenberg-Helfert in the essay of the same name published in *Alte und moderne Kunst* no. 138, of 1975.

It should be made clear, however, that the drawings discovered by Worbs show two variants of the same project. The greatest difference between the two versions lies in the addition of some elements to the basic cube. The first version, in particular, is characterized by a high prismatic chimney left visible on one of the sides, while the second shows the creation of a room on the roof giving access to the terrace, as well as a lateral balcony. What remains constant, though, is the lining of the walls with wood and the essentially closed appearance of the façades that are barely puncured by the most indispensable of openings. The internal arrangement is extremely simple and leaves room for a wide margin of distributive flexibility, easily obtainable with light and movable wooden panels.

The elemental cubic purity of this country house develops, in short, an extreme simplicity in the lines of its composition and in the material used that is in deliberate contrast to the conventional, backward «rural» image.

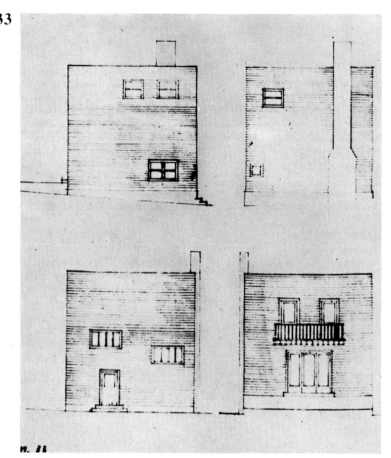

BIBLIOGRAPHY

J. KLINGENBERG-HELFERT, *Das «letzte» Haus von Adolf Loos*, in «Alte und moderne Kunst», Vienna, no. 138, 1975, pp. 30-31, figs. 1-12.

D. WORBS, *«Unbekannte» Bauten und Projekte von Adolf Loos in der Č.S.S.R.*, in «Alte und moderne Kunst», Vienna, no. 144, 1976, p. 23, fig. 15-17.

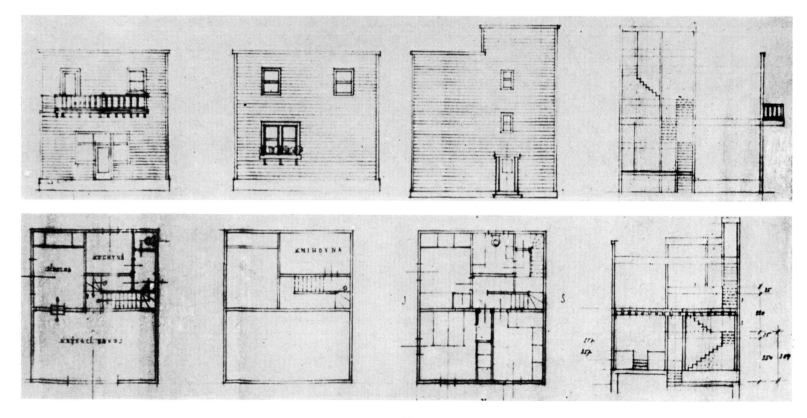

BIBLIOGRAPHY

In drawing up a bibliography of Adolf Loos it is first of all necessary to point out that his work has been the subject of much attention and critical evaluation from the principal «histories» of contemporary architecture: starting out with the first attempts to put the architectural trends of the 20th century into perspective (cf. A. BEHNE, *Der moderne Zweckbau*, Berlin - Frankfurt 1923; G. PLATZ, *Die Baukunst der neusten Zeit*, Berlin 1930), through the by now «classic» historiography on what has been defined as the «Modern Movement» (cf. N. PEVSNER, *Pioneers of the Modern Movement from William Morris to Walter Gropius*, London 1936; S. GIEDION, *Space, Time and Architecture. The growth of a new tradition*, Cambridge, Mass. 1941), and continuing with more recent volumes devoted to the analysis of contemporary architecture (B. ZEVI, *Storia dell'architettura moderna*, Turin 1950; H.R. HITCHCOCK, *Architecture: Nineteenth and Twentieth Century*, Harmandsworth, Middlesex 1958; L. BENEVOLO, *Storia dell'architettura moderna*, Bari 1960; R. BANHAM, *Theory and Design in the First Machine Age*, London 1960; G.C. ARGAN, *L'arte moderna 1770-1970*, Florence 1970; M. RAGON, *Histoire mondiale de l'architecture et de l'urbanisme moderne*, Tournai 1972; R. DE FUSCO, *Storia dell'architettura contemporanea*, Bari 1974; K. ROWLAND, *History of the Modern Movement*, New York 1974; M. TAFURI, F. DAL CO, *Architettura contemporanea*, Milan 1979).

Further documentation of Loos' work is to be found in publications dealing with Austrian and, more generally, German architecture of the 20th century (K. SCHWARZER, *Wiener Bauten 1900 bis heute*, Vienna 1964; G. FEUERSTEIN, H. HUTTER, E. KOLLER, W. MRAZEK, *Moderne Kunst in Österreich*, Vienna 1965; H. BOBEK, E. LICHTENBERGER, *Bauliche Gestaltung und Entwicklung seit der Mitte des 19. Jahrhunderts*, Vienna 1966; R. WAGNER-WIEGLER, *Wien, Architectur im 19. Jahrhundert*, Cologne 1977; G. SELLE, *Die Geschichte des Design in Deutschland von 1870 bis heute*, Cologne 1978). To these should be added the series of essays (of a critical, philosophical or literary nature) that contain significative discussions of Loos (T.W. ADORNO, *Funktionalismus heute*, Berlin, Heft 4/1966; W. BENJAMIN, *Illuminationen*, Frankfurt 1977, L. WITTGENSTEIN, *Vermische Bemerkungen*, Frankfurt 1977).

All this literature has been taken into account in the body of the text, but in compiling a bibliographical list it has been thought better to adopt a selective criterion that limits the titles quoted to those written by Loos himself or devoted specifically to his work. This has been done in order to avoid a selèction based on parameters of choice so wide as to inevitably turn out vague. The list is in chronological order.

WRITINGS BY LOOS

Collections of essays

Ins leere gesprochen (Essays 1897-1900), Paris-Zurich 1921, Second corrected edition, Innsbruck 1932.

Trotzdem (Essays 1900-1930), Innsbruck 1931. (This also contains the two issues of the review «Das andere» published in 1903 and drawn up entirely by Loos).

Sämtliche Schriften, edited by F. Glück, Vol. I, Vienna-Munich 1962.

Parole nel vuoto, Italian trans. of *Ins leere gesprochen* and *Trotzdem*, edited by S. Gessner, Milan 1972.

Ornamento y delito y otros escritos, Spanish trans. edited by R.L. Schachel, Barcelona 1972.

La civiltà occidentale, «*Das Andere*» *e altri scritti*, with an introduction by Aldo Rossi, Bologna 1981.

Writings not included in the above mentioned collections

Ein Wiener Architekt, in «Dekorative Kunst», year II, no. 11, Munich 1898. (Reprint in «Alte und moderne Kunst», no. 113).

Die alte und die neue Richtung in der Baukunst, in «Der Architekt», no. 3 Vienna 1898. Reprinted subsequently in «Alte und neue Kunst, Wiener Kunstwissenschaftliche Blätter», year II, no. 3, Vienna 1953.

Unsere jungen Architekten, in «Ver Sacrum», no. 7, 1898.

Die Ausstellungsstadt, Der neue Styl, in «Neue Freie Presse», 8th May 1898.

Myrbach-Ausstellung, in «Die Waage», no. 14, 1898.

Englische Kunst auf der Schulbank, in «Wiener Rundschau» III, no. 6, Feb. 1899.

Mitteilung, in «Illustriertes Wiener Extrablatt», Vienna 1910.

Vom Gehen, Stehen, Sitzen, Liegen, Schlafen, Essen und Trinken, in «Der Sturm», Nov. 1911 (previously published with illustrations, but unsigned in «Wiener Extrablatt»), Vienna 25th Mar. 1911.

Das Haus auf dem Michaelerplatz, lecture of 11th December 1911 (typescript).

Richtlinien für ein Kunstamt (divided into two parts: *Bildende Kunst* by Loos, and *Musik* by A. Schoenberg), Vienna 1919.

Kunst und Architektur, 1920 (manuscript).

The Chicago Tribune Column. (The International Competition for a new Administration Building for The Chicago Tribune MCMXXII), Chicago 1923. German trans. in «Zeitschrift des Österreichischen Ingenieur-und Architekten-Vereines» year 75, nos. 3-4, Vienna 1923.

Das Grand-Hotel Babylon, in «Das Kunstblatt», no. 4, Potsdam 1924, previously published in «Die neue Wirtschaft», Vienna 20th Dec.

Beauté de la destruction ou destruction de la beauté?, in «Paris Soir», 5th April.

Der Bildhauer Franz Zelezny, Zum 60. Geburtstag des Künstlers, in «Österreichische Bau- und Werkkunst», 1925-26.

Kunst und Gewerbe, in «Moderne Bauformen», 1930.

Projet de Sauvetage d'une Pinède, in «L'Architecture d'aujourd'hui», no. 7, Paris 1931.

Über Josef Hoffmann, in «Alte und moderne Kunst», no. 113, Vienna 1970.

Some essays by Loos collected in *Ins leere gesprochen* and *Trotzdem* were published in the following reviews: «Der Sturm», «Wohnungskultur», «Cahiers d'aujourd'hui» e «L'Esprit Nouveau».

Some letters by Loos are published in the letters of Lina Loos collected under the title of «*Du silberne Dame du*», Vienna-Hamburg 1966.

Two 'private' publications of Loos' works also exist: *Wohnungswanderungen*, Vienna 1907; *Antwort an den Bundes-Wohnngs und Siedlungsfond*, Vienna 1921.

BOOKS ON LOOS

MARILAUN K., *Adolf Loos*, Vienna, Leipzig 1922.

MARKALOUS B., *Adolf Loos*, Prague 1929.

MARILAUN K., *Adolf Loos*, Brno 1929.

VV.AA., *Adolf loos, Festschrift zum 60 Geburstag*, Vienna 1930.

KULKA H., *Adolf Loos, Das Werk des Architekten* (in collaboration with F. Glück and L. Münz), Vienna 1931.

GLÜCK F., *Adolf Loos*, Paris 1931.

AA.VV., *Hommage à Adolf Loos* (writings by G. Besson, L. Werth, Le Corbusier, W. Gropius etc.) in «Vient de Paraître», 11th year, Paris 1931.

LOOS C., *Adolf Loos privat*, Vienna 1936.

LOOS V., *Ein Gedächtnismal für den Erbauer A. Loos*, typescript kept in the «Haus der Technik», Vienna 1942.

MÜNZ L., *Adolf Loos*, Milan 1956.

MÜNZ L. e KÜNSTLER G., *Der Architekt Adolf Loos*, English trans., Vienna 1964; *Adolf Loos, Pioneer of modern architecture* (with an introduction by N. Pevsner and an account by O. Kokoschka), London 1966; New York-Washington 1966.

KUBINSZKY M., *Adolf Loos*, Budapest 1967, German trans. Berlin 1970.

ALTMANN-LOOS E., *Adolf Loos, der Mensch*, Vienna-Munich 1968.

PERUGINI G., *Perché Loos*, Rome 1970.

AMENDOLAGINE F., CACCIARI M., *Oikos: da Loos a Wittgenstein*, Rome 1975.

CZECH H., MISTELBAUER W., *Das Looshaus*, Vienna 1976.

CACCIARI M., *Adolf Loos e il suo angelo* (contains the reprint and the Italian translation of the two issues of the review «Das andere» and the *Festschrift zum 60. Geburtstag*), Milan 1981.

GRAVAGNUOLO B., *Adolf Loos. Teoria e opere*, Milan 1981 (I edition, preface by Aldo Rossi), trans. Vienna and New York 1982, Madrid 1988.

RUKSCHCIO B., SCHACHEL R., *Adolf Loss. Leben und Werk*, Vienna 1982.

VELOTTI S., *Adolf Loos. Lo stile del paradosso*, Bari 1988.

OPEL A., VALDEZ M. (edited by), «*Alle Architekten sind Verbrechen*». *Adolf Loos und die Folgen. Eine Spurensicherung*, Vienna 1990.

TOURNIKIOTIS P., *Loos*, Paris 1991.

DENTI G., *Adolf Loos, Architettura e città*, Florence 1992.

DENTI G., PEIRONE S., *Adolf Loos, uno spirito sociale*, Florence 1993.

CATALOGUES

Adolf Loos, Walter Gropius, Gewerbemuseum, Basle 1931.

Ausstellung Adolf Loos, Bauten und Bildnisse 1870-1933, Buchhandlung Perless, Vienna 1933.

Exhibition of the work of Adolf Loos at the Architectural Association, Bedford, England 1934.

Adolf Loos, Tel Aviv 1947.

Adolf Loos, Mensch und Raum, Darmstadt 1951.

Adolf Loos 1870-1933 (edited by Maria and Ludwig Münz), Würthle Gallery, Vienna 1961.

Adolf Loos, Galerie des Beaux-Arts (edited by the Arbeitsgruppe 4), Paris 1962.

Adolf Loos, Museum des 20. Jahrhunderts (edited by the Arbeitsgruppe 4), Vienna 1964.

Adolf Loos, Facoltà di Architettura (edited by the Austrian Cultural Institute in Rome), Rome 1965.

Adolf Loos 1870-1933, Graphische Sammlung der Eidgenössischen Hochschule, Zurich 1965.

Gottfried Semper, Otto Wagner und Adolf Loos (edited by Künstler G.), in «Das K & K Hoftheater-Kulissendepot», Vienna 1977.

Adolf Loos 1870-1933, Institut Français d'Architecture, Institut Culturel Autrichien de Paris, Lièges-Bruxelles 1983.

Adolf Loos 1870-1933. Raumplan-Wohnungsbau, Akademie der Künste, Berlin 1984.

The Architecture of Adolf Loos, Arts Council Exhibition, London 1987.

Adolf Loos, Albertina, Vienna 1989.

Raumplan versus plan libre, Delft University (edited by Max Risselada), Delft 1991.

OTHER WRITINGS ON LOOS

BAHR H., *Der englische Stil*, in: «Ver Sacrum», no. 7, Vienna 1898.

HEVESI L., *Kunst auf der Strasse*, in: «Fremdenblatt», Vienna 1899.

CLOETER H., *Das Dreilauferhaus*, in: «Neue Freie Presse», Vienna 1909.

SCHEU R., *A. Loos*, in: «Die Fackel», no. 283-284, Vienna 1909.

KRAUS K., *Das Haus am Michaelerplatz*, in: «Die Fackel», Year 12, Vienna 1910.

KRONSTEIN, *Die Mistkiste am Michaelerplatz*, in: «Die Neue Zeitung», Vienna 7th Dec. 1910.

GOLDMAN L., *Zuschrift*, in: «Zeitung unbekannt», Vienna 1910.

MARILAUN K., *Das Haus auf dem Michaelerplatz*, in: «Reichspost», Vienna 1910.

SCHAUKAL R., *Ein Haus und seine Zeit*, in: «Der Merker, Österreichische Zeitschrift für Musik und Theater», no. 5, Vienna 1910.

SPEIDEL F., *Vom modernen Haus*, in: «Neues Wiener Tagblatt», Vienna 1910.

STRZYGOWSKI J., *Wiener Bauten*, in: «Die Zeit», Vienna 1910.

TIETZE H., *Der Kampf um Alt-Wien, III, Wiener Neubauten*, in: «Kunstgeschichtliches Jahrbuch der k.k. Zentralkommission für Erforschung und Erhaltung der Kunst und bist. Denkmale», no. 1, Vienna 1910.

WITTMANN H., *Das Haus gegenüber der Burg*, in: «Neue Freie Presse», Morgenblatt, Vienna 1910.

DAHL H., *Michaelerhaus*, in: «Schlesische Zeitung», 17th May 1911.

ENGELMANN P., *Gedicht zum Michaelerhaus*, in: «Die Fackel», no. 317/318, Vienna 28th Feb. 1911.

SCHAUKAL R., *Nochmals das Haus gegenüber dem Michaelerhof*, in: «Reichspost», Vienna 1st Jan. 1911.

SERVAES F., *Wiener Wandlungen*, in: «Der Tag», Berlin 8th Mar. 1911.

STOESSL O., *Das Haus auf dem Michaelerplatz*, in: «Die Fackel», nos. 317/318, Vienna 1911.

WYMETAL W., *Wiener Weihnachtsbrief*, in: «Tagesbote für Mähren und Schlesien», p. 17, 23rd Dec. 1911.

KRAUS K., *Untergang der Welt durch schwarze Magie*, in: «Die Fackel», nos. 363/365, Vienna 1912.

KRAUS K., *Das Gfrett mit den Dienstboten*, in: «Die Fackel», nos. 381/383, Vienna 1913.

KRAUS K., *Der Löwenkopf oder Die Gefahren der Technik*, in: «Die Fackel», nos. 384/385, Vienna 1913.

KRAUS K., *Die Schönheit im Dienste des Kaufmannes. Offener Brief an Loos*, in: «Die Fackel», Vienna, Nov. 1915.

MANSCH A., *Adolf Loos*, in: «A. Mansch, Meisterarchiv, Galerie von Zeitgenossen Deutschland», Berlin 1915.

(anonymous), *Der «fremde Herr» im Damensalon*, in: «Neue Freie Presse», Vienna 9th Dec.

PATER F., *Adolf Loos und das Schicksal Österreichs*, in: «Der Friede», nos. 48/49, 1918.

OTTMANN F., *A. Loos*, in: «Der Architekt», Vienna 1919.

STEFAN P., *Adolf Loos zum 50. Geburtstag*, in: «Neue Zürcher Zeitung», Zurich 30th Dec. 1920.

FISCHER L., *Adolf Loos*, in: «Die Stunde», Vienna 7th Feb. 1923.

HENRY M., *Mon cher ami*, in: «L'Eclair», 24h Nov. 1923.

RAMBOSSON Y., *Le Salon d'automne*, in: «L'Amour des Arts», no. 11, 1923.

VAILLAT, *L'Art de la trompette*, in: «Temps», Paris 7th Nov. 1923.

VAUXCELLES L., *Le Salon d'automne*, in: «L'Eclair», Paris 3rd Nov. 1923.

FISCHEL H. (review of), *Ins leere gesprochen*, in: «Österreichs Bau- und Werkkunst», Vienna 1924.

MARKALOUS B., *Adolf Loos*, in: «Wohnungskultur», no. 1, 1924-25.

MARKALOUS B., *Adolf Loos*, in: «Prednasek o Architekture», no. 7, Prague 1925.

RAY M., *Adolf Loos*, in: «Paris Soir», n. 543, Parigi 1925.

HILDEBRANDT H., *Adolf Loos*, in: «Stuttgarter Neues Tagblatt», Stuttgart 9th Nov. 1926.

KLEIN O., *Loosovy preduasky na Sorbona*, in: «Tribuna», 25th Feb. 1926.

WEINER R., *Adolf Loos chavon*, in: «Lidove noviny», 3rd April 1926.

(anonymous), *La forme d'une ville*, in: «La Vie Parisienne», Paris 16th Mar. 1927.

(anonymous), *Das Wiener Weh*, in: «Kleine Volkszeitung», Vienna 21st April 1927.

ABELS L., *Ein Wiener Herrenmodesalon*, in: «Das Interieur», II, Vienna 1901.

KOSEL H. C., *Adolf Loos*, in: «Deutsch-Österreichisches Künstler- und Schriftsteller-Lexikone» I, 1902.

SCHÖLERMANN W., *Die «Wiener Richtung» in der Innenausstattung*, in: «Innendekoration», Darmstadt 16 Jr. 1905 Heft 1.

HABERFELD H., *The Architectural Revival in Austria*, in: «The Studio» no. XX, London 1906.

HEVESI L., *A. Loos*, in: «Fremdenblatt», Vienna 1907.

HEVESI L., *Der Neubau des Kriegsministeriums*, in: «Fremdenblatt», Vienna 1908.

SCHAUKAL R., *Gegen das Ornament*, in «Deutsche Kunst und Dekoration», year XI, no. 7, 1908.

SCHAUKAL R., *A. Loos, Geistige Landschaft mit vereinzelter Figur im Vordergrund*, in: «Innendekoration», year XIX, Darmstadt 1908.

WYMETAL W., *Adolf Loos*, in: «Tagesbote aus Mähren und Schlesien», 4th Jan. 1908.

(anonymous), *Adolf Loos über die Wiener Werkstätte*, in: «Neue Freie Presse», Vienna 21st April 1927.

(anonymous), *Das grosse Wiener Weh*, in: «Neues Wiener Journal», Vienna 21st April 1927.

(anonymous), *Kunst und Handwerk*, in: «Neues Wiener Tagblatt», Vienna 21st April 1927.

(anonymous), *Ich - der bessere Österreicher*, in: «Neues Wiener Journal», Vienna 23rd April 1927.

(anonymous), *Das Wiener Weh*, in: «Der Morgen», Vienna 25th April 1927.

(anonymous), *Das Marillenknödel-Derby des Herrn Adolf Loos*, in: «Neues Wiener Journal», Vienna 28th June 1927.

(anonymous), *Adolf Loos baut*, in: «Wiener Allgemeine Zeitung», Vienna 16th Sep. 1927.

(anonymous), *Adolf Loos ist gegen den Wiederafbau des Justizpalastes*, in: «Wiener Allgemeine Zeitung», Vienna 17th Sep. 1927.

GALEOTTI J., *La Nouvelle Architecture*, in: «Vogue», no. 4, Paris 1927.

K. N., *Der soziale Mensch und seine Architektur*, in: «Arbeiterwille», 9th Nov. 1927.

(anonymous), *Architeckt Loos kündigt der nunizierenden Amerikanerin*, in: «Wiener Allgemeine Zeitung», Vienna 19th Feb. 1928.

JACOB H., *Wer ist Loos*, in: «Prager Tagblatt», Prague 30th Nov. 1928.

POLGAR A., *Fall Loos*, in «Prager Tagblatt», Prague 15th Sep. 1928.

(anonymous), *Ausstellung «Der Stuhl»*, in: «Frankfurter Zeitung», Frankfurt 21st Feb. 1929.

(anonymous), *Der psychoanalysierte Loos*, in: «Die Glossen», no. 143, Vienna 23 Jg. 1929.

FISCHER L., *Siedlungen von Loos und Leopold Fischer*, in: «Wasmuths Monatshefte», no. 70, Berlin 1929.

(anonymous), *Der grosse Gott Loos*, in: «Die Stunde», Vienna 2nd Mar. 1930.

(anonymous), *Zwei Architektenbücher*, in: «Werkbundgedanken», Vienna 27th Mar. 1930.

A. M., *Adolf Loos*, in: «Arbeiterzeitung», no. 338, Vienna 10th Dec. 1930.

A. M., *Die Loos-Ausstellung im Hagenbund*, in: «Arbeiterzeitung», no. 354, Vienna 27th Dec. 1930.

BORN W., *Adolf Loos*, in: «Neues Wiener Tagblatt», Vienna 9th Dec. 1930.

ERMESD M., *Generations führer Adolf Loos*, in: «Wiener Tag», Vienna 10th Dec. 1930.

HOFMANN H., *Eine Villa von Adolf Loos*, in: «Prager Tagblatt», no. 46, Prague 22nd Feb. 1930.

ILG J., *Die Adolf-Loos-Ausstellung im Hagenbund*, in: «Wiener Allgemeine Zeitung», Vienna 12th Dec. 1930.

JARAY, *Adolf Loos*, in: «Sozialdemokrat», no. 129, p. 5, Prague 10th Jan. 1930.

KRAUS K., *Adolf Loos*, in: «Die Fackel», nos. 845-846, Vienna 1930.

KRAUS K., *A. Schönberg, Heinrich Mann, Valéry Larbaud, James Joyce. Aufruf zu Adolf Loos' Geburtstag*, in: «Prager Tagesblatt», Prague 4th Dec. 1930.

KULKA H., *An Adolf Loos unseren Lehrer*, in: «Wiener Allgemeine Zeitung», p. 5, Vienna 11th Dec. 1930.

LECHNER F., *Loos und Hoffmann*, in: «Prager Tagblatt», Prague 7th Jan. 1930.

MARKALOUS B., *Adolfovi Loosovi, iniciatoru moderni Architektury*, in: «Pestry Tyden», no. 6, Prague 1930.

MARKALOUS B., *Adolf Loos zum 60. Geburtstag*, in: «Prager Presse», no. 338 p. 3, Prague 10th Jan. 1930.

MICHAELIS K., *Der Überwinder des Ornaments*, in: «Vossische Zeitung», no. 288, 10th Dec. 1930.

MICHAELIS K., *Adolf Loos zum 60. Geburtstag, am 10. Dezember* in: «Neue Freie Presse», Vienna 1930.

SCHLEICHER G., *Zum 60. Geburtstag von Adolf Loos*, in: «Neues Wiener Tagblatt», Vienna 10th Dec. 1930.

SETNICKA I., *Sedesat let Adolfa Loosa*, in: «Stavitel XI», 1930.

STARY O., *Adolf Loos*, in: «Starba IX», 1930-1931.

STEFAN P., *Der sechzigjährige Adolf Loos*, in: «Die Stunde», Vienna 7th Dec. 1930.

WONDRACEK R., *Adolf Loos. Das Haus am Michaelerplatz*, in: «Österr. Bau- und Werkkunst», Vienna 1930-1931.

BAUER K., *A. Loos*, in: «Der Kunstwart», no. 6, Vienna 1931.

ECKSTEIN H., *Adolf Loos*, in: «Karlsbader Tagblatt», 6th Sep. 1931.

ECKSTEIN H., *Adolf Loos als Baumeister und Schriftsteller*, in: «Die bildenden Künste», Münich 28th Jan. 1931.

GABLOT G., *A. Loos*, in: «Revue d'Allemagne», Paris 1931.

GANTNER J., *A. Loos zum 60. Geburtstag*, in: «Das neue Frankfurt», no. 1, Frankfurt 1931.

GLÜCK F., *Karl Kraus, Peter Altenberg, Adolf Loos*, in: «Literarische Monatshefte», no. 9, 1931.

H. S., *Adolf Loos*, in: «Württembergische Zeitung» 28th Mar. 1931.

SCHLEICHER G., *Adolf Loos und sein Werk*, in: «Stuttgarter Rundschau», Stuttgart 24th Mar. 1931.

SCHLEICHER G., *Adolf Loos und seine Ausstellung in Stuttgart*, in: «Esslinger Zeitungen», p. 3, 25th Mar. 1931.

WIESNER E., *Adolf Loos*, in: «Die Wahrheit» no. 1, Prague 10th Jan. 1931.

(anonymous), *Adolf Loos in Karlsbad*, in: «Karlsbader Tagblatt», no. 130, Karlsbad 5th Jun. 1932.

FRANK J., *Internationale Werkbundsiedlung*, in: «Neues Bauen in der Welt», Vol VI, Vienna 1932.

(anonymous), *Adolf Loos gestorben*, in: «Die Stunde», no. 335, Wien 11.Jg. 1933.

(anonymous), *Adolf Loos Gedächtnisfeier*, in: «Neues Wiener Tagblatt», Vienna 28th Oct. 1933.

(anonymous), *Die Loos-Feier des Österr. Werkbundes*, in: «Volks-Zeitung», Vienna 2nd Nov. 1933.

(anonymous), *Unter den Anwesenden fehlten...*, in: «Der Morgen», Vienna 6th Nov. 1933.

AA.VV., *In memoriam A. Loos*, in: «Architectura» IIIrd year, no. 2, Ljubliana 1933.

DUESBERG A. C., *Adolf Loos*, in: «L'Equerre», Year 7, 5th Jan. 1933.

EIMERS M., *Gedächtnisfeier für Adolf Loos*, in: «Der Wiener Tag», Vienna 27th Oct. 1933.

F., *Adolf-Loos-Gedächtnisausstellung*, in: «Neues Wiener Tagblatt», Vienna 17th Sep. 1933.

FRANK J., *In memoriam Adolf Loos*, in: «Architectura III», 1933 Ses. 2.

HAAS W., *Erinnerungen an Adolf Loos*, in: «Prager Mittag», Prague 25th Aug. 1933.

HILDEBRANDT H., *Adolf Loos*, in: «Forum III», no. 9, p. 264, Brno 3rd Jr. 1933.

HOLZMEISTER C., *Bahnbrecher der Wohnkultur*, in: «Neues Wiener Journal», Vienna 25th Aug. 1933.

KOKOSCHKA O., *Der die Menschheit von unnützer Arbeit befreite*, in: «Wiener Allgemeine Zeitung», Vienna 25th Oct. 1933.

KRAUS K., *A. Loos, Rede am Grab*, in: «Die Fackel», no. 888, Vienna 1933.

KULKA H., *Adolf Loos*, in: «Frankfurter Zeitung», Frankfurt 31st Aug.1933.

KURTZ W., *Adolf Loos*, in: «Sonntagszeitung», no. 36, Vienna 3rd Sep. 1933.

LABÒ M., *Un architetto: A. Loos*, in: «Lavoro», 1933.

LHOTA K., *Architekt A. Loos*, in: «Architekt SIA», no. 32, Prague 1933.

MARKALOUS B., *Adolf Loos zaslouzil se o civilisaci*, in: «Pritomnost Prag», nos. 36-37, Prague 1933.

MARKALOUS B., *Za Adolfem Loosem*, in: «Pestry tyden 36», str. 2, 1933.

MATEJCEK A., *Adolf Loos zemrel*, in: «Lidove Moviny», 25th Aug. 1933.

PERSICO E., *In memoria di A. Loos*, in: «Casabella», Milan 1933.

RISMONDO P., *Adolf Loos*, in: «Wiener Allgemeine Zeitung», Vienna 25th Aug. 1933.

RISMONDO P., *Die Loos-Feier des Werkbundes*, in: «Wiener Allgemeine Zeitung», Vienna 28th May 1933.

SCHEU R., *Adolf Loos*, in: «Prager Tagblatt», Praga 25th May 1933.

SETNICKA I., *Adolf Loos zemrel*, in: «Stavital KIV», 1933-34.

STRESSL O., *Erinnerungen an Adolf Loos*, in: «Die Welt im Wort», no. 10, p. 2, Prague-Vienna 1 Jg. 1933.

URBAN B. S., *Tvarei duch moderni architektury*, in: «Narodni Listy», 26th Aug. 1933.

VETTER M. A., *Ein Licht ist erloschen*, in: «Profil», 1933.

ZINGARELLI I., *Il pioniere dell'architettura razionale*, in: «La Nazione», 16th Sep. 1933.

(anonymous), *Ein Adolf Loos Archiv*, in: «Tagblatt», 24th Apr. 1934.

(anonymous), *Für ein Adolf Loos Archiv*, in: «Prager Presse», Prague 26th Oct. 1934.

SHAND P. M., *Loos*, in: «The Architectural Review», London 1934.

LOOS C., *Adolf Loos privat* (review of the book of the same title), in: «Neue Freie Presse», Vienna 11th Dec. 1935.

MÜNZ L., *Schutz für ein architektonisches Meisterwerk*, in: «Wiener Zeitung», Vienna 1935.

GLÜCK F., *Die Gefährdung des Loos-Hauses auf dem Michaelerplatz*, in: «Wiener Zeitung», Vienna 1936.

GLÜCK F., KULKA H., MURY L., *Zum Gedenken an Adolf Loos*, in: «Wiener Zeitung», Vienna 23rd Aug. 1936.

MÜNZ L., *Die Gefährdung des Loos-Hauses auf dem Michaelerplatz*, in: «Wiener Zeitung», Vienna 10th Jan. 1936.

LIEBSTÖCKL H., *Los von Loos*, in: «Die Bühne», Vienna 5th May 1937.

MÜNZ L., *A. Loos und sein Franz-Josef-Denkmal*, in: «Wiener Zeitung», Vienna 1937.

BOURNOUD P., *Une construction d'Adolf Loos en Suisse*, in: «La demeure. Formes et couleurs», no. 4, Lausanne 1944.

GLÜCK F., *Eine wichtige Aufgabe*, in: «Wiener Kurier», Vienna 7th Nov. 1945.

LOOS L., *Adolf Loos und Ich*, in: «Wort und Tat», August 1947.

SCHLEICHER G., *Der Bekämpfer des Ornaments. Adol Loos zu seinem 80. Geburtstag*, in: «Stuttgarter Zeitung», Stuttgart 10th Dec. 1949.

COLIN R., *Mannerism and Modern Architecture*, in: «The Architectural Review», London 1950.

SCHLEICHER G., *Adolf Loos, zum 80. Geburtstag*, in: «Die Bauzeitung», Stuttgart 55 Jg., Year II, p. 55, 1950.

LEHMANN F, *Die ein fältige und die modische Baukunst. Loos, Tessenow, Le Corbusier*, in: «Die Österr. Furche, Die Warte», no. 9, Vienna 1953.

MÜNZ L., *Vorwort zum Abdruck Adolf Loos: Die alte und die neue Richtung in der Baukunst*, in: «Alte und neue Kunst», no. 3, Vienna 1953.

SCHLEICHER G., *Adolf Loos, der Wegbereiter für moderne Bau- und Wohnkultur*, in: «Die Bauzeitung», no. 55, Stuttgart 1955.

ECKSTEIN H., *Josef Hoffmann, der Wiener Jugendstil und Adolf Loos*, in: «Bauen und Wohnen», Munich 1956.

GRAF M., *Der Baumeister Adolf Loos*, in: «Die Weltpresse», 19th May 1956.

ANDL H., *Warum das Loos-Haus keine Fähnchen trägt*, in: «Der Abend», Vienna 9th Jun. 1956.

NHAM R., *Ornament and Crime*, in: «The Architectural Review», London 1957.

RFLES G., *Loos e la Secessione*, in: «Domus» no. 328, 1957.

CHER W., *Adolf Loos und seine Lehre von den reinen Formen*, in:

«W. Fischer, Bau-Raum-Gerät», Munich 1957.

GLÜCK F., *A. Loos 1870-1933*, in: «Der Aufbau», Vienna 1958.

KÖLLER E., *Die Überwindung des Ornaments*, in: «Arbeiterzeitung», Vienna 24th Aug. 1958.

MÜNZ L., *Über die Grundlagen des Baustils von A. Loos*, in: «Der Aufbau», Vienna 1958.

SCHEU R., *Erinnerungen an Adolf Loos*, in: «Arbeiterzeitung», Vienna 22nd Aug. 1958.

SOKRATIS D., *Adolf Loos*, in: «Der Aufbau», Vienna 13 Jg. 1958.

ZAHN L., *Adolf Loos*, in: «Das Kunstwerk», Venna 1958.

NEUTRA R., *Ricordo di Loos*, in: «Casabella», no. 233, Milan 1959.

ROGERS E., *Attualità di A. Loos*, in: «Casabella», no. 233, Milan 1959.

ROSSI A., *Adolf Loos 1870-1933*, in: «Casabella», no. 233, Milan 1959.

HILDEBRANDT H., *Anregungen für Generationen*, in: «Deutsche Zeitung», 10/11th Dec.1960.

HILDEBRANDT H., *Adolf Loos*, in: «Schwäbische Post», 15th Dec. 1960.

HIRSCH M., *Das Kapitel Adolf Loos*, in: «Neues Österreich», Vienna 10th Jul. 1960.

KULKA H., *Adolf Loos 1870-1933*, in: «Architects' Year Book 9», London 1960.

MRAZEK W., *Das Haus Müller in Prag (Zum 90. Geburtstag von A. Loos)*, in: «Alte und Neue Kunst», Vienna 1960.

SCHLEICHER G., *Adolf Loos attakiert Georg Trakl*, in: «Stuttgarter Zeitung», Stuttgart 9th Jul. 1960.

SCHLEICHER G., *Haus ohne Augenbrennen*, in: «Stuttgarter Zeitung», Stuttgart 10th Dec. 1960.

SCHLEICHER G., *Bau unter Denkmalschutz*, in: Stuttgart 10th Dec. 1960.

WÖRLE E., *Rettung einer Kostbarkeit*, in: «Der Bau», Vienna 1960.

GLÜCK F., *Briefe von Schönberg an Loos*, in: «Österr. Musikzeitschrift», no. 1, Vienna 1961.

HOFFMANN W., *Adolf Loos - Galerie Würthle*, in: «Werk», Winterthur, no. 5, 1961.

RAINER R., *Aus Anlass einer Loos-Ausstellung*, in: «Der Bau», Year 4, 16 Jg. 1961.

SCHIMMANN K., *Jedes Material hat seine eigene Formsprache, A. Loos in Wort und Werk*, in: «Österreich in Geschichte und Literatur», Vienna 1961.

SCHMELLER A., *Lebt Adolf Loos am Ende noch*, in: «Kurier», Vienna 7th Apr. 1961.

ACHLEITNER F., *Keinen Anspruch auf Adolf Loos*, in: «Die Presse», Vienna August 1963.

CLAUHS P., *Zum 30. Todestag von Adolf Loos*, in: «Baumeister», Munich 1963.

DELEROY R., *Adolf Loos*, in: «Knaurs Lexikon der modernen Architektur, Munich 1963.

LORENZ H., *Adolf Loos: Das Haus am Michaelerplatz*, in: «Aufnahmearbeit», Kunsthistorisches Institut der Universität Wien; manuscript, Venna 1963.

MATEJKA V., *Erst einmal Möbel? Erst einmal Loos!*, in: «Tagebuch», no. 4, Vienna 18 Jg. 1963.

POIDINGER G., *Adolf Loos*, in: «Arbeiterzeitung», Vienna 3rd Oct. 1963.

SUNDERMANN H., *Ornament, Kleinschreibung und Verbrechen*, in: «Die Furche», Vienna 1963.

THURNER, *Adolf Loos, Sämtliche Schriften* (review), in: «Der Bau», Year 4, Vienna 1963.

(anonymous), *Loos' Erbe*, in: «Die Presse», Vienna 2nd/3rd May 1964.

(anonymous), *Der Bummerang*, in: «Wochenpresse», Vienna 9th May 1964.

ACHLEITNER F., *Loos, Erbe und Erben*, in: «Die Presse», Vienna 2nd/3rd May 1964.

ACHLEITNER F., *Una grande mostra di Loos a Vienna*, in: «Domus», no. 418, Milan 1964.

B. A., *Loos fegte unter unseren Füßen*, in: «Kurier», Vienna 8th May 1964.

BANHAM R., *Adolf Loos und das Problem des Ornaments*, in: «R.

Banham, Die Revolution der Architektur», Hamburg 1964.

CZECH H., MISTELBAUER W., *Das Looshaus*, in: «Der Aufbau», nos. 4-5, Vienna 1964.

HARTMANN D., *Der Baumeister einer heilen Welt*, in: «Volksblatt», Vienna 5th May 1964.

KALIDOVA F., *Navrat Adolfa Loosa do Brna*, in: «Lidova demokracia», 15th Sep. 1964.

KALIDOVA F., *Adolf Loos v Brne*, in: «Veverni Rovnost» 7th Sep. 1964.

PODREKA B., *Ceska, Plecnik, Loos, Fuchs*, in: «Most», Laibach 1964.

SCHMÖLZER H., *Besuch bei Lina Loos*, in: «Die Presse», Vienna 10/11th Oct. 1964.

SOKRATIS D., *Der Architekt Adolf Loos*, in: «Der Aufbau», Vienna 19 Jg. 1964.

UHL O., *Adolf Loos in seinen Bauten und Projekten*, in: «Die Presse» Vienna 17/18th Oct. 1964.

BEER O. F., *Holz hat nicht violett zu sein*, in: «Die Zeit», no. 21, p. 20, Vienna 1965.

EISENREICH H., *Was ist modern?*, in: «Christ in der Welt», 22nd Jan. 1965.

FEUERSTEIN G., *Adolf Loos. Volumen und Säule*, in: «Bauwelt», Berlin 1965.

GIRARDI V., *Adolf Loos, pioniere protestante*, in: «L'architettura - cronache e storia», no. 115, Rome 1965.

SCHMIDT H., *Adolf Loos*, in: «Beiträge zur Architektur», Berlin 1924-1964, Berlin 1965.

ADORNO T. W., *Funktionalismus heute*, in: «Neue Rundschau», no. 4 Berlin 1966.

BIRKNER O., *Die Welt um Adolf Loos*, in: «Werk», no. 2, Winterthur 1966.

CZECH H., *Adolf Loos und Funktionalismus*, in: «Die Furche», no. 25, Vienna 1966.

KREBITZ H., *Adolf Loos - Unbekannte Bauten*, in: «Bau», no. 1-2, Vienna 1966.

MOOS St., *Zur Architektur von Adolf Loos. Besprechung des Münz-Buches*, in: «Neue Zürcher Zeitung», Zurich 21st Aug. 1966.

SOBOTKA W., *Adolf Loos*, in: «The New York Times», New York 1966.

(anonymous), *Haus Müller in Prag*, in: «Werk», Winterthur 1967.

GRADMANN E., *Adolf Loos*, in: «E. G.: Aufsätze zur Architektur; Schriftenreihe des Instituts für Geschichte und Theorie der Architektur, E. T. H. Zürich», no. 6, Bask-Stuttgart 1968.

HUNDERTWASSER F., *Los von Loos*, in: «Protokolle '68», Vienna 1968.

KOHLMAIER G., *Destillierte Materie. Anmerkungen zu Loos*, in: «Protokolle '68», Vienna 1968.

KÜNSTLER G., *Der «Traditionalist» Adolf Loos*, in: «Österreichische Zeitschrift für Kunst und Denkmalpflege», no. 2, Vienna 1968.

STEVENS Th., *Propriety and plainness*, in: «The Architectural Review», London Feb. 1968.

GUBLER J., BARLEY G., *Loos' Villa Karma*, in: «Architectural Review», no. 865, London 1969.

SCHACHEL R., *Ist Ornament Verbrechen?*, in: «Bauforum», Vienna 3 Jg. 1969.

SCHACHEL R., *Ins leere gesprochen*, in: «Die Furche», no. 16, Vienna 1969.

SCHACHEL R. L., *Bei einem Ohr hinein ins Leere gesprochen...*, in: «Werk», 1969.

UNGER Y. K., *Adolf Loos*, in: «The Architectural Review», London April 1969.

ACHLEITNER F., *Adolf Loos, pioniero y tradicionalista*, in: «Gaya», no. 95, 1970.

ACHLEITNER F., *Adolf Loos: Ärgernis und Hemmschuh*, in: «Bauforum», no. 21, Vienna 1970.

ALBINI A., *100-godisnjica wdenija Adolfa Loosa*, in: «Covjeki prosta», no. 213, 1970.

ALISPACH W., *Adolf Loos, ein genialer Architekt*, in: «Form und Geist», no. 12, Hergiswil 1970.

BEHALOVA V., *Die Villa Karma von Adolf Loos*, in: «Alte und mod-

erne Kunst», no. 113, Vienna 1970.

BEHALOVA V., *Pilsner Wohnungen von Adolf Loos*, in: «Bauforum 21», Vienna 1970.

CZECH H., MISTELBAUER W., *Das Looshaus*, in: «Bau», no. 1, Vienna 1970.

CZECH H., *Der Loos-Gedanke*, in: «Bau», no. 1, Vienna 1970.

CZECH H., *Fabriksgebäude und Villa in Hrusovany bei Brünn*, in: «Bau», no. 1, Vienna 1970.

DIMITRIOU S., *Adolf Loos. Gedanken zum Ursprung von Lehre und Werk*, in: «Bauforum», no. 21, Vienna 1970.

FRANK H., *Adolf Loos, Eine Bewältigung*, in: «Bau», no. 1, Vienna 1970.

GROLIG H., *Kein Denkmalschutz für Loos*, in: «I.b.f. - Reportagen», Vienna 3rd April 1970.

HERZMANSKY H., *Ein Skizzenblatt des Loos-Archivs*, in: «Bau», no. 1, Vienna 1970.

KOKOSCHKA O., *Mein Leben - Erinnerungen an Adolf Loos*, in: «Alte und moderne Kunst», no. 113, Vienna 1970.

KOSSATZ H. H., *Josef Hoffmann, Adolf Loos und die Wiener Kunst der Jahrhundertwende*, in: «Alte und moderne Kunst», no. 113, Vienna 1970.

KULKA H., *Bekenntnis zu Adolf Loos*, in: «Alte und moderne Kunst», no. 113, Vienna 1970.

KÜNSTLER G., *Das Menschenwürdige und das Schöne*, in: «Die Presse», Vienna 12th Dec. 1970.

KURRENT F., SPALT J., *Einige Merkmale*, in: «Bau», no. 1, Vienna 1970.

KURRENT F., SPALT J., *Unbekanntes von Adolf Loos*, in: «Bauforum», no. 21, Vienna 1970.

MARILAUN K., *Josef Hoffmann, die Wiener Werkstätte und Adolf Loos*, in: «Alte und moderne Kunst», no. 113, Vienna 1970.

PICA A. D., *Il centenario di Hoffmann e di Loos*, in: «Domus» no. 492, Milan 1970.

SCHACHEL R. L., *Zum 100.Geburtstag von Adolf Loos und Josef Hoffmann*, in: «Steine sprechen», no. 31-32, Vienna 1970.

SCHACHEL R. L., *Adolf Loos. Amerika und die Antike*, in: «Alte und moderne Kunst», no. 113, Vienna 1970.

SONNEK G., *Haus Moller*, in: «Paläste und Bürgerhäuser in Österreich», Vienna 1970.

SONNEK G., *Haus Scheu*, in: «Paläste und Bürgerhäuser in Österreich», Vienna 1970.

ZEVI B., *Adolf Loos iconoclasta - Diceva che sulla carta non dice niente*, in: «Cronache di architettura», Vol. 5, no. 558, Bari 1970-73.

WORBS D., *Knize - Beschreibung und Analyse eines Herrenmodegeschäftes von A. Loos (1909)*, in: «Bauforum», no. 21, Vienna 1970.

ACHLEITNER F., *Loos-Zerstörer am Werk. Weitere Demolierungen im Haus am Michaelerplatz*, in: «Die Presse», Vienna 10th Jan. 1971.

ACHLEITNER F., *Schüler, Mitarbeiter, Chronist*, in: «Die Presse», Vienna 23rd Jun. 1971.

GROSS P., *Los von Loos*, in: «Die Furche», no. 10, Vienna 6th Mar. 1971.

SCHALLENBERG W., *Loos-Haus in Paris*, in: «Die Presse», Vienna 1971.

ALBINI A., *Premisljanje o povijesnnj istini Adolfa Loosa*, in: «Telegram» 7th Jul. 1972.

GLÜCK F., *Adolf Loos*, in: «Österr. Biographisches Lexikon 1815-1950», Vienna 1972.

WACHBERGER M., *Schon Adolf Loos baute ein Terrassenhaus*, in: «Die Presse», Vienna 14th Apr. 1972.

(anonymous), *Wieder ein Bau von Adolf Loos bedroht*, in: «Kärntner Tageszeitung» Klagenfurt 9th Jun. 1973.

(anonymous), *Rettet Adolf Loos*, in: «Die Presse», Vienna 9/10th Jun. 1973.

(anonymous), *Letzte Loos-Bank wird umgebaut*, in: «Kleine Zeitung Graz 10th Jun. 1973.

(anonymous), *Schutz für ein Loos-Portal*, in: «Die Presse», Vienna 17th Jun. 1973.

BEHALOVA V., *Das Loos-Service von J. & L. Lobmeyr* «Bauforum», no. 39, Vienna 1973.

BONICALZI R., *Un maestro per i neorazionalisti*, in: «Casabella»

BEHALOVA V., *Adolf Loos: Villa Karma*, in: «unv. Dissertation an der Universität, Vienna 1974.

EISENMAN P., *To Adolf Loos & Bertold Brecht*, in: «Progressive Architecture», 1974.

KUDELKA Z., *Cinnost Adolfe Loos v Ceskoslovensku*, in: «Studia Minora», Faculty of Philosophy of the University of Brno, Prague 1974.

SCHOCK-WERNER B., *Das Loos-Haus am Michaelerplatz und andere Grossprojekte von Adolf Loos*, in: «Seminarreferat am Kunsthistorischen Institut der Universität», Vienna 1974.

DAMISCH H., *L'autre Ich ou le desir du vide, pour un tombeau d'A. Loos*, in: «Critique», nos. 339-40, Paris 1975.

KLINGENBERG-HELFERT J., *Das «letzte» Haus von Adolf Loos*, in: «Alte und moderne Kunst», no. 138, Salzburg 1975.

PAGANO G., «*Lettura critica: analisi di cinque opere di A. Loos*», in: «Quaderni dell'Ist. Dip. Urbanistico», no. 7, Catania 1975.

RISMONDO P., *Vergessenes um Adolf Loos*, in: «Die Presse», Vienna 1975.

WORBS D., *Das «Würfelhaus». Darstellung und Analyse eines Projektes von Adolf Loos*, in: «Bauforum», no. 49, Vienna 1975.

CZECH H., *A newly discovered bank by Adolf Loos*, in: «A+U», no. 68, Tokyo 1976.

FORTIN J. P., PIETU M., *Adolf Loos: Maison pour Tristan Tzara*, in: «Architecture Mouvement Continuité», no. 38, Paris 1976.

GLÜCK F., *Adolf Loos und das Buchdrucken*, in: «Philobiblon», no. 3, Hamburg 1976.

WORBS D., «*Unbekannte» Bauten und Projekte von A. Loos in der CSSR*, in: «Alte und moderne Kunst», no. 144, Vienna 1976.

GRAVAGNUOLO B., *A. Loos: Il linguaggio e la differenza*, in: «Controspazio», XIth year, no. 3, Bari 1977.

CZECH H., MISTELBAUER W., *The Loos House*, in: «A+U», no. 86, Tokyo 1978.

CZECH H., *The Loos Idea*, in: «A+U», no. 91, Tokyo 1978.

CACCIARI M., *Interno e esperienza (Note su Loos, Roth e Wittgenstein)*, in: «Nuova Corrente», nos. 79-80, Milan 1979.

SIBOUR E., *Adolf Loos: un «Sebastiano nel sogno»?*, in: «Nuova Corrente», nos. 79-80, Milan 1979.

WORBS D., *Die Wiener Arbeiterterrassenhäuser von Adolf Loos 1923*, in: «Architektur, Stadt und Politik; Jahrbuch des Werkbund-Archivs», no. 4, 1979.

CZECH H., *Kärntner, American-Loos-bar*, in: «Lotus», no. 29, 1980.

GUTTENBRUNNER M., *Kraus, Loos, Wittgenstein und Altenberg*, in: «Bau», no. 2, Vienna 1980.

RUKSCHCIO B., *Adolf Loos zum 110. Geburtstag*, in: «Bauforum», no. 81, Dec. 1980.

RUKSCHCIO B., *Adolf Loos analizzato*, in: «Lotus», no. 29, 1980.

SCHEZEN R., *Trasformazioni nel reale*, in: «Gran Bazaar», no. 6, Feb. 1980.

SCHEZEN R., *La definizione di un modello*, in: «Gran Bazaar», no. 10, Sep. 1980.

BERNI L., *Ristampa di «Das andere», la rivista di Adolf Loos* (recensione), in: «Panorama», no. 782, 13th Apr. 1981.

CACCIARI M., *Loos e l'angelo dell'effimero*, in: «L'Architettura - Cronache e storia», no. 310-311, Aug.-Sept. 1981.

MELCHIORRE A., *Schönberg tra Loos e Kandinsky*, in: «Casabella», no. 473, Oct. 1981.

382, Milan 1973.

KOSSATZ H. H., *Neue Filiale von Adolf Loos*, in: «Arbeiterzeitung», Vienna 5th Aug. 1973.

MESSINA M. G., *L'opera teorica di Adolf Loos*, in: «Annali Scuola Normale superiore di Pisa», 1973.

PÖTSCHNER P., *Rettet Loos*, in: «Die Presse», Vienna 15th Jun. 1973.

RITSCHAL K. H., *Adolf Loos fegte unter unseren Füssen*, in: «Salzburger Nachrichten», Salzburg 18th Aug. 1973.

ROTH A., *Begegnung mit Pionieren Adolf Loos*, Stuttgart 1973.

RUKSCHCIO B., *Studien zu Entwürfen, Projekten und ausgeführten Bauten von Adolf Loos (1870-1933)*, in: «unv. Dissertation an der Universität, Vienna 1973.

RUKSCHCIO B., *Sorgen um Loos*, in: «Die Presse», Vienna 23rd/24th Jun. 1973.

RYKWERT J., *Adolf Loos: The new vision*, in: «Studio International», no. 957, Vol. 186, 1973.

SCHACHEL R. L., *Eine Bank von Adolf Loos - Analyse eines Un-Glücksfalles*, in: «Steine sprechen», no. 43-44, Vienna 1973.

The publishers gratefully acknowledge
the following sources from which
illustrations have been obtained:

Photo Surwillo (pp. 90-91)
Photo Gerlach

Loos Archiv Albertina, Wien
Historisches Museum der Stadt Wien
Nationale Galerie Berlin - Charlottenburg

Würthle Galerie, Wien
Löcker Verlag: *Adolf Loos, Das Looshaus*

Schroll Verlag: *Der Architekt Adolf Loos*

«Alte und moderne Kunst»
«Bauforum»

The publishers have sought as far as possible, the rights of reproduction to
the illustrations contained in this publication. Since some of the sources are
unknown, the authors would be grateful to receive information from any
copyright holder who is not credited herein.